# Islands, Identity and the Literary Imagination

## Anthem Studies in Australian Literature and Culture

**Anthem Studies in Australian Literature and Culture** specializes in quality, innovative research in Australian literary studies. The series publishes work that advances contemporary scholarship on Australian literature conceived historically, thematically and/or conceptually. We welcome well-researched and incisive analyses on a broad range of topics: from individual authors or texts to considerations of the field as a whole, including in comparative or transnational frames.


**Series Editors**

Katherine Bode – Australian National University, Australia
Nicole Moore – University of New South Wales, Australia

**Editorial Board**

Tanya Dalziell – University of Western Australia, Australia
Delia Falconer – University of Technology, Sydney, Australia
John Frow – University of Sydney, Australia
Wang Guanglin – Shanghai University of International Business and Economics, China
Ian Henderson – King's College London, United Kingdom
Tony Hughes-D'Aeth – University of Western Australia, Australia
Ivor Indyk – University of Western Sydney, Australia
Nicholas Jose – University of Adelaide, Australia
James Ley – *Sydney Review of Books*, Australia
Susan Martin – La Trobe University, Australia
Andrew McCann – Dartmouth College, United States
Elizabeth McMahon – University of New South Wales, Australia
Susan Martin – La Trobe University, Australia
Brigitta Olubus – University of New South Wales, Australia
Anne Pender – University of New England, Australia
Fiona Polack – Memorial University of Newfoundland, Canada
Sue Sheridan – University of Adelaide, Australia
Ann Vickery – Deakin University, Australia
Russell West-Pavlov – Eberhard-Karls-Universität Tübingen, Germany
Lydia Wevers – Victoria University of Wellington, New Zealand
Gillian Whitlock – University of Queensland, Australia

# Islands, Identity and the Literary Imagination

Elizabeth McMahon

ANTHEM PRESS

Anthem Press
An imprint of Wimbledon Publishing Company
*www.anthempress.com*

This edition first published in UK and USA 2019
by ANTHEM PRESS
75–76 Blackfriars Road, London SE1 8HA, UK
or PO Box 9779, London SW19 7ZG, UK
and
244 Madison Ave #116, New York, NY 10016, USA

First published in the UK and USA by Anthem Press 2016

© Elizabeth McMahon 2019

The author asserts the moral right to be identified as the author of this work.

All rights reserved. Without limiting the rights under copyright reserved above, no part of this publication may be reproduced, stored or introduced into a retrieval system, or transmitted, in any form or by any means (electronic, mechanical, photocopying, recording or otherwise), without the prior written permission of both the copyright owner and the above publisher of this book.

*British Library Cataloguing-in-Publication Data*
A catalogue record for this book is available from the British Library.

ISBN-13: 978-1-78527-189-2 (Pbk)
ISBN-10: 1-78527-189-X (Pbk)

This title is also available as an e-book.

# CONTENTS

# ILLUSTRATIONS

# ACKNOWLEDGEMENTS

Research undertaken for this book was funded by an Australian Research Council Discovery grant, which was greatly enabling and for which I am very grateful. I also received research and conference grants from the School of the Arts and Media (2013, 2014, 2015) at the University of New South Wales (UNSW). I am very fortunate to work in an institution that supports research so well. I am also fortunate to have such great colleagues in the English program at UNSW, in particular Brigitta Olubas, with whom I have collaborated on numerous teaching and research projects. In addition to the inspiring dialogue of ideas, Brigitta invited me to speak on Shirley Hazzard's literary islands at the Hazzard conference she organized at Columbia University in 2012. I have benefitted greatly from multiple collaborations with Elaine Stratford at the University of Tasmania and Godfrey Baldacchino at the University of Malta, who have encouraged me to make connections between literary islands and their material and cultural conditions and expanded the aspiration and, hopefully, the reach of my work.

I have given many conference papers on literary islands and published numerous essays. I thank Vanessa Smith from the University of Sydney who was supportive in publishing my early work in this field. I have attended every annual conference of the Australian Association for the Study of Australian Literature since 2003, each year delivering a paper on Australia's literary islands. I thank the 2012 conference organizer, Lydia Wevers, who invited me to give the Dorothy Green Memorial lecture, on trans-Tasman literary geographies, at Victoria University, Wellington, New Zealand. I thank the interlocutors at these and other conferences and scholarly referees for their feedback, which increased my knowledge and sharpened my thought. Parts of some of these chapters have been published in earlier versions in several journals: a small part of the Introduction appeared in *Journal of the Association for the Study of Australian Literature* (*JASAL* 2013), another short section of Chapter 2 appeared in *JASAL* (2012), a small section of Chapter 3 was published in *The Novels of Alex Miller* (2012) and small sections of Chapter 5 were published in *Southerly* (2001) and *Island Studies Journal* (2013).

I thank my research assistant Laura Joseph, Jacinta Kelly for proofing a full draft and overseeing permissions and Kate Livett for reading and analysing drafts and preparing the extensive table of Australian–West Indian connections in the Appendix. I thank Hannah Fink for suggesting the wonderful Segar Passi image for the cover. I thank the Anthem Press team for their exemplary professionalism. I was advised of Anthem's high standards before this book was contracted and this assessment has been confirmed by my own experience. Any errors are mine.

My family have always been great supporters of my work over a lifetime: keenly interested, enabling and patient. This book was written over a period when my parents and my brother Michael died. They would have been so happy to see this work out in the world. This book is dedicated to them, and to Kate, for everything.

# Section 1

# ISLANDS REAL AND IMAGINARY

# INTRODUCTION

Generations of Australian schoolchildren learned to describe their homeland as 'the world's largest island and the world's smallest continent'.[1] It is such a pleasing construction. It comprehends the two major topographies of land, islands and continents, in a reversed relation of scale, for islands are meant to be small and continents large. This inversion of the norm fits well with the concept of Australia's upside-down status when viewed from the boreal perspective of Europe. Despite the implicit judgement of that northern perception, there is nevertheless an enchantment that attaches to living in such a perverse space: Australia is the biggest and the smallest as well as upside down and inside out.

These statements of geographical 'fact' and legend are also inherently literary: the juxtaposition of opposites is an *oxymoron*; it is also a *paradox* in that it requires the interconnection of opposing terms for its effect and these qualities are underscored by the syntactical repetition of the *isocolon* (a statement that repeats the same phrase structure). Further, the reflexivity of these two sets of binaries casts the construction as a *chiasmus*, for there is an inverted parallelism in the two statements of topography. In summary, this perception of Australia is of a space that interconnects geographical and rhetorical contradiction and inversion, a space that contains an otherness within itself. Such a space promises to be endlessly baffling and, hence, philosophical and creative.

This book examines predominantly Australian literature in view of the shifting cartographies of modernity and their constructions of space. Representational dynamism is no more or less a feature of Australian cartography than anywhere else, but Australia's unique status as an island continent and the particular terms of the relationships among its geography, politics and history present an especially fascinating dilemma of especial relevance to the Australian context with the potential to reframe broader questions about the lived and imaginary experience of space. Australia's status as an island continent has certainly occupied the Australian literary imagination, which has not only responded to this spatial particularity but profoundly shaped its imaginary energy. At various historical junctures since the European invasion of Australia, Australia has been described as being more one topology than another: sometimes the island-continent is more of an island; at others, more of a continent. Sometimes Australia is more part of the region – itself a shifting boundary – where it appears, accordingly, as more diffuse. At others times it is an impermeable sovereign state whose boundaries are defined by the coastline of the continent. This book investigates the relationship between Australia's seemingly contradictory geography and its literary imaginary to identify both specific effects and nodes of regional and global interconnection. The large ambition is to identify distinctive aspects of Australia's representations of itself as lived space, according to its designation as an island continent, and to contextualize these qualities in the genealogy of globalization and its literary archive.

The frameworks for this enterprise derive from both literary studies and island studies, this latter being a relatively new interdisciplinary constellation that became formalized at more or less the same time as a range of large-scale intergovernmental initiatives such as UNESCO's creation of the International Council for Island Development (INSULA) in 1989, followed up by the Barbados Action Plan in 1994. The period also saw the establishment of the Alliance of Small Island States (ASIS) in 1990 and the Association of Small Island Developing States (ASDS) in 1992. Closer to home, the Australian Small Islands Forum (ASIF) held its inaugural meeting on Lord Howe Island in May 2012 (Stratford 2012). In the academic context, the International Small Islands Association (ISISA) was established in 1992 and the Small Island Cultures Research Initiative (SICRI) was formed in 2004, with other discipline-specific organizations following. In the 2000s, two scholarly journals devoted to island research were initiated: *Island Studies Journal* (2006) and *Shima* (2007). Both of these online, free-access forums have promoted work from across the disciplines and also between researchers and practitioners. This book would have been impossible without the focus and shared research enabled by these academic associations and journals. It is worth noting also that they include numerous Australian scholars in key roles.

This recent re-visioning of islands has been especially necessary given the relegation of islands to an imaginary outside of the economies and narratives of modernity. In an ironic twist on the name of Thomas More's island utopia or 'no place', islands have become increasingly invisible from the nineteenth century. In the early modern period, islands were prized by European colonizers for their maritime access, which enabled transport and trade, and for the relative ease by which the delimited space of the island could be controlled. They lost this status, John Gillis argues, with advances in transport across continents and with the shift to continental power from the nineteenth century

(2004, 121*ff.*), a shifting cartography that coincides with the colonial settlement of Australia. Many island cultures of the twenty-first century are simultaneously demanding attention to the very real difficulties they face, including population decline, expensive utilities and rising oceans, while also insisting upon their evident capacity for resilience and creative adaptation. The temporal coordinate of modernity worked to obscure islands as topographies outside the modern, as sites against which continental modernity could be defined. The currency of this descriptor has waned with the rise of globalization, a spatial category that flattens out time into the networks and topologies of the present. This shift, like most, carries mixed fortunes. In some moods it constructs an imaginary inclusivity, a comprehension of the whole globe, by which islands are rendered partially visible. However, the conceit of a global surfaceal comprehension retains the reticulations of capital and power, as Gayatri Spivak and Fredric Jameson have memorably analysed.[2] Now that value has shifted onto mobile cultures, the seeming stasis of the bounded island presents another mode of exclusion, or merely recasts the earlier sense of its temporal anachronism into spatial terms.

Literary studies are an essential component of contemporary island studies in a number of ways. First, literature is a major site where the Western imagination repeatedly rehearses and develops the enthralment of the island. This island enchantment has created a kind of island ideogram in the collective psyche, one that connects identity, space and desire and which has fuelled colonial acquisition as much as it has provided a mental space of reflection. In this mindset, the island is a perfect object of control, where the onlooker imagines he [sic] can be king. From Prospero in *The Tempest* (Shakespeare 1611) to H. G. Wells's *The Island of Dr Moreau* (1896), the island is a realm of power and invention that exceeds the constraints of the world that lies beyond its borders. Such power is most often revealed as being unethical, solipsistic, even theomaniacal, and is sustained by the triumvirate of history, materiality and representation.[3]

The flipside of this desire for control is the lure of the island as a site of escape and luxury, a site where the fruit drops from the trees and lotus-eating islanders are free from the burdens of selfhood, labour and the outside world. This fantasy of apathy also functions in very material and political terms. The West's boundless desire for capital and leisure, manifest in colonialism, promoted the idea of the island paradise in part to disguise the various forms of unfree labour by which these idylls were constructed and sustained: slavery, convict transportation, indentured workers. So, too, as set out in Jamaica Kincaid's caustic reflections on her home island of Antigua, the transformation of islands into luxury resorts is a contemporary manifestation of the same myopic desire (1988). In his 1993 poem 'Malthusian Island' Robert Gray writes with biting irony of this touristic colonialism in the context of Australians holidaying in south east Asia.

> Paradise is always within walls: here it is in within hotel grounds,
> or around some few great bungalows, with their gardens
> and pools. Outside, there is purgatory. (1993, 31)

The dawning recognition of the island's self-travesty or contradiction, its *aporia* in literary critical terms, is an endemic component of the island imaginary, and in evidence throughout Australian literature. In *The Confessions of a Beachcomber* (1908), E. J. (Ted) Banfield presents a Thoreauvian account of a retreat from the world to a life of self-subsistence on Dunk Island off the north Queensland coast. Banfield and his wife Bertha retreated to an 'unprofaned sanctuary – an island removed from the haunts of men' in 1897 where they remained for 23 years until Banfield's death (1908, xv). Banfield's island may have been 'unprofaned', but it was not 'removed from the haunts of men', being the territory of the Bandjin and Djiru people of whom Banfield writes in his various publications. Hence the Banfields' retreat *from* the world is, in fact, a journey *to* the world of another culture, which, in fact, assisted the Banfields in their subsistence living. That the *Confessions* opens with an account of the demise of the local island people accords them a grotesque precedence of sorts and intentionally or otherwise frames Banfield's text as its predicate. Banfield defines the island as 'removed from the *haunts* of men', but the *Confessions* is very much a haunted text, as he himself knows at some level.

This capacity to incorporate a reflexive counter-image within its own boundaries renders the island complete and unassailable, like the yin yang ideogram of opposition and complementarity from Chinese philosophy. The reader or viewer of an island story knows that when a text presents an initial depiction of an island's perfection this ideality is an illusion and that the island's beauty and the sense of autonomy it accords to visitors will soon be matched by an equal measure of ugliness, evil and subjugation. A further, related complexity of the island's doubleness is its capacity to confound the separation of history and literature and their connected materialities. The island not only reveals the interconnection of these two categories but reveals the dynamism of their mutual constitution. In her study of the *isolario* (a pictorial and literary cartographic genre of islands) as one of the key foundations of early modern Iberian literature, Simone Pinet claims that literature and modern cartography are not only usefully considered in parallel but are structurally interrelated and that the 'overlaps are not mere coincidences, but are historically specific strategies that can be traced back to structural concerns' (2011, xii). In the Anglophone tradition also, we can identify many such connections between literature and history. Emblematically, John Donne's pronouncement that 'no man is an island' was written the very same year, 1623, that the British claimed their first island colony in the Caribbean.

Literal and metaphorical cartographies often appear to be poised in a balanced or spellbound reflexivity (McMahon 2011, 126). Rajeev Patke signals this reflexivity in the chiastic title of his essay 'The Islands of Poetry: The Poetry of Islands' (2004) and opens by remarking that 'Islands, like poetry, may be described in Marianne Moore's words as "imaginary gardens" with "real toads"' (177). Moreover, as neither the real nor the metaphoric domain has primacy, the two are in constant and perplexing contest. Modern instances of this interaction between cartography and literary structure include the two 'hemispheres' of Christina Stead's *For Love Alone* (1944), in which the first part of the novel is titled 'The Island Continent' and the second is 'Port of Registry, London' (2011, 3, 291). Randolph Stow's *To the Islands* (1958) overlays maps of Indigenous and settler cultures through place and identity, articulated in the questing drive of its title. From the poetry archive, geography and *poesis* overlap in A. D. Hope's first collection of poems, *The Wandering Islands* (1955), in which insular isolation is articulated in each separate poem. In another vein, New Zealand poet James K. Baxter connects island topography, creativity and interiority in a description of his poetry as 'part of a subconscious corpus of personal myth, like an island above the sea, but joined underwater to other islands' (1976, 6).

While the separation of art and life is routinely challenged in art – we know with Melancholy Jaques that 'all the world's a stage' – the island figures this relationship with a specific intensity, which is connected to the island's emphatic boundedness. As Godfrey Baldacchino writes, we always draw an island as a round formation that fits within the margins of a page (2005, 247). In this conception, the island is defined by boundaries and by its relatively diminutive size. It is like a miniature object which, according to Susan Stewart's characterization, attracts us by its graspable materiality; we can hold such objects in our hands and, so we believe, within the imagined borders of our minds (1993, 37*ff*.). Nettie Palmer also acknowledges this quality in the diary of Vance's and her writing retreat on Green Island in 1932. She writes that they wanted the island to 'be small enough for us to grasp as a whole' (Jordan 2010, 150). So, on the one hand, the island's status as a fetishized object epitomizes static materiality – and islands are often described as trinkets or jewels – but it also undoes this fetish fantasy by revealing an energetic volatility that belies the surface veneer of its allure.

The island-specific quality of this bounded construction is, however, complicated in the Australian context. For, as Libby Robin has discussed regarding the political and geographical relationship of Australia's continent, Australians also tend to draw Australia as one land mass that neatly fits inside the parameters of a page (2007, 205). This has also occurred in official representations, which have, on occasion, omitted Tasmania from the map, let alone other island territories. A recent article in Hobart's daily newspaper, *The Mercury*, lists seven recent instances of omission (Hope 2014).

Many topographical elements have deep psychic resonances, and the island is not alone in this connection: Gerard Manley Hopkins famously wrote that 'the mind has mountains' and Hans Blumenberg has tracked the 'nautical metaphorics of existence' in Western philosophy, discussed in Chapter 4. However, the island is unique in that it operates as a figure of the imagination, of the human subject and of literature, in and of itself. As many commentators have noted, in relation to the Western imagination at least, the island operates as a kind of metafigure, a key *topos* of the literary imagination. The island is a figure of another world, the site on which possibilities are created, rehearsed and tested, as occurs in a novel, play or poem. In seeming contrast to this other place of fabrication and the 'no place' of utopia, the island is variously the world in microcosm, the suspended promise of home or *Heimat*, and the site of new beginnings. Some texts play out this island imaginary in very material terms, iconically *The Tempest* and Defoe's *Robinson Crusoe* (1719), both of which also exploit the confusion between fictional and historical domains enabled by the particular status of the island. *The Tempest* includes multiple references to the recently discovered islands of the New World and a self-reflexive commentary on the artist/playwright as an old man on his island of exile. Defoe's real life model for Crusoe, Alexander Selkirk's own non-fiction account of his experiences, was in wide circulation in Defoe's time, creating a dialogue between these two texts and their historical and fictional narratives (Souhami 2002). Such reflexive and recursive relations relate to the island's duality and, in turn, each new instance of the fiction/history crossover further emphasizes the island's ungraspable, impossible doubleness. In contemporary Australian fiction, Andrew McGahan's *Wonders of a Godless World* (2009) provides a new take on the relationship between fact and fiction. *Wonders* is in some sense antirealist in that the island is a fantastical site. The novel's characters are abstracted into archetypes and the events are impossible. However, this hyper-fictive reality is galvanized by factual, historical and scientific data in a narrative of the earth island.

McGahan's antihero has already died five times at the novel's opening. On each occasion he is caught up in a momentous cataclysm from the earth's history. His fury brings him back to life. This pattern of rebirth is a common feature of islands in the imagination. The new beginning promised by the island, like the world Prospero constructs on his island of exile, is a man-made or cultural creation rather than an original, natural beginning. *The Tempest* is a play of the non-natural, unnatural or supernatural; it is a perverse and marvellous form of generation – like the new creatures created by vivisection in *The Island of Dr Moreau*. As this site of unnatural origin, the island is a figure of the written text itself, which is a second-order creation. The interconnections between the island, origins and writing are evident from antiquity, most notably Homer's *Odyssey*, as well as in the new literary genres of modernity. Pinet shows how the Iberian adaptations of British Arthurian legends replace the forest with the island as the site of adventure (experience) (2011). She identifies the ways the *isolario* comes to underpin the structure of Spanish *Amadís* (1508) and then, in turn, Cervantes' *Don Quixote* (1605 and 1615), which is considered the first modern novel. Pinet's genealogy offers a compelling argument for the presence of islands and archipelagic constellations in the formation of modern literature (Pinet 2003, 180).

In the Anglophone tradition Thomas More's island *Utopia* (1516) – the first utopian text – is, as Fredric Jameson describes, 'one of those rare works that, whatever its precursors, inaugurates a whole genre' (1977, 4). So, too, Louis Marin makes the connection between More's *Utopia* and secondary origins when he locates its publication 'at the very dawn of our modernity' (1993, 403). Two centuries after More, Defoe's narrative of the island castaway, *Robinson Crusoe*, is published – a text accorded the status of the first realist novel. At this time also Swift publishes *Gulliver's Travels* (1726), a narrative structured by the protagonist's voyages to islands of strange and foreign worlds and which became, inter alia, the prototype for science fiction. These texts are, of course, explicitly linked to the European Age of Discovery and underscore the connection between the shifting morphology of the island and the development of literary forms in colonial modernity.

Pinet also demonstrates the increasing capacity of islands to figure abstract and interior states of being from the early modern period, as with Donne's 'no man is an island'. The increasing metaphorization of the island in the early modern period, its gradual shift from material denotation to its role in representing more abstract states, is another way that islands and archipelagos are at the heart of modernity's literary structures (Pinet 2011, xxxiv–xxxv). The first volume of Janet Frame's autobiography, titled *To the Is-land* (1982), provides a more recent example of the ways islands structure literary interiority in the explicit links Frame forges between ontology and her real island home of New Zealand's South Island, with the island of the literary imaginary. The deep connection between islands and writing for Frame is highlighted by her ongoing engagement with *The Tempest* and her identification with Prospero. In *An Angel at My Table*, she writes: 'I had absorbed the spirit of *The Tempest*. Even Prospero in his book-lined cell had suffered shipwreck and selfwreck; his island was unreachable except through storm' (quoted in Caney 1993, 152).

There have been numerous and necessary checks to the Western imaginary of the island as a fetishized space of possession, including self-possession, and as a site where Western fantasies are projected and enacted. These responses have sought to distinguish between the island of Western desire and actual islands on the earth and their inhabitants who often map quite different circulations of imagination and desire. Unsurprisingly, most of these ripostes have come from islanders themselves who do not recognize themselves or their home places in the Western fantasy. The Tongan writer and theorist Epeli Hau'ofa's landmark essay 'Our Sea of Islands' (1993) stands as a key intervention in this process, as all subsequent island theorists identify. Hau'ofa turned the Western fantasy on its head in his description of his wider home place, Oceania, as the 'sea of islands', overturning the western habit of binary structures that makes a dichotomy of land and sea, and locating each island in a connected space across earth and water. This topological understanding is not new to Western thought, as Christy Constantakopoulou makes clear in relation to the ancient Aegean, which was also called *Adalar Denizi* or Sea of Islands in the Ottoman period (2007, 1). Following Elisabeth Malamut, Constantakopoulou argues that two conceptions of insular space coexisted in the ancient Aegean. The first is much like that we have already discussed, the island as a '*terre fermée*, a world closed to its surroundings' (2007, 3). The second perception of the islands as plurality is one which stresses their 'active networks of communications and exchange' (2007, 2), hence our modern understanding of 'archipelago', from its ancient denotation of the Aegean as the 'primary sea'.

The connection between Oceania and the Aegean does not diminish the radicality of Hau'ofa's intervention in contemporary, postcolonial understanding of islands; indeed, texts such as Derek Walcott's modern Caribbean *Odyssey*, *Omeros* (1990), strengthen this connection and its perceived possibilities. Rather, Hau'ofa's sea of islands stresses how the force of history, in particular the linked drives of colonialism and capitalism, obscured forms of connectivity and systems of exchange outside their own operations, seeing only objects in the sea and blind to their interconnections and alternative systems of relation. Hau'ofa reminded critics and theorists, too, that the very premises of their studies and the basic terms of their understanding need deconstruction. Further, Hau'ofa directed attention to islands and archipelagos, hitherto little heard of in international forums, as sources of a necessary alterity, creativity and mobility. It is one of the many ironies of the West's fantasy island that it is defined as a site of creative invention but only for the fantasist himself.

Suvendrini Perera performs a similar inversion of land and water in her critique of settler Australia's xenophobia, *Australia and the Insular Imagination* (2009). She opens with this provocation for her Australian readers:

> What if the ground beneath our feet turns out to be the sea? This book pursues the idea that what constitutes and defines Australia is not ground, as terrestrial land mass, but rather the variable element that envelops and overlaps it. (Perera 2009, 1)

Where Hau'ofa inverts the conventional value of land over water in order to reimagine the epic potential of the Pacific for its island inhabitants, Perera's inversion pulls the rug out from under the sedentarized certainties of settler Australian culture to destabilize the ground(s) of its self-definition.

Similar to their significance in postcolonial theory, Caribbean writers have provided the most sustained riposte to the ideas and practice of islands as reified totalized units: Kincaid's *A Small Place*, published in 1988, details the effects of Antigua's plight as a postcolonial holiday resort. Her opening parodies the illusion that one can comprehend the island by the force of a desiring gaze: 'If you go to Antigua as a tourist, this is what you will see. If you come by aeroplane, you will land at the V. C. Bird international airport [...] As your plane begins to descend you might say, 'What a beautiful island Antigua is' (Kincaid 2000, 191). Cuban writer and theorist Benítez-Rojo's formulation of 'the repeating island', derived from Chaos theory, offers a model of connection and separation between the Caribbean islands that denies the relationality of centres and boundaries, and originals and copies (1992); Barbadian poet Edward Kamau Brathwaite's theory of tidalectics disavows the binary of land and water in favour of tidal and cyclical flows between them (1983). He asserts the distinction and connection of islands: 'The unity is submarine' (Brathwaite 1974, 64). In essays and poetry St Lucian Nobel laureate Derek Walcott interweaves material and figurative archipelagos providing internal and external landscapes for the modern fractured globe with its brutal history and the subjects it has created. His Nobel address specifies this experience to the Caribbean but with much broader application. He declares: 'Antillean art is this restoration of our shattered histories, our shards of vocabulary, our archipelago becoming a synonym for pieces broken off from the original continent' (Walcott 1992). Martinican Édouard Glissant calls for the broad adoption of the archipelago's model of interconnected relation, a perspective that calls for monolithic continents to heed the Caribbean experience: 'The Caribbean may be held up as one of those places in the world where Relation presents itself most visibly' (1997, 33).

All of these island theorists argue for an archipelagic relationality to replace the stolid monadism of the island, and this book follows their lead in its juxtaposition of the singular island with the islands of plurality and interconnection. These two conceptions operate variously in complement, opposition and contradiction and further complicate Australia's status as an archipelago – it comprises 8,222 islands according to Geoscience Australia – and its sometime desire to be a single monolithic island continent (Geoscience n.d.). The island theorists outlined above are all writers of fiction and poetry working both to dismantle tropes deep in the rhetorical unconscious of modernity that suture the island to a possessive desire that degrades islanders as objects and is, hence, inimical to the subjectivity needed for literary invention (amongst much else). They work also to extend the island's unique creative status as a site and figure of literary production within specific local contexts and histories.

The modelling of these theorist-artists is especially important for, as Rod Edmond and Vanessa Smith noted in 2003, islands had 'tended to slip the net of postcolonial theorizing' (5) to that point. Edmond and Smith's edited collection, *Islands in History and Representation*, stands as a landmark publication in the field, not least because of their introductory essay, which maps and frames the issues for island studies in the humanities. Elizabeth DeLoughrey's literary critical work on Caribbean literature and on the comparison of Caribbean and Oceanic literatures in *Routes and Roots* has also broken new ground and has provided a model for many in the field including this author (2007). Of major significance is the way DeLoughrey organizes her reading and research of the Caribbean and Pacific writing according to Brathwaite's theory of tidalectics, thereby instantiating an archipelagic and oceanic relationality as her method as well as the object of her study. Pinet's theorization of the mutual constitution of literature and the cartography of islands in the early modern period is ingenious. In addition to her specific findings, discussed above, her work links history and geography to the literary imagination in ways that open up literary island studies. Finally, Perera's monograph, *Australia and the Insular Imagination: Beaches, Borders, Boats, and Bodies* (2009) provides a powerful and necessary analysis of Australia's brutality and paranoia regarding sovereign borders, which is only more pressing now than at the time of publication. I had the opportunity to participate in a forum on this book in *Political Geography*, with three other readers and Perera, and that extensive discussion and the enduring insights of the book itself inform this work also (Stratford et al. 2011b).

In method and approach this book is also informed by collaborative work I have undertaken with cultural geographers in the burgeoning field of the geohumanities (Stratford et al. 2011a; 2011b). These projects seek to bridge the material and imaginative consideration of islands and to draw upon contemporary conceptions of space from a range of disciplinary perspectives and the shared but distinctive engagements with theorists such as Michel Foucault, Gilles Deleuze and Peter Sloterdijk. This approach is undertaken here in recognition of the pressing issues facing many island communities in the wake of climate change and rising oceans, as articulated so powerfully by the poet Kathy Jetnil-Kijiner, from the Marshall Islands, in her address to the Climate Summit at the United

Nations in September 2014. She described the situation in her homeland, where the islands sit at an average of less than two metres above sea level:

> We've seen waves crashing into our homes and our breadfruit trees wither from salt and droughts [...] We look at our children and wonder how they will know themselves or their culture should they lose our islands. (Jetnil-Kijiner 2014)

This is true for many islands in the region which face inundation, including the islands of the Torres Strait. It remains to be seen how and when Australia, blinded by its own 'insular imagination' to use Perera's description, will assist its neighbours. Recent studies of Australia's archipelagic complexity within and without its borders complicate this insularity. Tim Flannery's account of his research travels in the Trobriand Islands, *Among the Islands* (2011) makes complex connections between Australia and its northern neighbours. It concludes, with Flannery looking across the ocean, to the next archipelago, following the lure of the islands. Michael Veitch's *The Forgotten Islands*, also published in 2011, explores the Bass Strait islands, the archipelago Stephen Murray-Smith titled 'Australia's last frontier' (1969). In a quite different vein, John Mateer's dual-language account (Bahasa and English) of the Cocos Keeling Islands in the Indian Ocean imbricates Australian and Indonesia through history, space and language (Mateer 2015).

The approach deployed here is also informed by the insights of Wai Chee Dimock's *Through Other Continents: American Literature Across Deep Time* (2006) and by the project that took up the potential for Dimock's thought in the Australian context, Robert Dixon and Brigid Rooney's *Scenes of Reading: Is Australian Literature a World Literature?* (2013).[4] Dimock's formulation of a 'national literature' insists upon the many and tangled connections across space and time that inflect literary production. Ancient texts such as *Gilgamesh* live in the national literatures of many countries as do contemporary works from far afield. The terms of Dimock's challenge to the parameters of any national literature are especially relevant to a study of literary islands, which have been the setting and the structure of ancient texts, such as the *Odyssey*. Islands also operate in the spatial metaphorics of self and world, from womb and shelter to cosmos, planet and ego. The profundity of this psychic and rhetorical unconscious requires a far-reaching consideration beyond national borders and across temporalities. Islands have also been at the forefront of epistemic shifts in modernity from the genesis of literary genres already noted to such momentous events as the Columbian discoveries; Darwin's theory of natural selection, which took shape on the Galapagos islands; and the Cold War nuclear tests in the Bikini Atoll, Marshall Islands, and the Montebello Islands of the north west coast of mainland Australia, as Robert Drewe has recently explored (2012). Currently in Australia, in the era of global mobility, islands are the focus of asylum seeker policy and practice, as Australia uses its (poorer) island neighbours in the bid to keep refugees out of its sovereign territory.

This current study attempts to read Australian literary texts from a variety of genres and across an extended period of time in the light of these local and global events and literary productions to show the continuities with older conventions, to identify specific experience and to habituate the discussion of Australian writing in global forums.

The book is divided into three main sections. This Introduction is followed by a study of John Donne's metaphor 'no man is an island' (1623), understood as a defining maxim of late modernity from the mid-twentieth century when it became, in the words of Gillian Beer, an 'instant cliché' (1997, 1). After lying nearly dormant for 320 years this metaphor was seized upon in the 1940s as definitive of the modern moment. This chapter speculates on the reasons for this rediscovery of Donne's metaphor and examines the relationship between the early modern and late modern contexts of its utterance, including Australian literature. The discussion of the relationship between Donne's man and island argues that the two terms become inseparable as an anthropomorphic map of Western modernity and the subject of the modern era who is reborn into a condition of alienation. The dialogue between the early modern and late modern contexts conducted in this chapter continues throughout the book.

The second section of *Islands, Identity and the Literary Imagination*, comprising Chapters 2 and 3, is titled 'Islands: Making the Planet, World, Globe'. The two chapters chart the shifting relationships between geography, politics and representation through the changing status of islands and continents from Europeans' discovery of the first New World, the Caribbean, and Australia as the last. Chapter 2, titled 'The First and Last of New Worlds: The Caribbean and Australia', traces connections between the two sites which bookend European colonial 'discovery' in view of the developing concept of the earthly globe. Integral to this process is the shifting status of continents and islands including their repeated misrecognition, their role in ideology and the role of the island in the figuration of the planet as a graspable whole. This discussion charts a number of reticulated lines between the Caribbean and Australia and compares the worlds discovered by Columbus and Cook according to their respective understandings of cosmos and globe and the constituent elements of islands, continents, sea and land. It examines the epistemic shifts within the era of 'world history', what Sloterdijk terms the period of the 'terrestrial globe', when the vertical cosmos is replaced with surfaceal cartography of the planet, which, in this study, is the particular globe of European colonization. (2013, 3–15).

The second part of this chapter focuses on the Australian colonial period when the first and last of new worlds are brought into simultaneous relation through imperial, carceral and mercantile economies. Juxtaposing the colonies of the Caribbean and Australia reveals the double logic of their relation. On the one hand the two are seen in sequence, a structure which generally relegates the West Indies to the past while the Australian colonies are the new (white) hope. However, their simultaneity also relates them as mutual alternatives, as occurs in the first novel published in Australia, *Quintus Servinton* by Henry Savery (1830) and in the comparative reading of figures such as Edward Eyre whose behaviour in one place does not seemingly accord with his actions in the other. An appendix of original research accompanies this discussion, which lists the extensive human traffic between the West Indies and the Australian colonies.

The second chapter in this section, Chapter 3, is titled 'Insular and Continental Interiors: The Shifting Map of Literary Universalism after the War' and reads a range of West Indian and Australian writing of the mid-twentieth century, the moment of the literary naissance of the Caribbean archipelago and of an Australian re-evaluation of its status as an island continent. The chapter begins with a discussion of the overdetermined significance of interiors in Modernist thought across the geographical categories of islands and continents from the search for planetary and domestic dwellings to understanding of the inner life. The chapter compares the diverse planetary imaginaries of the four Nobel laureates from the Caribbean and Australia: Patrick White, Derek Walcott, V. S. Naipaul and J. M. Coetzee. All four define themselves and their writing in terms of islands and continents, variously as home places and sites of alienation. Individually and in association, the four construct a shifting map of the globe, remaking the planet in response to the universalist remit of the Nobel Academy.

The chapter continues to distinguish between the related terms of globe, universe and planet in an examination of the postwar global fiction of Shirley Hazzard, whom Brigitta Olubas terms a 'literary expatriate and cosmopolitan humanist' (2012). Hazzard's fiction maps the spaces of the postwar world as a synthetic process in which islands are preferred sites where selves can be remade and, indeed, which map her own rhetorical unconscious. Hazzard's mobile globe contrasts with much of the new West Indian writing by women which so often maps an initial constitution of identity in and against colonialist cartography. The four novels discussed in this section, which span from the 1930s to the 1980s, all narrate the need to leave island homes. The heroines of Eliot Bliss' *Luminous Isle* (1934) and Phyllis Shand Allfrey's *The Orchid House* (1953) are both drawn and repulsed by the fetishizing gaze upon both island and self as white women in Jamaica and Dominica respectively. Merle Hodge's classic, *Crick Crack Monkey* (1970), exposes the conception of the island jewel as a nightmare of a colonial insularity that turns in on itself, fracturing its subjects. Hodge's heroine must also leave her island home, Trinidad, to undo the lockstep of self and (island) place structured by colonialism. Dionne Brand's novel, *In Another Place, Not Here* (1996) moves across the American archipelago from Trinidad and Grenada to Canada. Yet Brand's heroines are also islands of a kind. In their melancholy isolation and interconnection, the women in *In Another Place, Not Here* are exposed to the world in its brutality as well as locked within the confines of unrealized/unrealizable selves.

The following section on Australia's mid-century continental vision stands in stark contrast to the Caribbean narratives of becoming. Moving from the continental, monomaniacal hubris of Patrick White's *Voss* (1957) to Alex Miller's novels of continental complexity and diversity, the overlay of island and continent in these tales of the island-continent produces both nightmarish visions and spaces for negotiation of internal and cultural difference.

The third section is titled 'Dreams and Nightmares' and includes two chapters. Chapter 4, 'Accidents of Empire: Shipwrecks and Castaways', reads the proliferation of shipwreck literature during the colonial period as a symptom of the impending accident at the heart of empire. The chapter contends that shipwreck narratives from this period perform the dissolution of a series of long-standing literary pacts between writer, reader and subject. Moreover, these broken elements prove to be only partly salvageable and, even then, as we see though readings of both poetry and fiction, their imperfect reassemblage creates distortion throughout the text. The second part of the chapter moves to the land and illustrates the distinction between island and continental possession in the metaphorics of imperial ideology, which fosters island despotism. The literary analysis focuses on a series of Australian castaway stories from the colonial archive to contemporary fiction which chart the despotic potential of this distortion. The chapter concludes with discussion of 'The Castaways' (2009) by Darwin-based writer Marie Munkara, which unravels the history of island fetishization and acquisitional desire.

The final chapter, 'The Best and Worst of Times: Utopias, Dystopias, Archipelagos', examines the operations of the island dichotomy as both a paradise and a prison and as a supplement to the continental dominant. The discussion presents a range of ways these binaries are critiqued and undone. This undoing is necessary to break the fetishistic and possessive claims upon islands and the perception that they are inherently disconnected from the main. Deconstruction of the binaries of island and continent, land and sea, utopia and dystopia, identifies the dynamism of the island and its interconnections, which may be internal to islands, as in an archipelago. There is an urgent need to rethink the real conditions and imaginary capacities of islands and islanders on their own terms and in themselves. There is also the possibility that this understanding can provide models of interconnection that are urgently needed at a global level. This chapter presents alternatives to the island binary through utopian theory and recent debates about the topographies and topologies of archipelagic arrangements. It concludes with a comparison of an ancient and a contemporary story of the Torres Strait to show these interconnections across both space and time.

# Chapter 1

# WHAT'S IN A METAPHOR: 'NO MAN IS AN ISLAND'

> One thing is clear, the island, if it is to give us the satisfaction we want, must be small enough for us to grasp as a whole.
>
> Nettie Palmer, Green Island Diary (28 April 1932)
> (Jordan 2010, 150)

John Donne's famous pronouncement 'No man is an island' has proven to be a key coordinate in the map of modernity, particularly regarding the relationship between geography and identity. Donne's claim, first made in 1623, is poised on the brink of a new cartography of islands and continents taking form in his time and continuing to unfold into ours. As Donne's statement suggests, islands have a particular role in this map as both literal and imaginary locations: they were perceived as ideal colonies for primary production, especially given the difficulty of overland transportation until the nineteenth century, and as ideal prisons, as with Norfolk Island, Van Diemen's Land and Palm Island. Inseparable from these historical events is the powerful charge of the island in the Western imagination. As Yi-Fu Tuan has famously observed: 'The island seems to have a tenacious hold on the human [...] But it is in the imagination of the Western world that the island has taken strongest hold' (1998, 118). Gilles Deleuze's meditation on islands also identifies the lure of the island for the human imagination and its specific hold on the modern Western psyche, which resides in the island's capacity to represent the (illusory) possibility of a perfect harmony between man and space, where ego and geography appear to be perfectly aligned (2004, 10–11).

The ensuing discussion seeks to unravel the compacted set of meanings that attach to the man–island metaphor to show how and why this relationship assumed significance in the modern period and identify some of its implications in both history and representation. The chapter will investigate a range of ways the map of colonial modernity maps the modern man who is its proper and preferred subject. It argues that the island offers a figure of re-creation or rebirth which aligns with modern conceptions of identity formation – and the self-made colonial in particular. Through a study of both literature and history, I will show multiple ways this man-island takes shape according to racialized, gendered and literary formulations.

## Early Modern to Late Modern: Donne's Warning against Insularity

Two directives from Donne's Meditation XVII in *Devotions upon Emergent Occasions* (1623) became part of popular parlance in the twentieth century, though they are not always linked. One is the memento mori, 'never send to know for whom the bell tolls; it tolls for thee', popularized by Ernest Hemingway's novel *For Whom the Bell Tolls* (1940), much of which he wrote on the island of Cuba. The other, 'No man is an island', stands as a defining axiom of identity for Western modernity in its paradoxical capacity to refuse yet define the fantasy of self-origination and autonomy (Donne 1967, 100–101). The resonance of this man–island metaphor ranges across both its meaningful and ironic connotations. For while Donne cautions against this act of misrecognition – of mistaking oneself for an island – the metaphor of man and island nonetheless stands. The negative image shadows the statement. In her consideration of Donne's metaphor, Gillian Beer directs us to the psychic operations of language, specifically to Freud's claim that the unconscious mind knows no negative but can only structure desires in the affirmative: I want, I hate, I am. Accordingly, the reader's unconscious erases the negative cast of the metaphor, ironically affirming that man *is* indeed an island at the same time as their conscious mind registers that he is not (Beer 1997, 43). In this interrelation, the reader experiences both the positive impulse and the prescription against it.[1] Furthermore, and as is conventional of metaphor, the two associated terms, man and island, flicker between their reference to material reality and their figurative nationality, crisscrossing to produce numerous permutations of the real and imaginary subject of man and the real and imaginary object of the island. Lisa Gorton identifies a further and profound contradiction in Donne's use of space, which, she argues, simultaneously presents 'old and new ways of imagining the cosmos' so that man and space are located within both cosmographic and cartographic systems of ways of imagining the world, as incompatible as these may be (1998, 1).[2]

The contradictory valence of Donne's metaphor – its paradoxical interrelation of presence and absence, the material and the notional, cosmography and cartography – charts the lineaments of an anthropomorphized map that sutures man and geography in modernity. It identifies the man of Donne's

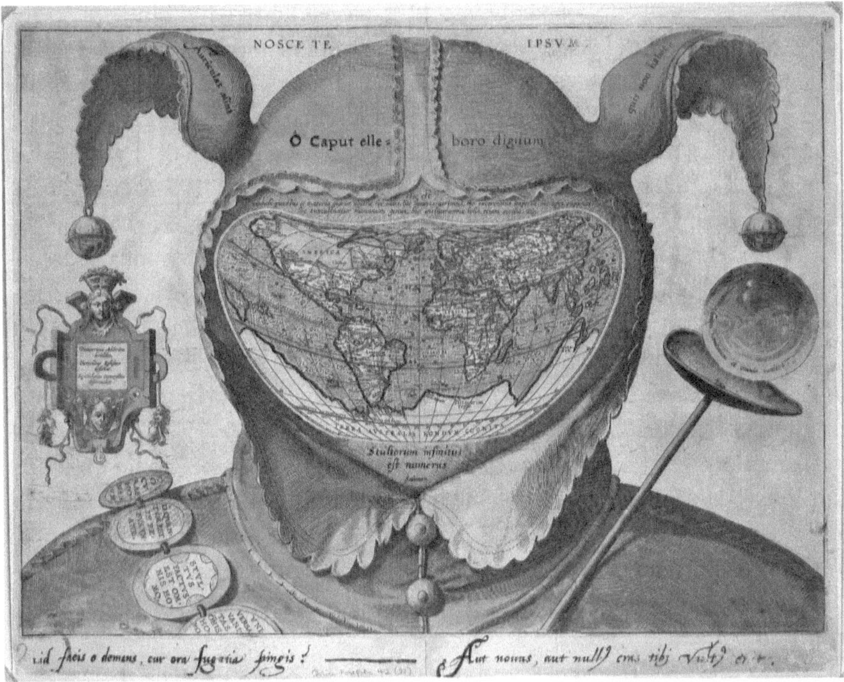


**Figure 1.1** Fool's Cap Map of the World (1580–1590). Courtesy British Library.

statement to be a gendered melancholic subject in the process of internalizing the loss of a passing sense of connectedness with the continental main, while looking forward to an imagined future autonomy as an island, anticipating both its freedom and its alienation. The internalization of loss and the projection of autonomy find a figure in island insularity, as this is variously understood: sanctuary, containment, separateness, incarceration, autonomy, solipsism. As we will see, the island is both the site and the means by which this new modern self is mapped at a defining moment of its constitution. This modern self is an overdetermined figure of melancholy, for the island will always disappoint the subject's desire for self-containment, for a perfect alignment of subject and object, of the human subject and space. Ultimately, as Deleuze has famously observed, the Western island imaginary seeks unity with the *élan* of the island's desertedness but is necessarily rejected by the island, which retains its perfection in separation (2004, 2, 10–11).

The mapping of this island-man in this discussion will first turn to Donne's subject, man, and then locate him in and through the associated term island. This approach is informed by the spatial turn in the humanities, now sometimes termed the geohumanities, by which real and imaginary geographies become a vital category of analysis, and are as contested and synthetic as the fields of history and society are now widely understood, rather than background setting or context. Related in part to this geographical focus, this study is also motivated by the new interdisciplinary field of Island Studies, which analyses the materiality, experience and representation of small islands, including their changing status in the history of European imperialism and in the newly globalized economies and geographies of the present. Studies by non-European islanders show a range of vastly different perceptions concerning space and inhabitation, highlighting, inter alia, the very particular, circumscribed spatiality of the island in the Western imaginary. These ideas will be canvassed for their challenges to Western thought, as original formulations of intrinsic value, and for the ways they overlay the globalized map with alternative relations, scales and dynamics.

Tom Conley claims, no doubt correctly, that '[t]he geographic imagination of early modern writing is marked by the wonder and enigma of the Columbian discoveries' (2007, 402). Donne's pronouncement about man and islands, uttered into the echo of the tolling bell of shared mortality, is so marked. Yet while Donne's metaphor reads as definitive of the modern condition, Beer has noted the long silence between the initial publication of Meditation XVII in 1624 and the twentieth century, when it was popularized by Ernest Hemingway's *For Whom the Bell Tolls* (1940) and when the two cautionary directives quickly became commonplaces (Beer 1997, 47). The 'rediscovery' of Donne by T. S. Eliot and the Modernists, and the publication of *For Whom the Bell Tolls* very specifically, ensured the currency of his work throughout the twentieth century and into ours, and has brought what John Gillis terms the two 'great eras of globalization', the Age of Discovery and our own, into a relation of ongoing becoming (2004, 38).[3] Accordingly, consideration of Donne's man-island requires a stereoscopic lens that moves between early modern and late modern contexts to consider the timeliness of Donne's spatial vision at these two historical moments. This comparison picks up from the suggestive insights of Beer's conclusion regarding the clichéd operations of 'No man is an island' from the twentieth century. Beer writes that cliché is a way of 'neutralising dreads and yearnings held within a community' and covers over matters that 'won't bear too analytical a scrutiny' (1997, 47). However, when these 'underground communal experiences cannot be contained or become the property of a different group, cliché retains the capacity to awaken as insight, perhaps as warning: No man is an island' (Beer 1997, 47). The task of unpacking what has become the cliché of 'No man is an island' is, then, a process of uncovering those matters that resist or deny analysis and how its redeployment from the mid-twentieth century has reawakened insight.

Ultimately, this analysis addresses the possible warning issued by Donne's 'Devotion' to the mid-twentieth century as it re-emerges from the midst of two world wars.

The investigation also proceeds on the understanding that such an inquiry is invited by Donne's text itself, though its use of imperatives appears to forestall argument. The instruction 'do not send to know for whom the bell tolls, it tolls for thee' is a commandment along Old Testament lines. However, the unequivocal injunction of the commandment can also be read as an invitation to speculation and debate rather than its refusal. Following Walter Benjamin's account of divine commandments in his 'Critique of Violence' and the subsequent engagements with this work by numerous influential thinkers (1978, 277–300), the discussion here will read Donne's proscriptive imperative as an opening rather than a closure.[4] For Benjamin, the divine commandment of the Bible, as distinct from the mythical law of Greek antiquity, cannot be used as a mode of judgement in instances of its transgression. He writes:

> The commandment exists not as a criterion of judgment, but as a guideline for the action of people and communities, who have to wrestle with it in solitude, and, in exceptional cases, to take on themselves the responsibility for ignoring it. (Benjamin 1978, 298)

For Benjamin the divine commandment – that is, for instance, Thou shalt not kill – precedes lived experience yet holds within itself the implication that transgressions will occur in that domain. He writes: 'The commandment precedes the deed just as God was preventing the deed' but 'the injunction becomes inapplicable, incommensurable once the deed is done' (Benjamin 1978, 298). In Benjamin's formulation, the temporalities of precedence and the present correspond with the domains of injunction and experience.

Donne's two statements also precede their (inevitable) transgression and indeed hold those transgressions within themselves, at the very level of figure and syntax, for, as indicated previously, the axiomatic wisdom is shadowed by empirical knowledge. In terms of historical precedence, we can also see how Donne's claim about the nature of man, yoked to an injunction regarding shared mortality, has played out in Western modernity in multiple ways since the time of its utterance in 1623. Accordingly, the interrogation of the operations and effects of Donne's metaphor 'No man is an island', undertaken here, views this claim to natural law and the attendant commandment not to heed the ringing bell of shared mortality as 'guideline[s]' we continue to 'wrestle with', not only in solitude but also with a new self-consciousness on the condition of solitude itself created by the contemplation of the man-island.

## The Piece of Work That Is Man

In a seminar on *Robinson Crusoe*, Jacques Derrida asked repeatedly: 'What is an island?' (2009, 3). We will come to that too, but heeding Derrida's attention to the basic terms of an inquiry we will begin with the subject of Donne's metaphor to ask 'What is ("No) man?"' For this (No) man is not universal, though he appears to be so by dint of his centrality in a statement of natural law and embedded in the certainty of its syntax and cadence. Rather, (No) man is culturally specific. Early modern writers furnish us with many definitions and doubts, including Hamlet's exclamation, 'What a piece of work is man' (Shakespeare ca.1600, 2.2.303) and George Herbert's poem 'Man' (1633) in which it is declared that 'Man is ev'rything' (2007, 332–33). As Leonard Barkan sets out in his detailed study on the topic of early modern man, man and the human body in particular are little worlds, microcosms and models of symmetry (1975, 1–2). In a similar vein, Andrew Gordon and Bernard Klein attest to the way that in 'cosmographical thought the world has always been imagined in terms of the human body, and the conceptual identity between cartographers and anatomists is one of the founding tropes of mapping' (2001, 7). This understanding of man as located and dislocated between cosmographical and cartographical understandings of the world is augmented by contemporary theories of space and subjectivity of the late modern era to which Donne's metaphor clearly resonates (see Figure 1.1).

First and foremost, Donne's man needs to be understood as a gendered term rather than designating the putatively inclusive understanding of man as humanity. Especially in its association with an island, (No) man is gender exclusive, for the identification of the self with an island is a fantasy and condition of the masculine subject. From Prospero and Donne to *Robinson Crusoe* and the industry of Robinsonades that ensued, there are very few texts, if any, in which women align their subjectivity with an island. There are a small number of projections of female characters by male authors, such as J. M. Coetzee's postcolonial Robinsonade *Foe* (1986), and there are feminist utopias, that operate quite differently. In their respective discussions of the female Robinsonade *The Female American* (1767), by the pseudonymous Unca Eliza Whitfield, both Hans Turley and Michelle Burnham point to key differences between this novel and its predecessor by Defoe, including, most significantly the fact that the female castaway is not alone: a hermit has preceded her to the island, there is a community of indigenous inhabitants and the novel ends in marriage (Turley 2004; Burnham 2001). Jeannine Blackwell's study 'An Island of Her Own: Heroines of the German Robinsonades from 1720 to 1800' sets out similar distinctions along gender lines and points to the profound difference in the notion of self-generation in these texts according to the hierarchy of gender (1985). Derrida, too, stresses the gender specificity of the Crusoe figure:

> [T]his man is a man, a human and a male human (not woman) let's never forget it; nothing equivalent or similar or analogous was ever to my knowledge (and I may be wrong) written about a woman alone: an island in an island. (2009, 2)

Despite numerous similarities in narrative structure and colonizing imperatives, woman is not 'an island in an island'. Unlike the masculine subject she is not aligned or commensurate with the island.

In his fable *Tale of the Unknown Island* (1997, 1999), 1998 Portuguese Nobel laureate José Saramago stages the gendered nature of the island aspiration as a dialogue between the main male and female characters. The pair has recently united in a plan to sail to the Unknown Island, or, more precisely, the woman has realized there are possibilities in attaching herself to the plan, which is of the man's conception. His is the first statement in the following dialogue where the first three commas indicate a change of speaker:

> I want to find out who I am when I'm there on that island, Don't you know, If you don't step outside yourself, you'll never know who you are, The King's philosopher, when he had nothing to do, would come and sit beside me and watch me darning the pages' socks, and sometimes he would say that each man is an island, but since that had nothing to do with me, being a woman, I paid no attention to him. (Saramago 1999, 32)

The woman's facetious but nonetheless astute recognition stalls the speculations of both the king's philosopher and her new companion. She is wise to do so, for acceptance of Donne's axiom would exclude her from the projected journey to the Unknown Island, as it only pertains to man. Indeed it would erase her from the narrative itself.

In addition to gender limitation, Donne's (No) man is nationally specific. He is the Western subject and, specifically, a subject of the emerging British Empire. Donne's position in English society led to first-hand experience of islands, other than his native Britain, including his participation as a volunteer in the Azores or Islands Expedition of 1597. This expedition, like the campaign for Cadiz the year earlier, aimed to weaken the Spanish fleet in its voyages to and from the New World, thereby enabling British access to the same. As has been amply recorded, most recently and compellingly by John Stubbs, the expedition and campaign against the Spanish in the Azores, led by Walter Raleigh and Robert Devereux, Earl of Essex, was a failure at multiple levels (2006, 70–80). The two poems Donne wrote on this expedition were to remain very popular in his own time, and they are now valued in part for their 'realistic' description of experience. The pair, 'The Storme' and 'The Calme', written to his friend Christopher Brook, records aspects of the voyage and his own tumultuous responses (1953, 175–78). The poem of the voyage, 'The Storme', dramatizes the events of a violent storm from within the experience and in a mood of fear. It has also been read allegorically as a poem of battle (Nellist 1964, 511–15). 'The Calme' partners the earlier poem, but the matter belies the title in that it is not a poem of relief or respite. Rather, it counters the frantic activity of 'The Storme' with stagnation in an account of the enforced and protracted stay on the island of Fayal when the English fleet is becalmed after they have laid siege to the island and the Spanish Fleet. 'The Calme' is often cited as a suicidal poem.[5] The poet mocks his own slight reasons for joining the campaign as well as those of the 'rotten state' of his own country. He concludes:

> What are we then? How little more, alas,
> Is man now, than before he was? He was
> Nothing; for us, we are for nothing fit;
> Chance, or ourselves, still disproportion it.
> We have no power, no will, no sense; I lie,
> I should not then thus feel this misery. (Donne 1953, 178)

In her reading of the two poems Linda Mizejewski argues persuasively for their significant difference from Donne's other works, and for the progressive disillusionment from 'The Storme' to 'The Calme' (1977, 217). In the elaborate figurative operations of much of his other poetry, she contends, a system such as science provides a ballast or counterlogic to balance or deflect a conceit of love or despair. Alternatively, Donne deploys discursive shifts, as in moving to physics from geometry in 'A Valediction Forbidding Mourning', to figure a form of resolution seemingly out of reach in the terms of the original argument. These two poems, however, deploy or import no other system to make sense of the experience (Mizejewski 1977, 217). Consequently, there is no fit, no harmony between man and the world. Mizejewski compares the two poems in terms of the blackness and obscurity of 'The Storme' and the light and clarity of 'The Calme'. This clarity, however, does not restore an inherited concept of the harmony of the world and man's place within it but enables a steely eyed appraisal that illuminates disharmony formed by the impersonal operations of nature and the unfitness of man.

The dramatized speaker in 'The Calme', whom the biographical references identify as comparable to Donne, is deeply implicated and undone by the English campaigns to gain the New World. What may appear to modern readers as the unlikely connection of colonist, soldier, slaver and poet is examined in the early poem of St Lucian 1992 Nobel laureate, Derek Walcott, 'The Ruins of a Great House' (1953–54) whose catalogue of 'Ancestral murderers and poets' includes 'Hawkins, Walter Raleigh and Drake'. Walcott's poem weighs the seeming contradiction that these Renaissance men included murderous conquest in their repertoire. It is Donne's Meditation XVII that mediates the poet-speaker's rage in the final two stanzas of the poem, for even against his will, his 'eyes burned with the ashen prose of Donne' (Walcott 1992b, 19–21). For Walcott, the irresoluble dilemma is to be so drawn to the writing – of Donne in particular – and so enraged and repulsed by the poets' participation in Britain's violent colonization of the New World. Donne's motto, *per Rachel ho servito, et non per Lea* (I have served Rachel (the contemplative life) not Leah (the active life)), is rendered highly ironic (Keynes 1973, 259–60).

'The Calme' may perform the poet's dilemma in that the speaker is rendered artless in the face of actual conquest, but Donne did indeed serve the active life and actively sought it, including a direct role in the colonization of the New World with the Virginia Company, as discussed in the following chapter. However both the activity and inactivity lead to intense introspection in these two poems and the poet's main question leads back to our own: what is man? If before he was nothing, now he does not even fit nothing. He is not fit, in that he is unworthy, and he does not fit, in that there is no longer a sense of emplacement.

The Azores, mid-Atlantic islands positioned above an active triple junction, where three of the world's largest tectonic plates meet, were a key location in various operations of colonization and slavery. Donne's contemporary, the geographer and cartographer Abraham Ortelius, was the first to hypothesize the theory of continental drift in 1596, but it was not developed until the twentieth century and not fully proven until 1968, our own time, and the second great era of globalization. The three plates that meet in the Azores are the North American Plate, the Eurasian Plate and the African plate: a triumvirate that comprises the three-stage triangular trade route from Europe to Africa to the Americas including the middle passage and the transportation of slaves, whose labour constructed the New World. Many years later, Australia's first major poet, another melancholic, Adam Lindsay Gordon, was born on this same island – another story of British interests in the New World.

In one of his earlier fictions on islands real, imaginary and unknown, Saramago's 1986 novel *The Stone Raft* brings this same colonial network into late modernity in a quasi-fantastical narrative, predicated on the calamity of the Iberian peninsula breaking away from mainland Europe and floating away, into the Atlantic, on course for a collision with the Azores islands, materializing Donne's conceit. Mark J. L. Sabine describes the journey of the promontory-turned-island:

> After near collision with the Azores, the Peninsula changes direction several times, following by turns a rectilinear, then a rotary trajectory before coming to an inconclusive halt between Africa and Latin America, roughly the heart of postcolonial Hispanophone and Lusophone world. (2005, 74)

Saramago's satire of modern European politics and his own adherence to a Marxist politics of utopia remap Spanish and Portuguese alliances in the twentieth century so that they are connected to the postcolonial Hispanophone and Lusophone worlds rather than, as Saramago's satire perceives, relegated as insignificant players in the European Union. It is the same triangulated space at the centre of European colonialization of the New World via Africa and the slave trade.

From 1597 at Fayal Island to 1623, when Donne coined his enduring metaphor of man as an island in the Devotions, he is involved in another connection between politics and poetics. For 1623 also marks English explorer Thomas Warner's claim to the first island colony in the New World for England, the island of St Christopher (St Kitts). The following year, in which Donne published the Devotions, an English colony led by Warner was established on the island. Further, in 1625 Warner allowed the establishment of a French settlement on the island led by Pierre Belain d'Esnambuc, hence enabling the first French island colony in the Caribbean also. In 1626 the English and French united against a real or fabricated uprising by the Carib peoples of the island leading to the Kalinago genocide in which many thousands of Carib people from St Kitts and surrounding islands were murdered. After this time, with the French and English now firmly established, the two communities divided the island and used it as a base to colonize neighbouring islands (Hubbard 2002, 14–25). Both introduced slavery from Africa as the bedrock of labour and industry.

Accordingly, Donne's metaphor is entwined in this history of British imperialism and the acquisition of islands as readymade colonies and as sites of racial genocide and slavery. This imbrication of figure and ground elucidates the ways Donne's man refers to racialized hu/man with very clear limits, and these limits were in the process of definition on the islands of the New World at this very moment.

The particular connection between islands, British imperialism, ethnicity and *poesis* is identified by Deleuze and Guattari in their discussion of national philosophical differences in modernity. They argue that the 'history of philosophy is [...] marked by national characteristics' or, what they term 'nationalitarians' (*nationalitaires*) and go on to compare the national characteristics of French, German and English habits of thought according to a tripartite model of Founding-Building-Inhabiting. In their account the French 'are always reterritorialised on consciousness', that is, preoccupied with the *cogito* in various formations. The Germans have not surrendered the Absolute and 'must clear and consolidate [the Ancient Greek] ground, that is to say they must lay foundations' (Deleuze and Guattari, 1991 104). English habits of thought are characterized in terms of the inhabitation of islands:

> The English are precisely those nomads who treat the plane of immanence as a moveable and moving ground, a field of radical experience, an archipelagian world where they are happy to pitch their tents from island to island and over the sea. The English nomadise over the old Greek earth, broken up, fractalised, and extended to the entire universe. (Deleuze and Guattari 1994, 104)

More than the French and German in this account, the English mode of conceptualization is defined by geography: it is linked to the Britons' ancient migration from the continent to the British Isles and their ongoing capacity to inhabit and habituate themselves in new places, especially islands. It is characterized, too, by a process of contemplation that contracts the object of contemplation; these contemplated objects are often 'the elements from which we come' (Deleuze and Guattari 1994, 105).

Donne's man–island metaphor figures the interlinked processes of inhabitation, contemplation and contraction by which Deleuze and Guattari identify the nationalitarian of English thought. The island is in many ways a synonym for home and inhabitation. In Australia, we are most familiar with the phrase 'My Island Home' from the song Neil Murray wrote for George Rrurrambu and the Warumpi Band about Elcho Island off Arnhem Land, and which was also modified and recorded by Christine Anu who sang of her family's island home in the Torres Strait (Murray and Warumpi Band 1986).[6] So, too, the island commonly figures contemplation through its inherent insularity or interiority. And, as a miniature world, the island is a figure of contraction. In such devices as epitome, Donne's poetry habitually contracts the contemplated object, as in the final stanza of 'The Canonisation':

> You, to whom love was peace, that now is rage;
> Who did the whole world's soul contract, and drove
>     Into the glasses of your eyes;
>     So made such mirrors, and such spies,
> That they did all to you epitomize. (2002, 6–7)

Here the eye-mirrors explicitly direct us to the reflexive qualities of such contractions and dilations, as each element alternately encompasses or is encompassed by the other. In relation to the man–island metaphor, the alternating contractions and dilations perform the incorporation or introjection of man into the island and vice versa. The resulting configurations of the man-island, of one carrying the other within itself, are concepts both of gestation and of mourning.

Derrida traces this connection of islands, gestation and mourning in his final reading of Paul Celan, another writer of the Second World War, a poet of the Holocaust and mourning. In his reading of Celan's 1967 poem '*Grosse, Glühende Wölbung*' ('Vast Glowing Vault'), Derrida writes: 'There is no world any more, only islands' for the world has been fractured irreparably by the War. As there is no longer any common ground, Celan concludes: '*Die Welt is fort, ich muss dich tragen*' (The world is gone, I can only carry you) (Derrida 2009, 9). Without world, with only islands, the only form of inhabitation possible is the process of carrying another in melancholic gestation. Without world – or an understanding of the human collective, as Donne describes at length in Meditation XVII – we can no longer associate as communities on shared ground but must take others into ourselves as we do lost loved ones in grief, for each and every other person is an island, impossibly separate and always lost to us.

This melancholic gestation is a perverse form of generation in its confusion of birth and loss. For if everyone is already lost to us, the act of taking them into ourselves in gestation reverses the sequence of birth and death, what in classical rhetoric is termed *hysteron-proteron* (latter before). Overturning logical or natural sequence in this way typically produces an unnatural effect, such as the supernatural phoenix rising to life from the ashes of death, or, more broadly, it signifies artistic creation. In its refusal of natural progeniture the melancholic gestation of an other who alternately seeks to contain us, also signals self-creation, for it replaces the sequence of generation with synchronic reflexivity: the sin of Milton's Satan; and so Donne cautions us: No man is an island.

If, as Deleuze and Guattari suggest, the contemplated and contracted objects that define English habits of thought are 'the elements from which we come', the island contemplated by man provides such materials. Island and man are made of the same stuff, further confounding the attempts to differentiate man from the island. To the reader who contemplates both man and island and their relation of alternating encompassment, the two terms appear coeval; neither begat the other, each is created *in* the other, returning us to Deleuze's argument in his essay on 'Desert Islands' that islands seem to offer the possibility of a perfect harmony between man and space, man and world so that man is the world (Deleuze 2004).

## Negative Generation and the Melancholy Subject

These paradoxes of birth and death, origin and lost origin also play out in the relation between Donne's man and his obverse identity as 'No man'. The definitional statement is in the negative, but this negation folds into the sentence itself, performing a form of self-cancellation. Hence the affirmative claim embedded within it, 'man is an island', is a double negative. Read meaningfully, the axiom claims the authority of self-evidence – clearly man is not a geographical formation – as if distancing itself from the far-fetchedness of metaphor's conventional mode of category crossing. The authority of self-evidence strengthens the claims of the statement's wisdom concerning man's inherent sociality as being in accordance with natural law. It is profoundly true also in the sense that Deleuze formulates in 'Desert Islands', that the Western island imaginary seems to promise a perfect alignment between self and geography, which is always necessarily disappointed, for man is *not* an island (2004, 10–11). Read conversely, the statement leads us to speculate that man *is* an island, even as we understand that this condition is somehow prohibited or improper. This converse statement does not provide axiomatic wisdom but is in the order of an empirical or experiential observation. Its status is lesser in terms of axiomatic Truth and greater in terms of empirical facticity.

The holographic alternation between negative and affirmative readings of '(No) man is an island' and between precept and experience also operates to construct the modern subject, who is not divinely created and named but fashioned from within the binaries of the fallen world. These binaries are in play in the proper noun of 'No man' which, like More's *Utopia* or 'No Place', designates a particular site even in its self-erasure. In a similar vein No man also recalls the punning trick Odysseus plays on Cyclops in Book Nine of the *Odyssey*, when he calls himself 'No-man' to conceal his name from the giant (Homer 800 B.C.). In Homer's island story, 'No man' stands in the place of the narrative's most positive presence, the hero himself. In Donne's island metaphor 'No man' stands in the place of the hero of modernity, namely the Western subject, who comes to view and is made present in the shadow of a negative.

The paradox of this negative presence is underscored if we read/hear No man as an allegorical figure like Everyman in the earlier morality play (Anon *The Summoning* 2011). Beer also makes this connection to argue that the 'controlling negative' of Donne's No man constructs an everyman in the general sense because the negation of exclusion creates inclusion and connection (1997, 48). However, the use of negative definition also signals a recalibration of the way the human representative is imagined and figured. The alteration from Everyman to No man shows the diminished capacity of one to represent the whole, a feature that Conley notes was of especial concern in Donne's time (2007, 404).

Donne turns to this dilemma repeatedly in his poetry, as David Hirsch documents in a study of the interrelationship of atomic and anatomic conceptions in Donne. Hirsch discusses the contradictory movements towards the unification of a body or self and the dissolution of (an)atomy into pieces in a range of poems including 'The First Anniversarie' and 'Upon Mr Thomas Croyats Crudities' (1991, 69–94). In Meditation XVII the context for the No man as a human representative is established by the opening paragraph which stresses the partial or atomic relation of each human to the anatomy of mankind.

> When [the Church] baptizes a child, that action concerns me; for that child is thereby connected to that body which is my head too, and ingrafted into that body whereof I am a member. And when she buries a man, that action concerns me: all mankind is of one author, and is one volume; when one man dies, one chapter is not torn out of the book, but translated into a better language; and every chapter must be so translated. (Donne 1967, 100)

However, this first image of a unified anatomy that coheres according to Christian doctrine is in tension with tolling bell of material decay and mortality that decomposes an atom at a time.

The shift from Everyman to No man also points to a process of definition via negation rather than by the absolute decree of creation, which again directs us away from the coherence of divine genesis to self-creation through an assemblage of worldly components. Perhaps most immediately, this process recalls the dialogue between Jesus and Satan in Milton's *Paradise Regained* (1671) and the process by which Jesus realizes his dual humanity and divinity through his refusals of Satan's temptations rather than by action or affirmation (1983, 460–513). Negation is the mode of attainment in a fallen world where identity is achieved through a secondary process and is not already complete. It is a mode of definition that recognizes the impossibility of absolute definitions. Rather, it understands that classification and naming are achieved in a relational system, by measuring one thing against others which it is *not*. Later in the modern era this method became emblematic of Freud's catalogue of human subjects in which definitions of perversions and deviations precede the norm or man, who is thus able to emerge from the shadow of perversion to be defined only by what he is not (2000, 2).

Such paradoxical inversions are, of course, stock in trade for the seventeenth-century poet and for Donne in particular (Finkler 1999, 207–8). Twentieth-century theories of language, also, alert us to the impossibility of fending off either term of any binary construction, as both terms are always in play, perhaps most especially when the attempt to block one and quarantine another is performed so insistently, as it is in Donne's statement (Derrida 1983). Through the dual lenses of early modern poetics and poststructuralist theorization of contaminated binaries, we see that even the island, that imaginary space of absolute and uncontaminated borders, mirrors the putative absolutism of Donne's statement in that it proves to be compromised by the presence of its own opposition within its own syntax. Furthermore, when one such contradiction is identified, those others parallel or attendant on this primary opposition become circumscribed within the same relentless process of oscillation and tension. In Donne's Meditation these other binaries include the relation between islands and continents, self and others, and, reflexively, the status of its own utterance and its location within domains of abstraction and materiality, precept and experience.

Donne's No man is the Western hero or subject and, as Freud theorized, this subject belongs to one gender, as noted previously. However, the gender specificity in Donne's Meditation is not only nominative but structural. The masculine subject whose rebirth is staged on and as an island is profoundly melancholy. The melancholy of Donne's conceit is accented by the theme of the Meditation as a whole, namely the memento mori and the unified body of the Christian community, which renders each death as partly our own, hence: 'never send to know for whom the bell tolls; it tolls for thee'. The timbre of sage and sober counsel is accompanied by an equally elegiac voice of felt experience that can also be linked to the shifting parameters of the world that he stages in the changed relations between the continent and the broken island.

The connection between geographical discovery and melancholy at this time is well documented: Patricia Vicari (1989) reads geographical discovery as a potential cure in Burton's *Anatomy of Melancholy* (1621), while Conley writes of this period that the 'abyss opened between individual experience of space and what received information might tell of it' actively produced melancholy (2007, 407). Donne's speaker is aligned with the latter experience, and he makes explicit that he is speaking from within the condition he describes. He writes that he is 'brought so near the door by this sickness', indeed he may be brought so low that he does not recognize his own imminent death. Accordingly, the Meditation's steely eye is motivated and animated, ironically enough, by the personalized distress of the speaker's enforced quiescence, and he presents himself as very alone in his illness amid the theorization of the communal body. He grieves for himself, as he believes he is witnessing 'a piece of himself [passing] out of this world' (Donne 1967, 101).

The play on presence and absence is in some ways akin to Freud's *fort/da*, the child's game of loss and recovery that mediates and metaphorizes the loss of the mother, except that *fort/da* is a process: first loss, then recovery in repeated sequence (2003, 52–55), whereas the temporality of presence and absence in Donne's metaphor is simultaneous. The synchrony and conflation of presence and absence defines the melancholic subject who, in Freud's formulation, incorporates the lost object-cathexis (lost loved one) into the self through identification that blurs the boundary between the self and its object (2003, 43–102). This may occur in a symbolic manner, as a kind of substitution of the real loss, but in Freud's theory, if the loss is denied it becomes in Tammy Clewell's words 'encrypted into the body' of the mourner (2004, 50).[7] Donne's sick body is an image of this denial. For he both denies and accepts the loss of the man who was connected to the community or continental main, the earlier self, in both historical and personal senses. Personally, it is the self before individuation and attendant self-division; historically, it is a moment before the emerging individualism of the axiom, from before man became an island.

This real or fantasmatic memory of an earlier, preindividuated man, who is in the process of passing out of the world, is internalized into the No/New man, creating the space of modern interiority. It is, as such, an interiority born of melancholy, of the former lost self who was not separate like an island but a component of the human body. This tautological construction is also a form of autogenesis; for man and No man construct both the interiority and exteriority of the subject. It is the theory of self-origination espoused by Milton's Satan who bases his claim on the absence of a memory of origin:

> rememberest thou
> Thy making, while the Maker gave thee being?
> We know no time when we were not as now;
> Know none before us, self-begot, self-raised
> By our own quickening power. (1983, 318)

Satanic self-creation relies on amnesia, the self is initiated at consciousness. Donne's No man, however, has too much memory. The felt absence of origins and the attendant melancholy of their impossible recovery are markers of the self made man. Into the vacuum left by lost origin is the interiority of the reborn, melancholic self.

## From Man to Island

The nature of this interiority leads us to ask, with Derrida, 'What is an island?' Like man a full response to this question crosses multiples discourses and requires many specifications.[8] Edmundo O'Gorman claims that in the sixteenth century, for the first time, 'the concept of insularity, in the sense of discontinuity, ceased to be the property applicable to great landmasses' (quoted in Gillis 2004, 62). Insularity, even though the word is now synonymous with islands, is only at this time becoming identified with geographical islands, lands surrounded by sea. The literal and abstract centrality of interiority is the pivot point for this discussion also, for the connected ideas of a self-defined and self-sensate interiority lead directly to a consideration of the island, which is, in its many forms, a figure of insularity and autonomy. Donne's Meditation is thus using a new lexicon of geography and cartography at a volatile moment of significant redefinition including shifting emphases between their real or metaphorical signification.

Studies of cartography in early modern literature identify oppositional trajectories for words moving between their figurative and geographical meanings. As certain words move toward increased material referentiality, others become more abstract and figurative. In her extensive study of medieval and early modern Iberian literature, Simone Pinet traces the increasing metaphorization of the island across this period, its gradual shift from material denotation to its role in representing more abstract states and providing implicit scaffolding for literary structures (2011, xxxiv–xxxv). An antithetical pattern is discernible in the English context, where Henry Turner records that the more general term 'map' in Renaissance poetry was deployed far more for its figurative operations and that the spatial sense of the map was very much the secondary meaning. He writes:

> For the Elizabethan poet the 'map' functioned as a conceit in a variety of figurative senses, all of which align it with the epitome, emblem, portrait, mirror or digest: it evoked a visual image that encapsulated, in condensed form, emotional states, abstract qualities, or metaphysical ideas. (Turner 2007, 412)

In terms of chronology, the figurative sense of the map predates the literal: figure heralds ground.

Donne, however, is properly a Jacobean poet and a Mannerist, writing later and after the Elizabethans, and his cartographic figuration of self renegotiates this relation so that each term is weighted more evenly. As occurs so frequently in his poetry, the holographic flickerings and reversals suspend the two terms of comparison; the literal referent and his abstract mirror are in unresolved tension in which neither term remains stable. Accordingly, the mapping of man and island in Donne carries the legacy of the conventional mirror or epitome, but it is also more indeterminate regarding its primary domain. It may present as a treatise on man and mortality, but this condition is now ineluctably inscribed into the cartography of the modern.

The volatility of Donne's statement, its retrospective and prospective salience, is evident at the basic level of the shifting denotation of key words in the Meditation, where we can trace their increasing application to geography.

The two spaces Donne deploys in his Meditation, the island and the continent, are historically contingent, and at the time of writing (1623) were at a moment of historic redefinition. In *The Myth of Continents* (1997) Martin W. Lewis and Kären E. Wigen claim that the current understanding of continents was only consolidated in the middle decades of the twentieth century. Gillis notes that the word 'continent' is first used in the modern sense of a large land mass in 1559 by William Cuningham in *The Cosmographical Glasse.* Cuningham writes that a continent 'is a portion of th' Earth, which is not parted by the Seas asounder' (quoted in Gillis 2004, 113). Some decades later Richard Hakluyt uses the term in *Principall Navigations* (1599) in reference to the Americas: 'That large and fruitfull Continent of the West Indies' (Lewis and Wigen 1997, 29).

The word *continent* is used repeatedly in Renaissance texts but more often in its older sense of a container, as we see in Act 2 of *A Midsummer Night's Dream* (ca. 1595) when Titania declares to Oberon that 'contagious fogs' have every petty River made so proud, / That they have over-borne their Continents (Shakespeare ca. 1595 2.2). So, too, in his sermon 'The White Devil, or The Hypocrite Uncased', preached at Pauls Crosse (7 March 1612), Thomas Adams uses the term in this sense when he writes: 'The Bag is a continent to money, and the world is a continent to the Bag' (1612, 253). Later again, in 1616, in Act Four of *Antony and Cleopatra*, Mark Antony instructs his heart to be 'stronger than thy continent, / Crack thy frail case!' (Shakespeare 1616, 4.14). Closer again to Donne's Meditation in numerous ways, Robert Burton also refers to the continent as a container in *The Anatomy of Melancholy* (1621) in which he sets out as the fundaments of his study a Laurentian understanding of the body, which is divided into 'parts *contained*, or *containing*' (1927, 128). This understanding of 'continent' as container fits easily with the relation between microcosm and macrocosm in the Principle of Correspondences and with a geocentric vision of the world, with each unit contained in a larger one in centrifugal expansion.

Donne's use of the term continent as a land mass is an early record of its usage in the modern geographical sense, and it necessarily carries the older understanding of the continent as a container, locating man and space at the centre of the universe in accordance with the Principle of Correspondences and the Ptolemaic system. This earlier meaning underscores the designation of the geographical continent as a proper container for man. Crucially, this locatedness within the cosmographical order is relational in that man occupies a known position in a pre-existing system. This is to say that the continental structure of inclusion advocated in the Meditation remains at least partly vertical, as the system of ever-increasing containers or continents amplifies to the macrocosm in a graduated series of contained centres or interiors. Ironically, this association of space and containment has become the property of islands – indeed it is in this very process in Donne's metaphor – but in island containment there is only the self, sensate to the felt borders of the island's delineation.

Gillis notes that the emergence of the geographical understanding of continent is coincident with the increasing delineation of the word 'island', which had hitherto referred to a multiplicity of separated spaces and peoples (2007, 62). The *Oxford English Dictionary* records that even in the sense of island in terms of land and water, the word was '[f]ormerly used less definitely, including a peninsula, or a place insulated at high water or during floods, or begirt by marshes' (*OED online*, 99986). Gillis suggests that the first 'use of the word in its modern sense was recorded in 1555, when Antonio Galvano, writing about a failed ancient project to dig a canal from the Nile to the Red Sea, noted that it would have made Africa "an island all encompassed with water"' (2007, 84). Hence before the geographical definition of 'island' as land surrounded by water the word referred to various forms of separateness and discontinuity. In the limitation of the word's meaning, what was once but one exemplum of separateness, land surrounded by water, now commandeers the whole term. In the first chapter of *The Colony*, Grace Karskens refers to the new settlements in New South Wales as islands. She writes that until the 1820s, the Europeans, who were a maritime people, used the rivers as the primary mode of transport and that their settlements were either coastal or 'inland islands' (2009, 23). Here again we can see that the older understandings of the word 'island' are in play in Donne's metaphor and that his usage is poised between old meanings and new, as used by Karskens in her description of European settlements and by Joseph Furphy in *Such Is Life* (1903) to refer to a habitable or contained space. In chapter 3 Tom describes a tract of land as an 'island of verdure, and no white man could track a horse through the labyrinth that led to it' (Furphy 1991, 84). In chapter 4 he refers to 'an island among the lignum, where the bullocks would be safe' (Furphy 1991, 160).

The identification of the shifting meanings of islands and continents, of their increasing specification as singular spatial designations, positions Donne's metaphor at a moment of literal redefinition. He is using terms that are especially volatile, animated by the movement of their meanings in the very moment of their alteration, a movement that has continued with the relentless changes from that time. Their particular movement towards the lexicon and semiotics of space and geography marks a fracture in the capacity to conceptualize the cosmic wholeness of the world. The world is broken into aggregate parts that do not articulate to produce a composite whole. The production of a whole is the task of the geographer, as Conley notes in his discussion of Peter Apian's 'emblematic rewriting of the first sentences of Ptolemy's *Geography*'. The dilemma that presents itself in this system is that the increased inclusion of multiple sites within national space produces the effects of 'fragmentation, of a limited point of view on the topic, and of singularities that do not fit in a greater or reassuringly self-contained picture' (Conley 2007, 404).

The identification with the island can be seen as symptom and compensation of this fracture, this non-fit. In the absence of this holistic order, the cosmic globe becomes epitomized as the miniature globe of the island. While in the system of correspondences Man was a cosmos, he becomes, in Donne's figuration, an island – figured as a substitute cosmos. This is not merely a change of scale according to the operations of microcosm and macrocosm but proves to be a changeling substitution, which undoes the pattern of amplification and diminution of the correspondences. In this case, the alteration of the globe as a cosmos to the globe as an island has shifted discourse from cosmography to cartography with all the attendant, if also inconsistent, shifts this implies, most especially from vertical vision to horizontal purview. Once altered, there is no true return, although the attempt is repeatedly rehearsed, as with the assertions of the Meditation. The effect is distorted and parodic as the axes of meaning and the multiplicity of semantics are dislodged from the anchor of certain presence in both word and world. In relation to the vertical and horizontal planes of meaning, this distortion refigures conventions of centrifugal deferral and centripetal precision. Where once vertical deferral related to a higher authority, a transcendence, and the centripetal target of precision nailed down meaning and confirmed the presence of each word, a form of immanence, both terms are flattened onto the horizontal plane of modern geography. The dichotomy is no longer vertical, between the earth and the heavens and the paradoxical interplay between them, but is now between inside and outside earthly planes and borders, onto which is mapped the interior and exterior conditions of man. The movement Donne's man makes is horizontal and contiguous, away from the continent but with an oceanic gulf between continent and island.

Pinet makes a similar claim for the horizontal plane as an index of modernity and cites the Francophone medieval scholar Paul Zumthor who 'asks if the word "modern", coined in 1100, can be in fact sutured to the change or reduction of perspectives to horizontality' (Zumthor 1993, 34, quoted in Pinet 2011, xvii). Reading Donne in relation to emerging cartography and space has been a keystone of Donne scholarship, and from their various positions and with particular emphases, most critics are in loose agreement that Donne is both committed to older images and representations of the universe, the Ptolemaic geocentric vision and other vertical cosmographical understandings of the world, at the same time as he is captivated and galvanized by more modern, horizontal cartography (Gorton 1998, 1–27).

It is the interplay and overlay of these two volatile terms, man and island, that produces an anthropomorphized map of modernity which promises to address the question of particular connection of Donne's 1623 text to its late modern context and the vast and vastly erudite body of work on Donne's engagement with both cosmological and cartographical knowledge and his direct use of ancient and modern maps.[9] Gorton argues he 'phrased ideas to himself in spatial terms' (1998, 10), pointing to the chiastic construction of space and writing in his work and highlighting the inseparable construction of self and space.

The links between geography, literature and subjectivity have been made clear by the spatial turn in the humanities over the last three decades. This approach has stressed the textuality of maps themselves, and Conley notes their increased relevance to literary critics who study them 'to detect how they mix observation and fantasy', elements vital to poetry and fiction and to representation in general (2007, 401). Importantly, this relationship is not only textual or metaphorical, but historical and structural, as Pinet claims for the relationship between Iberian cartography and literature. She concludes that the 'archipelagic narrative structure of the *isolario* is a model for Iberian prose fiction' culminating in *Don Quixote*, a founding work of modern Western literature (2011, xxxiv). So, too, the specific mutuality of geography and subjectivity has been made visible through the spatial turn. In his account of the new geohumanities, renowned geographer Denis Cosgrove argues that the conventional remit of the humanities, 'know thyself', has become interrelated with the new spatiality of geography resulting in a '[f]ocus on the human subject, and specifically on "imaginative geographies", [which] allows us to "map" the self into the world' (2011, xxiii).

Deleuze produces such a map of the self, writing and the world in his essay 'Desert Islands', which opens with reference to the relationship between the domains of geography and the imagination: 'Geographers say there are two kinds of islands. This is valuable information because it confirms what the imagination already knew' (2004, 9).[10] In the interconnection between their geographical and imaginary meanings, these two kinds of islands map Donne's melancholic subject replete with his solipsism, death drive and desire for rebirth. The first kind of island is the one Donne explicitly counsels against, namely the continental island that has broken away from the main. The second form of island is oceanic, the new island that has risen from underneath the sea, seemingly giving birth to itself. The first island is created by separation, the other by oceanic origination. However, as Deleuze states, in both cases, '*the island is also the origin,* radical and absolute' (Deleuze's italics) (2004, 10). Both separation and creation are forms and requirements of origin, as Prospero shows us in his exile and invention.

Deleuze argues that the island holds the (illusory) promise of a perfect accord between identity and space (2004, 10–11). The subject imagines it can be one with the *élan* of the island's desertedness but only manages to degrade the island by its presence, hence the dystopian reversal that so often unfolds on utopic islands. In attempting to mirror the island the ego imagines it can fully occupy delimited territory while remaining protected by the discernible, indeed *felt* borders that characterize islands of the imaginary. It feels both expansive and contained, autonomous yet held secure, as we clearly in D. H. Lawrence's fable, 'The Man Who Loved Islands' (1928), which opens:

> There was a man who loved islands. He was born on one, but it didn't suit him, as there were too many other people on it, besides himself. He wanted an island all of his own: not necessarily to be alone on it, but to make it a world of his own.
>
> An island, if it is big enough, is no better than a continent. It has to be really quite small, before it FEELS LIKE an island; and this story will show how tiny it has to be, before you can presume to fill it with your own personality. (2006)

We can see here the overlap between exilic withdrawal and the desire to originate as a sovereign self. In both the literature and history of modernity the identifications with the continental and oceanic islands are often entangled, so that dreams of rebirth lead to the experience of alienation and, conversely, narratives of enforced exile lead to originality and revitalization, as with Prospero's exile on the island and his secondary or artistic re-creation of a world. This self-birth, which is commensurate with locating an island that accords with the ego, recalls Milton's Satan, who has no memory of origin and so claims self-origination (1983, 318). The identification with the island as a mode of self-definition is not with the island as birth, which is an Edenic fantasy, but as rebirth and re-creation, the man who makes himself (anew) as does Robinson Crusoe.

Nor is this mutual spatialization between island and man limited to individual fantasy. This rebirth is evident also in the man-made utopian fantasies of More's *Utopia* and Francis Bacon's *New Atlantis* (1627), the latter written in the same year as Donne's Devotions, as fantasies of ideal commonwealths. Nor is the mirrored operation quarantined to literature but is rehearsed and developed across the culture, especially in colonial acquisition and settlement. From the vantage point of the twenty-first century, it is necessary to reimagine the status of islands in the early modern period to grasp their importance. In our time, small islands are largely disadvantaged by the operations of globalized modernity. So many are relegated to tourist resorts, offering sanctuary from the pressures of late modernity to wealthy continentals, and are, of course, the most vulnerable to climate change and rising seas (Niles and Baldacchino 2011). Continents are the powerful force in modernity, as exemplified by Mackinder's theory of heartlands (1904, 421–42), and as Lewis and Wigen have amply documented in their *Myth of Continents* (1997). But this was not the case in Donne's time when islands were prized as stepping stones across oceans, as manageable areas of arable land, and for their natural access to the sea, which enabled transport and trade (Gillis 2007, 125, 145; Flint 1992). Their natural boundaries also meant they were highly valued as colonies and prisons. The history of the colonial acquisition of islands, which Warner initiated in the Caribbean for the British Empire, bears this out. Donne, of course, supported the Virginia Company and the English aspirations on mainland America, and his sermon on its settlement stands as a manifesto of *ferae bestiae* and the 'natural' rights of European colonists (1953–62). However, the vexed beginnings of the Virginia settlements and its dissolution in 1624 point in part to the difficulties of continental colonization.

Islands were far easier to control and govern and epitomized a form of natural sovereignty. Indeed, as Stephen Royle records, there are only a handful of islands in the world that include more than one country and these are often disharmonious (2001, 150–152). Royle's study identifies the mutual constitution of defined geographical territory and cultural, political units. The link between the real and imagined sovereignty of islands has far-reaching effects. Philip Steinberg writes that 'the image of the [modern] territorial state closely resembles the representations of islands on sixteenth century portolan maps' leading him to suggest a 'historical link between the Renaissance-era of islands and the modern imagination of states' (2005, 253).

The specificity of the Western view of islands and sovereignty, including Donne's metaphor, is highlighted by its comparison with alternative understandings. Tuan's (1998) much-cited observation on Western islomania, cited previously, contends that this island-identification is largely confined to the Western imaginary. As numerous scholars in the field of Island Studies have shown, other cultures experience and figure islands very differently, often without the individualist identification or acquisitional drive of the Western construction, as noted in the Introduction. In his project of denaturalizing the Western view Gillis writes:

> The distinction between islands and mainlands is [...] an arbitrary one, good to think with but difficult to demonstrate from physical geography itself.

> Islands and mainlands belong to the same geological, biological, and cultural continuum (2004, 48).

However, as we know, received ideas shape and determine events even when they fly in the face of fact and evidence. The revivals of Donne's metaphor and of the island imaginary testify to this process, though the axiom may take on a grotesque irony in the disappearing islands of climate change, where no man can afford to stay.

The dialogue between the early modern and late modern Donne was in part enabled by the championing of Donne by T. S. Eliot. Eliot's 'rediscovery' of Donne is another myth, of course, as Donne was much prized by Robert Browning, Edmund Gosse and numerous late nineteenth-century writers (Haskin 2007). However, Eliot's deployment of the metaphysical poets in the service of an intellectual and 'difficult' Modernism, and as a form of conventional reaction against his immediate predecessors, created its own momentum which has variously limited and galvanized Donne into the present (Eliot 1932, 241–50). Across the twentieth century, in a way not seen hitherto, Donne appeared to epitomize modern experience, and from 1940 this perception has been especially concentrated on Meditation XVII. It announces the overdetermined currency of Donne at the time as the late modern subject hears the death bell tolling in Donne's axiom of identity, it wavering in presence and absence. The bell tolls for the death of the coherence of the Western subject or monad, the island maroon, whose demise is documented in the literature of High Modernism and who has long anticipated this passing from his melancholy origin. It is also resonates into the devastation of war, the world being broken into pieces; a time of unimaginable loss, when the world map is not only altered but shattered; as Derrida mourned, 'There is no world any more, only islands' (2009, 9). And like Walter Benjamin's Angel of History we look back from the unstoppable cataclysm of the present to those of the past. And such a cataclysm is present in Donne's Devotion with its long preamble of illness and death working akin to Benjamin's definition of allegory as 'the Hippocratic face of history as a petrified, primordial landscape' (1928; 1998, 166). Death precedes and frames Donne's 'primordial landscape' of the man/island dyad so that they too are fragmented emblems locked within the bounded map composed only of other fragments.

The island also promises the possibility of new birth within this devastation, but this birth knows its origin in fact rather than myth; it is compromised yet compensatory. As Deleuze writes, the island's signification as a figure of rebirth operates as a form of sacralized secularity.

> This second origin of the world is more important than the first: it is a sacred island. Many myths recount that what we find there is a perfect egg, a cosmic egg. Since it is a second birth, it is entrusted to man and not to the gods. (2004, 13)

The second birth is more 'essential than the first, since it gives us the law of repetition, the law of the series, whose first origin only gave us moments' (Deleuze 2004, 13). That is to say that the second birth, which is the island, ushers us into time; in the case of Donne's man/island this involves releasing man into the chronology of modernity.

To return to the image of Donne on the island of Fayal in the Azores, speculating on the nature of man, becalmed at the literal junction of the geography that would make New World colonization, this soldier poet will coin an endlessly productive metaphor about man and islands which is swept into the chronology of modernity and finds its moment in the mid-twentieth century: prescient and formative of the modern, despite and because of the trace of its own antecedence. As such this utterance is a dynamic emblem of the calamity that Benjamin's Angel of History looks back upon while impelled into the future, always promising the possibility of a new beginning of the same calamity (1968, 257).

# Section 2

# ISLANDS: MAKING THE PLANET, WORLD, GLOBE

# Chapter 2

# THE FIRST AND LAST OF NEW WORLDS: THE CARIBBEAN AND AUSTRALIA

> The islands saw it, and feared:
> the ends of the earth were astonished:
> they drew near and came.
>
> Isaiah 4:5 as quoted by Columbus in his *El Libro de Las Profecias* (1505)

> no new discovery of importance can be made, some few islands is all that can be expected while I remain in the Tropical Seas.
>
> James Cook, *Journals* (2 August 1773)

The title of this chapter comes from Paul Sharrad's description of the relationship between the Caribbean and Australia in view of the sequence of their discovery and colonization by Europe, which locates them as bookends of European imperial expansion (1993, 58). Columbus (it is believed) first landed on Guanahani Island, which he renamed San Salvador, in 1492, and which he thought was one of the 7,449 islands of the Sea of Cin, Japan and Cathay (Clay 1992, 617). Cook landed in Ka-may, which he renamed Botany Bay, on continental Australia in 1770 – nearly three hundred years later in a very different world and on a very different topology. The Caribbean/Australian connection focuses both the continuities and discontinuities between these two 'discoveries' and illustrates the process Mariano Siskind terms 'a genealogy of globalization', which 'begins with the territorial spatialisation of the universal premises of modernity; what is conceptually universal must be geographically universal' (2005, 2). This chapter examines the relationships among the concept, geography and literary representation to trace at least some of the formulations that have shaped successive understandings of universe, planet and globe. As Denis Cosgrove attests in *Apollo's Eye*, 'earthbound humans are unable to embrace more than a tiny part of the planetary surface. But in their imagination they can grasp the whole of the earth' (2001, ix).

The island is a figure of this graspable planet, the world as a coherent and comprehensible form, and the ensuing discussion will chart the shifting relationships among geography, politics and representation through the changing status of islands and continents between Europeans' discovery of the first New World and the last. The alignments and misalignments between conceptual and material accounts of these two topologies continuously form and re-form the world. Much is at stake in this grid of relationships. As Cosgrove claims, 'globalization is a hydra of modernity' (2001, ix), and the island simultaneously figures the globe and its fracture in line with Derrida's definition of the world after the Holocaust, discussed in the previous chapter: 'there is no world any more, only islands' (2009, 9). Once an image of unity, the island epitomizes unbridgeable isolation. This chapter traces the contradictory understandings of the island topography and topology as either a site of unity or fracture in the historical and imaginative construction of the modern globe.

Continents became the preferred global topology of the modern era, but they, too, are contradictory. Although defined against islands, they are also imagined as isolable units. As Martin Lewis and Kären Wigen have shown, while continents on maps appear so confidently inarguable, their delimitations are predominantly cultural (1997). Moreover, continental borders are often imagined in terms of islands. One significant and influential instance of the insular continent is Halford Mackinder's geopolitical theory of the continental heartland, published in 1904, in which he located the 'geographical pivot of history'. Mackinder divides the world into three 'island' groups: the first is the 'world island', which comprises the interlinked continents of Europe, Asia and Africa; the second group, which he calls 'offshore islands' is comprised of the British Isles and the islands of Japan; the third group or 'outlying islands' includes the American continents and Australia (1904, 434). In 1919 Mackinder returned to his theme in *Democratic Ideals* and summarized his theory:

> Who rules East Europe commands the Heartland;
> Who rules the Heartland commands the World-Island;
> Who rules the World-Island commands the world. (1919, 194)

The impact of Mackinder's theory on twentieth-century thought, history and policy is well documented (Fettweiss 2000). For present purposes, his formulation stresses the ways in which islands and continents are related by a constant dynamism and interconnection as well as real or imaged distinctions. In Mackinder's theory we can identify both the legacy of older, even ancient conceptions of the world island centred in and by Europe, which *Democratic Ideals* traces in detail, as well as pinpoint one key moment in Siskind's 'genealogy of globalization' structured around the distinction yet indivisibility of islands and continents.

Another of the key ways the island is central to the mapping of the new globe is its capacity to figure an alignment of self and space, of identity and world. In the terms proposed by the philosophical frameworks of modern teleology from Kant and Hegel, this island alignment mirrors the relationship between the individual and the universal, between specificity and the world, that underpins the Enlightenment view of history, human reason and the modern state. Such an alignment is rendered more problematic, indeed thrown back into history, when it is overlaid with the attendant operation of the island in the Western imaginary as a site of possessive and acquisitional desire; as Columbus writes: 'My desire was not to pass any island without taking possession' (1893, 43). The perceptual apparatus constructed by the various elements of history and representation, specificity and world, self and space – and all these in constant rearrangement – identifies the island as a site of the complex calibration of these broader issues, and one where these calibrations have been staged in the full horror of history.

The following two chapters focus on three historical moments that connect and dissect the Caribbean and Australia, all understood on the continuum of modern teleology/globalization and as the bookends of British imperialism. The first two of these moments are contained in this chapter, and the following chapter continues the discussion. The first focus is the moment of European 'discovery' and of first contact between Europeans and the Indigenous peoples. Second is the network of relationships between the Anglophone Caribbean (the West Indies) and the Australian colonies in the nineteenth century. The third focus is the postwar, mid-century moment of Modernist writings in both the Caribbean and Australia, in which the island is revisited as the site for new negotiations of self, space, history and world in both Caribbean and Australian literature.

Until recently, there has been very little written on the relationship between Australia and the Caribbean apart, of course, from cricket and, for Australia at least, the great significance of the 'Calypso Summer' series of 1960–61. At this time also, there was some analysis of colonial and political relations in view of the attempted Federation of the West Indies (1958–62), in which the former British colonies in the Caribbean joined in a political union modelled on the Canadian Confederation, the Australian Commonwealth and the Central African Federation. While geographically distant and topologically different, the two places have recently identified shared specific environmental concerns regarding the protection of the world's two largest coral reefs: the Great Barrier Reef and Mesoamerican Barrier Reef System (Rudd 2011).

The colonial archive records the movement of British officials between the convict colonies of the West Indies, New South Wales and Van Diemen's Land, and there are many instances where these men act to sever ties with their earlier experience and those where they explicitly bring prior experience to bear on the new colonial context. In the past 25 years historians have led the way in unearthing direct connections between slavery and convictism in the Australian and Caribbean colonies. Ian Duffield's groundbreaking work on Caribbean convicts transported to the Australian colonies has been taken up by Cassandra Pybus, Hamish Maxwell-Stewart and Diana Paton so that we now have a clear picture of the human traffic in slaves and convicts between these two sites, which were always traversed via Britain (Duffield 1986; Pybus 2002; Paton 2008). The Appendix to this book adds to this knowledge in a compilation of the movement of colonial officers, merchants and professional men between the two locations and shows extensive connections that challenge the dyadic conception of mother country to colony.

The major theoretical links between Australia and the Caribbean have circulated around postcolonial studies. One of the foundational texts of postcolonial theory, *The Empire Writes Back* (1989, 2002) by Australians Bill Ashcroft, Gareth Griffiths and Helen Tiffin, highlighted, and derived inspiration from, the imaginative theorization of Caribbean writers whose work underpins postcolonial inquiry, discussed in the Introduction. In particular, Caribbean writers have investigated and articulated the experience of living in an archipelagic, multicultural and polylinguistic region where the webs of connection are in constant flux (Brathwaite 1974, 1983; Glissant 1997; Walcott 1992a). As this chapter will later discuss, such a model is in stark contrast to Australia's historical investments in monoculturalism and its continental topology.

Russell McDougall's 2002 edition of *Australian Cultural History*, *To the Islands*, is the only cross-disciplinary collection of essays that considers Australian/Caribbean connections and ranges from consideration of systems of imperial governance to the development of scientific and ethnographic studies and literary crossings. This collection, including McDougall's Introduction, provides a wealth of primary data as well as astute analysis to which the ensuing discussion is indebted. *To the Islands* contains two of the small number of essays that link Australian and Caribbean literatures: Brigitta Olubas on Wilson Harris's reading of Patrick White (Olubas 2002, 81–88) and David Carter on the life and work of Ralph de Boissiere (Carter 2002, 97–106). Additional to this collection, Helen Tiffin and Diane Brydon's 1993 study, *Decolonising Fictions*, maps out some of the grounds for transnational readings of West Indian and Australian literature including shared language, genocidal policies and practices, the use of unfree labour, diaspora and exile.

A survey of the AustLit database indicates that numerous Australian writers cite West Indian texts in their own works and as epigraphs. These refer predominantly to Derek Walcott, making links to his mesmerizing lyricism, literary vocation, and multivocal, diasporic vision. Les Murray cites Walcott's *Omeros* (1990) as one of the motivations for writing *Fredy Neptune* (1998), and Line Henriksen compares *Omeros* and *Fredy Neptune* as modern epics that grapple with the dilemma of how to 'present humility as the most important of ethical values' in the grand and lengthy epic form (Murray 1999, 304–305; Henriksen 2001, 88). Clive James's poem 'Belated Homage to Derek Walcott' (2009) stages a dialogue between speaker and subject, James and Walcott, as between poets and colonials, linking the West Indies, Australia and Britain in triangulated relation. The poem opens by connecting the reading and writing of poetry with distinctive experiences of the British Empire and its legacies. These include, on the one hand, the internalized dread of a postslavery culture, and on the other, James's own (happy) expatriation from Australia to England:

> You made me think last night. Your lines about
> How people on those islands you evoke
> As easily as blowing smoke
> Could not look down from high ground to the sea,
> Or even see a cargo ship, without
> Fear of the worst, reminded me –
> Reminded me I still need the reminder –
> That my own ships and oceans linked a kinder
> Imperium. (James 2009, 36)

James's poem traces some of the connecting routes formed by empire and identifies radical differences between each place and each relation that will be followed in this chapter across the historical constructions of the Caribbean archipelago and the island continent.

## A New World of Islands: Some Real

Columbus's discovery of what Peter Martyr would term the 'New World' (1516) presents a grid of contradiction and paradox (1912). Fundamentally, as Columbus's son Ferdinand stresses, Columbus understood the significance of the capacity to travel west to reach the east (Columbus, F. 1992, 15). Columbus may or may not have ever understood the full significance of his discovery of what are now known as the American continents, but his act of connecting the regions of the globe both united and fractured understandings of the world island. Topographically, the world in Columbus's time was imagined in insular terms: the great earth island and two vast archipelagos. As John Gillis observes: 'As long as Europeans persisted in thinking about the world archipelagically, they were bound to find only islands' (2004, 46). In accordance with the archipelagic view of the earth landmasses of his time, Columbus was not seeking to discover another continent and, indeed, landed on numerous islands of an archipelago. Thus, the search for, and discovery of, islands also enabled the discovery of continents, which in turn began the continental cartography of the modern era.

The spatio-temporal paradox of Columbus's discovery, often noted, is that his mission was not so much to discover new places as old ones, namely the Asian countries that had become cut off from European trade by the Ottoman Empire, especially Cipango (Japan) and Cathay (China). In cosmological terms also, Columbus did not seek to find new places but to fulfil the biblical and Christian visions of the earth and history (Flint 1992; Gillis 2004, 45–81; Watts 1985). Gillis notes that in Columbus's time and language the word 'discovery' was more akin to our 'recovery' (2004, 46) in that the stress was on the revelation of extant but hidden realities, as there could not be new realities in a created world. For a revealed religion, like Christianity, the world is already realized and time and space unfold within the circumscribed limits of its creation. Discovery (as recovery) is thus conceived as a mode of fulfilment, of bringing time and space to completion. In the schema of Peter Sloterdijk's theory of globalization, or sphereology, Columbus is simultaneously trying to realize the unity of a metaphysical cosmos, within the terms of the first phase in the globalization process from ancient Greece, but he is overlaying this understanding of the cosmos with that of terrestrial globe which he, himself, is inaugurating (2013, 10).

By various logics, including the progress narratives of modernity, the globe was made more complete by Columbus's discoveries. Ironically, however, the globe also becomes newly anatomized by them, and dissected accordingly from the perspectives of metaphysics to geography and geology. Crucially, it effected a shift in Western understanding of the relationship between man [sic] and space, as microcosms and macrocosms related by systems of resemblance, to one in which both man and the world are comprised of constituent parts. Gary Rosenberg charts this shift in relation to the Scientific Revolution – which is understood as beginning with Copernicus and (the anatomist) Vesalius in 1543 and ending with Newtown in 1687 – to show, inter alia, the interaction between the arts and sciences in the development of stratified anatomies of the human body, the earth and the cosmos (2006, 2009a, 2009b). The human person, understood as and by the Western subject, is interimplicated in this new earth not only for the new understanding that must shape the location of the self and present new relations to space, but because man is inextricable from the very conceptions of earth, planet and globe. As discussed in the previous chapter in relation to John Donne's conception of the modern man, this subject is an island, simultaneously a complete world and a broken piece of an earlier and obsolete whole.

Columbus's concept of earthly completion denies such trajectories and consequences because his discovery was to achieve the end of history. Indeed eschatological purpose is everywhere evident in Columbus's journals of the four voyages and in his *El Libro de Las Profecias* (*Book of Prophesies*), the compendium of prophetic and apocalyptic texts Columbus compiled between 1502 and 1505. In the *Libro*, Columbus includes many passages from Daniel, Isaiah and Ezekiel, the Old Testament books of vision and apocalypse and the basis for John the Divine's Book of the Apocalypse in the New Testament, which share a divine view of history and prefigure the world's transformation and conclusion on the Day of Judgment. This millenarian understanding prevailed in Columbus's era and was of particular interest to him through his association with the Franciscan fraternity who espoused this vision (Flint 1992; Zamora 1993).

Margarita Zamora compares Columbus's understanding of his discovery with that of Amerigo Vespucci who, in 1504, only 12 years after Columbus's first voyage, demonstrated that Columbus's discoveries were not the outer regions of the Indies but a separate landmass. While Columbus wrote that he had found an 'other' world, Vespucci wrote of this same place that it was a 'new' world. Columbus insists that the world he has found is 'well known to the ancients' whereas Vespucci understands that South America is not connected to Asia and is unknown to Europeans (Zamora 1993, 131). From our vantage point in late modernity, the distinction between 'other' and 'new' marks a clear pivot point from one era to another and into the modern. Columbus's 'other' world is devoid of temporality, it is a coexisting plane of a different order. Vespucci's 'new' world belongs to the progressive and linear temporality of modernity. As if obeying Ezra Pound's directive, definitive of another moment of Modern, Vespucci made it new.

Vespucci's more accurate observation was, of course, enabled by Columbus's voyages and by Columbus's accounts, including the interlocked frameworks by which he presented and understood events. Modern distinctions between disciplines of knowledge, fiction and nonfiction, secular and religious word views did not pertain in the same ways in the world Columbus inhabited. *The Travels* (1300) of Marco Polo, based on his many journeys along the Silk Road, were deemed incredible while the adventures of fictional 'John Mandeville' (1356) were more widely believed. Since the 1980s there has been a wealth of scholarship that documents the range of textual influences on Columbus, which have fleshed out his motivations, interpretations and actions via the discursive interplay of his reading and writing. This more recent understanding has highlighted the limitations of using only one approach to reading Columbus, who was, at once, a late medieval Italian, an early Christian humanist, and a man of overt piety yet deeply ambitious and self-interested. Delno West and August Kling, the translators and editors of the *Libro*, argue for the authenticity of Columbus's personal piety, citing his personal writings and annotations (1991). Pauline Moffitt Watts (1985) turns attention to the raft of religious writings and doctrine that guided Columbus as surely as his compass and astrolabe. Valerie Flint (1992) has documented Columbus's reading and annotations across the wide range of sacred and secular texts he accessed.

From the secular archive, in addition to Marco Polo and John Mandeville, the annotations on Columbus's copy of Pliny's encyclopaedia *Naturalis Historia* (ca. AD 77–79) suggest it was part of his shipboard library (Flint 1992, 71–73). He also read Homer's *Iliad* and the *Odyssey*, Ovid's *Metamorphoses* and Seneca's tragedies; indeed Flint suggests that there is 'something to be said for the idea that Columbus saw his own first voyage as a species of the *Argonautica*, with himself cast as Jason and Queen Isabella as Medea' (Flint 1992, 86). Indeed, as Diskin Clay has detailed, Seneca's *Medea* was one of the most important and inspiring texts for medieval and early modern voyagers, especially lines 376–80.

> *Venient annis sæcula seris*
> *Quibus Oceanus vincula rerum*
> *Laxet, et ingens pateat tellus,*
> *Tethys que novos detegat orbes,*
> Nec sit terris ultima *Thule*
> – time shall in fine out breake
> When Ocean wave shall open every Realme
> The wandering World at willshall open lye
> And Thyphis some new found land Survay
> Some travelers shall the Countries farre escrye
> Beryond Small Thule, known farthest to this day.
> (Seneca, *Medea* 375–79, tr. John Studley 1581, quoted in Clay 1992, 617)

Columbus not only recorded these lines in the *Libro*, but as Clay notes, he also paraphrased this same text as a desperate petition of his achievements in a letter he wrote from the Caribbean islands to the Spanish monarchs when he was being prepared to be transported home in chains. He may indeed have seen himself as Jason or, as Clay suggests, a modernized version of Jason's pilot, an update of the great classical navigator.

Columbus also drew practical inspiration from the maritime narratives of Christian hagiography, including its adaptation of the Irish immram, or sea story, developed in the eighth century, the most influential being *Immram Brain* and the legend of St Brendan's voyage (Dathorne 1994, 95). Other maritime saints who inspired Columbus with confidence for the long voyage included his namesake, St Christopher, famed for his carriage of people and the infant Christ across water. He was also inspired by St Ursula and the account of her voyage from south west Britain to Brittany in a single day accompanied by 11,000 virgins (Montgomery 2010, 45). These exemplars were understood in very concrete terms: Columbus used the signature Christoferens (the Christ carrier) in an identification with the legendary Christopher, which became part of the iconic representations of Columbus. So, too, in the journal of his first voyage he records passing St Brendan's island, and he names the Virgin Islands after St Ursula's entourage.

It would be hard to overstate the role played by these imaginary islands in the voyages of the Europeans at this time. The data and rationale may be flawed but, as Rosenberg is at pains to stress in relation to scientific discoveries at this time, erroneous premises led to many correct conclusions, with Copernicus as a telling case in point (2001, 145). As Gillis notes, by filling the oceans with imaginary islands, Europeans 'lessen[ed] the fears of the void that had prevented [them] from venturing offshore' (2004, 48). These imaginary islands shared the same status as those found in (what we would term) factual accounts of other Atlantic islands such as the Canaries, Azores and Cape Verde archipelagos, which had proliferated since the thirteenth century. From the perspective of our present we can see that both real and imaginary islands provided necessary stepping-stones across the 'dark ocean' of the Atlantic (Gillis 2004, 45–81).

For Columbus and other Europeans of this time the interplay of figure and ground that constructed these 'other' worlds preceded and shaped their actual discovery. The rich textual palimpsest of thought, ideology and *poesis* not only propelled the actual voyages but also framed what they 'recovered'. In the words of Yi-Fu Tuan, 'landscape is not defined by itemizing its parts' (quoted in Rosenberg 2009b, 14). Rather, the parts are, in Rosenberg's terms, 'clues to an integrated landscape already in mind' (2009b, 14). The power of the textual history that constructed this mental landscape is thrown into relief when we read of the most improbable of findings, such as islands of Amazons and hybrid creatures, which, ironically, are used to validate rather than discredit voyagers' accounts because they echo earlier texts and hence accord with existing beliefs. Conversely, the strength of an already integrated conception of the world goes some way to explaining the misreading of encounters with truly exotic places and peoples as if they were already known. The most significant of these is Columbus's belief that he had discovered the Indies when his encounters with the Taíno peoples of the Caribbean would have indicated very great differences from earlier accounts of the Far East.

In additional to the textual influence of others, textual power is also evident in the writings of the explorers themselves.[1] Columbus's writings were determined by the textual contract set out in the letter addressed to Queen Isabella and King Ferdinand that prefaces the journal of the first voyage (Zamora 1993). The first component in sequence and importance is the elaborate statement positioning Columbus and his voyages within the Spanish Crown's proselytizing project of Christian millenarianism. The second term of this contract pertains to Columbus's rewards, namely his rise to the position of 'Don' and 'Chief Admiral of the Ocean Sea' who would be 'perpetual Viceroy and Governor of all the islands and continents that I should discover and gain'. Furthermore, this role will pass by patrilineage to his eldest son. Thirdly, he undertakes 'to prepare a book, and to put down all as it were in a picture, by latitude from the equator, and western longitude' (Columbus 1893, 18). That is, he will provide the Crown with the textual cartography by which it could complete divine history by ruling the terrestrial world. He would give them the world and the book of the world.

This framing compact establishes what Flint calls the 'creative tension' evident throughout Columbus's writing between his desire for both God – in the proselytizing mission of Christianity and the realization of the terrestrial destiny – and the desire for gold and glory. In addition to any personal hypocrisy that this may illuminate, its importance is far reaching in that its figuration around harmony and concordance sits at the core of the history of colonial justification. Columbus's journals and letters attempt to present his own different objectives as harmonious, a harmony realized in and by Columbus's actions, what we might now understand as textual performativity. That is to say that the harmony is not pre-existing but is being brought into being by Columbus himself. Accordingly, he repeatedly stresses the quest for, and discovery of, the terrestrial paradise (Flint 1992, 140–44), and the location of a gold seam that would lead to the mines of Solomon. From this distance across the centuries there is a discernible anxiety regarding the misalignment of these objectives in Columbus's increasing assertions of divine achievement rather than material gain, such as the discovery of Eden in lieu of precious metals and, in the journal of the third voyage, the increased interest in the reconquest of Jerusalem to effect the second coming (Flint 1992, 185; Greenblatt 1992, 79). Akin to the riddle of an oracle in Greek mythology, meaning slides across and between these discourses confounding original expectations, so that the terms of one objective (gold) become displaced onto another (Christian fulfilment) and vice versa. These shifts fabricate an *ersatz* harmony or correspondence between the diverse objectives of the voyages and draw attention to the crucial role of language in weaving together Spain's desires with those of Columbus and their collective construction of a hall of mirrors.

There is, more broadly, a strongly performative sense in Columbus's writing, *performative* in the sense of theatricality and in the understanding within speech acts theory as utterances that change reality itself. Stephen Greenblatt has analysed the ways these declared realities, such as Columbus claiming new territory via a symbolic gesture with a flag and the pronouncement of certain words unintelligible to the local people, stand in lieu of actual agreements or treaties or even dialogue (1992, 139). The accounts of these formalities achieve meaning by their textual distribution across Europe. Columbus's writings were the means by which these self-referential symbolic gestures, in themselves meaningless, became self-fulfilling prophesies: the territory does indeed become the property of Spain, apparently verifying the power of the original ritual and pronouncement rather than the power accorded to it through discursive production and circulation. As noted above, Columbus was deeply drawn to prophetic texts and casts himself as a prophet whose words, as well as his deeds, command authority, have presence. This is a world where words spoken by anointed parties have the power of transubstantiation.

However, Columbus's rhetoric of persuasion, including self-persuasion, cannot make the world cohere into a seamless globe. The discovery or recovery of the Americas does not result in the alignment or fulfilment of the world, or a concordance of self and space. At the heart of this momentous occurrence in the mapping of the planet is a fracture that divides secular and religious conceptions of the earth. It also instantiates a new futurity, beyond the finitude of Christian millenarianism. It is the moment, also, when the conception of earthly unification is exposed in the rupture of hitherto discursive harmonies to be the lockstep of cognate discourses. The islands of the Caribbean become the site of this violent disharmony.

## British Reason and Other Acts of Rhetoric

If Columbus's rhetoric strains to perform the unification of history, geography and religion to bear witness to the shared presence within word and world, British colonial discourse of the following century might be said to be characterized by a negotiation of sameness and difference. Andrew Fitzmaurice reads the English accounts of the New World of the late 1500s and early1600s as acts of promotion, written to persuade their readers of the benefits of the New World and its colonization. He shows how these writers deployed classical and humanist rhetoric as a way of presenting new discoveries and opportunities in a mode that did not alienate audiences with overwhelming strangeness but created curiosity and excitement and provoked positive emotions. Hence, as Fitzmaurice claims, writing was a device of converting the audience's viewpoint; it was an act in itself (1997, 243).

These acts of persuasion are not performative in the same way as Columbus's discourse, a distinction that indicates a radical shift in the movement Foucault theorizes from monarchical power to the disciplinary power of modernity (1975). Where Columbus always addresses the crown to lay his discoveries at their feet, the British texts address potential colonizers, enticing them to the New World. Accordingly, John Donne opens his Virginia Company Sermon (1622) with an address to the potential colonizers: 'By your favours, I had some place amongst you, before: but now I am an adventurer; if not *to* Virginia, yet *for* Virginia; for every man that prints, adventures' (1667a, 3, italics added). By a slip of preposition from 'to' to 'for', the writer and his writing are rendered extra-textual, thrown into the facticity of politics and history (Fitzmaurice 1997, 242–43). Walter Raleigh's *Discovery of Guiana* (ca. 1595) attests both to the power and the peril of this rhetorical aim, for while it is true his book stood in place of any actual territory or gold, he eventually paid with his life when the absence of any gold was perceived as treason. Like Columbus, textual discovery and resolution was not enough.

Hence we can see that both Columbus and the English rhetoricians share an understanding of language as active and embodied, but there is a significant modification from Columbus to Donne regarding the quality of language's presence. This distinction may be understood in terms of temporality. For Columbus, there is a simultaneity of ritualistic utterance, divine decree and historical occurrence. In Donne's text, the simultaneity resides internally in the coherence of its own logic. Presence and action are identified in the slip of a preposition, a self-conscious conceit, and its effects are consequent; people will leave Britain and move to the New World because of his words. So, too, we can witness in the failures of Raleigh and Columbus, misreadings of the growing distinction between legend, myth and empirical facticity as these are played out in literary texts. Imaginary islands may have guided Columbus to the Caribbean, but textual truths – even those of the Bible – are not sufficient benefit. Likewise, Raleigh's claims to have located the mythical El Dorado thrill his readership but leave the authorities sceptical. He needed to heed the growing empiricism of Francis Bacon rather than the legend of Martinez and the city of gold.

These ongoing shifts in the relationship between language and the New World are symptom and cause of new perspectives, new ways of seeing in the textual relationship between author, readers and subject. This shift from monarchical to disciplinary power departs radically from the trajectory and dynamics of Columbus's accounts, an Italian/Spanish Catholic perspective of the previous century. In Columbus's accounts and despite their distance from the actual site, the gaze is upon the monarch, and the New World is textually harnessed and arranged for the monarch. As Mark Koch shows, a century later, the Protestant English gaze is that of the ruler upon the colony, the imperial centre gazing out, like the watchman of Bentham's panopticon (1998, para 4). It is also the inductive Enlightenment gaze, from Bacon and Locke, the evidentiary authority of empiricism.

The atomization of knowledge and the shift to disciplinary power are, according to Foucault's schema, key indicators of an epistemic shift into our own modernity. The combined forces of James Cook and Joseph Banks exemplify this pivotal movement, each the living embodiment of modern Men of Reason with their specializations in 'pure forms of knowledge', geography and botany respectively. With Cook and Banks we can identify a literal bifurcation of knowledges comprehended by Columbus – albeit on very different terms – and see their integral role in the developing conception of the island continent by the colonizing authorities, as W. C. Wentworth's famous colonialist poem 'Australasia' (1823) makes clear in the naming of the disciplines by which the new colony is conceived:

> And thou, fair Science! pure ethereal light
> Beam on her hills, and chase her mental night;
> Direct her sons to seek the perfect day,
> Where Bacon trac'd, and Newton led the way;
> Till bright Philosophy's full orb arise,
> To gild her noon, and cheer her ev'ning skies.

## Words, Sea, Land: Rites of (Dis)Possession

Both Columbus and Cook presumed the right to claim inhabited lands for their respective monarchs, though according to different understandings of the inherited laws of possession. As Fitzmaurice sets out, there is a fundamental difference between the Spanish and British understandings of *ferae bestiae* (the law of the first taker) and *res nullius* (nobody's property) (2007, 1–15). Importantly, Roman law, which structured so many European systems and institutions, was understood as a written form of natural law with evident implications for both legal and 'natural' or universal human rights. Spanish theologians Vitoria and Las Casas explicated the law to argue that the Spanish conquests were unjust and that the Spanish had as little right to take the lands of the peoples of the Americas as those people had to take Spanish land. Brian

Tierney argues that the theologians' position was informed by 'an interplay of jurisprudence and philosophy' which informed Las Casas's deployment of the legal term '*quod omnes tangit*' ('What touches all is to be approved by all') – the First Nations peoples had equal right to all decisions (Tierney 1994, 11; Fitzmaurice 2007, 6–7). Despite this clear judgement in Spain, it had little effect on actual events in the Americas.

British promoters of colonization also invoked natural law of possession but in this case to justify their endeavours. For the British, the Indigenous peoples of the New World had not properly taken possession of the land they inhabited, as they had not exercised human labour to transform the natural world into human communities (Fitzmaurice 2007, 7–9).[2] There are two forms of possession at stake here: the possession of the land from undeveloped cultures and the corollary that such people will themselves enter into the economies of monetary exchange and thereby acquire more possessions. In the eighteenth century this idea was propelled by John Locke's *Two Treatises of Government* (1689) which he formulated in relation to the American colonies, Locke's thesis was, however, already in force well before the publication of *Two Treatises*, as we see in Donne's Virginia Colony Sermon of 1622:

> There is a power rooted in nature, and a power rooted in grace; a power issuing from the law of nations, and a power growing out of the Gospel. In the law of nature and nations, a land never inhabited, by any, or utterly derelicted and immemerially abandoned by the former inhabitants, becomes theirs that will possess it […] That rule which passes through all municipal laws in particular states, *Interest reipublicæ ut quis re sua bene utatur* [it is of interest to the state that no man shall make ill use of his own (tr. Ballantine 2006, 246)]. The state must take order, that every man improve that which he hath, for the best advantage of that state, passes also through the law of nations, which is to all the world, as the municipal law is to a particular state, *Interest mundo*, the whole world, all mankind must take care, that all places be improved, as far as may be, to the best advantage of mankind in general. Again if the land be peopled, and cultivated by the people, and that land produce in abundance such things, for want whereof their neighbours, or others (being not enemies) perish, the law of nations may justify some force, in seeking, by permutation, of other commodities which they need, to come to some of theirs. Many cases may be put, when not only commerce, and trade, but plantations in lands, not formerly our own, may be lawful. (1967, 2)

So, for Donne, it is lawful to take territory if it is not deemed to be appropriately exploited and if there is a need for its benefits. These actions are made on the basis that the needs of the whole world must be privileged over one community; that is, he endorses a principle of universalism that is indivisible from material gain. Donne's painstaking performance of reason here is crucial to his argument and its desired effects. For, as Siskind argues of Enlightenment thought, reason and universalism are 'two sides of the same token' (2005, 23). In Donne's sermon, the superior reason of the British subject, which he embodies and performs, is properly a universal property shared by all humanity and could be made to be so in the course of colonization. Thus Donne calls on natural law and *Interest mundo* when he is, in fact, quite specifically calling on British authorities and British subjects to colonize a part of north east America. He pre-empts Charles Kingsley's conclusion that 'the welfare of the Teutonic race is the welfare of the world' (1864, 338). Donne, like Locke, is mapping capitalist colonialist modernity.

The controversy around the term *terra nullius* in Australia relates to whether the British Crown took possession of Australia on the basis that it was uninhabited. Andrew Fitzmaurice and Michael Connor have traced the origin and use of the term *terra nullius,* which was, in fact, not current in Cook's time (Fitzmaurice 2007: 1, 15; Connor 2005, 11, 47). *Terra nullius* came into use in the nineteenth century around the 'carving up' of Africa and in relationship to the Antarctic. Fitzmaurice concludes, however, that its contemporary use is consistent with the natural law used to dispossess indigenous people (2007, 1, 15). Cook carefully notes the Australian inhabitants' use of land according to the criteria of *ferae bestiae.* Further, the Governor of New South Wales Richard Bourke's proclamation of 1835 claimed all Australian land from top to bottom, east to west and inclusive of islands, for the British Crown, denying prior ownership and in direct response to Victorian Governor John Batman's attempts to enter into a land treaty with Aboriginal people (Bourke 1835). To the contemporary reader comparing the various attitudes of the European powers to the rights of First Nations peoples, there is a glaring disparity between the long legal and moral arguments undertaken, the theoretical disagreements of colonial powers and the shared practices of invasion and dispossession.

The European explorers and colonists formalized declarations of ownership in the act of naming. Where Columbus names islands according to religious designations (San Salvador), imperial possession (Hispaniola) and legend (the Virgin Islands), Cook's names are secular and most often refer to patrons, notaries and colleagues. However, both explorers do use metaphorical naming practices. Columbus, for instance, memorialized the conflict he encountered in (what is now) the Dominican Republic with the name 'Bay of Arrows'. Paul Carter's extensive consideration of Cook's metaphorical naming practices complicates the cold empirical view of Cook. He cites Pigeon House Mountain and Repulse Bay as evidence of an impressionistic mode not conventionally associated with the navigator who epitomized the Age of Reason (Carter 1987, 4–8, 18).

Whether metaphorical or arbitrary, both Columbus and Cook name space in performative speech acts where utterance is possession. Sloterdijk notes that 'the *coincidence* of sighting, landing, appropriating, naming, mapping and certification is what constitutes the complete, legally consequential act of discovery' (2013, 101, italics added). Indeed, Cook's journals are a compendium of naming as ownership. Doris Pilkington highlights the absurdity of this practice in *Follow the Rabbit Proof Fence* (1996) in relation to Fremantle's claim upon Nyungar land in Western Australia:

> Those Nyungar men about whom Yellagonga was speaking had no idea what was happening when they met Captain Fremantle. The Captain told the men, the traditional owners who had gathered on the muddy banks of the river, 'My government has advised me to meet with you and seek your approval before giving your country an English name.'
>
> [...]
>
> 'I take it we are all agreed and that I have your consent,' said Captain Fremantle, nodding to the Nyungar men who stood motionless, staring blankly at him. (2002, 9–10)

Palawa writer Jim Everett's recent uncompromising essay 'Savage Nation' refuses the fundamental terms of European law, surveying, topography and naming. He opens:

> Firstly, to introduce myself: I am a *plangermairreenner* man of the First Nations of north-east Tasmania. I am not Australian Aborigine, nor am I Indigenous, nor am I an Australian citizen. My mountain is *turbunna*, my river is *meenamatta lienta* through *menamatta walantanalinany*, my grandmother is *wapperty* of the *plangermairreenner*, and my grandfather is *manalargenna* of the *leetermairremene*. My mother is Ena Everett (nee Maynard) and my father is Keith Everett. I am known as Jim Everett. I am puralia meenamatta. My home is on Cape Barren Island off the north-east coast of Tasmania, and one of the fifty-two islands of the Furneaux Group. (Everett 2014, 27)

In addition to the many terms of affirmation and rejection here, the transcription of language, including its italicization and its exclusive knowledge, stands against the arcane Latin of the West's legal heritage. It is a powerful statement – the missed introduction between cultures.

Carter's account of colonial nomenclature champions Cook, whom he juxtaposes with the naturalist Joseph Banks, who, with his 'suite' of eight scientists, accompanied Cook on his first voyage. Contrary to the association of Banks as the appreciative eye upon the marvellous sights of New Worlds – a fascination in contrast to Cook's spare accounts – Carter finds Banks's approach hollow. If Cook's role in the process of globalization was to (nearly) complete the navigation of the globe itself, Banks's role, in view of Carter's reading, performed what Siskind terms the Universalist premise of modernity to make 'what is conceptually universal' also 'geographically universal'. In Carter's view, this universalizing framework is embedded in the Linnaean taxonomic method which, by definition, categorized flora and fauna into types based on one indicative species, a framework all too easily applied to human species and which, inter alia, assures the centrality of the British subject as the original indicative type.

Certainly a version of this Linnaean view is evident in W. C. Wentworth's poem 'Australasia' (1823), quoted in part above, in which the speaker lauds the colonies as 'a new Britannia on another shore'. This particular quality of this newness recalls the distinction between Columbus finding an 'other' world and Vespucci's recognition of the Americas as a 'new world'. Australasia might also have been thought to be a New World in this way. But Wentworth's claim is not of a New World but of a new satellite of the old world, and so, unexpectedly, creating a link to Columbus's world view. It is as if there can be no utterly new place, only one that consolidates the ethos and reach of the old. Columbus's view was informed by a cosmological transcendence. That of the British colonists of 'Australasia' was also transcendent, but it was the transcendence of the unholy nexus of Reason, Universalism and Empire.

Cook's approach as a geographer, according to Carter (1987, 27–33), is more concerned with specificity, which the Linnaean model does not permit and which is necessary for the geographer. Although Nicholas Thomas presents quite a different reading of Cook to Carter, his reading shares this recognition of Cook's assiduous focus on detail. He writes that Cook was a man whose 'business – which he carried out almost automatically – was to know precisely where he was in the world' (Thomas 2003, 58).

Looking back from Cook to Columbus's high blown rhetoric of personal achievement and millenarian fulfilment, Cook's journals are diligent and workaday records. Looking forward to the consequences of his discovery, he conveys little sense of momentous impact.[3] The drama and the heroism of the journal is reserved for maritime incidents, such as the near shipwreck in the Great Barrier Reef, which John Hawte Beaglehole argues were based on Banks's journal in any case (Carter 1987, 18). Nor does Cook record any sense of moment regarding his first encounters with Indigenous peoples. As Thomas discusses, throughout his many and involved encounters with Indigenous peoples, Cook's accounts are detached, though increasingly anthropological, and the meaningful charge of such encounters is most often missed or elided. Further, as Thomas observes, Cook was not prepared for the ways in which many of the Aboriginal people in Australia preferred to ignore him, his crew and his ship – a somewhat deflating response for the world navigator, one that took the wind out of his sails, so to speak (2003, 57), or one that, Carter argues, fascinated Cook by indicating 'complete detachment' (1987, 23).

One of the effects of Cook's omniscient and empiricist perspective on Australia, the *un*remarkable tone of discovery and first encounter, is to remind us that Cook's discovery and claim upon Australia is sandwiched between the other purposes of his voyage, namely the observation of the Transit of Venus on the island of Tahiti and the secret instruction given to Cook to locate and claim the southern continent of the Antarctic.[4] Viewed as such, Cook's textual rendering of the island continent of what is now Australia appears stranded between two topographies: the island of Tahiti that enabled the cosmic planetary vision; and the Antarctic continent which was the mythic ballast of the earth island. As Siskind details, what is most prized for Cook and his masters is (the elusive) continental discovery (2005). Carter remarks that 'the chief discovery of the Endeavour was its discovery of nothing, of the nonexistence of the great southern continent' (1987, 23). Located as such within the Western cartography of empire, Australia appears variously incidental, accidental, locked in ambivalence. It is neither one thing nor the other. Columbus's discovery was *accidental* in the sense of both error and chance, as he thought he was voyaging to the Far East, whereas Cook's discovery is *accidental* in the sense that it is parenthetical and tangential to his primary purpose.

In relation to the shifting status of islands and continents in the genealogy of globalization, there is a revealing parallelism in the relationship between the topographies and topologies discovered by Cook and Columbus, their status as real or imaginary, and the fulfilment of the ideological contracts with which each was charged. Columbus landed on islands, which were the outlying lands of continents, but his cosmological world view obscured the reality and possibility of those landmasses from sight. Instead he understood that he was reconnecting the old world, leading him to understand the magnitude of the Orinoco River as a sign of the island of the Garden of Eden rather than the South American continent. Cook sought to complete the globe by the discovery of the southern continent 'which has at times ingrossed the attention of some of the Maritime Powers for near two Centuries past and the Geographers of all ages' (1971, 186). Alternatively, he could disprove its existence, and he sets out this case in detail in his journal in March 1770 (Cook 1971, 59–60). He, too, had a directive to complete the world, but it is no longer Columbus's cosmos but the modern globe. In opposition to Columbus, he is driven by and towards what he cannot see, cannot reach.

Where Columbus sought islands – and found them, albeit a different archipelago than that planned – he also misunderstood the magnitude, in all senses, of locating the American continents. Cook discovers an island-continent – an undecided and contested topology, itself an in-between landmass – while he is in between the two main objectives of his journey, one the island that will reveal a cosmic event and will be the site of his death, the other the continent that forever eludes him. In different ways, both Columbus and Cook miss the reality or significance of continents: one sees what is now the South American continent but cannot read the scene in his desire to realize the metaphysical cosmos; the other cannot reach the continent that occupies the final undiscovered place on the terrestrial globe.

Siskind reads Cook's inability to discover Antarctica as constituting the 'implosion' of the universal premises of modernity, which reaches a limit to its territorial spatialization of conceptual 'universals'. He argues that the 'radical sublimity' of the Antarctic is more powerful than reason, this aligning the material failure with the failure of reason. The picture of the globe he presents to his patrons and to the world is both complete – as he and reason must be – and incomplete. Certainly the question of the Southern Continent promotes extensive reflection and deliberation on his voyages. He writes:

> I had now made the circuit of the Southern Ocean in a high Latitude and traversed it in such a manner as to leave not the least room for the Possibility of there being a continent, unless near the Pole and out of the reach of Navigation; by twice visiting the Pacific Tropical Sea, I had not only settled the situation of some old discoveries but made there many new ones and left, I conceive, very little to be done even in that part. Thus I flatter myself that the intention of the Voyage has in every respect been fully Answered, the Southern Hemisphere sufficiently explored and a final end put to the searching after a Southern Continent, which has at times ingrossed the attention of some of the Maritime Powers for near two Centuries past and the Geographers of all ages. (Cook 1971, 186)

Sloterdijk terms the second stage of globalization the 'terrestrial globe', which he describes as the phase of 'travelling the world in ships', and which replaces cosmic transcendence with horizontal transcendence (2011, 50; 2013, 23). This is the familiar shift from a cosmological to a cartographical world view, which is often traced in early modern scholarship.[5] Sloterdijk's insight into this change is the identification of how humanist universalism shifted its territorial imperative. For overlaying the globular image of circumnavigation, such as that achieved by Cook, as navigator and embodiment of the Man of Reason, are mono-directional pathways. Unlike Columbus's 'recovery' of the created world is the *discovery* of the new from which there is no retreat.

These cartographical lines travel in one direction, at least from the perspective of European colonization – until the diasporic movements much later. They rehearse and give evidence to the trajectory of ignorance to knowledge, of enlightenment. This phase is characterized by an epistemology of *alatheia*, as Heidegger has it, the process of unveiling or disclosing that which is unknown, which necessarily effects change.[6] Hence in real and imaginary terms we can say that the circumnavigations that materialized the circular globe were accompanied by a linear movement of progression, travelling ever forward.

While Cook epitomizes the Man of Reason who travelled the world in ships, Cook's drive for unity recalls the cosmic globe of Columbus. This unity persists as a travesty in the enveloping circumscription of empire, which becomes the transcendent term, both inside and outside the colony. Ironically this unity, imagined as globe or island, can be seen to break down into smaller and smaller spherical units, smaller and increasingly disconnected islands.

Cook's completion of the globe (minus Antarctica) in the project of British imperialism reframes the purpose of voyaging and its literary correlative of the quest. For the imperial centre, if not all the peoples it controlled, monodirectional pathways enacted a contradiction; they were propelled by the imperative of progression that could no longer provide a revelation at the point of destination. The empire's mobilization of populations across the globe thus ushers in an era of mobility without progress, activity without chronology and change without temporality. In this periodization or, more properly since time is no longer the measure, in this spatialized condition, the imperial comprehension has evicted any exterior domain. There is nothing outside itself: no God, no space, no time.

Ironically, this diminishment of the exterior and the sense of its passing depletes the capacity for habitation, for nesting inside space. Deleuze and Guattari's characterization of an English philosophical habit of thought, discussed in the previous chapter, is relevant here in historical terms in its reformation of history to space. They define the English as nomads who 'pitch their tents' on island after island in an ongoing process of fractalization (Deleuze and Guattari 1994, 104). The island is both figure and ground of this process as one nation's universalism is realized in territorial terms on different scales, in other dimensions and in proliferating relations. This complexity compounds, intensifies, in that the island is also the figure and ground of the longing for a place beyond or outside the deadening comprehension of totality. The island also figures inhabitation; as discussed in the previous chapter, the common phrase 'my island home' is a multiple tautology, for each of the three words invokes the other two.

## First and Last, Before and After, Coincident

From the 1780s the first and last sites of the New Worlds are brought into relation via the network of Empire at the moment of this confusion between historical time and globalized space. Clearly, Australia is cast as pertaining to (Britain's) modernity while the West Indies are increasingly cast as belonging to its past. This temporality, while immensely powerful and with major ramifications, is also at odds with the new simultaneity of the spatialized globe in which both colonial sites now coexist. Ironically, this simultaneity is used to enforce narratives of chronology, supersession and obsolescence. The juxtaposition of the two in a static image bears witness to their oppositionality. Taken together, the new coordinates mapped by the West Indian and Australian colonies complicate accepted measures of pace and scale, as events and people are too fast or slow, too big or small, too early or late for the shifting dimensions of each location and its position on the new globe.

The subjects who materialize this epistemic shift, those who are caught in this moving stasis, exhibit a range of behaviours and symptoms in their textual accounts, which are the focus of the following discussion. Each of the texts examined tracks movements between the two colonial sites in genres that negotiate the personal experience of history: an autobiographical novel, a private/professional journal, commissioned colonial commentary, a historical travelogue and a historical novel.

Underpinning the construction of these sequences and alternate parallels are two of the main operations of the British Empire in the nineteenth century: the adamant insistence on causality in its justification of national expansion, specifically in convict transportation which relies on criminal cause and promises reforming effects; and the temporalization of racist discourse. In each and all the texts we can discern confusion regarding the relationship between cause and effect, of experience in one place *then* the next – a progressive teleology. This progression is overlaid with the contemplation of the alternate lives in each place –a relation of simultaneous juxtaposition, of a parallel universe.

The first novel written and published in Australia was *Quintus Servinton* (1830), scripted in part in the confines of the prison at Hobart, on the island of Van Diemen's Land by transported convict Henry Savery (1791–1842) though published anonymously by Henry Melville. The novel is a three-volume bildungsroman that details the development and education of young Quintus from childhood, through schooling, his early infatuations then marriage, and his professional career in business. The reader can detect fundamental flaws in his generally likeable character that prepare us for his downfall when he is driven to forgery. It is in this dimension of his life, also, that the novel traces visible and invisible lines between and across the empire from the West Indies to Britain and Van Diemen's Land. A somewhat challenging tome for the modern reader in both style and length, *Quintus Servinton* is autobiographical, and narrates the vicissitudes that lead its author/hero to crime, conviction and transportation (Miller 1957; Hadcraft 1962; Howard, 2011). Like his author, Quintus's crime of forgery attracts the death sentence which is commuted 24 hours before execution to transportation to Van Diemen's Land. The novel was partly written during Savery's reimprisonment in Hobart for further crimes of forgery, prompted by yet another financial collapse.

The novel's eponymous hero is directed into the world of business by his parents, who are threatened with financial ruin when Quintus is a boy and so determine to shape Quintus to take up the family's financial burden. After his schooling, itself tailored to achieve this result, Quintus's ability and interest recommend him to the company of a 'West India' merchant where he quickly proves his worth. His skill and diligence result in a proposal for Quintus to travel to the West Indies, which he initially accepts, albeit reluctantly, for he does not want to leave his wife and young child, a romantic facet of his character that is as dangerous as it is endearing. When, seemingly miraculously, another offer presents in England, he changes plans and stays at home. This proves a fateful decision, as from this point he becomes involved in a complex plot of financial deceit, which leads to his arrest and transportation.

The first of the novel's transnational ties in terms of textual sequence is between Van Diemen's Land and Britain, which Savery sets out in his Preface to the novel. These links are, on one hand, clear and direct and stress not only the ties to the mother country but also its replication in a far distant island, so that the colony is, in Wentworth's famous phrase 'a new Britannia on another shore' (1823). However, the two sites are also impossibly distant, and Savery reverses his own viewing position in the trajectory of this gaze to accord Britain the prerogative of imperial perspective, thereby also aligning his 'true' perspective with the imperial home. He describes Van Diemen's Land as 'a little speck upon the Southern Ocean', though in actuality it is 40 per cent as large as the island of Great Britain and 80 percent as large as Ireland. Its size is, of course, determined by distance, according to the convention of imaginary islands, as Van Diemen's Land would have been to Savery's English readers. It is determined also by the perceived relative significance of the islands, which magnifies Great Britain and diminishes Van Diemen's Land.

A key reason Savery dwells on the question of distance in the Preface is its justification of the decision to publish the book locally in Hobart rather than in Britain (see Figure 2.1). Savery sets out the advantages of local publishing at some length in order to soften the possible charge of his 'temerity' in writing and publishing a novel from the new colony, which is returned to Britain as a finished product. Such temerity is aesthetic – he is a first-time novelist – as well

**Figure 2.1** Andrew Bent's Stanhope press, on which Australia's first novel, *Quintus Servinton* by Henry Savery, was printed, on display in the Tasmanian Museum and Art Gallery. Courtesy Tasmanian Museum and Art Gallery.

as colonial, for the local production of the book runs the risk of claiming an independent, even contrary viewing perspective from that of the imperial and penal centre. Savery understands the danger of appearing to return the imperial gaze, bearing out Foucault's identification of the shift from monarchical to disciplinary power taking place at this time as well as its deep implication in the surveillance of the modern penal system. Foucault's argument centres on the panopticon of Foucault (1975), which is used as the structure for the 'Model Prison' opened at Port Arthur, Van Diemen's Land, in 1853.

The temerity of colonial self-production highlights one of the contradictions of the penal colony, which is both highly surveilled but also removed from view. The subject's imagined transformation is a process, a pupal stage of development, not the end product. Savery wards against such accusations by framing the novel with a version of a found manuscript device, which casts the events of the narrative as past and resolved. Moreover, the temporary and transitional nature of the convict life in the colony is proleptically foreclosed by a gypsy prophesy early in the novel, which contains Quintus's misfortune to the decade of his thirties, so it is always already contained – as contained as an island penal colony.

As Morris Miller documents, Savery and Melville were right to be apprehensive about the reception of the novel on these grounds. A reviewer in *La Belle Assemblee* (1832) performs confusion about the authorship, provenance and production. Miller glosses the review:

> The reviewer takes a facetious turn, referring to the novel as 'one of a very extraordinary character; nothing less indeed, than a three-volumed tale, with "Hobart Town, Henry Melville, printer," on the title-page. With "the sweetly-romantic name," one might imagine the printer to be the hero of the tale. The hero, however, is entitled "Quintus Servinton".' The reviewer goes on to say: 'We are much more attracted by the quality of the paper, the respectability of the type, the solidity of the covers, and the beauty of the yellow labels, than by any of the woes and wonders of the story itself.' Yet he hopes 'novel-loving readers will have curiosity, enough to glance at a work that is ushered in under such unusual auspices.' (1957, 2)

Savery's anxiety around the temerity of process and product is astute also in that their relation is becoming one of the most charged distinctions of his time, especially within Britain's global empire. As a completed account and artefact, it may appear to deny Britain its right of authorization. It may also circumvent the primacy of its industry of secondary production, the right to fashion the raw materials of its colonies on British soil, as suggested by *La Belle Assemblee*'s focus of the materiality of the book as composite material object: 'the quality of the paper, the respectability of the type, the solidity of the covers, and the beauty of the yellow labels'. For one of Britain's innovations as an imperial power and global trader was the transportation of raw materials from their sources back to Britain for refinement and manufacturing. It is this innovation that redraws the single line between the Australian colony and Britain to the Caribbean.

Savery's failed venture into sugar refinement or 'sugar-baking' in Britain, using transported cane from the West Indies, charts another line between the islands in both the life and the narrative. This is true also of his subsequent involvement in copper mining, a major industry in South West England, where Savery was born, but increasingly global in its operations. In their documentation of the role of copper in the globalization of the industrial revolution,

Chris Evans and Olivia Saunders quote French metallurgist Frédéric Le Play, writing in 1848, who claimed that copper manufacturing from the late 1820s had transformed and expanded Swansea so that it 'had no limits but the globe itself' (2015, 4). While copper mining and smelting had once required proximity, new maritime transport meant the processes could be bifurcated. Swansea, for instance, had the coal for smelters but no copper. The South Wales smelters not only processed copper from the south west of England but 'ores from around the European littoral, from the island of Cuba, from Mexico, from Colombia, from Peru, from Chile, from Australia and from New Zealand' (Evans and Saunders, 2015, 4).

*Quintus Servinton*'s map of the modern globe casts the West Indies as a site of mercantile possibility. In narrative terms, the West Indies also represent shadow alternatives to the plot and are linked to 'Providence', as is clearly the case with Quintus's decision not to take up his business opportunity in the West Indies, which leads to his undoing. So, too, when Quintus attempts to evade arrest in England by fleeing to the Isle of Wight, he boards a frigate bound for the West Indies. This attempt is foiled. A similar issue of will and destiny is set out later in the novel, when Quintus is sailing to Van Diemen's Land and is befriended by the ship's surgeon, Mr Bruce, who counsels Quintus with a moral tale in which, once again, the West Indies are the path not taken. Mr Bruce describes how he tried in vain to be assigned to a frigate sailing for the Caribbean, as he longed to be with his 'brother officers, who were endeared to [him] by long acquaintance' (235). He was so disconsolate by the refusal that he nearly 'retired from the service'. Subsequently he reads that the frigate was wrecked and all on board perished. The ship and shipmates he did not seek but was assigned all prospered.

The West Indies operate in *Quintus Servinton* as a parallel universe. They are an other world – *not* a new world – in an unexpected link between Columbus and the nineteenth century, which in fact marks the beginnings of the end of the terrestrial globe. In this other world the British subject can have an other life. There is no longer anything to be 'discovered' in this once-New World. Voyaging no longer discloses, for the world is revealed as Columbus's Christian cosmos. However, it does promise a destination with the (illusory) capacity to enclose the subject. Importantly, in the context of a narrative of transportation and incarceration, this other world is imagined as a refuge, the island home where one can be sheltered. In Sloterdijk's terms, the terrestrial globe, like the cosmic globe, has no outside because it incorporates everything. Quintus's dilemma is that there is no escape from the newly global empire. The structure appears to offer opportunities, but these are tied to the construction of a ubiquitous condition of exteriority, exposure and homelessness. *Quintus Servinton* attempts to circumscribe this negative potential – to enclose itself – by its (inconsistent) temporality of retrospection, which asserts England as the first and final home. Savery himself did not ever realize this *nostsos*. He died, possibly by his own hand (he had tried twice before), in 1842, in Van Diemen's Land at the Port Arthur penal settlement, where he had been sent for reoffending. He is buried on an outlying island of the settlement named the Isle of the Dead, his final island-prison-home.

The Commandant of the Port Arthur at the time of Savery's arrival was Charles O'Hara Booth (1800–1851), who kept a journal from 1815 to 1838 detailing his career as a military officer across the colonies of the Empire. The journal includes events, reflections, poetic transcriptions and poetic compositions. Although they are clearly very different men, a study of Booth's journal indicates points of connections with Savery in their common dislocation and dispersal across the islands of empire. Both Savery and Booth died prematurely at age 51 in Van Diemen's Land, never returning to Britain. And while Booth's journals reveal a great sense of purpose and his growing attachment to Van Diemen's Land, he also records the contradiction of feeling exposed in a culture of incarceration, a contradiction encapsulated in the reality and the figure of the island.[7] Both convict and gaoler are caught in the ever-diminishing circles of island containment.

In 1838, 'heart broken and miserable' over a disappointment in love, Booth travels to a small island off the Port Arthur peninsula. He writes: 'would it were mine with a good tempered little partner' (Booth 1981, 221). He craves an island home, understood as a shelter from the world. Booth's simple desire in fact maps an intricate web between the West Indies, Britain and Van Diemen's Land and raises a series of questions about the utter separation yet connection of the colonies. In the years before arriving in Van Diemen's Land he had completed a six-year stint in the West Indies, including Demerara, Berbice and St Vincent, followed by a three-year period back home in England and then Ireland. On the island of St Vincent, Booth had a common law wife, a Creole woman named Caralin Douglas Wharton. They had two children, whom he left behind and never saw again.[8] Booth eventually married Elizabeth Charlotte (née Eagle), the stepdaughter of his regimental surgeon at Port Arthur, and the couple had two children: a mirror of another life on another island, one he tried repeatedly to replicate before his marriage.[9] Booth's pattern of repetition, a cloning of self across space, is another connection to Savery and his history of repeat offences and convictions for the exact same crime in England and Van Diemen's Land.[10] In the terms of global connection of empire, this pattern of behaviour across space enacted by Savery, Quintus and Booth highlights a confusion between repetition, cause and effect, and alternatives in a newly cotemporal globe. Each island is (almost) a separate world.

This same question informs Rochester's bigamous attempt to marry Jane in *Jane Eyre* (1847) On the one hand, Rochester is the wealthy yet embittered man he is *because* of his connections in the West Indies, and yet he wishes to leave that self behind, contained within the other island. Jane's strength derives from her refusal to change herself for any person or circumstance. This sheltered, parochial young woman knows her place in the world wherever she is. She is, therefore, precisely the person Rochester needs yet she is also the one who would feel his incoherence most acutely, as both a moral issue and as a threat to her own self-consistency.

Importantly, the relationship of cause and effect in the global British Empire, as Booth's journal shows, includes surrogacy and displacement. As father to the children with Eagle, in establishing the children's prison at Port Arthur and later as the Principal of the Hobart orphanage, Booth's abandonment of his first two children on a Caribbean island, is replicated, distorted and extended in another place and time – on another island. This part-repetition is a form of self-mimicry, further compounding the ironies of Homi Bhabha's famous formulation of mimicry in postcolonial discourse. The endless irony created by the forked tongue of colonized peoples speaking the language of their colonizers is the 'the same but not quite, the same but not white' (Bhabha 1994, 85). The self-mimicry of the colonizers themselves both denies and reinforces the sequence of original and copy. It is the constitutive split in being – of self from self, colony from colony, that actively produces the modern global (imperial) subject, who is freely mobile, but whose travelling produces no discovery, and whose sense of home becomes increasingly ideational. It is also a form of disaggregation that produces meaningful difference between the colonies, the borders necessary for the crossing of capital and racial segregation.

The patterns of progression, repetition and parallelism enacted in the individual narratives of Savery, Quintus and Booth are impressed on and by Britain's colonial carceral globe. From the historical archive we witness a range of causes and effects travelling mostly from the Americas to Australia, beginning with Britain's perceived need for a new convict colony after American independence. The transportation of convicts also only went one way. In addition to the 160,000 white convicts transported to Australia, Ian Duffield documents that there were 202 black convicts from the West Indies (1986, 25).[11] More West Indian convicts might have ended up in the Australian colonies were it not for the different conceptions of the racial destinies of each place. Diane Paton writes:

> [T]he decision to end this particular form of population movement indicates a growing sense, among the empire's British-based administrators, of the colonies

> as a set of racially differentiated spaces. Some colonies, including Australia, were in the process of becoming white places, soon to achieve Dominion status. Others, including those in the Caribbean, were increasingly marked as 'black', and would, a generation after the end of inter-colonial transportation, become Crown Colonies. (2008, 450)

The same policies were in force, though more formally, when the Australian Government enacted the *Pacific Island Labourers Act* (1901) to repatriate all Pacific Islander labourers – many of whom had been forcibly brought to Australia as indentured workers – as part of its White Australia Policy. Like the Caribbean, this labour had been imported for the production of sugar cane. Unlike the Caribbean, the vision for Australia, as a 'new Britannia on another shore', was white.

The other binding connection regarding unfree labour concerns the cessation of convict transportation to Australia (1842 in New South Wales, 1853 in Van Diemen's Land and 1868 in Western Australia). These decisions were hastened by the Molesworth Committee of 1834, which understood transportation as a form of slavery, for which they took the West Indies as their ultimate model (Duffield 1986, 25). Certainly, the conditions on the Second Fleet to Port Jackson (1789) were modelled directly on the slave ships of the middle passage. The company subcontracted by the British government to transport the convicts, Camden, Calvert & King, had previously transported slaves to North America. Of the 1,026 convicts embarked on the Second Fleet, 267 (256 men and 11 women) died and a further 124 died shortly after they landed.

The movement of 'free' people between the West Indian and Australian colonies was considerable. The majority were the personnel of empire, including the judiciary, career army officers and regimental soldiers, including veterans of the Napoleonic Wars who were caught up in the economic crisis that faced Britain concerning war pensions and so had limited options in any case. The Appendix to this book is a compilation of this traffic and shows how extensive it was. Every aspect of life in Australian colonies was informed by the West Indian experience. The first judge appointed in New South Wales in 1814, Jeffrey Bent (1781–1852), who was recalled to Britain in 1817 at Governor Macquarie's insistence, nevertheless went on to judicial senior roles in Grenada, Trinidad and British Guiana.[12] In the other direction, Archibald Burt (1810–1879), born to a plantation family in St Kitts, became the first chief justice of the newly created Supreme Court of Western Australia in 1860. Numerous members of the military, with experience in the Caribbean, hence aware of colonial operations and their benefits, made substantial land grabs once they arrived in the Australian colonies.[13] Many merchants and professionals used their experience of the colonial system in the West Indies to launch new careers and ventures in Australia.[14] Some, like medical doctor John Hampton (1810–1869), moved across the spaces and the roles of the empire. He served in numerous ships between Britain the Americas and wrote 'his observations on the diseases of the West Indies' to great approval. He was surgeon on several convict transports to Van Diemen's Land where, in May 1846, he was appointed as comptroller general of convicts. In 1862 he was appointed governor of Western Australia, overseeing the last six years of transportation (Boyce 1966).

With specific reference to the development of Australian literary culture, the link to the West Indies is fundamental, and its recognition meaningfully complicates the dyadic relationship between colony and the imperial centre. George Howe, who founded Australia's first newspaper, *The Sydney Gazette* (1803–1842), was born into a printing trade family in St Kitts. Howe was also Australia's first book publisher (McDougall 2002, 11). Gilbert Robertson (1794–1851), from Trinidad, published Van Diemen's Land's first daily newspaper, the *True Colonist and Van Diemen's Land Political Despatch and Agricultural and Commercial Advertiser*. Robertson was a strong critic of Governor Arthur, which landed him in prison for a time and affected the production of the newspaper. In her detailed essay on Robertson, Cassandra Pybus notes that while he was 'referred to as a gentleman in public, in private he was reviled as a mulatto' (2011, 5).

As we have already seen, Australia's first novel mapped connections to the West Indies. Australia's 'first true poet' also had deep connections to the West Indies. Adam Lindsay Gordon was born on Fayal in the Azores Islands – the same island on which the earlier poet John Donne fought the Spaniards for colonial advantage. Gordon's mother was the daughter of a Barbadian planter and former Governor of Berbice and Demerara. As is often noted, this colonial network is further underscored by the fact that Gordon's father taught at Cheltenham School, a preferred institution for colonial families, where Adam attended, as did Australian Nobel laureate Patrick White.

The categories of official roles and literary culture overlap in two of the most notorious cases of transcolonial movement between the Australian and Caribbean colonies. Both Edward Eyre (1815–1891) and James Froude (1818–1894) were celebrated in Australia and became notorious in the Caribbean in connected ways. Both are also deeply embedded in the writing cultures of Australia and the West Indies. In Australia, Eyre is known as a remarkable explorer and as an effective 'Protector of Aborigines'. His extraordinary journeys and his remarkable accounts of them, including the relationship with his companion and guide, Wylie, are part of both Australian history and myth. His journals have inspired generations of Australian writers: a survey of the AustLit database shows 163 single literary works on Eyre. Writing of his time in London during the Blitz, Patrick White writes:

> Other remembered reading was Eyre's account of his walk from Adelaide to Esperance. Falling bombs and Eyre's journal started in me a longing for Australia and some kind of creative urge I could not yet channel or even define. (1981, 83)

Exactly one hundred years after their publication, Eyre's journals summon White home – or construct an idea of what his home might be – and initiate creative, literary desire.

So for Australians, Eyre's subsequent history has been viewed as discordant. After his time in Australia and New Zealand, Eyre was appointed Lieutenant Governor of St Vincent (1854) then the Leeward Islands (1860), where he was known for his humane governance. He was appointed acting Governor of Jamaica in 1861 and assumed full responsibility in 1864. In this role, in 1865, he brutally suppressed an uprising, the Morant Bay Rebellion, in which 608 people were killed or executed, another 600 were flogged and 1,000 dwellings burnt to the ground. He was recalled and proceedings were brought against him three times but dismissed. These proceedings are embedded in British literary culture of the time and Jamaican culture to this day. The group calling for his prosecution, the Jamaica Committee, comprised notable lawyers, parliamentarians, scientists and philosophers including, inter alia, John Bright, Thomas Hill Green, John Stuart Mill, Charles Lyell, Charles Darwin and Thomas Huxley. The limited number of literary figures in this group included Thomas Hughes and Leslie Stephen. The Eyre Defence Committee, established by Thomas Carlyle, was heavily comprised of writers including John Ruskin, Charles Kingsley, Charles Dickens and Alfred, Lord Tennyson – and one scientist, the physicist John Tyndall. The literary establishment supported Eyre.

Theories abound as to how to account for the apparent discontinuity of Eyre's behaviour. In his summary for the *Australian Dictionary of Biography*, Geoffrey Dutton focuses on the conundrum in individual terms:

> The poignant contrast remains between the friend of Wylie and humane protector of the Aboriginals [sic] in Australia, and 'the monster of Jamaica'. The obstinacy that gave him his endurance as an explorer was his undoing as a governor in Jamaica. (1966, n.p.)

Dutton's viewpoint is clarified further by Peter Linebaugh and Marcus Rediker who have shown how the colonial enterprise in the Atlantic utilized the rhetoric of singular heroism of the colonizer against the mob. They trace the recurrent deployment of the classical myth of Hercules in colonial fiction and nonfiction of the Atlantic and its deployment in the justification of violence against hostile subordinates including slaves. In this tropism Hercules is pitted against the monstrous Hydra with proliferating heads. Linebaugh and Rediker argue that Hercules provided a model of strength, progressive ambition and the unification of a centralized territorial state (2000, 1–7). This view is certainly supported by the discussion of the West Indian islands in the copious travel accounts published in the nineteenth century.

In accordance with Linebaugh and Marcus Rediker, Julie Evans disputes any reading of Eyre's actions as 'extraordinary' to either himself or colonial governance. She writes:

> Eyre's actions in Jamaica are extraordinary only insofar as they represent the full realisation of the correlation between race, resistance and repression that was common to colonial governance. [...] Eyre's writings about Aborigines, for example, were an early indication of how the correlation operated throughout the Australian colonies, where race initially upheld dispossession. (Evans 2005, 139)

Evans argues also that 'race' operated differently in shared spaces, as in Jamaica, and cites Patrick Wolfe's analysis of the shift in perceptions of race, from its role in the pre-emancipation period as the justification for slavery, to the process of 'racialization' – the production of racialized subjects – after emancipation (Evans 2005, 139; Wolfe 2002, 58).[15] The nexus of racialization and population ratios is born out directly in the defence offered for Eyre. John Tyndall on Eyre's Defence Committee argued not only that the races are separate species, but also that Eyre's violent suppression of the Morant Bay uprising was legitimate on that basis, as long as such impositions of martial law were restricted to Jamaica, and, by implication, other imperial territories with white minority populations (Winter 1963; Semmel 1963, 125–26).

In his account of the division caused by Eyre's actions within British society, Robert Fraser (2011) proposes that his defenders were influenced by contemporary conceptions of the modern Hero formulated by Carlyle and attached to Eyre from his earlier feats of exploration on the Australian continent. No doubt Kingsley was influenced by the Australian experiences of his novelist brother, Henry, author of *Geoffrey Hamlyn* (1859), who had spent five years in Australia from 1853 to 1858 and who wrote an extensive account of Eyre's explorations (H. Kingsley 1865). The Morant Bay massacre created another (official) national hero, this time in Jamaica. George William Gordon, member of the Legislative Assembly, activist on behalf of the 'coloured' people of Jamaica, was executed by Eyre as one of the instigators of the protest. There are many literary treatments of Gordon and the massacre in the Jamaican archive, iconically Claude McKay's 'George William Gordon to the Oppressed Natives' (1912; 2004, 282), Roger Mais's play *George William Gordon* (1938) and V. S. Reid's novel *New Day* (1949).

One of the attendees at the first meeting of parties wishing to defend Eyre was the novelist, historian and biographer James Froude (1818–1894), long-time friend and future biographer of Carlyle, and brother-in-law of Charles Kingsley. Froude did not take a public role in this matter, given his editorship of *Fraser's Magazine*, but he, too, is deeply implicated in the racialized literary networks that connected the Australian and West Indian colonies at this time.

A life of fiction and nonfiction writing already behind him, Froude became interested in the future of the Empire and the fate of the colonies in the 1870s. On Lord Canarvan's quasi-official suggestion related to the project of federating groups of colonies, he visited to South Africa in 1874 and 1875, which proved disastrous for the Cape Colony and its administrators, as he advocated introducing a forced labour system onto the Xhosa people and the redistribution Xhosa and Basotho lands to whites. He strongly argues for white supremacy and colonial rule, exhibiting the same anxiety regarding population ratios in the governance of the West Indies (Koditschek 2011, 151*ff.*). He contrasts this situation in Africa with that in Australia, which he had not yet visited.

In 1885 he came to Australia to see for himself. In reverse of Quintus Servinton, Van Diemen's Land was the path not taken for Froude, as he had accepted a teaching post in Hobart as a young man but the offer was retracted after the scandal caused by his novel *The Nemesis of Faith*, published in 1849. In 1875 he was fêted in Australia during his visit, as his literary works had preceded him and he was considered one of the foremost of Victorian writers. He, in turn, wrote very favourably of his experiences in *Oceana: Or, England and Her Colonies* (1886), published after his return to England, and in which he opined at length on his vision for a Pacific federation of British colonies. Australians and New Zealanders did not respond well, and *Oceania* was criticized and lampooned in the Australian and New Zealand press (Teale 1972). This included the Australian coinage of the descriptor 'froudacious' (Markus 2005, 243).

In 1887, 22 years after the Morant Bay massacre and nearly 20 years since the proceedings against Eyre, Froude visited the West Indies. His Jamaican visit included a stay on an estate owned by the manager of the Colonial Bank. The estate was of especial interest to Froude as it had previously belonged to George William Gordon. Froude published his impressions – and again, his lengthy theories on colonial federations and sustaining colonial ties with Britain – in *The English in the West Indies: Or, The Bow of Ulysses* in 1888. In this account, Froude authorizes his perceptions of the West Indies through his prior experience as a colonial observer in the Pacific colonies, a framework that overlays the temporalities of simultaneity and sequence to construct a racist comparison and progression:

> I had visited our great Pacific colonies. Circumstances led me afterwards to attend more particularly to the West Indies. They were the earliest, and once the most prized, of all our distant possessions. They had been won by the most desperate struggles, and had been the scene of our greatest naval glories. (1888, 1)

This discussion continues for some pages and includes consideration of the view of a senior colonial official, voiced 17 years prior, that the British should conclude their connection with their Caribbean colonies:

> They were no longer of special value to us; the whole world had become our market; and whether they were nominally attached to the Empire, or were independent, or joined themselves to some other power, was of no commercial moment to us. It was felt, however, that as long as any tie remained, we should be obliged to defend them in time of war; while they, in consequence of their connection, would be liable to attack. The sooner, therefore, the connection was ended, the better for them and for us. (Froude 1888, 5)

Froude contrasts this view, with which he strongly disagrees, to the earlier value and role of the Caribbean for the Empire, using the conventional figure of island jewels:

> At one time the West Indian colonies had been more to us than such casual seedlings. They had been precious regarded as jewels, which hundreds of thousands of English lives had been sacrificed to tear from France and Spain. The Caribbean Sea was the cradle of the Naval Empire of Great Britain. (1888, 6)

The island jewels, which have lost their shine, mark the shift from islands to continents as preferred topologies in the nineteenth century, though this broader pattern cannot be seen by Froude within the purview of his imperial history.

Froude concludes his first chapter of historical visions by advocating for Britain's continuing role in the Caribbean on the basis of British history and its proper immortalization in epic:

> If ever the naval exploits of this country are done into an epic poem – and since the *Iliad* there has been no subject better fitted for such treatment or better deserving it – the West Indies will be the scene of the most brilliant cantos. For

> England to allow them to drift away from her because they have no immediate marketable value would be a sign that she had lost the feelings with which great nations always treasure the heroic traditions of their fathers. When those traditions come to be regarded as something which concerns them no longer, their greatness is already on the wane. (1888, 10)

Here, as throughout Froude's account, all matters refer back to Britain. He talks of thousands of lives lost, but the only deaths visible to him in the carnage of the Caribbean history are British. In a poetic figure, the West Indies are cantos in an English epic.

In his Nobel speech, 'The Antilles: Fragments of Epic Memory' (1992a), Derek Walcott takes up both issues of epic form and its relationship to the Caribbean, but the epic in question is the *Ramayana* and it is in fragmented in and by its transportation from the Indian subcontinent to the islands of the Caribbean, as he later deploys the *Odyssey* for his 'epic of the dispossessed', *Omeros* (Walcott 1990; Hamner 1997). In his Nobel address Walcott also directly addresses the perception of Caribbean people as fragments of other (putatively) whole cultures: '"No people there," to quote Froude, "in the true sense of the word". No people' (1992a). The imperial eye, which Froude assumes with some ceremony, organizes the syntax of every sentence in which the actual place and its people are cast as objects, figments of its dominant discourse of history and conquest. Alternatively, they are ritually elided; they are the expected predicate needed to make sense, but are bypassed as the subject once again turned in on itself.

As even a beginning student of the West Indies knows, Froude's study has come to epitomize imperious imperial perspectives in and of itself and in view of Jamaica's recent past. It was swiftly and thoroughly repudiated by John Jacob Thomas's *Froudacity*, published in 1889 in Britain. *Froudacity* is a distinctive intellectual work that inaugurated a particular mode of resistance writing in the West Indies while retaining significance in itself, as C. L. R. James claims (1969, 23*ff.*), and as Walcott's reference also indicates. It would be nice to think that the coinage *froudacious* passed from Australia to become *froudacity* in Grenada where Thomas wrote his eloquent and thoroughgoing riposte – a fleeting ironic moment shared between the two colonies – a moment, too, of mutual contemporaneity against the relational temporality of empire.[16] However, while Australians have a long tradition of satirizing English (and other) authority, it is sobering also to think that many Australians may not have taken issue with Froude's racism; Australia was founded on dispossession and, in 1889, was only 11 years from instigating the White Australia Policy.

From the perspective of the twenty-first century, Froude was clearly furthering the concerns of a faction in the British debate regarding ongoing colonial rule, which he disperses with writerly flourish of personal and historical narratives. Crucial to all of these is racism based on skin colour. He applauds Australia, Canada and New Zealand, which are white, and is appalled by the racial ratios of the Caribbean. In all fairness to Froude, it needs be said that he was also appalled by the white Catholics in Ireland, especially the unseemly poor, reminding us of John Beddoe's phrenological study *The Races of Britain* (1862), which links the Irish, Welsh, the 'Africinoid' peoples and the poor as sharing similar physical traces of subintelligence. Froude's good friend Charles Kingsley wrote of how dreadful it was to witness the 'white chimpanzees' of Ireland while his other great friend Carlyle thought they should be classified 'with the niggers' (Gibbons 2000; Duffy, 2007, 25). Froude praised the brutal practices of English colonists in Ireland, even Cromwell, and advocated an increase of the English population in Ireland as a way of redeeming its fortunes. With that noted, however, there is a particular racism reserved for dark-skinned people in Froude and it becomes characterized as a form of anachronism, as it does for Australian writer Mary Gaunt, discussed below.

This temporality of racism is, of course, linked to genocide in that it denies people both their present and future. In Australia, this manifested in a range of genocidal practices, linked by the conception that First Nations people belonged to the past, to prehistory. These practices are explicitly brutal as shown with disregard for life in conquest, dispossession and transnational slavery, and became embedded in social Darwinism, as if modern subjects passively wait for the demise of premodern peoples. The anachronism in Froude's racism is related to these conventional operations, but it is also significantly different. In his discussion of Grenada he fears that the withdrawal of the British would result in a reversion to savagery – the lines are not worth repeating (Froude 1888, 49–50). He also relegates the West Indies to Britain's past, and hence to the global past. He acknowledges Britain's ongoing responsibility but admits that there is no possible return to white-dominated cultures in the islands, hence no modern future. This exclusion from modernity enforces the imagined timelessness of the island paradise.

For Froude, one important reason for Britain's proper acquittal of its duties in the Caribbean is that it will give the new, white colonies confidence in their ongoing dealings with Britain: they are the future. The white Australian is the 'Coming Man' of a Darwinist-Nationalist model. From the Australian perspective at least, the comparison of these temporalities refigures the accepted dyadic relationship between twilight and dawn, which, in literary history of the late nineteenth century, has been read as a dynamic between European decadence and Australian emergence. The very title of Louisa Lawson's literary journal *The Dawn* (1888–1905) is evidence of this, as is her journal for children *Young Australia* (1889–1903). However, if we triangulate the relationship of emergence and decline to include both the first and last of the New Worlds, a different dynamic becomes visible. The 'decline' Froude and other colonial observers witness in the Caribbean – and in the construction of the Irish 'twilight' of the late nineteenth century – is a means by which the imperial globe constructs an ideology of time by which the impress of its own history becomes naturalized through mortality and seasonal cycles as global history.

There is a sense of belatedness in Froude's account of the West Indies. He himself is an old man whose personal habit of retrospection reinforces the historical framework that measures present decline against past glory. We find a similar anachronistic imperial zeal in the works of Australian writer Mary Gaunt (1861–1942), though she had little time for the English in the West Indies and advocated a kind of alliance of colonials across the globe. Gaunt was staunchly Australian, an identity that commonly included disdain for Britain, but she was also a fierce defender of the Empire. She was a nationalist, an imperialist and a colonialist, leading Angela Woollacott to claim that she showed how 'Australianness could be constructed in multiple parts of the globe'; that is, as a mobile identity. Moreover, Gaunt indicates that for many Australians in the early twentieth century, there was no contradiction between strident nationalism and loyalty to the empire (Woollacott 2003, 194).

Gaunt visited Jamaica in 1919 and again in 1931 and wrote two nonfiction books: a history titled *Where the Twain Meet* (1922), and a travel book titled *Reflection – In Jamaica* (1932). She also wrote a novel titled *Harmony: A Tale of the Old Slave Days in Jamaica* (1933). By this time she had published many works of fiction and nonfiction, the volume of her output determined in no small measure by the fact that she lived by her pen. This energy, ingenuity and enterprise is a quality of her heroines such as Phoebe Marsden, the heroine of her most successful novel, *Kirkham's Find* (1897), which tells the story of a young woman who defies convention and becomes independent via beekeeping. The opening chapter is framed by an epigraph from Southey on the relationship between ambition and contentment:

> It is not for man to rest in absolute contentment. He is born to hopes and aspirations, as the sparks fly upwards, unless he has brutified his nature, and quenched the spirit of immortality, which is his portion. (Gaunt 1997, n.p.)

In Australian literature Gaunt's reputation rests mainly on her early writings. Her Jamaican writings occur later, after she had left Australia for London in 1901 to eke out a living as a writer. From there she travelled extensively including extended stays in China and Africa, and she published numerous accounts of her experiences.

Her two trips to Jamaica occurred more than ten years apart in 1918 and 1931, and the travel accounts of each trip were published the following year. Her novel *Harmony* appeared after both. This pattern is significant in its indication of Gaunt's resourcefulness. She habitually utilized and recycled her experiences across genres, stretching their economic potential as far as she could. In this way she embodied her own ideal of the enterprising white colonial woman. In her Preface to the 1915 collection of her previously published (recycled) short fiction, *Ends of the Earth, Stories*, Gaunt makes explicit the connection between real events and writing fiction:

> I do not know how other people write short stories, but for myself I seldom do it unless I come across an incident that interests me deeply or some scene that cries out to be illustrated. I know I never write a successful short story unless one of these conditions is fulfilled, so it comes that in collecting together this book I seem to be going step by step through my own life. (2002, 3)

She supported herself by her writing and sought to support the British Empire in the published observations of its colonies and its peoples.

Gaunt announces her fascination with the history of the Caribbean, which was prompted by her earlier visits to West Africa and witnessing the remnants of the transatlantic slave trade, which she reprises in the opening sections of her first Jamaican book, the historical *Where the Twain Meet.* That title is from Kipling, of course, establishing both her colonial affiliation and a nonracist understanding of human differences. Indeed, while many her ideas appear anachronistic, Gaunt's novel *Harmony: A Tale of the Old Slave Days in Jamaica* (1933) has been included in discussions by Jamaican commentators of slavery resistance narratives. Verene A. Shepherd and the pseudonymous 'All Woman Writer' in the *Jamaica Observer* both cite Gaunt's novel as one of the few texts to represent female resistance to the slavery system (Shepherd 2007, 273–74; All Woman Writer 2001).

Gaunt's texts on Jamaica are anachronistic in significant ways. Additional to her future hopes for the Empire in the face of its perceived decline, she is also stranded between what Sloterdijk terms the terrestrial globe, the age of discovery and world history, and the age of the global foams, in which spaces are brought into mutual relation. This dilemma manifests in Gaunt in her contradictory assessment of the strengths of empire. Gaunt would have had little time for Froude or Trollope as she considered the English as lacking the mobility and adaptability needed to revive the fortunes of Jamaica. She complains that Britons can only take their country with them, they cannot enter into other cultures. She also writes that Jamaicans are compromised in their capacity to realize prosperity. The subject best equipped to effect necessary change is the enterprising white colonial woman – exactly like herself. Her colonial perspective recognizes connections across the globe and, whereas Froude divided the colonies according to a black past and a white future, Gaunt suggests that Australia may lend some of its futural energy to Jamaica. Certainly there was some offence taken by her 1932 accounts of her travels ('Mary's Little Lamb' 1932, 12).

However, Gaunt, like Froude, is of an advanced age (67) by the time she writes *Reflection – In Jamaica* (1932). The travel and the book occur late in her life and in her *oeuvre*. She has travelled widely, seen, written about and fictionalized numerous continents and islands. She combines elements of the belated discoverer shooting across the terrestrial globe – she describes herself as being in the wake of Columbus – and of the modern mobile subject for whom discovery is no longer possible and relational dynamics are determined by the internationality of empire. There is a further effect that surprises Gaunt herself, which is that she cannot sympathize with the people that she encounters in Jamaica. She has no difficulty identifying with the historical past as she announces in the opening pages on *Where the Twain Meet*:

> Perhaps in a former life I too was a slave, or perhaps I was one of those careless folk who lived in one of the death-traps they called Castles on the Guinea Coast, and something in me made me wish to see them again, and having seen them, something certainly stronger than myself made me finish with Jamaica, the lovely island where Britain, though she does not seem to know it, is experimenting in negro rule. Yes, surely, some haunting memory of a past life has shaped my career. (Gaunt 1922, 2)

Gaunt finds the past much easier to manage than the present and often erases the present scene before her by superimposing imaginary past events over it:

> On the country roads of Vere it does not take the night and a motor light to bring back the past. It stalks along beside you in the broad daylight. The peasants step back from the roads with their hoes in their hands. They are road gangs, men and women, mending the roads, but I think of the slaves who came along when these roads were mere tracks. They hold in their hands uplifted as weapons, tools of a like description and cry 'Kill! Kill!' (1922, 29)

She then reproaches herself and questions her thought processes. Here and elsewhere the answer she gives for her response is that she cannot enter the interior lives of the Jamaican people. She cannot understand them. She writes:

> I tried to talk to them. I wished them well but I could not think, rack my brains as I would, of anything to say. There was no single point, it seemed to me, where our lives touched and we could meet on common ground. (Gaunt 1922, 45)

For Gaunt, at this juncture, sympathy and affect are only possible in the domain of textuality, in history and fiction. She is variously too close to her fictional fantasies – as with the identification as a slave or slaver – or too distant from the actual world around her. In this discourse of belated discovery, actual contact is deflected by the interpolation of stock tableau from the colonial archive. Gaunt's identification of this breakdown in her text and in her own subjectivity can be read as a confusion between the various roles, voices and genres through which she represents self and world. She is a victim of her own energy and enterprise. This incapacity is also meaningfully understood as an endpoint to Columbian world-making. The admission of difference beyond understanding, of only understanding the scene of the present through the textual past, the textual performance of failure – all mark the end of discovery and the dawning consciousness of that conclusion. Gaunt may be in the business of presenting marvellous and exotic otherness, but these images have to be recycled from the past. Not only is there no New World to discover, but there are no new images to provide her reader. Her futural ambition is undone by this repetition, the one-way progress narrative has turned in on itself and needs to wait for the possibility of reciprocation, a co-mobility and mutual locatedness within the new globe.

# Chapter 3

# INSULAR AND CONTINENTAL INTERIORS: THE SHIFTING MAP OF LITERARY UNIVERSALISM AFTER THE WAR

> But had Columbus returned to Cairi [Trinidad] in 1935 he would have found her still beautiful as on that July day four hundred years before [...] the stars would shine like those jewels in the El Dorado of dead men's dreaming.
>
> Ralph de Boissiere, *Crown Jewel* (1952)

In his grand, three-part narrative of globalization Peter Sloterdijk dates the middle stage as occurring from 1492 to 1945 when, he argues, the globe became a philosophical concept. Material expansion created the terrestrial earth, which effectively ejected the cosmological domain from its coordinates so that the ancient cosmos or sphere became the globe (Sloterdijk 2013, 3–15). Sloterdijk describes his formulation as 'the para-Nietzschean proposition: The Sphere is dead' (quoted in Alliez 2007, 318). This second phase overlaps with its predecessor in time, if not in thought, for as Sloterdijk notes, it retains 'metaphysical quirks that like to hide beneath the veneer of the ordinary' (Sloterdijk 2013, 6). This second era was that of 'world history', of global exploration and colonization, which was characterized in European history and thought by unidirectional, nonreciprocal 'discovery' of new places, peoples and ideas (Morin 2008, 64–66), as examined in the previous chapter.

This chapter is concerned with the moment this second stage of globalization gives way to the third and final epoch that Sloterdijk terms 'global foams', which he dates from the end of the Second World War and which continues to fold into the present. 'Global foams' evokes qualities of relationality, permeability, mobility, plurality and ephemerality in what is, in many ways, a spatialization of theories of postmodern simultaneity and surface. The era of global foams, the globalized globe of our own time, is defined by relationality because all (terranean) places have been discovered. The unidirectional trajectories of world history have given way to dynamics of action and reaction.

Sloterdijk's particular metaphorics (or metonymics) of globes as encapsulated worlds are especially productive to a consideration of literature's role in the remaking of world and globe in the postwar period. Specifically, the model of global foams enables the tracking of vectors and interactions between multiple conceptions of inner and outer worlds across/on/through topologies and topographies at a moment of radical global transformation. Derrida argues that from this time, '[t]here is no world any more, only islands' (2009, 9). Sloterdijk's spatialized formulation of Being as different kinds of spheres derives explicitly from Heidegger's concept of *Dasein* (literally 'there-to be' or 'being-there'), which identifies and explores the spatial quality of being. *Dasein*'s intimate relation to the accompanying concept of *In-der-welt sein* (Being-in-the-World) stresses the interconnection of existence and world, the osmotic flow between inner life of each subject and the interiority of their 'world'. George Steiner glosses the flow between these interiors as Heidegger claiming that 'to be is to be worldly'. Further, as the 'meeting up' of *Dasein* and world effects their mutual constitution, each of the terms provides knowledge of the other (Steiner 1989, 85).

As the ensuing discussion will demonstrate, the postwar renegotiation of interiority and habitability – of Being-in-the-World – is conventionally mapped through real and figurative topographies, predominantly islands and continents. As argued in the previous two chapters, the collocation 'my island home' is a tautology, for each word of the three is a declaration of self and possession, pointing to an inherent *in*ness of the island as a figure of both self and world. However, despite this overdetermination of interiority, islands are not inherent shelters, as writer Peter Conrad flags when he describes the experience of growing up in Tasmania as the feeling of being 'unhoused' (1988, 57). Furthermore, and in seeming contradiction, continents may also signify interiority; the etymology and earlier usages of the word stress the connection between *continent* and *containment*, as discussed in Chapter 1. In the literature of the postwar period examined in this chapter, continental interiority turns on the perceived capacity of a capaciousness that accommodates and enfolds the self within diversity.

Deleuze's model of a philosophical archipelago, which he develops in his essay (1997) on Melville's 'Bartleby', explicitly invokes networked pluralities or 'foams' over the topographical imaginary, taking its cue from the dexterity of Melville's navigation over and between land and sea. This section of Deleuze's essay discusses American pragmatism – which, like Sloterdijk's foams and Heidegger's 'Being-in-the-World', stresses the interactive dynamic between organism and environment in topographical terms. Deleuze writes of an epistemic crossroads evident in Melville's fiction, which may be also understood as an intimation of the age of foams:

> Western knowledge was the skull, or the paternal spirit that realized itself in the world as totality, and in a knowing subject as its proprietor [...] A contemporary of American transcendentalism, (Emerson Thoreau), Melville is already sketching out the traits of pragmatism that will be its continuation. It is first of all an affirmation of a world in process, an archipelago. Not even a puzzle, whose pieces when fitted together would constitute a whole, but rather a wall of loose uncemented stones. Where every element has a value in itself but also in relation to others: isolated and floating, islands and straits, immobile points and sinuous lines – for Truth always has 'jagged edges'. (Deleuze 1997, 86)

Each 'uncemented stone' is separate but interdependent, like islands in an archipelagic chain or one of Sloterdijk's 'ensouled bubbles' (Morin 2008, 61). It is an interior or home located amongst many others whose containment is not insular but provided by external multiplicities.

Walter Benjamin's theorization of the permeable flow between the relative interiors of being and world identifies a potential claustrophobia. In the *Arcades Project* (1927–40), he identifies the correlation between the domestic interior of the bourgeois dwelling and the imagined interior life of its inhabitant. In these connections, Benjamin historicizes the 'eternal' image of the human abode as pertaining to the conditions of a particular time and space. He writes:

> In the most extreme instance, the dwelling becomes a shell. The nineteenth century, like no other century, was addicted to dwelling. It conceived the residence as a receptacle for the person, and it encased him with all his appurtenances so deeply within the dwelling's interior that one might be reminded of the inside of a compass case, where the instrument with all its accessories lies in deep, usually embedded violet folds of velvet. (Benjamin 1999, 220)

Benjamin's image of the human shelter as a compass case evokes its capacity to orientate the human subject within the world, but the case with its folded velvet is also like a coffin. In view of Sloterdijks's global epistemes, it, too, captures a point of transition between the age of men travelling in ships and the current era of global foams, as these are marked by their respective understandings of interior spaces, of home. Charles Rice describes Benjamin's paradoxical dilemma in the characterization of the bourgeois dwelling as 'the difficulty in capturing the eternal conception of dwelling as a precise historical condition of the nineteenth century (2005, 172). While Benjamin acknowledges that there 'is something age-old' – perhaps eternal – about the image of the abode, it is also definitive of modernity in the nineteenth century, which turns the domestic home into the 'primal' 'shell' (1999, 220).

In literary terms, these modern dilemmas of dwelling and interiority were theorized by George Lukács in *Theory of the Novel* (1920), specifically his identification of the 'transcendental homelessness' (1971, 29, 41), which he argues characterizes the modern novel, which is itself a product of the 'era of world history'. Lukács' theory of the novel is structured on the 'rift between' 'inner' self and 'outside' world that has emerged since the cosmos became the terrestrial globe (1971, 29). For Lukács, a chronic symptom of this lack of home rehearsed repeatedly in the modern novel is the nostalgic draw to an imagined originary home place, which he argues manifests in what Novalis described as the impossible 'urge to be at home everywhere' (Lukács 1920, 29).[1]

Anglophone literary Modernism writes the dilemma of the rift between inner and outer worlds as fiction and poetry repeatedly rehearse the transition from the terrestrial globe into global foams.[2] Tellingly for the current discussion, this shift often deploys the figure and ground of the island, as in Virginia Woolf's *To the Lighthouse* (1927), where transition across epochs is mapped on and through the Isle of Skye which is, for the Ramsay family, an alternative, ambiguous home. D. H. Lawrence's satire on Compton Mackenzie, 'The Man Who Loved Islands' (1928) charts both his own unsuccessful search for an island home and the perils of aligning personal interiority with that of the island.

W. H. Auden's sestina, originally titled 'Paysage Moralisé' (1933), represents 'islands' as an escape from the 'cities' of Depression-era England. A decision to travel to the islands would, in Jonathan Bolton's reading of the poem, constitute the privileging of personal life over public responsibility, foregrounding a tension between the world of self and the broader interior of society (1994, 57).[3] Louis MacNeice's poem 'No More Sea' (1947) expands and inverts Auden's question and Lawrence's fear of solipsism. Set on Achill Island, off the coast of Mayo in Western Ireland, 'No More Sea' questions the place of human subjects on the planet at a historical moment when the speaker fears mass 'uniform[ity]' and mental 'coagulat[ion]' in an 'age of mainlanders'. The poet imagines an alignment of self and geography when he describes 'islanders whose hearts themselves are islands' (23). They are both their 'own king and castle', masters of self and world, their own island homes or shells.

Where MacNeice's islanders experience no 'rift' between inner and outside worlds, the very title of Auden's 'Paysage Moralisé', derived from Erwin Panofsky's coinage of the previous decade, announces the predicament of self-translation. In this way, *paysage moralisé* connects to T. S. Eliot's influential promotion of art's search for the 'objective correlative', an equivalency between the inner, opaque experience of being and that of the observable world. While this undertaking performs and accentuates the artistic labour necessary for the correlation between inner and outer worlds, the process can also be understood ironically as the invention of a boundary between the two domains. In the achievement of the externalizing and locating image the writer manufactures an imaginary 'outside' from which the self can be sheltered, not only harbouring this self but affirming the very existence of an invisible, untranslatable inner reality.

Heidi Hartwig observes of Auden that his later poems move from the *paysage moralisé* to the '*maison moralisé*', from correlatives of landscape to those of domestic interiors, chiming with Benjamin's claim regarding the domestic interior in the *Arcades Project* and foregrounding the connection between islands, homes, the globe and interiority. Hartwig reads Auden's 'Thanksgiving for a Habitat' (1963) through Henry James's idea of the artist's 'Great, Good Place', the shelter in which they can write away from the world. However, she also cites Auden's own account of the poem as framed by the concept of 'what worldliness really means' (Hartwig 2012, 9); the home is not disconnected from the world but is an 'ensouled bubble' (Morin 2008, 61), a floating island within it: 'to be [in the late modern era] is to be worldly' (Steiner 1989, 85). James's 'Great, Good Place' can be extended from its imperative in relation to artistic production and the housing of the creative subject to a more general sense of literature's role in enabling inhabitation and providing shelter. Literature, too, can be the 'great good place' of Being-in-the World.

The following examination of literary texts continues the cartographic project of the previous chapter at the junction where the era of world history transforms, fractures and reforms to become the era of global foams. Continuing the dual-perspective on Australian and West Indian writing, as their relationship moves further away from the chronologies of world history, I will chart the various ways writers from these cultures map the twentieth-century globe via the shifting borders of islands and continents and their fluctuating capacities for inhabitation. These writers occupy the already globalized globe that requires the construction of interiorities to align self and geography, to identify a place one can house oneself. In both contexts the longing for a habitat is connected to the displacing, dispossessing operations of colonialism and to variable material conditions. Poised at the juncture when world history gives way to global foams, these writers and their texts exhibit the resilient residue of universalism as it is challenged by the complex formations of diaspora, plurality and the differend. As we will see, these new constructions themselves can be folded into the universalizing processes of Western culture, especially as these are embedded in colonialism, 'world literature' and Modernism. However, this project becomes fractalized producing, in its repetitions, telling variations: resistance, travesty, independence, distortion, monstrosity. These new spaces of possible inhabitation also proliferate cartographies that redraw geographical and historical connections as both organism and environment continuously change to create habitable space in their co-fragility.

The discussion begins with the Nobel laureates from Australia and the West Indies to demonstrate how the Nobel Academy constructs the literary globe through the unidirectional discoveries and universalist drives of the era of world history, which is, in turn, overlaid with the relationality of the globalized globe presented by each author as he moves between islands and continents. From here I move to a detailed consideration of Australian expatriate Shirley Hazzard's fiction of global reconstruction after 1945 to trace the vertical but secular cosmos of her global imaginary and her rejection of continental power for the small island as the site of possible reinvention. A very different conception of island possibility and limitation follows with a reading of four disparate West Indian writers who explore the particular and various interiorities of their island homes and the shared necessity to leave their islands. The final section of this chapter deals with the continental interiority of Australia, the island continent, which is 'discovered' by white Australia in the early decades of the twentieth century. In this section I consider iconic texts of this imaginary from A. D. Hope's early poetry to Patrick White's *Voss* (1957). The chapter concludes with a detailed consideration of Alex Miller's continental imaginary which, like Hazzard's island, is offered as a site on which to reconceive and reconstruct global relationality.

## The Nobel Prize and the World

The Nobel Prize for literature, founded in 1901, is an institution of the twentieth century explicitly designed according to universalist aims to effect its cosmopolitan purpose. Pascale Casanova discusses the Nobel's charter in precisely in these terms and describes the process as one which identifies 'works deserving of being universalised'. She writes:

> Having put itself in the position of acting as an impartial tribunal whose judgments will be universally accepted as legitimate, the Academy finds itself forced to rigorously establish standards of criteria for literary excellence and to openly acknowledge the consequences for the unification of world literary space of supporting international writers in their struggles with national writers. Indeed the history of the prize since its inception can be seen as an ongoing attempt to develop explicit standards of universality. (Casanova 2004, 148)

James English's examination of the Nobel Prize in *The Economy of Prestige* (2005) also pertains to the current discussion in two key ways. First, the Nobel Academy was the institution that inaugurated the modern culture of literary prizes and, hence, the global circulation of literary texts in line with univeralist conceptions of literary value. Secondly, it is the institution we identify as being along the continuum of our own historical moment, as part of globalized modernity, our globalized globe (English 2005, 28–29).

The related arguments of Casanova and English frame a question regarding the role of the topography and topology of islands and continents in the project of unifying literary space within the recent genealogy of globalization. Specifically, a reading of the Nobel addresses of Caribbean and Australia laureates promises to construct a particular globe shaped by the imbricated construction of space, subject and writing, and the colonial cartography produced by the imperial machine. More specifically still, as the ensuing discussion sets out, the authors figure the island as the container of authorship and literature, moving between the monadic island of individual, text and cultural location to the world island of universalism.

Between them, Australia and the West Indies have produced four Nobel laureates for literature over 30 years: Patrick White in 1973, Derek Walcott in 1992, V. S. Naipaul in 2001, and J. M. Coetzee in 2003. All four were either born or have been resident for long periods of time in countries other than their place of birth. Indeed they all write of the modern global world formed by colonialism, predominantly British colonialism, and the communities and subjects it has created. They are vastly different writers in terms of genre, style, intellect and sensibility. Yet grouping them together enables the identification and calibration of shifts in the ways literature imbricates the geographical and conceptual understandings of the modern globe as these are framed by the Nobel Prize's humanist agenda and its role in constructing postwar literary cartographies.

White, an Australian born in England, moved between these two 'homes' (the first is 'home', the second is 'Home') until settling in Australia after the War, a return that was prompted in part by reading the journals of Edward Eyre during the London Blitz (White 1981, 83), as noted in the previous chapter.[4] By this time he had already published *Happy Valley* (1939) and *The Living and the Dead* (1941), but it is his postwar novel *The Aunt's Story* (1948) which is considered to be his first major work. His novels over the next three decades rehearse the process of negotiating key Modernist dilemmas regarding meaning, presence and identity – so-called *universal* concerns – in a range of Australian contexts. Indeed Simon During strongly criticizes White and Australia's championing of him on the basis that he fulfilled the national need for a 'universal' literary representative (1996, 18, 35). Unlike his predecessors valued in the Australian canon, the literary nationalists, so the (too-simple) story goes, White located Australia within global modernity in and by its links with the universal. Tellingly, the Nobel committee summarized his achievement as 'an epic and psychological narrative art which has introduced a new continent into literature', once again bearing out the link Mariano Siskind identifies between conceptual and geographical universality in the globalizing directives of modernity (Nobel Committee 1973; Siskind 2005, 2).

From the vantage point of 2015, the Nobel committee's recognition of White's continental vision can be understood in part as an event of the *détente*, a remapping of the globe, indeed bringing the globe to fulfilment by including a new continent; White thus appears as the literary equivalent to Captain Cook. In stark contrast, Walcott's award 20 years later is given 'for a poetic oeuvre of great luminosity, sustained by a historical vision, the outcome of a multicultural commitment' (Nobel Committee 1992). Walcott's archipelagic, rather than continental, vision understands the world as assembled fragments. It discountenances the idea of a unified globe, which is now understood as a figment of continental 'universalism': monolithic, monological and monocultural. Accordingly, Walcott's speech on the occasion is titled 'The Antilles: Fragments of Epic Memory' and opens in Trinidad, not Walcott's home island, to describe a performance of the Ramayana enacted by the East Indian community of the island. Walcott invites us to contemplate the transportation of the Ramayana from the Indian subcontinent to the Caribbean islands: 'Consider the scale of Asia reduced to these fragments'. For Walcott, these migrations and re-enactments have the vitality and resilience of dialect, the strength of the grafted offshoot. Walcott recognizes the fabrication of any concept of unification and values acknowledged fabrications that occur now that the postmodern globe is understood as fractured, like fragments: 'Break a vase, and the love that reassembles the fragments is stronger than that love which took its symmetry for granted when it was whole'. These fragments constitute the real and figurative archipelago: 'Antillean art is this restoration of our shattered histories, our shards of vocabulary, our archipelago becoming a synonym for pieces broken off from the original continent' (Walcott 1992a).

Darwin was the first to make the distinction between oceanic and continental islands during his *Beagle* voyage (Darwin 1873, 323–24; Wallace 1895, 242–43). Deleuze picks up on the distinction, which, he argues, confirms what the imagination already knew. Continental islands are very knowing, fallen topologies. Unlike oceanic islands, which are 'originary' and 'essential', continental islands are 'born of disarticulation, erosion, fracture: they survive the absorption of what once contained them' (Deleuze 2004, 9). This describes Walcott's archipelago, literally and as a figure. Ironically, however, the continents to which to the islands are connected are not only defined by geographical proximity, as they also include, most significantly, Africa and India.

Naipaul's speech nine years later, titled 'Two Worlds' (2001), is also anchored in the East Indian community of Trinidad, Naipaul's people and home place until his migration to the United Kingdom at the age of 18. Naipaul's globe is also fractured but in very different ways to Walcott's archipelagic chain. Naipaul begins the account of his life from inside a dislocated culture, namely the descendants of indentured labourers from the subcontinent, mostly from the Gangetic Plain, who came to the Caribbean from the 1880s, on the promise of future land grants after the terms of working contracts. Like Walcott, Naipaul constructs this opening scene as a palimpsest, but one of compounded absence: the first layer comprises the Indigenous peoples who were systematically annihilated by European colonists and who name his hometown of Chaguanas, and this first silence is overlaid with his own family's displacement and its maintenance of a resolute silence about India and the past. In Naipaul's account, which directly addresses the diasporic globe, there is little joy in disconnection and discontinuity, though isolated memories of a living, textured culture are recounted with the tenderness of minute attention:

> We lived on the Chaguanes' land. Every day in term time – I was just beginning to go to school – I walked from my grandmother's house – past the two or three main-road stores, the Chinese parlour, the Jubilee Theatre, and the high-smelling little Portuguese factory that made cheap blue soap and cheap yellow soap in long bars that were put out to dry and harden in the mornings – every day I walked past these eternal-seeming things – to the Chaguanas Government School. (Naipaul 2001)

The global movements charted by Naipaul's 'two worlds' do not trace out island fragments or mobile spaces and selves, as in Walcott, but a series of dialectical and antinomical tensions that cannot cohere. Tellingly, given the controversies of his personal life and views, he opens by insisting on the distinction between the writer's life and work, between the writing and nonwriting selves of the author, on the nonalignment of self to self. Following Proust, these selves are imagined as bifurcated: the exterior self and the 'innermost self which one can only recover by putting aside the world and the self that frequents the world'. Place and space are also described according to interior and exterior divisions. He writes: 'My grandmother's house in Chaguanas was in two parts [...] So as a child I had this sense of two worlds, the world outside that tall corrugated-iron gate, and the world at home – or, at any rate, the world of my grandmother's house' (Naipaul 2001).

Naipaul's globe is, accordingly, inherently anachronistic. The moment where self, culture, place and writing might have aligned is continually missed or elided. He characterizes himself and his work as out of space and time: in one sense he is a belated subject of his culture, yet somehow this lateness casts him perennially as an orphan child. Vilashini Cooppan makes a related point in her analysis of Naipaul's sense of colonial belatedness. He longs for the imagined securities of an earlier world 'in which the notion of the "purely literary" is thinkable, if only as fantasy' (Cooppan 2009, 87). Cooppan discusses Naipaul's essay 'A Bend in the River', where he describes the new postcolonial world as providing no ground: 'But in the new world I felt the ground move below me' (Cooppan 2009, 87).

Naipaul's description of his grandmother's house also captures the way he is caught in temporal logic of *hysteron-proteron*, the reversal of sequence from classical rhetoric. He writes: 'I feel – and the anxiety is still vivid to me – that I might easily have failed before I began'. In spatial terms this paradox of identity, experience and writing finds its figure in the island of Trinidad itself. He writes:

> My background is at once exceedingly simple and exceedingly confused. I was born in Trinidad. It is a small island in the mouth of the great Orinoco river of Venezuela. So Trinidad is not strictly of South America, and not strictly of the Caribbean. (Naipaul 2001)

This confusion or misrecognition of continental or archipelagic definition curiously repeats Columbus's experience of the third voyage. Columbus 'discovered' and named Trinidad on this voyage and used it as base for exploration in the Gulf of Paria between Trinidad and the South American continent. It is here that he sees the mouth of the mighty Orinoco River, a freshwater river so large it could only be found on a continent. Columbus recognized its great significance, not as evidence of continental discovery but as the original Garden of Eden, which he understood from Pierre d'Ailly's *Imago Mundy* to be located in the Fortunate Isles (Tuan 1990, 119).

As if held by the spell of that original misrecognition, bound by its repetitions and distortions, Naipaul is also caught between a continent and an archipelago, always between one thing and another. Unification is not possible, though he does find genuine connection when he returns to the Gangetic Plain of north India, in the midst of his ancestral subcontinent. Here he feels is no longer *between* but *within* place, not the four walls of the island but a location of depth as well surfaceal containment.

In his reflection of *Reading and Writing* (2000), published the year before he won the Nobel Prize, Naipaul figures his fictional production in terms of a dilemma not so much of dislocation but of scale. Again, unlike Walcott's epic fragments, whose breakages and imperfect reconstitutions create the fractures of possibility, Naipaul's experience of the related fragments of island and culture becomes that of an oversized subject peering into the miniature house of childhood. For Naipaul, this came to prohibit the writing of fiction:

> Fiction had taken me as far as it could go. There were certain things it couldn't deal with. It couldn't deal with my years in England; there was no social depth to the experience; it seemed more a matter for autobiography. And it couldn't deal with my growing knowledge of the wider world. Fiction, by its nature, functioning best within certain fixed social boundaries, seemed to be pushing me back to worlds – like the island world, or the world of my childhood – smaller than the one I inhabited. Fiction, which had once liberated and enlightened me, now seemed to be pushing me towards being simpler than I really was. For some years – three, perhaps four – I didn't really know how to move; I was quite lost. (2000, 15)

Naipaul is shut out from his island home that mapped his fictional coordinates. His self-prescribed treatment for this exclusion was the itinerancy of travel and travel writing (Naipaul 2000, 16).

This island of writing is the subject of J. M. Coetzee's address in his Nobel lecture two years after Naipaul. Born and raised on the continent of Africa, and now resident on the island-continent of Australia, Coetzee's address does not explicitly discuss his own experience or his craft but displaces both in a story or allegory that revisits his engagement with Defoe's *Robinson Crusoe*, which he first explored in *Foe* (1986). Coetzee's fable retains the pattern, if not the meaning, of insistent dualisms which underpin Naipaul's account of self and writing, as flagged by the title 'He and His Man' (2003). With Coetzee, however, these two pronouns and the one, two or multiple subjects of 'Man' carry many inflections and overlays between Coetzee, Defoe and Robinson Crusoe – notably not Man Friday (Cornwell 2007, 99). The island in question is also multiple, being, inevitably, the one on which Crusoe was wrecked, and Great Britain, for the story also contains numerous excerpts from Defoe's *Tour thro the Whole Island of Great Britain* (1724–1727) and the island of writing. As Gareth Cornwell observes, Coetzee is reprising the conflation of author, character and island that he performed in his introduction to the 1999 Oxford World's Classics edition of *Robinson Crusoe* (Cornwell 2007 100). In this introduction Coetzee queries what he suggests may have been the original allegorical reading of Defoe's novel, namely that 'Crusoe is Everyman, that every man is an island, and every life, seen in an allegorical light, a life of isolation under the scrutiny of God' (Coetzee 2001, 18). Rather, Coetzee refers to the novel's preface in which Crusoe – in these words very close to Defoe – writes: 'I can affirm that I enjoy much more solitude in the middle of the greatest collection of mankind in the world, I mean, at London, while I am writing this, than ever I could say I enjoyed in eight and twenty years confinement to a desolate island' (Coetzee 1999, 21; Cornwell 2007, 100). For Crusoe – and probably

Defoe and possibly Coetzee – the isolation of author and text is an exposed insularity, just like the island open to the weather.

Coetzee's story invites an allegorical reading of the 'business of writing' – of writing as mimetic repetition – and illustrates both the necessity and impossibility of retaining boundaries between the worlds of writing and the worlds outside it. The story reveals the commensurability of human relations, of human tyranny and of himself as the island monad who may write of 'his man' in a gesture reaching out from that inherent solitude, which is not the interior of a shelter.

In a number of ways, Coetzee's island story returns us to the Modernist monadic subject (masculine, isolated, non-national, unowned and unownable) of Patrick White. There are many connections and severances in the progressions and reversions from White through Walcott and Naipaul to Coetzee but, however different, their various accounts of their being-in-the-world – as these are circumscribed by the Nobel Academy and as the writers meet them – are reflections, refractions and obversions of each other. Across the various topographies and the mapping of selves through these spaces, there remains a recurrent tension between the inside and outside of self, world and writing, figured and narrated through islands and continents. Viewed together, these accounts illustrate the ways Western universalism continues to draw in geopolitical regions of the planet in the bid to align the geographical and conceptual coordinates of the globe and maintain currency with the multiple ways literature effects and enables these cartographies. Their collection also alerts us to the contradictory experiences of any one topography. Despite the dichotomy constructed between island and continent, both *topoi* have dynamics of centre and margin, interior and exterior, that are constantly re-forming in the wake of specific historical experience. Together, the anthropomorphic charts mapped by these writers of the British Commonwealth also mark the break from Sloterdijk's terrestrial globe into the time of global foams: unidirectional, nonreciprocal 'discovery' has become a recognized dilemma or has given way to diasporic mobility: flight, migration, repeated departures and returns, asymmetrical reciprocity.

## Islands, Continents and Catastrophe in Shirley Hazzard

This moment of fracture and reconstruction in the wake of two world wars is the *locus* of Shirley Hazzard's fiction as each text revisits the process of mapping the self in and on the broken globe. Hazzard is profoundly occupied with the ways the world and has been made and unmade in the postwar era, as her actors are caught up in processes of mutual invention of self and world that are tested and mirrored across the arc of her own oeuvre. Brigitta Olubas has shown the close links between Hazzard's fictional exploration of this dilemma and her nonfiction, specifically her writing on the United Nations, another universalist institution seeking to promote a conception of common humanity across the globe (2012, 31–72). Hazzard's vision of earth and globe is strung on a secular verticality, and the topography of her thought and invention stages a thoroughgoing rejection of continental power. In its place is the continental island, broken from the main, a knowing site of possible reconstitution.

Hazzard is one of Australia's most attentive postwar literary cartographers. Much of her writing addresses questions of the new global relations and subjectivities in the wake of World War II and throughout the Cold War, as Brigitta Olubas has recently shown (2012). Hazzard sees herself, too, in cosmopolitan terms and refuses to be bound by national definitions, though Nicholas Birns notes that Hazzard identified herself as 'an Australian writer' at an Australian literary event held at Australian Consulate in New York in 2009 (2014, 112). Whatever the (inconstant) claim, Olubas argues that Hazzard writes of Australia through 'a kind of disavowed expatriatism, locating itself in an expanded rather than nationally circumscribed world' (2012, 15). Olubas elsewhere cites Jay Parini's tribute to Shirley Hazzard as a 'world novelist' whose fiction crosses 'the entire world' (2013, 127). Hazzard left Australia in 1947, aged 16, and since then has lived in New Zealand, Asia, Europe, Britain and the United States. Her literary works draw directly on these experiences. Hazzard's drive to what Olubas describes as a 'cosmopolitan humanism' found everyday expression in her employment at the United Nations in 1953, as she describes in an interview with Jan Garret in 1984:

> I was 20 and I was part of that feeling of hope that came into the world with the end of the war. I went, like many other people then, to apply to the United Nations in a spirit of idealism, little dreaming indeed that idealism was the last thing that was wanted there. (Garret 38 quoted in Olubas 2012, 6)

Hazzard's short story collection, *People in Glass Houses* (1967) is based on her experiences at the United Nations, as are two of her nonfiction monographs. All of her fiction, from *The Evening of the Holiday* (1966) to *The Great Fire* (2003), is caught up with questions of how to make the self and the world in the postwar era. These complex processes are achieved, at least in part in her work, through the superimposition of planet, earth and globe. Hazzard maps the spaces of the postwar world as a synthetic process, one that assembles and rearranges material and figurative resources. Her narratives are often predicated on cataclysms, natural and man-made disasters, frequently some combination of both, and repeatedly the devastation of the Second World

War, which has destroyed space, time and the human subject. Their aftermath requires a realignment of time, space and subject constructed from both the residues and traces of the past and the unformed coordinates of a new world order. Further, the lives she narrates of personal and domestic experience, and often emplotted through feminine genres such as romance and melodrama, are always inextricably woven into global, planetary events, as Olubas and Fiona Morrison separately observe (Olubas 2012, 164–173; Morrison 2014, 22).

Hazzard's fiction plots these realignments along both vertical and horizontal axes: our gaze is directed upwards to the peaks of mountains, to aerial and astronomical revelations, and it is cast downward to the subterranean depths of seismic instability.

Hazzard's geographical imaginary creates spaces for possible inhabitation, experience and being in this newly fragmented world. These sites reveal some continuities with earlier cartographies; indeed their representation and figuration rely on a range of conventional tropes, but these are deployed in ways that overturn the imagined structures of their coherence. So, too, Hazzard's fiction eschews continental heartlands, the most contested sites of the two world wars, for the fragmentary and contingent spaces of islands and archipelagos. Islands are favoured sites in Hazzard for their imagined comprehension, their epitomic inversions, as sites of contemplation and renewal, and for their promise to make the self one with geography – all conventional properties of the Western island imaginary. The space of the island in Hazzard, from Capri to Etijama and Hong Kong, commonly follows the convention of the epitome, the world island, but the global view is always reparticularized so that material topography distresses the round completeness of the globe integral to its reification as a totalizing abstraction.

This postwar remapping is vertical as well as surfaceal and recharts seismic and subterranean dimensions, from the 'slurping' movement along the volatile plates of the Japanese islands, exposed by the bombing of Hiroshima in *The Great Fire*, to the aeronautical disasters that litter her stories and the astronomical phenomenon that titles *The Transit of Venus* (1980). This latter invokes and inverts James Cook's first voyage, for the discoveries of life and love experienced by the two Australian sisters begin when they make the voyage from Australia to England. The vertical axis of Hazzard's fiction, which spans from the depths to the heavens, recalls premodern cosmologies, and the overlay of human experience with topography in Hazzard's universe appears at first to resemble the patterns of Platonic correspondences; certainly the pulse of thought and action in her stories dilates and contracts in patterns of centrifugal and centripetal movements, between the most private thought or emotion and historical events. But Hazzard's late-modern cosmology is avowedly secular, and the patterns of analogy and interconnection across the categories of the human, history, geography and astronomy cannot be aligned by virtue of divine authority or cosmic design but only within the components of the broken world itself. It is for this reason also that the island is an enabling space in Hazzard's fiction, for as Deleuze observes, the island 'has been entrusted to man and not to the gods' (2004, 13). The island is the site of a new beginning, a synthetic, compromised, worldly renewal.

Hazzard's fiction performs a resistance to a totalizing view of the globe at all levels of textual construction: figuration, syntax, plot and characterization. Perhaps the most explicit instance occurs in the opening scene of Part One of *The Transit of Venus* (1980), titled 'The Old World', in which scientist Sefton Thrale holds forth to family and guests the dissolution of the social structure in the postwar era:

> 'There has been a global order of a kind. Say what you like.'
>
> That of course they could not do.
>
> When Sefton Thrale said the world 'global' you felt the earth to be round as a smooth ball, or white and bland as an egg. And had to remind yourself of the healthy and dreadful shafts and outcroppings of the world. You had to think of the Alps, or the ocean, or a live volcano, to set your mind at rest. (Hazzard 1980, 10–11)

'Globe' here shifts from the discourse of politics to geography, topography and geology, and in the process, the text undermines Thrale's totalizing understanding of the smooth globe by adding the textures and irregularities of height, surface and depth. This corrective move, which also shifts across the binary designations from culture ('global order') to nature ('the Alps', 'ocean', 'volcano'), and their synthesis ('set your mind at rest') slides across discursive categories in a sardonic critique of the imperative to align conceptual and territorial universalism. These shifts are presented as associative, for they are set in train by a feeling engendered by Thrale's particular use of the term 'global', which is then riffed along alternative vectors of figuration. Moreover, the comic movement from the bland egg of ideology to the vitality of natural phenomena undermines the foundation of the global figure itself. The refusal of the 'smooth ball' of the globe is deemed necessary to identify spaces where the mind may be 'at rest', spaces one can inhabit. Ironically, the nominated elements of the terraquaceous globe – alps, ocean, volcanoes – are decidedly unrestful, indeed defined by volatility and danger. This contradiction, itself a form of dynamism and friction against the 'bland egg' of the globe, marks the complete difference between Thrale's world view and that of the novel's key thinkers, Ted Tice and Caro Bell, who share the counter perspective presented in this passage.

A similar shift but along different figurations and narrative line is evident in Hazzard's short story 'Sir Cecil's Ride' published in the *New Yorker* in 1974, which Olubas describes as centring on the 'bounded space' of the 'island as colonial interiority' (2012, 23). Set on Hong Kong Island, the narrative traces an arduous walk on one side of the island undertaken by Constantin (aged 36) and Elizabeth (aged 18) – one of the many relationships between a young woman and an older man in Hazzard's work (Olubas 2012, 23). As the title suggests, the location and the narrative of the couple's walk are circumscribed by related borders: colonial history, island topography and the dynamic of mastery. The walk concludes with their arrival at the peak, surveying the world below. In the long descriptive passage that gives duration to their viewing, she writes:

> In the arc of new-peeled sky and late ocean, the dark innumerable islands extended far out towards Lantau. Like flung stones – or as countries might look, set on the curve of the earth, if only you could see the globe entire.
>
> 'The whole world before you.' Constantin was saying.
>
> [...]
>
> Winding round and round one gets the illusion of distance, as if one were not on an island, the filament going back to there and forward from here at apparent random. She knew she would not marry this man and that it would come about in grief not to be mastered in advance, enlarging as the earth raised its stakes. (Hazzard 1974, 32)

The couple's walk and its culmination at the mountain summit conform to the conventional allegory of the experiential journey and its progression towards knowledge and understanding. However, the journey in 'Sir Cecil's Ride' is also emphatically literal, and much of the description is given to the material world and the physical hardship of the walk. Akin to the meditation on Thrale's 'globe' in *The Transit of Venus*, 'Sir Cecil's Ride' breaks down the distinctions between figure and ground, but in this instance they are complicated by their chiastic formulation. The story presents knowledge, including self-knowledge and proleptic foresight, as achieved in and through the sublime experience of the summit. Elizabeth progresses schematically through Kant's three stages of sublime experience – prehension, apprehension and comprehension – in her vertiginous encounter and its promise of mastery (Makkreel 1984, 310). The summit scene presents the earth in miniature, as if viewed from space. This planetary earth is significantly different from the bland egg of Sefton Thrale's globe, which is constructed by a geopolitics that cannot allow particularities to complicate an undifferentiated whole, for here the world in miniature enables perspective on her individual situation. In 'Sir

Cecil's Ride' the epitomical manipulation of scale combines with the allegory of knowledge to produce both an overdetermination and a displacement of *comprehension* in line with Denis Cosgrove's claim that the earthbound human can only embrace 'a tiny part of the planetary surface but in their imagination they can grasp the whole of the earth' (2001, ix).[5] The moment of apprehending 'the whole world before [her]' leads to a comprehension of herself and her life. Ironically, however, this moment of comprehension is, itself, a form of prehension leading to a proleptic realization: 'She knew she would not marry this man and that it would come about in grief not to be mastered in advance, enlarging as the earth raised its stakes.'

The illusory mastery suggested by the panorama of the miniature earth enables Elizabeth's realization that she cannot achieve 'mastery' of the future in advance. The collapse of allegory and reality accords her the capacity to read her own short walk as a miniature, a frame narrative for what is about to unfold in her life. Hence the conclusion of the story is inverted into a beginning – another characteristic manoeuvre in Hazzard's fiction (Olubas 2012, 25, 56).[6] In so doing, character, event and context are rendered open and vulnerable, a moment of literal and figurative exposure to the elements and to unknown futures. Finally, the conclusion of the story limits the capacity of human comprehension or abstraction to contain the earth and experience. Rather, these are understood to be subject to historical and material forces. Echoing the progression in the passage on the 'orb' in *The Transit of Venus*, abstraction yields to the material: 'the earth raised its stakes'.

While Hazzard's islands are not the smooth eggs of the Thrale's globe, they are akin to the island eggs of renewal described by Deleuze. For Deleuze the island's self-generation and ovate form cast it as a 'parthenogenic egg', a secondary formation of the world:

> The island is the necessary minimum for this re-beginning, the material that survives the first origin, the radiating seed or egg that must be sufficient to reproduce everything. Clearly this presupposes that the formation of the world happens in two stages, in two periods of time, birth and re-birth, and that the second is just as necessary and essential as the first, and this the first is necessarily compromised, born for renewal and already renounced in catastrophe. (2004, 13)

Islands in Hazzard's fiction are sites of the second birth after the catastrophe of the first. Most profane is that the bombed city of Hiroshima on the island of Honshu, which is, as Olubas writes: 'a consequent topography of war and [...] the point of origin of Cold War modernity' (2012, 197). The novella *Bay of Noon* (1970), set after the catastrophe of World War II and under the volcanic threat of Vesuvius, also charts numerous visits between Naples and

Capri in its negotiation of continuity, of loss and renewal, of second chances and displaced love. The narrative concludes decades after the main events of the story with the protagonist Jenny's return to Naples to her friend Giaconda. This reunion is, however, displaced and deferred from Naples to Capri, and the novella ends mid voyage. The projected meeting with Giaconda, Jenny's return to the past of memory and desire, is thus suspended, circumscribing Jenny and her past within the text's striations of loss and longing. In the figuration of this deferred longing, the island becomes a continent. The novel concludes: 'We are like the early explorers of Australia who died of thirst on expeditions to the dead centre of a continent, always thinking they must come ultimately to water' (Hazzard 1970, 154).

The shift from island to continent here is a conventional dilation by which the small island comprehends continental enormity. It also performs, at the level of metaphor, the same displacement of Jenny's reunion, taking us away from Europe to the other end of the earth, overturning comprehension even as its insists upon it by distance and difference. For the only comprehension possible for Jenny is *of* the past, and this is ironically deferred into the future. This understanding of self is imagined in terms of 'territory', 'region' and the coordinates of 'bearings', 'landmarks' and 'positions'. This territory of the self and experience, clarified by retrospection, does not provide the ground to stand on in the present. Its effect is not 'to direct, but to solace us; not to fix out positions, but to show us how we came' (Hazzard 1970, 154). The renewal promised by the island is never tested.

Hazzard's most extensive mapping of the postwar globe in terms of islands and continents is undertaken in *The Great Fire,* which deploys the island as a site of renewal in a range of perverse forms. The narrative moves across islands like stepping stones. The novel opens with a voyage from the large island of Honshu, Japan, to Etajima, the island off Hiroshima, and moves to the island of Hong Kong and to Britain, and concludes in the 'Shaky Isles' of New Zealand. Continents are located in the background and in the past in *The Great Fire*: the hero Aldred's journey across mainland China pertains to the past, to the world before he meets Helen Driscoll; Helen records her journey across continental Australia in shorthand; Ben is sent to the United States ostensibly for a cure but really to die out of sight. The acts of remaking self and world occur in the spaces of the island.

Aldred Leith's journey to Hiroshima and the island of Etajima repeats Ted Tice's journey in *Transit of Venus.* In both novels the horror of the site comprehends and destroys metaphorics: Ted sees islands that are 'fragments of a cataclysm', which is literally true; metaphorical language is deemed inadequate. Aldred's visit to Etajima and his sojourn among the occupying forces provides a window of graduated renewal or rebirth as variations of perversity and monstrosity. On Etajima the first or natural state of the island has been 'compromised [...] renounced in catastrophe' (Deleuze 2004, 13).

In *The Great Fire*, as in *Bay of Noon*, foreign occupation is presented as a travesty of inhabitation. The alternative society ruled by the Driscolls on Etajima is tyrannical, according to the convention of island despots. The Driscoll family is also portrayed along various permutations of perversity: the parents' disregard of their children and their disgust at their own sick child, the incestuous closeness of the relationship between the siblings – one of the centres of beauty in the text – and, eventually, the intergenerational love of Aldred and Helen. This renewal cannot be fulfilled in Etajima, for reasons proposed by the circumstances of narrative and because, in ethical terms, it would turn Etajima into a site of renewal for Western occupational forces; global cataclysm and atomic annihilation redeemed by an individual love story.

The renewal is deferred and displaced onto the 'Shaky Isles' of New Zealand. It is here, in an outpost, on a volatile and volcanic archipelago, away from the continental heartland, where individual identity can be examined and, unlike Elizabeth in 'Sir Cecil's Ride', where Helen can envisage a future with her lover. In the logic of Hazzard's topographical metaphorics, this vista is made possible from within the island itself, rather than the imagined mastery of self, space and time of Thrale's global egg or Constantin's despotism. Alternatively, this New Zealand section of the novel could be read as an understanding of inhabitation as waiting, waiting for the world to begin, just as Elizabeth's experience on Hong Kong Island in 'Sir Cecil's Ride' pre-empts her own experience, which becomes, though prolepsis, known in advance. Helen's waiting also recalls Jenny at the conclusion of *Bay of Noon*, except that *The Great Fire*, in the ultimate prolepsis of Hazzard's fiction, takes us back to the beginning of Hazzard's own expatriation from Australia through New Zealand, the beginning of her own project of remaking the world.

Hazzard's cartography rejects continents as Mackinderesque monoliths of power. It foregrounds the island for two key and related reasons. First, with Derrida, Hazzard agrees that 'There is no world any more, only islands' (Derrida 2009, 9). Any attachment to the universal over the particular and to the collective of nation runs the risk of repeating sectarianism, hysteria and collective barbarism. The island is the topology that enables reconstitution and reconstruction. It also scales down the enormity of the globe and the destruction of twentieth-century history to dimensions graspable by the human mind. Secondly, the island is the topography where Hazzard thinks best. It maps her own rhetorical unconscious: its habitual dilation and contraction; the miniaturized frames of narrative presented as omens or prolepses and from which stories and characters unfold; inversion, circularity and paradox. The island, in and as the world, is a key conceit by which to imagine habitable locations and possible lives in the entanglement of deeply personal experience with history.

## Island Place, Small Place, Other Place

The postwar period was also a time of original constitution as well as reconstitution for the writers of the Caribbean islands, for it marked the moment of a collective literary naissance. It is a truism that this beginning is marked by exile, indeed founded upon it, and many narratives sketch the impossibility of island lives and the movement away to Europe, Canada and the United States. These are narratives of the global diaspora rather than the cosmopolitanism of Hazzard, part of the global trend of population movement from islands to continents, from imagined margins to the metropoles. Australian writers and artists have long spent extended periods in Britain and Europe (Patrick White's two 'homes'); it was/remains a rite of passage (and sometimes survival) that was accelerated and diversified after the War. However, Australia did not share the same economic and social imperatives of the Caribbean islands that were at the forefront of large-scale migration as great numbers of people sought work, education and opportunity elsewhere. Australia, on the other hand, more commonly became the new home for Europeans brutalized by the War.

As recorded in both fictional and nonfictional accounts, relocation away from the Caribbean was necessary to break away from economic and colonial structures that limited all aspects of life, including literary creativity. The exciting and painful experience of West Indian migration, recounted across genres from George Lamming's *The Pleasures of Exile* (1960) to Curdella Forbes's *A Permanent Freedom* (2008), sutures diasporic movement with literary production and identity formation in what is also a transformative moment in the genealogy of globalization. It is one where the trajectories of empire are reversed, reticulated and entangled. It is a time of mobilization, sometimes desired, other times necessary, of people once forcibly transported then restrained within the islands. The creative outpouring of people long denied is radical in its originality and its transformative potency. Ironically, the 'world' has come to rely on it for its ongoing reanimations. Caribbean literature and philosophy from the 1950s is a site of this intensity. From the purview of the current discussion about globalization and the 'interior', this renaissance is mapped by the reimagining of the relationships between the most basic coordinates of time and space and their role in the formation of individual and collective identity.

A comparison with Australia's literary renaissance of the 1890s is instructive here. From the Australian vantage point more than 120 years later, we can see that the Australian literary flowering was part of a national coming of age leading up to Federation in 1901, with all the attendant formulations regarding the origins of white culture in the colonies. This focus, shared by other white-majority colonial contexts, plays out in Australian fiction in the repeated rehearsals of coming of age stories and myths of the fall (McMahon 2000). These two *topoi* are at the centre of the Australian classic *Such Is Life* (Furphy 1903), for instance, in which the novel's figure of the 'coming Australian', Mary O'Halloran, dies in the bush (disappears 'into' the continent) as a consequence of her parent[s'] inability to resolve political acrimony carried over from the old world. The story is a loss of innocence, a version of the myth of the fall into sin and death, into chronology and, hence, history. Paradoxically, although the narrative rejects the old world history that has caused this death, 'history' is imported nonetheless, validating white settlement and supporting Australia's aspirations for inclusion within modern history and the modern globe.

In literature of the West Indian renaissance we can read a similar overdetermination of a coming of age narrative bound up with the lived experience of island identity and the movement to political independence, as identified from the early critics such as Victor Ramraj (1971) and Gareth Griffiths (1978). This story is distinctive, which is not to say that the literature is a national allegory because the archipelagic topography refutes such categories. This coming of age story is about exile, displacement and the renegotiation of each subject's multiple selves across space. This is not a myth of the fall – the history of genocide and slavery disallows such a confection – but of dislocated origin and of exile. Daryl Dance writes:

> [T]he narrative of the journey away from home to Europe or Canada or the United States and the later efforts to return may be said to be *the* Caribbean story, as suggested in the subtitle of Wilfred Cartey's wide-reaching study of Caribbean literature *Whispers of the Caribbean: I Going Away, I Going Home* (1991), which argues that while in Caribbean literature there is much movement away, there is also a of literature 'in which the motion of away and images of movement are replaced by images of return' (Cartey xiv). (2010, 1)

Dance goes on to list a string of writers whose story of leaving the island is an overdetermined rite of passage in that it is that is both the subject of the narrative and the author's own induction into fiction.[7] These literary island beginnings recall Naipaul's observation in his Nobel address regarding his experience of the relationship between fiction and islands: 'Fiction, by its nature, functioning best within certain fixed social boundaries, seemed to be pushing me back to worlds – like the island world, or the world of my childhood – smaller than the one I inhabited' (2000, 28). The diasporic rite of passage in West Indian literature of the postwar period could be viewed as a contrary movement to that which Naipaul seeks to regain, a pushing beyond social boundaries and into a world larger than the one inhabited, which is to say it is an image of birth. Conversely, it may also be that the distance of a foreign location provides a perspective on the island, whose image as a miniature world accords with the scale of imaginative literary creation. This was certainly the experience of Ralph de Boissiere, the Trinidadian-Australian writer, who claimed that it was his immigration to Melbourne that enabled him to write about Trinidad (Sayer 1981, 26).[8] Moreover, it is no coincidence that the primal story for Caribbean literature is one of exile, a narrative that questions origins, for this is the origin of all but the indigenous cultures, and the Caribbean experience of exile from Africa was the middle passage and slavery.

In terms of the ongoing completion of the globe, the emergence of West Indian literary culture at this moment appears like a response to a call. As discussed in the previous chapter, small islands are often perceived as ahistorical or premodern in comparison to the monolithic modernity of continents and their metropoles. West Indian literature profoundly disputes the centrality of these outworn categories. Certainly, it portrays impossibilities of island living, laying to rest any residual fantasies of the island paradise, and it details the brutal conditions that force migration. But it also maps and models an archipelagic consciousness that can retain interiority in dispersal, a definition of a postcontinental modernity. This way of being figures the 'universal' condition of postwar modernity in ways, ironically, that the universal could not imagine.

The experience of women and women writers marks this movement in particular ways for multiple reasons including the conventional association of the feminine with interior space and their roles in gendered culture. The texts discussed here present the necessity for women (who are able or compelled) to leave their island homes. The selection covers a span of time and includes writers from different islands and from different backgrounds. All, however, stage the impossibility of the living *within* familial and societal structures and institutions, restrictions enforced by the boundedness of the islands themselves.

The earliest of these narratives, Eliot Bliss's *Luminous Isle* (1934), is an introspective, autobiographical novel that narrates the heroine's two-year return to her Jamaican home, the unnamed 'luminous isle' of the title. The young woman, Em, has been at school in England, and her sojourn back in the island leads to her decision to leave forever. This decision is a refusal of the class, gender and racial politics of Jamaica, which she finds untenable in the suffocating insularity of the white community on the island. The world that both character and author travel to at the end of the novel is the bohemian heart of Modernist Europe where Bliss changed her name from Eileen to Eliot in homage to both George Eliot and T. S. Eliot and published two novels. Some years later, incidentally, Bliss formed an intimate relationship with the British-Australian poet 'Anna Wickham' (Edith Alice Mary Harper, 1883–1947), who had fled Sydney as a 21 year old for similar reasons.

Within the broader narrative arc of the journey from England to Jamaica and back are two related island-specific trajectories. The first is the telescopic perspective that moves from the periphery to the centre of the island. Gillian Beer identifies an exemplar of this line of sight and its relationship to acquisitional desire in Stamford Raffles's *History of Java* (1817). Beer quotes Raffles:

> There is a country, where there is a sea, in which there is an island, in which there is a mountain, on which there is a fort, in which there is a palace, where there is a jewel of brilliant lustre. (2003, 32)

Raffles's eye penetrates to the jewel that is nested within multiple outer layers.[9] In *Luminous Isle* the movement to the island's 'jewel' is to the top of a mountain, to people and experience beyond the evacuated protocols of Kingston society and where Em identifies the possibility of another life. This event, central in terms of its placement in the novel and along the trajectory of Em's journey of self-knowledge, is occasioned by a visit to an aunt who lives in the mountains outside of Kingston. On the journey she befriends a young black woman, Rebekkah. They organize a future 'tryst' for the exchange of gifts, and Rebekkah comes to work for Em when she returns to the town. The community of friends and family Em stays with in the mountains is a microcosm of a progressive, artistic society, which is her true home. It is here, at the core, that she locates an intense concentration – a jewel – of her desire. Ironically, it is this discovery of self that accelerates her departure from the island. Standing on the deck of the boat that will take her away, she formulates this desire in spatialized and universalist terms: 'To be sexless, creedless, classless, free. A soul swinging wide across the universe – out of a small dark space' (Bliss 1984, 371).

Like the centripetal movement to the island core, the second island trajectory mapped in the novel is also circular. However, this journey has no centre, no point. The endless 'round' of chaperoned social occasions and sporting events designed to while away time are, to Em, not a viable option as a way of life. For Em, this circularity of both space and time denies the future. Em's challenge is to break the nexus between the self-recognition and others' knowledge of her, whether in the tedious social round or recognition by the artistic community in the mountains. The mountain community may have given her a sense of her true home, but she needs to dislocate this belonging from the knowing gaze upon her. As the boat begins to move away from the island, she looks around and compares herself to the other voyagers:

> There was a maddening ache in her heart – a gnawing maddening ache. But far below it, somewhere in her being, she could not control another feeling – she too agreed with these other people who, unlike herself, were not leaving anything they cared for so greatly behind – a feeling of expectation and relief. She was going towards the future. (Bliss 1984, 372)

The journey home to the island and its core has enabled Em to read her own innermost being, 'below' the heart, her centre. It is this identification which equips her for the future as she 'swing[s] wide across the universe'. The 'jewel' of self-knowledge and desire is transportable. The visit to the island interior has enabled the introjection of interiority, which is independent of the island's specific conditions. Hence, the readers know that she will find another artistic community, other relationships with women, in another place beyond the island.

The connection between expatriation, homecoming, transition and island time is also at the heart of Phyllis Shand Allfrey's *The Orchid House* (1953). The novel is primarily focalized by Lally, a black nurse to three white sisters on Dominica. She is a figure who is both inside and outside the family – a problematic construction as a number have observed, but one that accords a black woman a central voice and, literally, the first and last word. The girls have grown up, married and left the island: one to America, one to Britain and one to Trinidad. These three trajectories follow Allfrey's own travels and her increasing social activism. The sisters' stories are thus a combination of sameness – all have left, married, had a son, and each is still in love with their cousin – and of the differences within this sameness. Like variations on a theme, each plays out a set of responses to their personal and historical circumstances.

The island home of *The Orchid House* also contains jewels at its centre or core. The eldest girl Stella complains:

> 'I wish they wouldn't make any more roads in this island'. It was a thought she had often nursed. The great glory of the island was its beautiful secrecy. The further into the interior that the 'good' roads crawled, the less safe the secret would be. (Allfrey 1982, 83)

This 'secret' is real in that Stella is partly describing the incursion of tourists. It is also a metonym for the core of the island, the perfection of its islandness, which Deleuze claims is retained by the island's rejection of human projections upon it. Stella's unconscious sense of class privilege in this desire is brought to the fore when her young son queries whether she would prefer all roads to be of the same poor quality of the one on which they are walking. Stella corrects him that the current 'road' is in fact a private track, which, we understand, operates according a separate economy to the public road.

The girls' cousin, Andrew, is another of the jewels at the centre of the island and the novel. Each of the sisters loves him, and he draws them home in an overdetermination of island desire and possession. The final 'jewel' of island and novel is the orchid house of the title; as an enclosed centre of tropical beauty it is a microcosm of the wider island.

The novel ultimately critiques these jewels of island desire while acknowledging their intensity in a passing social structure. It looks past its own colonial desires into the future and concludes with a promise of continuity in the form of social activism. Unlike *Luminous Isle*, where the future is necessarily elsewhere, *The Orchid House* takes the future into the text and into the island. Like Allfrey herself, who lived and died on Dominica, *The Orchid House* perceives the future in terms of radical change. As such, it cannot be forecast because its appearance will constitute a break with the present. For Em in *Luminous Isle* personal fulfilment for a woman and an artist is impossible in white Jamaica. In *The Orchid House* it is the social contract that is most important. These two decisions are not unrelated, and Allfrey is reported to have declared in later life that 'Politics ruined me for writing' (Paravisini-Gebert 2004).

Published 17 years later, in 1970, Merle Hodge's first novel, *Crick Crack Monkey*, is a classic of West Indian literature and marks a new era in Caribbean women's writing. Caroline Rody notes that 1970 'was the same pivotal year that Toni Morrison, Alice Walker and Maya Angelou published their first books' (2001, 118). Like *Luminous Isle* and *The Orchid House*, *Crick Crack Monkey* negotiates the dichotomy of two cultures across generations; however, *Crick Crack Monkey* is located in the black community on the island of Trinidad and its coming of age narrative is intimately bound up with broader issues of the culture and politics. Hodge has commented that the figure of the child is a 'symbol' of Caribbean culture at the time, when the culture was as yet unnamed and unrecognized (Balutansky 1989, 653).[10] We can compare this child with that of Furphy's *Such Is Life*, who dies in the bush. Both are 'symbols' of national becoming, but where Australia's myth of the fall requires a white figure of innocence, of unrealized perfection, to be buried in its soil to claim its majority, the Caribbean narrative fosters children into the foreign country of their own becoming.

In Hodge's novel the process of individuation occurs across multiple domains that are confusingly entangled, but the narrative eventually shares the conclusion that the female subject must leave the island. The novel is structured around the split within one extended family according to the related structures of class and race. The young protagonist, effectively an orphan, is raised by her two aunts in succession. Named Tee by her lower class Aunt Tantie and Cynthia by her aspirational Aunt Beatrice, Tee/Cynthia is torn by the incommensurability of these two contexts that are supposed to be homes, her shelter in the world. Moreover, she is distant from her grandmother, who is the character most connected to their African heritage. All of the worlds Tee/Cynthia inhabits on the island are neither viable on their own terms, nor in their relation to one another.

*Crick Crack Monkey* prizes apart the homogenizing categories of race and class to show their internal diversity and division. The novel does not only to show difference within presumed sameness but exposes the manner in which the racism of skin colour, with its the endless assessments and calibrations, has commandeered and obscured actual personal difference within a community. This is made explicit in scene after scene and is ingrained in the education system. During one dinner time family spat, Cynthia's cousin Jessica complains that there is no point to ambition as the nuns who teach her prefer the lighter skinned girls (Hodge 1989, 83). Beatrice, Jessica's own mother, accepts this reality not only in its facticity, but is complicit in its criterion of value. Beatrice is a successfully colonized subject who exhibits no resistance, indeed actively reinforces the racism that victimises her own child. Cynthia also is variously overlooked or the subject of cruel attention on the basis of her skin colour. Although she is always in the top three of her class, her achievements are ignored. However, when she absent-mindedly causes a noise by running her ruler along the room partition, her teacher uses the opportunity to tell her that she is 'one of those who will never get very far' (Hodge 1989, 98). Personal distinction is dismissed by the teacher who calibrates value by skin colour.

In the terms of the topologies of inside and outside, *Crick Crack Monkey* exposes the intensity of the island jewel as a nightmare of a colonial insularity that turns increasingly in on itself. As the skin assessment demonstrates, the finer and finer gradations of skin colour are a compacted implosion of colonial views which have turned inward. It is a mode of viewing that is locked in circulation of insularity. This internalization of colonial ideology is enacted by Tee herself when she assumes the perspective and values of her Aunt Beatrice against Aunt Tantie and her world. She becomes riven by the colonized interior of her being, and her response is desperate. Tee's situation is echoed by Jamaica Kincaid's first novel *Annie John* (1985), which narrates the life of its heroine from age 10 to 17, on Antigua. Despite her happy early years, centred around her relationship with her mother, Annie becomes increasingly alienated until she suffers a complete breakdown. The novel ends with her in the cabin on a boat sailing to England to study nursing. She, too, must leave the island.

As has been much commented, the last sentence of *Crick Crack Monkey*, which signals Tee's urgent desire to leave the island, does not represent a resolution of its dilemma. Tee ruminates: 'I desired with all my heart that it were the next morning and a plane were lifting me off the ground' (Hodge 1989, 111). At this point in the narrative – and perhaps more broadly – departure suspends the dilemma of how to negotiate the experience of racialized class hostility within the island. The text offers no answers within the island/novel. However, the book itself signifies the achievement of knowledge and perspective needed to understand and address the dilemma. Hodge herself reinforces this reading when she describes her experience of leaving Trinidad to study in England, where she thought she would find the 'real thing', the authentic and original source of her own culture. Up to this point she had not differentiated Trinidadian and West Indian culture from that of Britain. It was the discovery of (hierarchized) difference between her culture and the dominant English one that allowed her to identify the specificities of Trinidad. For Hodge – and, she speculates, for other West Indians in England also – this recognition prompted a process of 'turning inward', a deep reflection on identity and colonial inheritance and the naturalized operations of culture.

Tellingly, Hodge began to write the novel while she was studying in England. For both writer and character, it is this second cultural separation that provides the requisite insight and the distance of individuation. In Hodge's subsequent reflection on the ending of the novel 20 years later, she affirms the hope that 'the whole conflict would be resolved by her experience in England' (Balutansky 1989, 654). Significantly, this perspective is not a reversal of the colonial gaze, from dominion back to empire, but the (oblique, refocused) assumption of the parental gaze itself, that is from the 'mother country'. The gazing subject is thereby enabled to be both and neither child and parent within the colonial economy. Ultimately, both become discovered places, locations – 'foams'.

A generation later, Dionne Brand's semi-autobiographical novel *In Another Place, Not Here* (1996) also maps the impossible complexity of intricate distinctions, shared histories, and collective and personal subjectivities on an island. Brand's island is an amalgam of Trinidad, where Brand (born 1953) lived until 1970 when she left for university in Toronto and where she still lives, and Grenada, where, in 1983, she worked for 10 months in the Agency for Rural Transformation until the American invasion. The novel moves between this composite island and Toronto on the north continental mainland. Brand's own experience and her imaginary sweep range along this archipelagic line, shadowed by the African past she cannot access.

In her prolific output across genres, Brand repeatedly redraws the map of place and identity in ways that insist on the specificity of experience, history and community, which confound conventional divisions of inside and outside, island and continent. In an interview in 1990, Brand rejects the expectation for fiction by people of colour to be universalist and describes her own placement inside a pan-island-continental community:

> If you read my work you have to read Toni Morrison, you have to read Derek Walcott, Rosa Guy, Jean Rhys, Paule Marshall, Michael Anthony, Eddie Brathwaite and African writers and poets [...] Bessie Head. I don't consider myself on the 'margin', on the margin of Canadian literature. I'm sitting right in the middle of black literature because that's who I read, that's who I respond to. (Brand quoted in Daurio 1990, 14)

In this litany of writers from the Americas and Africa, Brand, like Walcott, constructs an archipelago linked across space and history. The continental islands of the Caribbean are imagined in their fractured connections to continents – again both the Americas and Africa – denying the rigid borders of any one topography. In the context of the current discussion of modern cartography, it is significant that Brand insists upon an interior position for herself and her work. The movement across space and borders is not conceived as moving to an exterior location. The map is a cultural construction made between its actors. Brand concludes her 'book of discovery', *A Map to the Door of No Return: Notes to Belonging*, with the realization that, for her personally and perhaps for others who share her history: 'A map [...] is only a life of conversations about a forgotten list of irretrievable selves' (2002b, 226).

In a separate interview Brand disputes the frame of immigration as a means of reading her work. For Brand, this categorization is a way of perpetuating the outsider status impressed upon recent arrivals and of absolving the hegemonic mainstream of participation within the complexities of context. Instead, she offers a mobile map of connections in which there is no accepted conception of inside (home) or outside:

> 'I don't see my work as being about immigrants,' Brand says. 'I see it as an exploration of the psyche in the Americas. [The idea of home] is such a complicated question – how can we say where we are from? Is it just "this town" or is it all the experiences you've been through? Does it represent our family's hopes for us?' (Brand 1990, 272)

In her 1996 novel, *In Another Place, Not Here*, however, the restrictions of the island home are felt intensely. The novel's narrative and respective interiorities are presented by two main voices, Elizete and Verlia, two very different women who become lovers. Although both islanders, they are of different worlds, characterized by their distinctive experiences of such fundamental dimensions as time and place and marked absolutely in the text by language and voice. Yet each is also an *imago* for the other; that is, the lineaments of half-remembered, loved figures from the individual and collective past. Each is also a figure of each other's lost self, again as this is imagined in both personal and cultural terms. Elizete says of Verlia:

> She looked like the young in me, the not beaten down and bruised, the not pounded between my legs, the not lost my mother, the not raped, the not blooded, the not tired. She looked like me fresh, fresh, searching for good luck tea, leave my house broom, come by here weed. It ease me. It sweet, sweet. (Brand 1996, 15–16)

And she articulates Verlia's assessment of her:

> Her look say, 'Elizete, you is bigger than me by millennia and you can hold me between your legs like rock hold water. You are wearing me away like years and I wonder if you can see me beyond rock and beyond water as something human that need to eat and can die. (Brand 1996, 5)

The overlaying of imagos and lost selves constructs their relationship by the dynamics of melancholy, as Freud describes it, the incorporation of the lost other into oneself. It recalls Celan, discussed in Chapter 1, whose poem concludes 'The world is gone, I can only carry you' (Derrida 2009, 9). In this post-war world of islanded beings, the only form of inhabitation possible is to be carried by another in melancholic gestation. Brand's novel plays with the temporality of this process, of past, present and (proleptically) future losses which may occur, to show the profound confusion of embodiment in the presence of such internalized ghosts. The personal tragedy of the novel, connected to its political tragedy, is that the internalization is unsustainable and Elizete is left to inhabit the haunted places where Verlia once lived. In a perverse figure of inversion, this haunted existence, where internalized loss is the strongest reality, leads to complete exposure in the world, to a literal state of homelessness in Toronto.

Brand's avatar, Verlia, is the woman of abstraction called to political action. She describes the panic of growing up on the island and her desperate need to leave. Like many island texts, including those discussed above, this sense of imprisonment is ineluctably linked to constructions of time, as Em at the conclusion of *Luminous Isle* sets out for the future – a place where futurity is imaginable. Verlia describes her family as locked in a condition of anxious waiting: 'they expected peril, listened for it at the window on nights without lamp oil [...] they were so vigilant' (Brand 1996, 124). This condition – which is an effect of the internalization of slavery and colonization – cannot imagine a future, except of violence and death. The family can only imagine more of the same, repetitions of their past, which is their true fixation. Verlia resolves:

> She'd go away from these people who could not predict the future even if it were a minutes from now of this very second. Who could never take care of anything except grief. Which they did with pageantry, all the money they could borrow and headlong plunges into the graves of their lost, wailing and fainting into the muddy holes of the dead. (Brand 1996, 123)[11]

It is only when Verlia arrives in a continental city that she can finally let go of the responsibility of time. In Toronto 'time is tended to' (Brand 1996, 152). It does not need her vigilance. From the life of waiting, she moves to the life of action, of activism.

The dilemma of time on the island is central to the Verlia's – and the text's –revolutionary agenda. The detailed descriptions of the personal and cultural experience of time sutures time and history and shows their mutually constitutive trauma. As Brand asks in her poem 'Thirsty', 'how come / I anticipate nothing as intimate as history' (Brand 2002a, 1). Giorgio Agamben has argued that 'modern political thought has concentrated its attentions on history and has not elaborated a corresponding concept of time' (1993, 91). He writes:

> Every culture is first and foremost a particular experience of time, and no new culture is possible, without an alteration of this experience. The original task of a genuine revolution, therefore, is never merely to change the world, but also – and above all – to change time. (Agamben 1993, 91)

In the novel *In Another Place, Not Here*, the time of the island, which cannot imagine a future and must keep vigil, is an internalization of history, which, paradoxically, produces paralysis. Again, Agamben clarifies this point. He first rejects the notion that history is 'man's servitude to continuous linear time' (1993, 104). It is precisely the opposite, namely 'man's liberation' from history. The 'time of history' is when 'man' chooses 'freedom in the moment' (Agamben 1993, 91, 105). Hence the 'time' in history is the site of revolution. It is this moment, denied to slaves, which truly denies their history. Not only are the facts of slave history elided by dominant narratives of world history's progression but the condition of slavery prohibits the choice of 'freedom in the moment'. Verlia's description of her family's endless waiting is the condition that cannot exercise this freedom. So, too, their inability to conceive of futurity inhibits both activity in the present but also the conceptualization of the past. As Benjamin writes in the 'Theses on the Philosophy of History', 'Nothing is completely lost to history, but the past is comprehensible only from the position of redemption', which is to say on the continuum of amelioration and of revolution (1968, 247).

*In Another Place, Not Here* links time, history and redemption as a revolutionary project. Verlia becomes involved in radical politics in Toronto and the revolutionary struggle takes her back to the island. This ultimately fails, and like the characters in Bliss, Allfrey and Hodge, Verlia also leaves the island. However this second departure is not the expatriation of the first leaving. It is, rather, the death that follows fighting to make the island an inhabitable space. The text does not proffer the redemption of history. There is some suggestion, however, that time and history coincide in the freedom 'bubble' of the (final) moment:

> She's flying out to sea and in the emerald she sees the sea, its eyes translucent, it back solid going to some place so old there's no memory of it. She's leaping. She's tasting her own tears and she is weightless and deadly. She feels nothing but the bubble of a laugh each time she breathes. Her body is cool, cool in the air. Her body has fallen away, is just a line, an electric current, the sign of lightning after lightning, a faultless arc to the deep turquoise deep. She doesn't need air. She's in some other place already, less tortuous, less fleshy. (Brand 1996, 247)

## Continental Interiors and the End of World History

In the middle to late decades of the twentieth century, which witnessed the nascence of West Indian writing and the attendant remappings of the globalized globe, Australia was also reconstituting its identity along spatialized lines. Specifically, the geographical status of Australia as an island continent became variously reassociated. Bearing out Lewis and Wigen's argument about the cultural rather than geographical categorization of islands and continents and the raft of attendant contradictions this implies (1997), we can trace a shifting emphasis on either one or the other of Australia's topographies – island or continent – as the new nation forms and re-forms through the twentieth century. So, too, we find that the stress on one term may inadvertently, and perhaps inevitably, invoke the other thereby denying their separation.

These shifts in definition, in the borderlines of the nation, are determined by historical pressures and opportunities. In 1901 Australia's first Prime Minister, Edmund Barton, stressed the continental rather than island topography of

Australia. He is recorded to have declared: 'For the first time in history, we have a nation for a continent and a continent for a nation' (quoted in Morris 1996, 58). In the chiastic relation set up by this pronouncement, two monumental objects, *nation* and *continent*, are related reflexively to appear as mirror images. This self-reflexivity invokes self-containment, independence and monumentality, an image that befits the occasion marking the unification of the Australian colonies and their separation from Britain (McMahon 2010).

The neatness of this reflexive view is compromised if we consider the continent in geological terms. For the Australian continent actually comprises the Australian mainland, Tasmania, New Guinea and all intervening islands that sit on the same continental shelf. But such multiplicity and crossing of political territory disrupts the seeming perfection of Platonic form between political state and geographical space. Ironically, this rhetoric of natural sovereignty is a feature of island states rather than continents, and indeed there are only eight islands in the world that house different political units and these are generally fraught with tension (Steinberg 2005, 254). Barton's continent is a monological, monocultural construction, as his government's inauguration of the white Australia policy made clear. He imagines the continent as a large island.[12] Barton's rhetoric also aligns with the burgeoning age of continents, as set out by Halford Mackinder in his Heartland Theory of 1904, discussed in the previous chapter. It continues the promotion of Australia as a continent to prospective British immigrants in the nineteenth century (Johnston and Anderson 2005, 43–49). There have always been sceptics regarding Australia's continental status. The *Oxford English Dictionary* (*OED*) cites Samuel Butler's 1813 dismissal of the claim and is, itself, somewhat begrudging of this definition, viewing it as a kind of geographical and colonial hubris (OED 1989).

In the popular literary field at this time, as J. J. Healy, Robert Dixon and Roslynn Haynes have separately detailed, the impact of Rider Haggard's *King Solomon's Mines* (1885) spawned many Australian imitations of continental exploration. Healy argues that these texts 'opened up Australia as a continent *in* space and time, as a continent *of* space and time' (Healy 1978; Dixon 1995, 63). These narratives operated by stock formula including a range of discoveries from Leichhardt's remains, lost white cultures in the centre of the continent and gold (Healy 1978; Dixon 1995; Haynes 1998).

The middle decades of the twentieth century witnessed a re-evaluation of Australia's continental status, with particular focus on the deep interior or centre. This rethinking is attributable to a range of factors. As Haynes and Libby Robin have separately shown, the interior, which had defeated Europeans since their arrival, became increasingly accessible from this time and was sought after for pastoral development and mining (Haynes 1998; Robin 2007).

Hence, this period witnessed a new onslaught of colonial land grabs and created a new arena of Indigenous dispossession including the implementation of the Aboriginals Ordinance by which light-skinned children were removed from their families. Tiwi Islander and politician Marian Scrymgour presented her father's experience of this policy in her 2007 Charles Perkins Memorial Oration (2007). Her father, like Charles Perkins, was born in central Australia and removed from his family. Scrymgour's father was eventually relocated to Croker Island off the coast of Darwin.

Scrymgour provides the background to the white push into the interior and describes the 'benign neglect' of Aboriginal people of the interior until the 1920s. This situation altered profoundly with the shift of responsibility for Aboriginal people from state to commonwealth at around the same time as the increasing interests of pastoralists and miners. She nominates this 'point in Australia's history' as one when 'Aboriginal tribes in central Australia were a newly subject people, to whom settler language, culture, and morés were foreign' (Scrymgour 2007). She describes the change:

> But by the early 1930s large cattle station domains had been established across the Centre, Alice Springs was a permanent town, and the Commonwealth mounted police patrolled regularly throughout those parts of the region to which the cattlemen and miners had laid claim. (Scrymgour 2007)

It was the police who 'determined how far the Federal Government's writ would run in the heart of the continent' (Scrymgour 2007).

The centre of the Australian continent was declared a 'dead heart' by John Walter Gregory, the inaugural Professor of Geology and Minerology at the University of Melbourne, in his account of the expedition around Kati Thanda-Lake Eyre, published in 1906. Though the coinage was new, it followed the assessment of European explorers beginning with Eyre and Sturt (Gregory 1906, 20). This 'dead heart' is nonetheless alluring. Gregory describes the draw of the interior as an instinctive reaction. Whereas in Sydney, he observes, the imagination is captivated by water and islands, in Adelaide – where the 'view is taken in with a glance' – the eye 'turns instinctively from the Adelaide Plains, and follows along the gullied face of the hills until, far in the distance, all is lost in the soft northern haze' (Gregory 1906, 18).

Gregory's phrase has proved enduring even in the face of the European ingression into the interior in the following decades. Cynthia Nolan refers to the 'Dead Heart' in her record of the Nolans' 1948 trip to central Australia, as a point of debate. She uses the drama of the term but also cites contrary views and details the damaging exploitation of the land by pastoralists to stress the lack of Europeans' knowledge of how to live in the centre (Nolan 1994, 5).

**Figure 3.1** Sidney Nolan, Burke and Wills Expedition (1948). Courtesy Canberra Museum and Gallery, Nolan Collection.

In the literary context the 'dead centre' can be seen to echo Marlow's voyage into continental Africa in Conrad's *Heart of Darkness* (1899). When Marlow arrives to sign up for the voyage, he describes the map of Africa on the wall of the waiting room as being 'marked with all the colors of a rainbow'. He is most excited by his own destination, coloured yellow. 'I was going into the yellow. Dead in the centre' (Conrad 2007, 283). Following Conrad, Australia's 'dead heart' combines the dual meaning of 'dead' as 'absolute' and lifeless. It is, accordingly, a mystic and pure place, as with the deserts of the Bible and with Kurtz's final utterance in *Heart of Darkness*, which Marlow describes as 'eloquence thrown to me from a soul as translucently pure as a cliff of crystal' (Conrad 2007, 353). As with Kurtz, in Australian literature also, this clarity may require, for Europeans at least, death across literal, metaphorical and spiritual domains.

This 'crystal' jewel, at the dead centre of a continent, superficially resembles the jewel encased in the interior of the island, discussed previously in relation to the novels of Bliss and Allfrey. It is, however, significantly different. Whereas the island jewel draws the gaze farther inside itself to a microcosm of the island's intensity, the continental centre draws the gaze in only to open out again in an image of completeness. It is encompassing rather than microcosmic. As Marlow says of Kurtz's final stare, it 'could not see the flame of a candle but was wide enough to embrace the whole universe' (Conrad 2007, 354). Understood as the point of coherence, the pivot that holds and organizes the 'world', the 'heart' that pumps life, the continental centre is a universalist imaginary, in accordance with Mackinder's identification of the 'continental heartland' as 'the geographical pivot of history'.

The political, economic and aesthetic claims upon the Australian centre mark the 'unification' of the continent under settler rule. They also signal a move to national self-possession in repudiation of the wider 'world' of two world wars in the act of becoming a complete world in and of itself. Within this continental comprehension the recognition of the distinctive otherness of the centre also provides evidence of difference within the boundaries of the continent. This 'new' space is defined by its distance – in all senses – from the coastal population 'centres' where, A. D. Hope wrote in 1939, 'second hand-Europeans pullulate / Timidly on the edge of alien shores' (1966, 13). Though literally more proximate than the cities, the desert is equally distant from the Bush of colonial legend, an imaginary space forged in literary realism around homosocial connections. Both the city and the bush are profane spaces and involve community. The desert centre, like an anthropomorphic map, instantiates heart and soul into the European Australian subject, into each interior self. The desert connects the new country with two mystic traditions where space and subject are in dynamic and reciprocal constitution: the desert prophets and saints of the Abrahamic faiths from the Middle East and the ancient culture of Indigenous Australia. Haynes cites Mircea Eliade's definition of the 'Centre' as a conventional 'zone of the sacred' and that the arduous journey from periphery to the centre is one from the profane to the sacred, from illusion to truth (Haynes 1998, 261).

Given the connection between topography and world view, it is no surprise that two of the main exponents of this journey in the postwar period are writers with declared religious affiliations: Francis Webb, particularly the latter two of Webb's explorer sequences 'Leichhardt in Theatre' (1952) and 'Eyre All Alone' (1961), and Patrick White, whose *Voss* (1957) was influenced by Webb's Leichhardt sequence and by Eyre's own journals. In both Webb's and White's texts, the protagonists experience the arduous journey from periphery to the interior, from the profane (and mundane) world of historical reality to a resacralized cosmos in and by which they are humbled. The extreme conditions of the desert provide the ballast to counter the short-sighted materialism of Australian culture with the 'horizonal' vision of an ascetic drive.

As the pivot of cohesion the continental centre is also the site where universalist conceptions may be dissolved: 'things fall apart / the centre cannot hold' as Yeats's 'rough beast' slouches through the desert to be born (Yeats (1920) 1994, 189). In *Heart of Darkness* Kurtz's final utterance simultaneously unifies and dissolves the world. For his naming of 'the horror' is accorded the status of a universal truth though truth is, itself, paradoxically in question in these two words. The irrefutable, universal truth Marlow discovers at the 'dead centre' is spoken by the 'manager's boy', who reports 'Mistah Kurtz – he dead', for death is certain (Conrad 2007, 354). Marlow remains loyal to Kurtz's unflinching vision of 'truth', but this is only observed not experienced.

The 'dead heart' of the continent is taken up in Australian literature and art in the mid-century period in an overlay of these various political, geographical, aesthetic and spiritual drives to the 'dead centre' or dead heart. Haynes argues that understandings of Australia's 'dead' centre gave way to the 'red centre' and then the 'mystic centre' in the period between the wars (Haynes 1998, 163). She accords Sidney Nolan's paintings of central Australia, from his 1948 travels (see Figure 3.1), as changing the perception of the centre irrevocably (Haynes 1998, 160). Haynes's account of this transformation is no doubt true. However, the notion of the dead centre persists in various guises in Australian literature and is integral to its literary cartography. As Laura Trevalyan proposes in the final pages of *Voss*:

> Knowledge was never a matter of geography. Quite the reverse, it overflows all maps that exist. Perhaps true knowledge only comes of death by torture in the country of the mind. (White 1960, 446)

Here is the *paysage moralisé* of Panofsky and Auden and a displaced version of Benjamin's domestic interior that reveals its inhabitants. In *Voss*, however, the categories of the 'home' are universal, national and personal rather than domestic. It is the desert outback rather than the bourgeois dwelling, a contradictory space where vastness and fatal exposure to the elements are the means by which geography is charted and a home identified. This point is underscored by *Voss*'s opening scene in which Laura receives Voss in her Uncle's home, a nineteenth-century bourgeois dwelling, such as those Benjamin describes. This house, which is indicative of its subjects, does not align with the interior lives of either Laura or Voss. It is not natural to them or of them, as if they originated elsewhere, which of course all non-Indigenous Australians do. In relation to the desert imaginary, this issue of provenance, of a true home is resolved by the way the desert *topos* reverses the direction of the journey. From the Bible we know that the prophets come *from* the desert. As Francis Webb writes in his poem 'Poet' (1961), 'I am *from* the desert country' (2011, 227). The desert, then, is a site of unnatural or supernatural birth, a second birth like that of the island.

This unnatural quality of the imaginary desert origin – and hence home – is foregrounded in A. D. Hope's poem 'Australia' (written 1939, published 1943), which casts the centre of the ancient continent as incapable of sustaining life, through that most extrinsic of beings, a postmenopausal woman:

She is the last of lands. The emptiest,
A woman beyond her change of life, a breast
Still tender but within the womb is dry. (1943, 42)

Yet this barrenness, which is the target of most of the poem, is finally, for Hope at least, preferable to Europe because it contains 'an Arabian Desert of the human mind'. It is the imagined emptiness on the vast scale of a continent that fuels this imagination. As Hope's poem performs in its accretion of reversals and paradox, it is the desert as the dead centre – imagined as incapable of sustaining organic life – that is sought by the poet to foster the life of the mind and the spirit. While the journey in Hope's poem is from Europe to Australia, a conventional *nostos* in settler literature, it is also claiming that the poet is from the dead centre desert of Australia, not the cultural deserts of its peripheries. The timing of this claim connects with the white colonization of the continental interior, with the turn away from war-torn Europe and with the interior turn of Modernist aesthetics. Its *nostos* is also the return to a sacralized conception of the poet who writes Truth.

The narrative of the mid-century discovery of Australia's continental centre by white Australia is complicated by the simultaneous re-'discovery' of its status as an island. Prime Minister John Curtin's wartime speeches align Australia with its island neighbours, and it appears as vulnerable, especially after the Japanese occupation of New Guinea and then Singapore in 1942, leading to the bombing of Darwin only four days later. The islands surrounding the Australian mainland provide stepping stones for the Japanese invasion as they are later perceived as falling dominos in the march of Communism during the Cold War. Most recently this rhetoric has been reanimated by Australia in its representation of asylum seekers arriving by boat since the 1990s (McMahon 2003, 2005, 2011; Perera 2009).

The coexistence of these perceptions and imaginaries in Australian literature, of both terms of the *island continent*, is indicated by A. D. Hope's first collection of poetry, titled *The Wandering Islands* (1955). The title poem opens:

You cannot build bridges between the wandering islands
The Mind has no neighbours, and the unteachable heart
Announces its armistice time after time, but spends
Its love to draw them closer and closer apart. (Hope 1955, 16)

The poem depicts the monadic, masculine artist-subject familiar from Romanticism to Modernism, figured as an island. This figure can be read as a realization of John Donne's prophetic declaration 'No man is an island' and of Derrida's assessment that the postwar globe is comprised only of islands – a connection underscored by Hope's lexicon of war, 'armistice'. In its particularity of *wandering* islands Hope constructs a relational and dynamic world of monadic entities, that can now be read as both prehension and underbelly of Sloterdijk's 'ensouled bubbles', floating, separate minispheres. In Sloterdijk's formulation, however, each floating foam is saved from alienation and solipsism by porousness, dynamism and the interdependence of co-fragility, more akin to Walcott's poetic archipelagos than Hope's islands of isolation.

The juxtaposition of Hope's two poems, with their explicit cartographies of self over a continent then an island, illuminates their coexistence within other works of this period. Stow's *To the Islands* (1958), for instance, is a narrative set in the north-west of the continent overlaid with the quest to the islands announced by the title. Bernadette Brennan's recent essay on *To the Islands* focuses on the disputed status of Stephen Herriot's final words as he gazes out to islands in the Arafura Sea, the islands of the dead for the Aboriginal people of this country (2014). Herriot's ultimate revelation is that 'My soul [...] my soul is a strange country' (206). Brennan, following Tony Hassall's lead, takes issue with Leonie Kramer's reading of this statement as being misplaced. Kramer objects that such a self-evident statement belongs at the beginning of a quest rather than its end. Brennan argues that the statement can only be uttered at the end of the novel as the revelation is the recognition of nonbelonging (Brennan 2014). It is a revelation of strangeness and estrangement, a white man in a strange country. If we view Herriot's quest and his ultimate self-knowledge in topological terms we can trace a movement through and away from the continent, away from white myths of the centre to its periphery. The islands of Aboriginal belief function problematically for Herriot as the island of Western longing, the primal homeland always on the horizon, the 'eternal' home. The 'strange country' of his soul is caught between a Western teleology mapped on the topologies of its desire, and the sacralized spaces of Aboriginal culture, a coherence of self and world that he cannot enter.

The confused overlay of topographies also provides an optic for reading Australia's iconic quest narrative of this time, *Voss*, published the year before *To the Islands*. Akin to the monadic protagonist of Stow's novel, the eponymous hero of *Voss* seeks an alignment between self and Australian space, which, in *To the Islands,* is figured according to the conventional figure of the island, where the (Western) subject seeks his mirror. In *Voss*, in a kind of topological misreading and error of scale, the hero seeks this same identification with the continent. This hubristic and possessive quest is epic in scale – like his real-life namesake, the nineteenth-century poet Johann Heinrich Voss, who translated the classical epics – as well as the epic imperial hubris of European colonization. The terms of Voss's quest are revealed as being unknown to him and beyond his control – relinquishments which are, in fact, the achievement of the quest.

Voss's death alone in the desert on a mission to impress his ego across the complete extent of space is an operation of island desire. His is a *desert* island fantasy of possession and alignment transferred to a continent. And like the desert island castaway the earth refuses him. However, this desert centre is a space of unnatural (supernatural or perverse) and oblique rebirth, just as Laura adopts Rose's child in the final section of the novel. Voss is the island monad whose multiple and epic misrecognitions are played out in the continental interior. He was looking for an island despotism in a continent where this illusion is magnified to the full scale of its error and its 'horror'.

Voss is saved from insular solipsism by the (mediated, oblique) connection with Laura. They are not quite Sloterdijk's ensouled bubbles, but the world being 'explored' in *Voss*, as with Webb and Stow, is no longer wholly understood by the operations of the terrestrial globe with its unidirectional, nonreciprocal 'discovery' of new places though these processes are still evident. Indeed these texts can be read as performances of their collapse. Primarily the narratives of discovery of the interior landscape of self, according to the Modernist *paysage moralisé*, coincide with the colonization of Australia's continental interior from the 1920s. So, too, like Marlow and Kurtz, there is a unidirectional journey or quest and an unveiling of the truth of self that leads to universal epiphany. Moreover, this unveiling relates to the exposure of the self, in and to the world where there is no shelter.

At this juncture, however, the journey and the revelation are in transition to pluralized perspectives as the narratives stage debate and counterviews that frame and critique the dominant driving subject. The move towards the globalized globe, the world of global foams, is advanced by the deaths of these monadic pilgrims and questers who enact its impossibility in and for the present. The glorious deaths they perform are the necessary break with the 'horror' of world history and the imperative to align geographical and conceptual universalism. The ending of *Voss* directly recalls that of *Heart of Darkness* in that the survivor or witness converses with the hero's lover. In *Heart of Darkness*, Marlow shields Kurtz's fiancée from the horror with a lie. In *Voss*, however, Laura is, herself, the knowing witness to the 'truth' of Voss and the expedition. Her continuance in the knowledge of the horror of history and truth locates her in the globalized globe of late modernity. Her genius in this context is the capacity to house the truth within herself and within the social world of the narrative that will, some 100 years later, come to recognize itself within it.

The overlay of islands and continents maps the worlds of Alex Miller's fiction and the discovery of self-knowledge through the 'truth' of others. By his own admission Miller's world is the 'fractured modern one' (Caterson 1994, 10) of late modernity, and his novels commonly perform a destabilization of imagined centres, especially the certainties of the metropole and the modern metropolitan subject. Many of Miller's novels are populated by characters who are repeatedly displaced across the Australian continent and across the globe. Characters from the city centres are displaced into the outback, others cross the world, continent to continent, as both conscious quests and unsought experience. Others still are lost in conditions of drift.

Yet for all this displacement, Miller's fiction is also structured and organized around centres, journeys to the heartland, to the interior, to the originary intensity of the core, which Steven refers to in *The Ancestor Game* (1993) as an 'internal homeland', the 'extensive and complex landscapes' deep inside the self (Miller 2003a, 10). For Miller this centre is a mirror between the matter and drive of the narrative. In 'John Masefield's Attic' he writes:

> With a novel, as with the exploration of a maze or a labyrinth, it is not a matter of reaching a conclusion, but of finding a centre. It is the centre that satisfies us. When it is reached the novel is abandoned. It may look finished but that is artifice, craft. (Miller 2009, 263)

Miller explicitly conceives of this centre in the topological terms of islands and continents. In his own reading of *The Ancestor Game* he observes that it 'retells again and again the story of a person who is marooned on some kind of island of metaphor and who comes upon the tracks of another self' (Miller 2003a, 6). These 'tracks' recall Brand's conception of a map as 'a life of conversations about a forgotten list of irretrievable selves' (Brand 2002b, 224). Also like Brand, these tracks and maps chart the negotiation between ethical processes and personal drives that lead the subject to action beyond their isolation and insularity. For Miller, this is achieved by the movement between inner and outer worlds or, more properly, from the inner world of the subject to the broader interiority of the world and thence to that of another subject and their world. In Miller's novels this process is commonly figured and narrated as the movement from the island insularity of the maroon to the continental interiority of another. It is this double action, this double exchange, that, in Sloterdijk's lexicon, locates us in the globalized globe of 'foams' – elastic porous entities endlessly negotiating their relationship with each other without self-certainty.

In Miller's world, the continent is not the monolith of modern power but the space of plurality and diversity where the maroon can enter *into* the centre of another. For Miller, this is the site where the modern subject can be housed. This quest moves towards self-knowledge, like Kurtz, Herriot and Voss. So, too, the self-knowledge is about the prison house of self. However, Miller's wanderers (rather than explorers from the age of world history) shift attention away from the self. This is not a magical panacea – enormous questions remain – but it does establish a relational and mobile site of possibility. The pattern of Miller's world-making is clear from four of his continental novels: *The Ancestor Game* (1993), *Conditions of Faith* (2000), *Journey to the Stone Country* (2002), and *Landscape of Farewell* (2007). Crucial to this transformation is the leap from the abstraction of metaphor into the grounded realities of history and culture – and back again. This movement follows Stow and White and also reflects back on them to identify the work they performed in staging the ethical imperatives of their moment of writing.

A brief outline of each text's journeys clarifies this pattern of double dislocation. In *The Ancestor Game* the protagonist Steven moves from England to Australia and then, via narrative, to Shanghai and Hangzhou. The protagonist of *Conditions of Faith*, Emily Stanton, moves from Melbourne to Paris, which she imagines will be the site to take her out of herself and beyond the constraints of her current life. However, it is only when she moves from Paris to Tunisia that a creative inner life is revealed to her, and this can only occur when she accepts the full weight of its personal cost. In *Journey to the Stone Country* the protagonist, Annabelle, leaves Melbourne for her childhood home town of Townsville, North Queensland when her husband (temporarily) leaves her for another woman. This first, planned homecoming is salutary, but the real transformation takes place when she embarks on a second journey to the more distant past of her family and that of Bo Rennie, an old friend from an Aboriginal family.

*Landscape of Farewell* pushes the number of displacements necessary for revelation, which is fitting given the historical issues of Australian and German genocide at the core of the novel. The chief protagonist, Max Otto, leaves his native Hamburg, where his wife has died. He is retiring from his work at the university and is on the brink of suicide. His journey to Queensland, on the invitation of a young Aboriginal academic, Vita McLelland, is only the first of his displacements. He then goes to stay with Vita's uncle Dougald Gnapun in Mount Nebo. But as even this second journey is planned, it does not provide the site of transformation. The real journey into the unknown occurs in the terrain of the Expedition Range, Dougald's people's home place. This experience, which is beyond Max's control, has the power to finally release Max from himself in the place, self and story of another.

The space beyond the known chart of self, space and experience is akin to the mariner described by Lyotard in *The Differend* (1983), in which he theorizes a model of irresoluble difference between parties who do not share the same 'idiom' or values (1988, 7). Lyotard advocates the role of the 'mariner' who travels between the islands of an archipelago negotiating between them but having no ground (no ideological base) of his or her own (1988, 131). The process of negotiating otherness requires this suspension of self and history. However, Miller's continental travellers, bounded as islands within their own traumas, must do more than negotiate. They must actively enter into the centre of another, at this other's invitation and on their terms.

This move again recalls Derrida's reading of Celan that, as islands in the wake of the world's fracture and of genocide, we can only carry another in melancholy (Derrida 2009, 9). In so doing Miller's travellers will have to sift through the fusion and confusion of real and imaginary domains, to identify the 'islands of metaphor' on which they are marooned, and which prohibit the mutuality of this carrying and containment. They learn to become lost in the continental complexity of at least one other and are bound by the co-fragility of land and friendship.

Returning to *Voss* through Miller's continental vision of connection further clarifies the significance and timeliness of Voss's epic failure. Perhaps more than any other Australian text *Voss* performs the transition from the era of world history to that of global foams. It is a text of compound anachronisms. In Lukács' terms, *Voss* is a philosophical novel framed in a prephilosophical cosmos. Linked directly to the unified metaphysical cosmos of the Greeks by his historical namesake – Johann Heinrich Voss, the translator of Homer – White's Voss is belated by millennia. Lukács' account of the demise of the Greek universe reads as a description of White's physical and psychical landscape:

> Once this unity disintegrated, there could be no more spontaneous totality of being. The source whose flood-waters had swept away the old unity was certainly exhausted; but the river beds, now dry beyond all hope, have marked forever the face of the earth. (Lukács 1920, 3)

But Voss is doubly belated, for he is also the nineteenth-century explorer, driven by unidirectional discovery, attempting, like James Cook, to complete the terrestrial globe and impress himself across it. Voss's dual belatedness highlights the time of writing and publication, 1957, as the condition beyond both cosmos and world history. It is, rather, the complex negotiation of the reimagining of these conceptions into the world of the internalized cosmos and relationality, as played out in the relationship between Voss and Laura. There is truth in During's criticism of both White and his Australian champions concerning the national drive for a universalist literary hero (1996). Whatever the intentions, however, what we can now read in *Voss*, 58 years after its publication, is a text that performs the painful and incomplete transformation from obsolete conceptions of self and globe into the condition of postwar modernity and the remaking of interiority.

Pulling back our focus even further, we can also see how all the texts examined in this chapter negotiate the interconnection of two interiorities, of existence and world, in their attempts to construct dwelling places in the inherited yet shattered topographies of history and fiction: the fractured islands, continents, spheres and globes of the postwar period. The literature of Anglophone Australia and the Caribbean examined here records and rehearses the misrecognitions, identifications, overlays and reconstructions in the search for ground on which self and world can be placed in meaningful and sustaining relation. The labour of literature may be understood as itself providing a transitory dwelling place in that the process of its creation is a shifting shelter for the writer and for present and future readers.

# Section 3

# DREAMS AND NIGHTMARES

# Chapter 4

# ACCIDENTS OF EMPIRE: SHIPWRECKS AND CASTAWAYS

The Sea is History

Derek Walcott (1986, 364–367)

The fish, the birds, and gradually a coast
At first a mirage in the mist.
  The island
Grew like those insights that show the self.
And then I read the lack of green, the rocks.
The loneliness from hill to hill.
I knew my days of deserts and droughts had begun.
More fish than man, I lost the grip of water.

R. A. Simpson, 'Castaway' (1972, 76)

A popular maritime story from the Australian archives:

> *In 1791 a group of convicts, including Mary and William Bryant and seven others, escaped from the Port Jackson colony in one of the governor's cutters. They sailed up the eastern seaboard, through the Torres Strait, across the Arafura Sea to Koepeng in Timor, some 5,237 kilometers in 69 days. On arrival, the party posed as shipwrecked castaways to the Dutch authorities but were eventually found out. A few weeks later, Captain Edward Edwards arrived on the island – a genuine castaway after the wreck of his frigate, the HMS* Pandora, *on the Great Barrier Reef. The* Pandora *had been sent from England to locate the mutineers of the* Bounty, *and when Edwards arrived in Timor he had 10 of the mutineers in tow. Another four had died with 31 of the crew when the* Pandora *was wrecked. Edwards took the masquerading castaways to Batavia with him when he left the island.*[1]

This well-known Australian story combines elements of extraordinary maritime achievement, though by convicts rather than naval officers. It records an inspiring bid for freedom, which was how it was popularly viewed. It combines confusion across colonial territories and the deployment of readymade aliases as castaways from the burgeoning annals of maritime misadventure. The arrival of Captain Edwards further extends the spectrum of castaway identities, as he was truly shipwrecked on the voyage home from capturing the *Bounty* mutineers. His crew included Thomas Hayward, who had been a midshipman on the *Bounty*, so this voyage was Hayward's second experience as the castaway of an open boat in treacherous seas. The captured mutineers represent another type of castaway, the willing lotus-eating dreamers of tropical fantasy, which they had achieved by making castaways of Bligh and his supporters.

Imagined together and from this distance across time the scene on Timor seems like as a stage farce about the colonial Age of Sail, along the lines of Caryl Churchill's *Cloud 9* (1979) and Edward Bond's *Restoration* (1981) with the absurdist repetitions of Tom Stoppard and role-playing of Joe Orton. For there is scarcely a character in the Bryant story who is not a castaway of some kind, and some characters are several kinds at once. There are costumed characters playing at history, deploying maritime stories as disguises, characters appearing without notice from another play entirely and all entering and exiting from left and right having crossed wide oceans, enduring (unjust) imprisonment and shipwreck and perpetrating mutiny. The epic scale of their actions, the historical reach of the events, the equal measures of achievement and failure for each player, all direct us to the historical force of the sea and its capacity for the profound derangement of the colonial machine, which seems to persist through a litany of accidents.

## Shipwreck and Its Insular Aftermath

This chapter charts the ways in which the literature of colonial modernity, in its rehearsal of shipwrecks and island castaways, is founded on a series of broken contracts between author, subject and reader. The residual fragments or wreckage are rearranged and soldered together on the castaway's island to produce replicas of the earlier, putative cohesion. This discussion links ships and islands in their shared metaphorics of the state and, in seeming contradiction, as the fantasy antidotes or escapes from its confines. In this latter mode, both ship and island also figure human interiority: the ship has long served as a metaphor of the mind, specifically the mind of the poet (de Gasperin 2010, 81–82), while the island is a figure of both desire and will, id and ego.[2]

Overlaying these shared and contradictory metaphorics is the causal or narrative relationship of ship to island in castaway stories; the ship leads to and from the island, and its voyage is a conventional device of narrative temporality, momentum and teleology. This chapter shows that when the island and the island castaway become isolated from these forms of dynamism, that is, from a narrative propeller, the figurative load carried by the static object becomes compacted and implosive. Together, the web of figuration and the narrative (im)mobility create a field of meaning in which the castaway island is both the mirror and the consequence of the shipwreck as well as the site where the broken literary compacts are calibrated and re-formed. As we will see, the relationship between the fundamental elements of literary construction – specifically, time and narrative, place and description, rhetorical figuration, characterization and tone – have to be reassembled in the scene of wreckage and in the re-creation of the new world or text that follows. These processes are evident in the Australian literary archive, where real and symbolic disasters from the colonial period and the two world wars as well as contemporary Australian policies and practices motivate literary production while challenging its very foundations.

Accordingly, the island castaway narrative can be identified as a specific kind of postcatastrophic writing. Following Maurice Blanchot's analysis of the disaster and literature, it can be characterized as writing that de-scribes as well as inscribes its subject (1986). Josiah Blackmore makes this point in specific relation to shipwreck narratives of the early modern era which, he argues, set up a relationship between 'calamity and writing' (2002, xxi). Conceived in this way, the castaway story also relates to Jason Mohaghegh's concept of the 'chaotic imagination', which he formulates in the context of the new literature and philosophy of the Middle East. As a creative matrix and as hermeneutic, the chaotic imagination comprises a 'will to cruelty' (Mohaghegh 2010, 2), which is also witnessed in agonized and agonistic forms in shipwreck and castaway tales. The chaotic imagination is premised on 'a conceptual matrix of fatality', itself comprised 'of extremity, excess and exhaustion' (Mohaghegh 2010, 3), by which the old is broken down and the new is wrested into being, another chain and process directly resonant of the wreckage and re-formation rehearsed in castaway stories of the modern era. Indeed, Carl Thompson argues that shipwreck texts of the Romantic era, including those of colonialist expansion, played to an increased desire for excess and suffering in travel narratives (2007). Mohaghegh expresses this mode of creativity and interpretation in the nautical, mobile, thieving figure of 'piracy' (Mohaghegh 2010, 4–5), which leads directly back to the focus of this discussion, namely the European Age of Sail, colonialism, shipwrecks and island castaways.

In this mood, the ship-island is a site where various forms of authority and sovereignty are contested, from authorship and the sovereign self to colonial, national and divine power. In the context of the shifting epistemes of modernity, the ship-island operates as an overdetermined figure of the tension between what Foucault termed monarchical power and disciplinary power, the former requiring public spectacle by which all meaning refers back to the sovereign, while the latter, epitomized by Bentham's panopticon and instituted on the island of Van Diemen's Land in 1853, operates by the internalization of social structures and the knowledge of ubiquitous surveillance. The broken contracts performed in and by island castaway narratives necessitate a continuous renegotiation of these systems of power and in that process reveal their tension in the ideology and rhetoric of empire.

Integral to the island's capacity to intensify the dilemma regarding the modality of power and the generation of social order is its promise to align self and space in seamless (self) possession. Crucially, this alignment, unlike continental claims of possession, excises all forms of otherness: between self and self, as well as gender and ethnicity. In this way the monadic castaway, often ironically, animadverts conceptions of sovereignty and challenges literary subjectivity and form, for these structures all rely on conventions of difference. Published in 1782, the period between Cook's discovery of the Australian east coast and the first British colony there, William Cowper's poem 'The Solitude of Alexander Selkirk' is an emblem of this dilemma and frames the ensuing discussion in a range of ways. It opens:

> I am monarch of all I survey,
> My right there is none to dispute,
> From the centre all round to the sea,
> I am lord of the fowl and the brute.
> O solitude! Where are the charms
> That sages have seen in thy face?
> Better dwell in the midst of alarms,
> Than reign in this horrible place. (Cowper 1913, 311)

This famous opening resonates throughout literary history, Australian history and postcolonial critique in a range of related ways. First, the inspiration for the poem, the account of Selkirk's four solitary years on Más a Tierra Island, published in 1712, was the model for Defoe's *Robinson Crusoe* (1719), the prototype for modern castaway narratives and the first realist novel in English. In terms of its subject, Selkirk is directly linked to British colonial operations and Australia via his connection with William Dampier, the commander of the buccaneering expedition that resulted in him being marooned on the island. Dampier was, of course, the first Englishman to explore part of the western coastline of what is now continental Australia.

The speaker's self-description as 'the monarch of all I survey' has become a mantra of sovereignty and autonomy over the last two centuries with varying degrees of relation to its original context. Thoreau quotes the claim in *Walden* (1854), for instance, to stress the benefits of nonmaterial ownership of place. For him, the ownership enacted by the gaze is ownership enough and is understood in contradistinction to materialist possession (Thoreau 2008, 59). Another American, artist William Herbert Dunton, reworks the phrase to displace the first person human prerogative. His 1909 painting *Monarch of All He Surveys* presents the sovereignty of the bear, metonymic of the wilderness, atop the New Mexico mountains in ironic echo of Caspar David Friedrich's painting *Wanderer Above the Sea of Fog* (1818).

Cowper's phrase has also become embedded in postcolonial reading practices since Mary Louise Pratt's deployment in her analysis of the rhetoric of travel writing and its implication in Europe's imperial project. In her groundbreaking analysis of the colonial gaze, Pratt identifies this colonial *mise en scène* as a conventional act of masculine territorial possession in which the colonizing gaze presumes the right to frame, objectify and comprehend the scene in view (1992, 166, 197). The word 'survey' also links us directly to colonizing processes in its reference to land valuation and the mapping of territory, especially relevant to Australia, which was so unknown to Europeans at this time. Rebecca Weaver-Hightower takes up Pratt's argument in relation to the *topos* of the island castaway to identify a key transformative moment when the castaway becomes a colonist. She argues for the connection between the 'castaway colonists' sense of the mutual boundedness of the island and the male body that enables a particular kind of gendered identification of ego and space (Weaver-Hightower 2006, xviii), a theory that accords with conventional island tropes from Shakespeare's Prospero (1611) to D. H. Lawrence's eponymous Man Who Loved Islands (1928). Pratt's emphasis on the possessive operation of the western gaze continues to provide a necessary and productive frame through which to review colonialist rhetoric, and Weaver-Hightower's specification of this process further refines this focus for the colonial island context.

Cowper's poem also exposes a dilemma of power and selfhood at the heart of that project, one that connects imperialism to fascism and thus undercuts the achievement or shows its human cost. The island-castaway narrative further exposes the development of the rigidly sovereign or fascist subject born in the collision of monarchical and disciplinary power. The 'monarch of all I survey' encapsulates this dilemma, for the monarch cannot be a true monarch without spectacle, without the eyes of his subjects upon him. Furthermore, his empty and pathetic claim is mindful not only of his displacement but also of his anachronism. Like Matthew Arnold a century later, the 'monarch' is caught 'between two worlds, one dead, / The other powerless to be born' in the shift from monarchical rule to the internalizing processes of biopower (1961, 187). He is simultaneously the outmoded sovereign and the emergent subject at once: a travesty or epitome of the sovereign self.

For the purposes of the current discussion, it is also significant that Cowper's final and other most famous poem, 'The Castaway' (1799), tells of another sea-voyager, though this hapless figure drowns at sea. Like 'The Solitude of Alexander Selkirk', 'The Castaway' records Cowper's painful identifications with the collateral damage of travel and empire. Both the drowning castaway and Selkirk are connected by their maritime experiences, their isolation and their despair. Selkirk's isolation resulted from his decision to stay alone on the island rather than risk further travel on a ship that did, indeed, later founder. The castaway is a victim of shipwreck, and he, too, is utterly alone bar the poet's intense sense of identification.

The connection between castaway and monarch in Cowper's poems gestures to the claims of this discussion that the monarch cannot be fully understood without the shipwreck as its precursor and base of meaning because it establishes the tentative nature of the castaway's claim to sovereignty. The shipwreck is the dissolution that predicates the reassertion of self by the castaway. As 'The Solitude of Alexander Selkirk' makes explicit, the castaway monarch may in fact have no one to rule and his [sic] monarchical self-perception is revealed to be a solipsistic delusion. The monomania Cowper describes proves to be a feature of self-appointed island monarchs more generally whether others are present or not.[3] It effects a form of blindness by which the monarch cannot see anything other than the image of the self in everything around him, a mode of sight with devastating consequences for other island inhabitants. The castaway condition ranges across the various denotations of the word castaway from its specific maritime references – the ship that is cast adrift and the shipwrecked person – to the broader understanding of the discarded object and the outcast and to Kristeva's 'deject' who cries 'Where am I' as s/he is 'ingrossed' by 'catastrophic' space (Kristeva 1982, 8).

In tension with the figure of sight as territorial possession in Cowper's poem is the mirror figure of blindness, for this monarch cannot see the charms of solitude's face, which are obscured by his solipsism. The castaway is, then, both the monarch of all he surveys and, ironically, the one-eyed king in the land of the blind. In H. G. Wells's narrative of the old proverb, 'The Country of the Blind' (1904), the blind inhabitants of an insulated but Edenic society, originally founded by refugees of Spanish colonialism, refuse the light (enlightenment) embodied by Nuñez, the modern hero-traveller (whose name directly echoes the early Spanish explorer of South America). Like the castaway of a shipwreck, Nuñez arrives in this hidden community after experiencing a devastating accident. He discovers that his 'gift' of sight is unwanted and his belief that he could be the king of the land is impossible. His only option, if he wishes to stay and marry his lover, is to undergo a ritual to blind him; he must surrender his gaze and become one of the community. He cannot, so he leaves and dies in the wilderness. In Foucault's terms, Nuñez cannot exercise the spectatorial authority of monarchical power because the community is blind. But nor can he exercise the disciplinary power of modernity, which requires social subjects to understand the power of ubiquitous surveillance, epitomized by Bentham's panopticon. He is a lone figure without language whose system of cultural meaning is rendered powerless.

This oscillation between these two epistemes signals the profundity of Nuñez's crisis, one which represents a homologous breakdown in literary and narrative teleology. Ironically, this hesitation between old world and modern narrative was enacted by Wells himself, in that his original 1904 ending saw Nuñez unable to resolve the situation and lost to exile and death. However, later, in 1939, Wells rewrote the ending so that the village is destroyed by a volcano but the two lovers escape together. The timing of this rewrite, the outbreak of World War II, rehearses the collapse and restoration of political, social and narrative cohesion, and given its historical context, figures itself as a utopian imagining.

Wells's fable connects the constellation of elements brought into focus in this chapter which identifies recurring patterns formed by the reticulations of literary, political and territorial sovereignty. This process will reveal the paradox of generative and nongenerative literary production at the heart of shipwreck and island castaway stories. For the island tales battle to rekindle creativity from a predicament premised on broken bonds of literary, political, religious and philosophical coherence. From this violent chaos, new writing emerges with frightening coordinates mapped on an imaginary coherence of self and place, self and world.

## The Wrecked Ship and the Broken Story

Shipwrecks and their literary treatments are, of course, ancient. In the Western archive, Odysseus and St Paul are early exemplars. There are numerous genealogical accounts of the shipwreck from different disciplinary and cultural perspectives including history, philosophy and literature, though these are inevitably interrelated. Together they provide some sense of enduring and formative understandings from antiquity to the present while also underscoring the crucial breaks enacted in modernity and the era of colonialism including the colonization of Australia.

At the most basic level, the proliferation of maritime and shipwreck narratives follows the related processes of national expansion and global trade from the early modern period. In his study of Iberian shipwreck narratives from this time, *Manifest Perdition*, Blackmore claims that while shipwrecks have been a staple of literature from antiquity, their consolidation as a genre is a product of modernity and has its origin in Iberian accounts that formed part of Portuguese imperial expansion from 1415 and with greater purpose from Vasco Da Gama's voyage of 1497 (Blackmore 2002, x). Blackmore shows how the publication of the *Histórica Trágico-Maritima*, a two-volume anthology of shipwreck narratives published in 1735–36, is the basis of the genre in modern Western literature. Similar to Simone Pinet's identification of the early modern Iberian *isolario* (island narrative) as one of the key scaffolds for modern literary narrative (see Chapter 1), Blackmore's claim for the *Histórica Trágico-Maritima* traces a modern literary form back into Portuguese cartography, geography and politics.

Writing of British shipwreck narratives of the eighteenth century, Margarette Lincoln identifies a similar connection between what had become the everyday occurrence of shipwreck and the upsurge in narrative treatments. Lincoln cites one Jonathan Wilkinson MD, writing in 1761, who estimates that approximately 4,200 Britons a year perished at sea in the middle decades of the eighteenth century, many in distant oceans (1997, 158). George P. Landow records that 1,645 people were drowned in British waters alone in 1859 (2014, 41), and Terence Grocott estimates that 2,000 wrecks occurred worldwide each year from 1793 to 1815 (in Titlestad 2009, 794). The Australian National Shipwreck Database (ANSD) shows a total of exactly 3,000 shipwrecks off the coast of mainland Australia and Tasmania during the colonial period (1788 to 1901).

A recent volume edited by Carl Thompson, *The Shipwreck in Art and Literature* (2013), maps some of the lines of continuity between antiquity and the present while also pointing to the specificity of the modern context and the European Age of Sail, where shipwrecks occurred in unprecedented number and to distinctive literary effects. Further, the identity of the 'misadventurers' – a coinage from Thompson – becomes more diverse in this era (Thompson 2007, 6). Colonial settlements and the transportation of slaves, convicts, indentured labourers and colonizers across the globe meant that more women, children and whole families sailed long distances. Maritime history across this period celebrates the increased capacities, strength and safety of ships, which, nevertheless, continued to be wrecked by storms, reefs, icebergs and unforeseen calamities. These often occurred on or around islands, as with Australia's most devastating shipwreck, the *Cataraqui*, which was wrecked off King Island in 1845 with the loss of over 400 people, including numerous whole families (Lemon and Morgan 2014; ANSD 2014).

Shipwrecks are central to Paul Virilio's discussion of the logic and temporality of the industrial accident in the postindustrial era Steve Redhead terms 'accelerated modernity' (Virilio 2007, 5, 8; Redhead 2006). For Virilio, to invent the ship is also to invent the shipwreck, as technological inventions contain the impending accident within them. Accordingly, the modern era of mobility and speed – dromology in Virilio's lexicon (1977) – proliferates not only the machines that enable this mobility but also their inevitable accidents. Moreover, it is the accident, such as the shipwreck, rather than the working vessel that can instruct us as to the properties of the ship, its construction and its makers. It is the accident that allows assessment and dissection of the limits of a vessel's seaworthiness and its capacity to fulfil its desired functions.

By extension, it is the text of the accident that can instruct us as to the properties of textual meaning and its various makers: authors, cultures and ideologies. It is the text of the accident that allows us to dissect the limits of both the text and its subject, which, in the current context, include both the narratives of empire and nationalist expansion itself. Blackmore makes a similar point when he claims the early modern Iberian shipwreck narratives in fact recast the practice of prose writing. Hence we can read the shipwreck as a symptom of the literary engine that produced it; *symptom* here drawing on its derivation from the Greek *σύμϖτωμα* meaning an accident, mischance or disease. In chiastic reflection, the shipwreck narrative is not only the writing of disaster but constructs the scene of writing as site of disaster. Blackmore argues that these narratives inaugurated 'a practice of prose writing, defined not solely by the presence of shipwreck in a text but by a relationship between calamity and writing, where a certain kind of experience generates a certain kind of text' (2002. xxi). He concludes that the increasing impossibility of a redemptive reading of the shipwreck 'presents the greatest blow to the predetermined success of national expansion and its textual analogue [...] They show that Empire contains disaster at its core' (Blackmore 2002, xxi–xxiii). This is not to say that Portugal's national expansion did not continue any less than did that of Britain, but that the shipwreck is an event, a site, of its personal and persistent cost where we may look to its ongoing making and undoing.

One of the key literary elements undone in modern shipwreck stories and articulated through them is tone, the profound compact between author, reader and subject. This relationship is the subject of Hans Blumenberg's famous study *Shipwreck with Spectator* (1997), which traces humanity's 'nautical metaphorics of existence' (7) in Western philosophical discourse from antiquity to the late twentieth century. Blumenberg's reading of literary shipwrecks in philosophy identifies the significance of the shifting relationship between the wreck and the spectator or narrator who is safe and on dry land. As he shows, one of the main ways this relationship changes over time is in regard to the diminishing distance between the viewer and the catastrophe.

Michael Titlestad and Mike Kissack (2007, 191–193) distil four key moments from Blumenberg's account. The first is exemplified by the shipwreck of the Socratic philosopher Aristippus (435–356 BCE) who is untroubled by the experience of his shipwreck on a foreign island because he is equipped with the requisite understanding to help himself. The second moment is characterized by the French Renaissance essayist Michel de Montaigne (1533–1592) who more self-consciously performs his capacity to distance himself from catastrophe as a philosophical quality. The third, which brings us into recent modernity, is Friedrich Nietzsche (1844–1900), for whom shipwreck is a precondition of existence; we are all castaways and maroons, an understanding which denies the solid ground needed for conventional theorization and perspective. To this we could add the Spanish philosopher José Ortega y Gassett (1883–1955) who claimed we must always remember that 'Life is, in itself and forever, shipwreck', lest we imagine we are safe and culture becomes 'lymphatic' and 'parasitic' (Ortega y Gassett 1989, 112). As Blumenberg and Robert Pogue Harrison separately discuss, in the binary of water and land on the terraqueous globe, Western thought repeatedly invokes the solidity of land for both perspective and foundation (Blumenberg 1997; Harrison 2003, 4).

This immersion in the scene of shipwreck chimes with relationships in art as well. One emblematic instance is discussed by Christine Riding in relation to Géricault's gruesome shipwreck painting, *The Raft of the Medusa* (1818–1819). During the Paris Salon of 1819 Géricault asked for the painting to be lowered to enable the viewer's immersion in the scene. Riding observes that the lowering of the painting meant that the 'viewer's feet were already in the water' and that the viewer needed to see the painting 'close up to appreciate its accomplishment' (Riding 2013, 122).

Blumenberg's account ends in the postmodern era where there is no qualitative difference between the spectator and the wreck; both are held in relation. Blumenberg epitomizes this moment in the figure of German philosopher Paul Lorenzen (1915–1994) for whom even the ship is built on the sea (Titlestad and Kissack 2007, 192–193). To this list, and in the specific discourse of counter-imperialism, we could add Walter Benjamin's citation of Rilke's deterritorializing riposte to imperial possession figured as 'the longing to be amidst the waves / and have no homeland in time' (Benjamin 1999; Conv S4a, 2: 551). For Rilke and Benjamin, to be amidst the waves is to write freely, to step aside from historicist progress. Subsequent to this immersion and denial of subjectivity, both Lyotard (1988) and Deleuze (1997) posit an archipelagic subject, a temporary assemblage created in and by the narrative and with the complicity of reader's/spectator's suspension of disbelief. This subject is a deliberately artificial position that enables the mobile voyaging throughout the archipelago. On each of the islands is one of Nietzsche's shipwrecked subjects or one of Lorenzen's boat builders, but these are no longer on the sea but isolated island castaways. Lyotard's formulation of the philosopher-mariner sailing between the islands of an archipelago in *The Differend*

(1983) negotiates the incommensurability of difference between and across cultures – each an island – and this temporary subject must have no solid ground of their own, no fixed vantage point or stable perspective or their task will fail (1988, 130–32).

Accompanying the utopian possibilities of ungrounded relationality is the shadow anxiety of the lost compass. For the coemergence of spectator, ship and wreckage denies the prerogative of origin. It creates a potentially calamitous scene of writing by rearranging and deranging the relationships between author, subject and reader, variously creating bonds of microscopic intensity or dissociations of unbridgeable distance. These derangements take various forms: the observer or writer may identify too closely with the victims of the disaster, an attachment that results in his surrender to the paralysis of melancholy. Alternatively, often simultaneously, the means of resolution are beyond reach. This derangement exposes the paradoxical status of the imaginary centre of world and text, which was thought to structure and stabilize textual meaning. As Derrida identified, this centre is imagined to exist at the core of the text, thereby according the text the authority of presence, while also being outside the text, according the text a transcendental authority beyond the play of meaning (Derrida 1978, 351*ff.*). In literary terms, the shipwreck can be read as is a figure of the dislodged centre within the text and gestures to authorial absence, to the elusiveness of an external and transcendent origin and destination.

In a similar vein, Blanchot conceives of the disaster in terms of the absolute to argue that the disaster is not an absolute in itself: 'on the contrary it disorients the absolute. It comes and goes, errant disarray, and yet with the imperceptible but intense suddenness of the outside' (1986, 4). Its force and effects are so great that it appears to come from the outside – the location of the absolute – so can be misrecognized as being the central or transcendental term in and of itself. The disaster occupies the space of the evacuated centre and the hermetic perfection of external transcendence.

A second element embedded in this issue of tone, both a cosymptom and its corollary, is the threat to narrative continuance based on the pact of author and narrator, reader and subject. This pact too, has a long tradition in the nautical metaphorics of writing. Vilma de Gasperin notes the link of momentum between writing and nautical metaphors in Virgil, in which 'to compose' is figured as setting sail and 'to conclude' the literary work is the task of 'furling the sails' (de Gasperin 2010, 81). For Virgil the nautical voyage, which launches out from one port and arrives in another, structures and charts narrative progression and resolution. Still earlier, in the *Odyssey*, the shipwreck off the island of Charybdis, whereby all but Odysseus are drowned as punishment from the gods, does not constitute a narrative rupture but enables a digressive episode, a narrative delay that acts to forestall closure. So, too, the shipwreck of St Paul on Malta marks the beginning of Christian conversion of the Roman Empire in a narrative that resolutely defies finality (Acts 28). These ancient wrecks generate narrative and extend its parameters.

From the early modern period, however, and coincident with the mobilization of Europe's colonial enterprise to commandeer the continents and islands of other peoples, the shipwreck more commonly arrests narrative in two ways. First, the progress of voyage and narrative is stalled by long description of the wreck, whose demise may challenge any kind of continuance at all. Secondly, the wreck denies the possibility of meaningful narrative closure within its own terms, namely the convention of the voyage or quest with a known point of departure and a planned destination. At the very least, these initial premises have to be altered or displaced in order to continue; they may transform into the narrative of survivors cast adrift or marooned on an unknown land. They may also require the insertion of another non-narrative discourse, such as an aphorism or prayer, in the place of a conclusion consistent with the dominant mode of the text.

By instilling doubt as to the possibility of narrative continuance, the shipwreck inverts an ancient narrative pact emblematized in the relationship between the Shahryār (king) and Scheherazade, in which Scheherazade is motivated to produce narrative extension and embellishment to prolong her life (*Tales* 2008). So, too, each of her 1,000 stories metaphorically undoes the death of the 1,000 wives the Shahryār executed, fearing they will be as unfaithful as his first wife, thereby bestowing Scheherazade's stories with a recuperative power over death. Her narrative also creates the duration necessary for the king to believe in her fidelity, thereby linking storytelling with trust and faithfulness. The pattern of their relationship creates closeness and distance, which are variously synonymous and opposite, for each night reprises the terms of the original nuptial intimacy and creates greater trust while also requiring the invention of unknown and unexpected narratives.

Where Scheherazade's fidelity is to her husband as audience/reader, the *Odyssey* (Homer 800 BC) figures the faithful marriage in terms of the female writer and wife, Penelope, and Odysseus, the male subject and husband. This pact is between author and subject. Penelope weaves and unweaves a shroud of death for a period of three years to fend off her suitors and preserve her fidelity to her husband, tactics which are synonymous with his narrative continuance and the precedence of the metastructure over incidental opportunities or events. Given the etymological link between making text and weaving, Penelope's craft identifies her as the storyteller, one who is literally faithful to her subject, and like Blumenberg's spectator and Harrison's thinker, she is safely on land while her subject is on his voyage home. Penelope's weaving and unravelling also creates textual duration and charts the temporality of storytelling alongside the actual story of Odysseus's journey. Here, too, is the dual movement of the making and unmaking of stories, the remembering and the forgetting, that fends off death. This double perspective of actor and author effects also the double layering of two stories: one of the action, the other a metanarrative of the fidelity between author, subject and reader.

In both these ancient texts, also, the marital pact acknowledges that the sovereign self (literally the king in *1001 Nights* and the hero-ruler in the *Odyssey*) is neither solitary nor self-sustaining. Scheherazade's stories are a means of reconstituting the King into a relationship of self and other that breaks the repetition of annihilation he has performed since his first broken marriage. The entire structure of the *Odyssey* is the narrative of the hero returning home, and it is the strength of the tie between Odysseus and Penelope that effects its success. Odysseus does not confuse himself with the islands inhabited by Calypso or Cyclops to become one with them, as John Donne fears will happen to the modern subject. The assertions of marital fidelity in these tales no doubt carry cultural significance of the tribe and genealogy, but in the specific terms of narrative contracts and conceptions of sovereignty, the cross-gendered union stresses duality as a necessary quality, whether this is within the self, between the self and a primary interlocutor, or between author, auditor or reader and the subject of the tale.

The modern shipwreck narrative overturns all the components that structure these ancient archetypal stories; they disrupt the logic of narrative temporality including the narrative's protection against death; they break the author's pact of fidelity to subject and reader; and they excise the admission of self-division. They also confound narrative time. Virilio's formulation of the relationship between invention and the accident leads us to identify the accident as the inbuilt futurity of the ship (Virilio 2007). As the ship's unknown future, and as inevitable and as unfathomable as the future, the accident figures futurity within the present, as an integral component of the existing technology. Consequence is hidden but present. Yet, as consequence or effect, the accident is also posterior, subsequent to the present. As both present and future the shipwreck overturns the structures of cause and effect.

A further paradox of shipwreck time and the reason for its potentially crippling effect on narrative itself is that its futurity – the wreck – in fact forestalls progression, halts movement onward. It is a rupture in time, the interruption of the voyage. It delays, often permanently, arrival at a destination, producing not only its cessation for those who perish but also an endless suspension of the time of arrival at the point of destination. Time continues but has become unanchored (literally) from the systems of meaning by which it becomes meaningful such as narrative causality, the mutual constitution of time and space and the calibration of *durée* (the long term) and history. When the accident is also a disaster, its temporality is further distorted. For, as Blanchot writes, 'the future, as we can conceive of it, belongs to the disaster and disaster itself has no future' (1986, 1–2).

In summary, the modern shipwreck narrative dislodges the centre of meaning, indeed is a figure of that centre in free fall. It disarticulates the pact between author, reader and subject, thereby disregulating affect and isolating each category – as islands. In transferring both experience and perspective from land to sea, it removes the stable ground, which is fundamental to human meaning. Finally, by disrupting the sequence and logic of time it becomes locked in a contradictory temporality of inevitability where, however, the future is denied. In each and all these ways, the Western shipwreck narratives of the modern era deny the power of narrative over death, for the story leads its subjects to their demise and the witness is unable to relocate the event in a structure of meaning or coherence. The fidelity of the narrative pact, like that enacted by Scheherazade and Penelope, which fends off death, is broken and is replaced with the paralysis of horrific apprehension and interminable suspension, as we see in the images that often accompany literary text. These visual images are not extraneous or ornamental. They capture this paradox of static movement in all its horror within the simultaneity that is conventional to its medium. Literary narrative, however, performs the rupture of its subject across its entire architectonics. Read alongside one another, the images teach us how to read the narrative and point to its dilemma of the broken link between temporality and telos.

These matters of literary form return us, ironically enough, to questions of history because they are bound up with the relationship between literature and the representation of the real, which discountenances fantastical means of resolution. The general populace's greater proximity to a greater number of shipwreck events in reality determined the demand for textual proximity also. As Lincoln observes, from the late eighteenth century, readers generally preferred 'eyewitness accounts' as the immediate and authorizing perspective for both factual and fictional shipwreck narratives (1997, 155). The link between fact and fiction is also evident in the practice of future voyagers reading both factual and fictional accounts of shipwreck survivors for practical advice in case they met similar fates (Titlestad 2009, 794).

The juxtaposition of this crisis in literary meaning and form with the deep connection between narrative account and historical event identifies shipwreck and castaway narratives from the late eighteenth century and nineteenth centuries as rich sites on which to enact a range of anxieties and debates, as Thompson has argued in detail (2007). Hence we need to read the shipwreck literature reflexively, heeding the facticity of the accounts with their self-evident horror and as accidents of the imperial machine, at the same time as identifying their more metaphoric deployment as vessels of cultural anxiety. The complexity resides in the inseparability of these two functions. However, their imagined separation enables the interpretation of a contradiction at the heart of these accounts concerning the limits of realism.

Given the greater expectation of realist representation and of the proximity of the narrator to the scene of shipwreck, it might seem that the writer cannot resort to a magical *deus ex machina*. However, this is exactly what many attempt to do. The increasing movement to realism – the preference for 'real' accounts and experience – carries a great cost in narrative terms, for it disallows anything but a superimposed resolution, given that the real events often offer none. This may take the form of a philosophical or religious distillation interpolated into the place where the narrative resolution should properly play out. It requires the text to cross genres, to perform the same fragmentation of textual elements that is the subject of the narrative itself.

Another articulation of the fidelity of continuance is the general Providence of Christian theology. Other terms for authorial authority and the transcendental signified are God and State, this latter in the Australian colonial context being linked but bifurcated components of the British Empire, at 'Home' in Britain and at 'home' in Australia. Accordingly the shipwreck necessarily brings these authorities into question, as Thompson has examined (2007). Conversely, the genre may also be used as a means by which to critique belief in religion and the state. Additionally, as we will see, the disorientation of former absolutes – God, State, textual meaning, authorial control – necessitate various forms of reconstitution from literary form to the remaking of author, narrative subject and reader. One of the effects of this new Frankensteinian creature is the internalization of absolutism into the self in fascistic despotism.

## Too Close and too Far: The Disorientation of the Absolute

In theology, God's Providence is understood as operating in two modes. The first is God's general Providence in maintaining the world's continuance, and the other is the special Providence of divine intervention. Variously, shipwreck narratives may question the seeming failure of special Providence to still the storm, or, conversely, may view the storm as an active intervention of special Providence, which has brought about the tempest as a penitential trial by which people are cleansed, a gruesome distortion of the baptismal immersion of Christianity and the oceanic nativities of mythology. Either perspective questions the relationship between Providence and accident, namely, the capacity or failure to recuperate the accident into the teleology and linear temporality of continuance, of life. The questioning of God's Providence, provoked by shipwreck, rehearses a breakdown of fidelity and trust in both literary and religious terms, and the implications of this collapse play out across all the elements of textual construction.

Unlike the careful choreography between intimacy and distance in *1001 Nights* and the *Odyssey*, the questioning of Providence effects suffocating closeness or impossible distance. God may be understood as being too distant for direct involvement to save the wreck. Alternatively, He is too close, actively bringing about a targeted catastrophe. Likewise the speaker or narrator identifies too closely with the fate of the misadventurers or absents himself [sic] entirely, not so much by philosophical distance *a la* Montaigne but by seeking recourse to the theology of Providence, which effectively replaces his own eye completely with that of God. This displacement occurs in the final stanza of one of the eighteenth century's most popular shipwreck poems by William Falconer, 'The Shipwreck' (1762). Falconer was well known as both a poet and a sailor himself, which underscores the authority of first-hand and proximate perspectives. However, by the final stanza, the first-person perspective has given way to the words of Jesus at Gethsemane:

> Disastrous day! what ruin hast thou bred!
> What anguish to the living and the dead!
> How hast thou left the widow all-forlorn,
> And ever doom'd the orphan child to mourn;
> Thro' life's sad journey hopeless to complain!
> Can sacred Justice these events ordain?
> But, O my soul! avoid that wondrous maze
> Where Reason, lost in endless error, strays!
> As thro' this thorny vale of life we run,
> Great CAUSE of all effects, Thy will be done! [bk. 3, 11. 899–908]

As Landow observes, the speaker of Falconer's poem has abandoned hope of finding the presence of God in the event and must, instead, accept the will of God without understanding (2014, 80). William Cowper's final poem 'The Castaway' (1799) also finds no theological explanation. The poem opens in the midst of describing the ghastly fate:

> Obscurest night involv'd the sky,
>         Th' Atlantic billows roar'd,
> When such a destin'd wretch as I,
>         Wash'd headlong from on board,
> Of friends, of hope, of all bereft,
> His floating home for ever left. (1913, 430)

And concludes with what Eve Sedgwick terms the final 'ravishing lines' (1990, 147):

> No voice divine the storm allay'd,
> No light propitious shone;
> When, snatch'd from all effectual aid,
> We perish'd, each alone:
> But I beneath a rougher sea,
> And whelm'd in deeper gulfs than he. (Cowper 1913, 431)

For Cowper the horror does not resolve or conclude, and the first-person identification diminishes the distance between the drowning man and the poet. Though Cowper had famously found consolation in evangelical religion and had become a major hymnodist of his time by the time he wrote 'The Castaway', his poem offers no consoling moral lesson, no recollection in tranquillity, no distance of either his own or of God. The subject, the speaker and the reader are each left isolated and in the midst of the experience. Nor is there any form of providential reasoning or wisdom. Providence here is understood in line with Calvin's theology of predestination and reprobation, the preordained fate of the damned (1538). The world and temporality of the poem are those of chance and accident. Viewed though Blumenberg's chart of the diminishing distance between shipwreck and spectator, the poet-speaker in Cowper's poem retains none of the spectator's grateful separation from the destruction of the wreck, and the inseparability of the poet from the drowning man removes access to the dry land needed for the philosophical perspective.

Various understandings of God's Providence and of human behaviour *in extremis* are in evidence in the shipwreck narratives and poems of Australian newspapers in the colonial period, reflecting both the historical facticity of the many shipwrecks around the coasts and islands of Australia – the data provided on the Australia government's shipwreck database are overwhelming and indicate a total of 8,200 shipwrecks to date (ANSD 2014). In addition to the representation of loss, the literary treatments of these events also participate in various master narratives of the sea voyage and the shipwreck in telling ways. Australia's worst shipwreck, the *Cataraqui*, occurred on 4 August 1845, and its passengers were emigrants from Britain, mostly young poor families from the English midlands, on their way to Melbourne. Their immigration was part of a social engineering project to increase the population and redress the proportionate number of Irish in the colonies. The barque foundered on the rocks off King Island in Bass Strait between Tasmania and the Australian mainland only hours before its destination point and 400 died. The few survivors spent the next two days burying the drowned in mass graves as they washed onto the shore of King Island. The shock was felt on both sides of the globe, and there were no further chartered voyages for several years (Lemon and Morgan 2014).

This temporary cessation bears out the truth of Blackmore's claims that the shipwreck 'presents the greatest blow to the predetermined success of national expansion and its textual analogue' (2002, xxi). Clearly the shipwreck did not stop immigration or social engineering in Australia, for these linked processes were resumed. However, even this limited effect provides the retrospective reader with a sense of the competing authorities being brought into question by this disaster. Literature that seeks meaning from the catastrophe is framed by the central question of divine Providence. However, it is the very temporal power of colonial trade and expansion that has caused the wreck. The elements of nature have not changed; hence, God is as constant or inconstant as ever. It is the perceived need to traverse the globe and to move populations that causes the wrecks.

Australian literature does not neatly align with European Romanticism – the temper of revolution and melancholy is differently valorized in a collection of convict colonies in the New World, and much of the early literature declares ongoing affinities with eighteenth-century genres and styles (Smith 1983, 30). In relation to shipwreck poetry, the Australian poems follow Falconer and Cowper more often than Coleridge or Byron. This is nowhere more evident than in the two poetic treatments of the *Cataraqui* wreck published in the Australian press at the time. The first, by one Samuel Prout Hill, was first published in the *Australian* in November 1845, four months after the event, and reprinted in the *Colonial Times and Tasmanian* the following month. The poem includes long, graphic descriptions of the drowning voyagers, its centrepiece a young family:

> Though his children are weeping – they scarce know for why;
> His faith is unshaken, and death he can dare;
> But 'tis horror to watch his young budding hopes die.
> Yet louder still louder the storm rolls around—
> All frantic and madly the ship rushes by—
> When hark! God of mercy! that terrible sound,
> The storm stands abash'd, so piteous the cry.
> Then shriek upon shriek rent apart the wild air
> The mother and child, oh! how fondly they clung;
> And above the rude wind might be heard the faint prayer
> The death-speaking wail of both aged and young. (Hill 1845, 4)

All but the final six lines of this 60-line poem are given to description of despair and terror. The final lines provide a moral lesson of a kind, but this does little to mitigate the extended depiction of the catastrophe that precedes it:

> Ye that pass that sad spot drop a tear on their grave,
> And breathe one deep sigh o'er their watery bed.
> Then their spirits shall guide you across your wild way
> Shall warn you of danger, when danger scowls near:
> And, oh! think of their fate when to Heaven ye pray
> Then your prayers for its guidance must needs be sincere. (Hill 1845, 4)

Rather than distil or extract Providential design from the incident, these lines instil fear into the survivor/reader, throwing them back into the scene of the wreck, thereby ensuring humility and sincerity in the readers' own quests for deliverance. The poem does not offer the wisdom of aphorism or a panoptic perspective from on high or through deep time. Rather, it offers a hellish scene to shore up (literally) the faithful through fear.

A very different understanding of Providence is offered by the second poem published on this shipwreck, also titled 'The Cataraqui'. Written by the pseudonymous 'Vox', it was published first by the *Sydney Morning Herald*, and then by the *Launceston Examiner* in March 1846. While this poem also records the despair of the voyagers, it is more distant in its perspective, more explicitly resigned to the ways of Providence. It concludes:

> Great God! How shall an erring worm
> Thy wond'rous ways explore?
> Thou ridest forth upon the storm
> Or check'st the tempest's roar.
> Oh! for each tie of kindred broke,
> Do thou a balm impart;
> We bow beneath thy chastening stroke,
> 'Bind thou each breaking heart'. (Vox 1845, 1)

The use of common metre, as well as the language and cadence of the poem, echoes the formality of a prayer or hymn, and the final line paraphrases the exaltation of the afflicted in the Book of Isaiah (61:1–3; 147:3). In Isaiah's formulation, divine justice reverses the misfortunes of the distressed so that prisoners are made free, the blind are given sight, the poor are nurtured. In Vox's poem, however, the interpolation of Isaiah points to the dilemma at the heart of Providential understanding. For in Isaiah's text, divine justice overturns the inequities of the earthly plane. In Vox's poem, as in many other shipwreck accounts of this time, both the affliction and its correction are acts of God's intervention, seemingly without contradiction. The poem's resolution does not allay the dilemma of the misalignment between justice and Providence, which remains an unresolved conundrum at the conclusion, against the preceding horrors the poem has described. Indeed, the recourse to the biblical text can be read as a form of despair, for it signals that the event is beyond words, and the quotation marks perform a kind *aposiopesis*, the act of the speaker becoming silent, turning away from language itself. In Blumenberg's terms, the spectator's inclusion of the biblical text attempts to reconcile the relational derangement effected by the shipwreck by which both the speaker and reader's identification with the fate of the misadventurers bring them too close and in which the Divine Providence is variously too near – causing the shipwreck – or too far removed to intervene.

A later poem titled 'The Castaway' (1884), published locally by Angus and Robertson in a collection titled *The Castaway and Other Poems*, also seeks meaning in divine Providence, as one might expect from its author, the Reverend Sydney Glanville Fielding, curate of All Saints Cathedral, Bathurst. However Fielding's poem is in many ways more convincing, if not in its cosmology, at least in the ways it relates emotion, experience and faith. The (amended) epigraph from Coleridge's 'The Rime of the Ancient Mariner' establishes the poet's engagement with the Romantics' deployment of nautical metaphorics and with their intense sensibility:

> Alone! Alone, this soul hath been
> Alone on a wide wide sea.
> So lonely 'twas that God Himself
> Scarce seemed there to be. (Fielding 1884, front cover)[4]

Ironically, in Fielding's poem, unlike the sustained emotive power of Cowper's despair, the high emotion of the experience is thrilling as well as terrifying – 'a rapture kin to awe' – partly because the voyage has reunited former lovers. The speaker of the poem is one half of the couple, the one who survives the ordeal. He describes his experience of the storm as he stands on deck with his lover:

> I felt an arm around my neck
> Cling close as stood on the trembling deck.
> Hand in hand in love we glide,
> Lip to lip, and side by side,
> O'er the dark and foaming tide.
> O God! It was sweet agony

To roam with her upon the sea,
When the storm had set our spirits free;
To feel that on the stormy ocean
A soul could share my soul's emotion,
And, 'midst its outward war and din,
The peace of love could reign within (Fielding 1884, 13).

In the two poems of the *Cataraqui*, despite their explicitly different positions on the relationship between Providence and shipwreck, the reader is equally unconvinced by the argument of a divine design in the gruesome and tragic events. If there is a God in operation, as these works attest there is, His malicious means far outweigh the human tragedy that results. It is not so much that the theodicean dilemma of evil and suffering in the world has to be accepted with resignation but that the elements of the poems are discordant; the particular combination of tone, narrative, metre and rhyme produce set pieces that render the biblical texts and theological arguments as evacuated formulas. Although the conclusion of Fielding's 'The Castaway' also makes sense of the wreck and the human loss by the argument of special Providence, this is mediated by the speaker's experience of both the uplifting and the terrifying elements of the sublime. This capacity for Romantic transport casts the speaker as always having belonged to both this world and some other. Thus his 'darling Helen' haunts him; she must 'ever be / Hovering near on land or sea', a closeness denied the separated pair before her death (Fielding 1884, 35).

The energy of the final lines performs a dogged insistence on the acceptance of divine will:

And I mix once more with humankind
To the will of a living God resigned,
An omnipotent will, that wills all for the best;
Why not in the will of the All-wise rest
In patience awaiting th' eternal love
Towards which all kindred spirits move? (Fielding 1884, 36)

The repetition of 'will' effects a semantic confusion that reveals the speaker's need for a sustaining mantra in the face of his suffering. So, too, it reveals an unwitting irresolution within these final statements of conviction, which end in any case with a question.

It will take a poet as consummate as Gerard Manley Hopkins in 'The Wreck of the Deutschland' (1875–76) to weave a poetics and theology that construct an internal coherence regarding random suffering and the shipwreck within Christian theology. In 'The Wreck of the Deutschland' this is achieved by the structure of the poem, an ode, in which the opening section details the poet's personal experience of God's wrath and seeming absence. This section frames the account of the shipwreck, and, in particular, identifies the speaker with the five nuns on board who were fleeing persecution for their beliefs. The opening establishes a world view wherein the identification of God's will is always agonized and is never resolved but ongoing, constant:

> THOU mastering me
> God! giver of breath and bread;
> World's strand, sway of the sea;
> Lord of living and dead;
> Thou hast bound bones and veins in me, fastened me flesh,
> And after it almost unmade, what with dread,
> Thy doing: and dost thou touch me afresh?
> Over again I feel thy finger and find thee. (Hopkins 1978, 34)

Derived in part from the Ignatian meditation of the Jesuits, the opening stanza establishes imaginative sympathy and intensity of experience – from beauty to suffering and death – as the meaningful register, indeed the core, of life. Metaphorical shipwreck is present before the account of the Deutschland itself; indeed it is overdetermined in the deployment of Blumenberg's 'nautical metaphorics of existence' in line three and by the poet's particular experience of affliction. In this way, Hopkins is also in the tradition of Pascal for whom 'inherited religious belief is wracked by doubt and the believer is brought face to face with intimations of nothingness' (Brenkman 2013, 1). The poem's theodicean inquiry, the imaginative sympathy which connects the poet to those on board the ship and the valorization of intense experience and meaning are interwoven by the intricate interplay of metaphor and facticity which, as with all metaphor, moves between radical difference and original and idiosyncratic connection. The labour and pain of this meditation, of the enterprise of language and metaphor, is rendered compelling by Hopkins' startling prosody, which denies the distinction between inner and outer worlds and between viewing subjects and the worlds around them, an understanding which he theorized as inscape and instress (Hopkins 2009, 210–30), and which his language seeks not only to represent but embody. Hopkins' achievement does not remove doubt; rather, it performs doubt as a constant, if painful, process of his faith. Furthermore, and in direct contrast to the biblical interpolation in Vox's poem, it rehearses this dilemma in and through its own linguistic struggle, forcing language to reach for the inscape and instress (specificity and life force) of the particular event and people. If there is a God in this poem, He resides in this linguistic activity, in the fracture, the terrible grace within sound, image and rhythm, which labours for presence.

The national designation, Deutschland, in the title of Hopkins' poem leads back, in part ironically, to the second broader cultural anxiety Thompson identifies at work in shipwreck narratives of the Romantic period, that of political governance, which is in fact deeply interconnected with Providence, and not only in the ways it explicitly claims. For the shipwreck poems call to God, but it is not God who created their circumstance; it is the state. The desperate shrieks and vivid scenes of horror are, in fact, a blind for the actual perpetrator, the machinery of national expansion, imperial rule and global trade. In the British context, as Saree Makdisi reminds us, over 150 million people were brought under British Imperial control in the Romantic period (1998, xi). These new colonies included Australia and New Zealand, South Africa, West Africa, Singapore and the Indian subcontinent. Shipwreck was part of the collateral damage of this expansion and both symptom and sign of its vulnerability, *symptom* again here drawing on its derivation from the Greek σύμϖτωμ meaning an accident, mischance or disease (symptom, n. *OED Online,* 96320).

God's presence or absence may be questioned in earnest, but Providence is not the correct framework for seeking meaning from the devastation of shipwreck. The question of Providence is an alibi by which metaphysics disguises the collateral damage of empire. Hopkins's poem is saved from his delusion by the admitted circumstance of the poem – namely, the explicit necessity for the nuns' voyage because of persecution by the state. In the poems of imperial wreckage, however, what Horace termed the 'impious boats' of state and capital have relegated God to a trope of imperial ambition (Blumenberg 1997, 11). The misadventurers call out to God as the absolute authority, but this position has been ceded to the state. So, too, they call to God for comfort, and, as we will see in the ensuing discussion, the state responds with an image of a model citizen who accepts the fate the state contrived for him. Moreover, these model citizens are accorded the capacity to exercise free will and choice in the face of the catastrophe. Indeed, the shipwreck scene plays out the connection between fear and liberty that Hobbes formulates in *Leviathan* (1651), in terms of shipwreck.[5]

If we read through the choices made by the model misadventurer, we can see that, whatever their position, it is the act of choice itself that signals the resilience of the subject. Lincoln explains that in the British context, shipwreck narratives from the eighteenth century 'record moments of crisis in which social conventions are tested in isolation from the conditions that normally support them' (1997, 155). Without the ballast of institutional surveillance and customs, categories of gender, class, nation and religion are challenged by extreme circumstance; sometimes they endure and at others they are abandoned. Often times, as we saw in Hill's poem of the *Cataraqui* wreck, it is the figure of the father and the father-captain who carries this figurative load, who is both a model of love and of honour, acquitting himself according to both private and public value systems and showing their concordance.

One of the most lamented shipwrecks of this time, the *Halsewell* in 1786, occurred at the beginning of the voyage from London to Madras, on the Isle of Purbeck off the Dorset coast. Of the 240 on board, 166 were drowned. The ship was an East Indiaman and the passengers included a large contingent of soldiers who were to be reinforcements for the East India Company. As Lincoln and Thompson each discuss, the event became the topic of survivors' accounts, performances and religious pamphlets as well as literary renderings and pictorial sketches and paintings (Lincoln 1997, Thompson 2007). I would venture that a poem by Henry Parkes – architect of Australian Federation who arrived in New South Wales in 1839 – titled 'The Last', may well be an adapted retelling of the *Halsewell* disaster, as it refers to a number of the stock images.

In many of these, the focal point is the fate of the captain and his two daughters, all of whom drowned (Lincoln 1997, 156–58; Thompson, 2013, 94*ff.*). As Lincoln notes the two young women are commonly portrayed as immobile, unable to do anything to save themselves, and the father is protective of them but also hampered by their gendered inaction. He might have saved himself if not for his love and loyalty to his daughters. As Thompson argues, this father becomes, in the prolific retellings, a model of Englishness. Significantly, this national superiority is linked to trade rather than exploration or adventure (Thompson 2013, 100), thereby connecting selfless heroism with British colonial mercantilism.

Another tale structured by the morality of fathers, also part of the East India Company, is William Mackay's *Narrative of the Shipwreck of the Juno*, published in 1798, which has been discussed in detail by Titlestad (2009, 795–96). This account presents a macabre distortion of the (already macabre) test of true maternity in the Book of Solomon. In Mackay's narrative, rather than two women arguing over a new baby, we are presented with two men presented with the impending deaths of their sons: one man, a servant, does nothing to aid his child; the other, lovingly tends his boy for five days until his death and then lies down to die himself. One is a false father, the other true. And while there is no Solomon present to arbitrate, and perhaps no law of state has been broken, natural law, the bond of father and son, is disregarded and respected in turns. Moreover, the inscription of social class into the account identifies the natural order of the class structure in its equation of natural law with social order (Titlestad 2009, 796). Mackay's commentary states that those who observed the men and boys were deeply affected by these events, showing that they, too, have not been desensitized to morality or sentiment and can be swayed by the behaviour of a superior person. The capacity of the observers on the Juno to feel and assess those around them, like the captain-father of the *Halsewell* to choose love – hence death – demonstrates that the civilized man can exercise a degree of free will even in this dire circumstance. Just as the fellow misadventurers take comfort from the ethical and humane behaviour they witness, so does the reader or viewer.

A similar juxtaposition of alternatives and choices in the situation of shipwreck and maroons is exposed by New Zealand maritime historian Joan Druett in her study of two groups of island maroons, *Island of the Lost: A Harrowing True Story of Shipwreck, Death and Survival on a Godforsaken Island at the Edge of the World* (2007), which compares the extraordinary coincidence of two shipwrecks on Grafton Island, 300 miles south of New Zealand, in 1864. Neither community was aware of the other: one survived for two years and developed the resources to effect its own rescue; the other descended into anarchy and only 3 of the 19 survived until they were rescued a year later. The account summons the island's association as a natural laboratory, from the significance of the Galapagos for Darwin's theories to the horror of H. G. Wells's *Island of Dr Moreau* (1896). In the Grafton Island episode, the island operates like the control by which the separate cases are tested.

The representative fathers of shipwrecks and the comparisons of makeshift island societies partake of the conventional tropes of ships and islands as figures of the state. The metaphor of the ship for the polity and government has a long tradition, from Plato's *Republic* (ca. 380 BC) to Horace's Odes (23–13 BC) (Thompson 2001, 167). It is thought the metaphor entered English in a translation of Machiavelli's *The Prince* in 1675 (*OED online*, 178226. Blackmore claims that in Iberian colonialism, the ship 'never relinquishes its status as icon of European culture or iterative nature of expansionist, ideological action' (Blackmore 2002, 553; Titlestad 2009, 790). The connection between the metaphorics of ship and island resides in the figuration and representation of governance in that the static ship of the island is also the site of utopian social speculation, as with More's *Utopia* (1516). Further, as Philip Steinberg has demonstrated in his analysis of portolan maps, in use from the thirteenth to the seventeenth centuries, there is a strong link between the early modern imaginary conception of islands and the development of the modern imagination of nation states (2005).

Shipwreck thus presents an image of the state in a bounded laboratory context and under siege or, *in extremis*, an extension or amplification of the single captain-father. Blumenberg identifies this metaphor as not only ancient but fundamental. He cites Horace's description of the wrecked ship of state in terms '"impious boats" that rashly connect what divinity has sundered'

(1997, 11); human hubris has caused it to over-reach itself and upset the elemental distinction of land and water. Hence, Blumenberg continues: 'When the sea throws itself against a fragile vessel, it is only protecting this original division established by the gods' wisdom and overleaped by human pride' (1997, 11). Blackmore's argument about the destabilizing effect of shipwreck for discourses of national expansion updates this reading to the early modern period (2002, xxi).

Thompson makes a similar observation in relation to Romanticism and the Age of Revolution (1790–1830). Shipwreck is everywhere and at the heart of the Romantic archive. In British visual art, Turner's many maritime studies, including numerous shipwrecks, are synonymous with the period, as Christine Riding has recently shown (2013, 112–32). Géricault's *The Raft of the Medusa* (1818–19) may be the most famous visual work of this kind. It depicts the fate of the French naval frigate that foundered off the West African coast in 1816 on its way to Senegal to effect the handover of the colony back to Bourbon rule. The total loss of the ship and the infamy of the fate of the survivors cast adrift in a raft caused huge public embarrassment for the French monarchy, which had only recently been restored to power after Napoleon's defeat in 1815. The boat was 'captained by an officer of the Ancien Régime who had not sailed for over twenty years and who ran the ship aground on a sandbank' (Louvre 2014). Lincoln notes that plays written about the incident were banned until a change of government in 1839 (1997, 161). The strong public emotion generated by the horror story ensured that Géricault's painting of the incident attracted wide interest and became, of course, an icon of French Romanticism.

Subsequent periods of volatility and war have also been represented by wreck and marooning. In the postwar, mid-century period this scenario was epitomized by William Golding's *Lord of the Flies* (1954), which charts the disintegration of a group of schoolboys who are gradually stripped of 'civilized' protocol and commit murder. There are two exceptions to the mob: one is the rejected 'weak' target of the new social engineering who is killed; the other retains his moral sense and capacity for sympathy, much like the fathers discussed previously.[6] Golding's novel is a product of the postwar, postnuclear, Cold War period, and war is the premise for the boys' air evacuation from Britain in the novel, which looks back to the recent horror of World War II and speaks to the tensions of its present.

In Australian literature also, a number of writers examined the barbarity of World War II through the *topos* of shipwreck and the marooned community. In each instance the calamity of shipwreck is a literal event and a metaphor of the calamity of war. The first of these is Martin Boyd's eighth novel, *Nuns in Jeopardy* (1940), which tells of shipwreck and the fortunes of shipwrecked survivors on a Pacific Island. The company includes six nuns, a group of sailors, an orphaned child and the thirteenth member of the party, a mysterious Mr Smith, who is variously a kind saviour and a demon. It is a kind of Agatha Christie-like assembly. (Thea Astley's island castaway narrative *A Boatload of Homefolk* (1968) is structured in this way also.) The idea for writing the novel came from Boyd's cousin, Joan Lindsay (author of *Picnic at Hanging Rock*, 1967). Boyd records the event:

> In 1938 Daryl and Joan Lindsay were in London. One day, when she was lunching with me in Holland Street Joan said: 'It's no good writing today a novel assuming that society is stable. You must either deal with the mess we are in, or else write of something quite fantastic, say, a lot of nuns wrecked on a desert island and call it Nuns in Jeopardy.' I said: 'Very well, I will.' And I did. (quoted in Kramer 1985, v).

The novel is an escape from the escalation of tension in Europe and a supposedly ahistorical fable about the very same tyranny and freedom but the War is everywhere present. As Leonie Kramer points out in her Introduction to the 1985 edition: 'Boyd was one of the first novelists to recognise that the First World War changed the course of European civilisation', and was deeply and rightfully fearful at the prospect of its sequel (vi). (Ironically for a novel about catastrophe, most copies of the first edition of *Nuns in Jeopardy* were destroyed in the 1940 Blitz.) The novel's abstract allegorical structure is clearly evident as its proleptic longing, for it subsumes the historical catastrophe taking place in reality onto a postcatastrophic island which can reconstruct social structures and institutions as well as human relationships.

A quite different connection between an island castaway story and the War is presented in Douglas Stewart's play *Shipwreck*, written in 1947 and first produced in 1949. Citing Nancy Keesing's biography of Stewart, Susan McKernan notes that 'Stewart claimed that *Shipwreck* was his response to the Japanese advances in the Pacific and news of conditions in Changi prison' (1989, 128–29). The play is an allegorical melodrama of tyranny and violence based on the actual wreck of the Dutch merchant ship, the *Batavia*, in the Houtman Abrolhos archipelago off the coast of Western Australia in 1629 and the ensuing bloodbath in which 125 people were murdered (see Figure 4.1). In the slippage between the related (but distinct) imaginaries of ship and island, we can say that the fragile governance maintained on board a ship distorts to a despotic mania when space and time are dislocated on the island. At this juncture of temporal arrest and this unmapped place of unwanted detour occurs one of the bloodiest incidents of the castaway sojourn in modernity perpetrated by a mutineering cohort led by the religious fanatic, Jeronimus

**Figure 4.1** Engraving of the massacre that followed the *Batavia* shipwreck – from the Jan Janz 1647 edition of *Ongeluckige Voyagie*. Courtesy Western Australia Museum.

Cornelius. The captain and a small crew had left the majority to sail to Jakarta for assistance. On the captain's return, the perpetrators were punished, and the remaining voyagers eventually arrived in Batavia (Jakarta). A number died soon after and an even smaller number eventually returned home to the Netherlands. The stone fort built by some of the party to resist the mutineers on what is now West Wallabi Island is the oldest remaining structure by Europeans on Australian territory, and the remains of the wreck were discovered in 1974 and are held in two branches of the Western Australian Museum: the Shipwreck Galleries in Fremantle and Geraldton.[7]

Like numerous subsequent treatments of the Batavia story, Stewart's staging of barbarity foregrounds the inexplicable evil of the main mutineer and murderer, Jeronimus Cornelisz (Cornelius in Stewart's play), whose reign of terror is only checked when the ultimate and legitimate authority returns from seeking help in Batavia (Jakarta) and forcibly captures him and his cronies. So, too, Henrietta Drake-Brockman's novelistic treatment of the Batavia story, *The Wicked and the Fair* (1957), contrasts benign and corrupt authorities as each responds under pressure and at a remove from the national centre. Brockman casts the ship's ultimate authority, Francisco Peseart, as a good man whom history has treated poorly, and she pits him against the evil pretender Cornelisz, who uses circumstances to advance his despotic dreams of wealth and power. Both Stewart and Drake-Brockman calibrate assumed power against legitimate power, seeming authority against rightful – and ultimate – authority. Accordingly, the reassertion of rightful authority is a form of faith in the resilience of social structures and of humanity in the face of ruthless savagery. It asserts that circumstances may enable radical evil but that there is a more powerful authority that will ultimately contain it. The relationship to the despotism of war and the dictators at its centre is clear, as is the belief that human despotism is less powerful than the broader social structures built to contain it.

There have been many literary treatments of the Batavia story. The earliest Australian fictionalization is a children's adventure story titled *Marooned on Australia* written by the explorer and writer Ernest Favenc in 1896, which was reprinted five times until 1925 (AustLit, Favenc). Favenc's story, however, focuses on the two marooned men, left as punishment for their involvement in the mutiny, on the north-west Australian mainland. It is thought that the two men were taken in and cared for by local people, and recent research has indicated that this may indeed be the case. Peter FitzSimons notes that the two communities in the world with the highest rate of polydactylism are the north western Aboriginal people and the Dutch religious sect, the Mennonites, who were included in the passengers and crew of the *Batavia* (2011, 435). Subsequent treatments of the story for children and young adults after Favenc, dating mostly from the 1970s, deal with the shipwreck, treasure and the events of the massacre.

Western Australians are the most exercised by the Batavia story, as one might expect, as its marks Western Australia's distinctive colonial history, often overlooked in the dominance of the mythologies of the eastern seaboard.[8] Their output includes fiction, nonfiction and drama by notable authors such as Randolph Stow (1971), Nicholas Hasluck (1984), Robert Drewe (2009b) and Gary Crew (1990, 2001), and poetry by Lee Knowles (2008). There is also a significant cluster of narratives and poems by a diverse group of writers in the period from the late 1990s to the early 2000s. The first of these is Arabella Edge's *The Company: The Story of a Murderer* (2000), which won the Best First Book Award of the 2001 Commonwealth Writers Prize for the South East Asia and South East Pacific region. Kathryn Heyman's novel *The Accomplice* was published in 2003. In 2002 HarperCollins re-issued Hugh Edwards's *Islands of Angry Ghosts*, originally published in 1966, and English historian Mike Dash published *Batavia's Graveyard: The True Story of the Mad Heretic Who Led History's Bloodiest Mutiny*. Simon Leys' nonfiction account, *The Wreck of the Batavia: A True Story* (2003) won the Prix Guizot, a prize of the *Académie française*. Lee Knowles published the poetic sequence 'Batavia Islands' (2008). Robert Drewe wrote a survey account of Batavia texts (2009a), and Peter FitzSimons published an extended full-length study in 2011, though he writes in his Preface that the book was first suggested to him in 1999, so had been brewing for more than a decade (2011, xi).

Numerous works for performance were written at this time also. Dramatist and activist Graham Pitts's play *Edge* was first produced in Perth in 1994. The radio play *Southland* written by the former National Head of ABC radio drama, David Britton, was produced and broadcast on BBC Radio 4 in 2000, and Patrick Carr's play *Batavia* was first produced in Brisbane in 2005. In 2002 the opera *Batavia* by Peter Goldsworthy and Richard Mills was staged by Opera Australia, and the production won the Helpmann Awards for Performing Arts in Australia, Best Opera section for 2002 A survey of the AustLit database reveals that, to date, there have been 5 performance works on the Batavia story, 4 plays and 1 opera; 9 works of prose fiction, of which 4 were written for young adult readership; 8 works of nonfiction; and more than 20 poems, with 2 significant poetic sequences.

I list these works and their accolades in detail to stress the significance and value attached to the Batavia story in Australia's literary and cultural imaginary. However, the Batavia story occupies an ambivalent position in the psyche of modern Australia, for while it so compelling it is not part of the national mythology of the country, possibly because the events occurred before the European invasion. So, too, the status of the Batavia story emphasizes the regional inflections of Australia's self-narrativization. This is an Indian Ocean story, not the eastern seaboard of British 'discovery' and the first settlements. However, its oblique status, literally to the side of the continental mainland in the Indian Ocean, also affords the Batavia story a particular symbolic charge. FitzSimons concludes his account of the Batavia events with a description of flying over the islands, 400 years after the events. He writes:

> you can still see clearly the exact imprint of the shape of the ship, a pale shadow on the ramparts of the reef in the bluey-greyness all around [...] That exact shape of the reef is alike a photographic negative, the reverse image of something vibrant and fantastic, which gives you a strong clue of what once was. (FitzSimons 2011, 466)

This fantastic image of a residual impression and a reverse image encapsulate the ways in which the Batavia story is a site of a shadow alternative where brutal possibilities and fears are tested out. This island is another laboratory where potential brutalities are rehearsed within defined limits including the extremes established by the original story and the boundaries of the islands and separated from the actual events of history. This status only raises more questions regarding the preoccupation with the Batavia story from the 1990s. It is as if this sunken wreck, this horror narrative of the Australian psyche, has surfaced in a sublimation and literalization of the horror of the new wrecks in the Indian Ocean of this time, namely the asylum seekers: Tampa, children overboard, the castaways of this time; the current disaster at the core of empire, the current dislocations of space and time, current forms of sovereignty (Marr 2004; Perera 2009).

Two of these recent Batavia narratives are symptomatic of this recent history around the idea of the 'accident of birth': Arabella Edge's *The Company* (2000) and Kathryn Heyman's *The Accomplice* (2003). Edge's novel echoes Süskind's *Perfume* (1985), and indeed they share the subtitle: 'The Story of a Murderer'. The novel is focalized through the eyes of the chief mutineer, who is cast as monstrous from birth – he is, himself, a figure of the accident at the core of the Empire and the Dutch Mercantile economy.

Heyman's *The Accomplice* is voiced by a female member of the ship, Judith, one of the few survivors. This narrative also opens with an overdetermined figure of untimely birth. Judith's daughter arrives at her house, heavily pregnant and grief-stricken at the recent death of her husband. She persuades her mother to tell her the story of the *Batavia*. The narrative proper also begins with a birth. It opens: 'Birth: It is always best to begin with birth' (Heyman 2003, 3). In this opening scene, Judith witnesses, with some horror, her mother give birth to her younger brother. This brother inadvertently, by dint of an accident, brings about the father's decision that the family will to travel on the *Batavia* to Jakarta. So we have two births, one impending and parthenogenic, the other a primal scene. The disruption of natural generation in these two novels dislocates time and space. It refigures relations between potentiality and inevitability in perverse permutations. These variations and dislocations are figures of the integral accident at the heart of empire, which inherently distorts genealogy and time, as the novel plays out.

The question of natural and 'unnatural' birth and moral choices is also at the centre of M. L. Stedman's acclaimed debut novel *The Light between Oceans* (2012), which continues the deployment of the island to structure allegorical, moral debate as a choice. *The Light between Oceans* is also set on an island off the coast of Western Australia, on this occasion a fictional island called Janus Rock off the coast of 'Partaguese', a fictionalized version of Augusta in the state's south. The name of the island signals the choice to be made between two understandings or perspectives that lie at the heart of the story, which is also a meditation on the brutality of World War I. The hero of *The Light between Oceans*, Tom Sherbourne, is a self-exiled castaway as the lighthouse keeper on Janus Rock, an isolated role he seeks after the brutalization of the War.[9]

During his short stays on the mainland, he meets and then marries a young woman, Isobel Graysmark, who comes to live with him on the island. The pair is heartbroken by a series of miscarriages, and one day Isobel finds a dead man and a live baby in a boat that has washed up on the island. In a decision that structures the moral dilemma of the novel, the couple keeps the child without notifying the authorities, causing great distress to the child's mother. Here again, we have a dilemma even more directly related to the story of Solomon's judgment of true maternity, a kind of uber-allegory about the possibility renewal (rebirth) after war and the misrecognition of the form such renewal will take.

This gendered metaphorics does not continue from ship to island in the figuration of state and polity. On the island, the usual figuration of subject, space and culture is emphatically and exclusively masculine. It is here, on the static space, that the castaways confront the sustained breakdown of pre-existing social order. In this context, the island is the catalyzed crisis of providence – faith in continuance – and the attendant crisis of subjectivity.

## From Ship to Island: Flying Solo

The dilemma of birth on the island also alerts us to the elision of the feminine and the maternal in castaway narratives, a move that marks one step in the formation of a particular formation of island possession. In some ways the castaway on the island can be read as epitomizing the process of colonial acquisition and possession, in line with Weaver-Hightower's thesis of the 'castaway colonist' (2006). Certainly, the island can operate as a site on which broader cultural operations are intensified. Despite many differences within the castaway genre, the grounds for the castaway's claim to the ownership of land are shared, even overdetermined. First, as the castaway's arrival is brought about by forces of nature rather than human design, his presence and settlement are authorized by the logic of the accident rather than direct intention. The lines of teleology appear to have been broken by an accidental occurrence, although, as discussed previously, Virilio's identification of the impending industrial accident within the ship itself traces a latent teleology from ship to shipwreck (2007). So, too, the island castaway, such as Robinson Crusoe, is an exemplary colonist, for his diligence in creating a habitat, in gathering, raising and killing food performs the claim to property by the law of *ferae bestiae*, which the English colonists repeatedly denied to indigenous peoples (Fitzmaurice 1997).

However, there are profound differences, evident in the Australian archive at least, between the writing of continental and island colonization. Critics and theorists, from Derrida's islander in the *Beast and the Sovereign* (2009) to

Weaver-Hightower's account of the 'castaway colonist', note the gendered specificity of the Western island castaway. Unlike much European colonial rhetoric, the island does not signify feminine land to be conquered and exploited. Two iconic examples from the Australian archive of the more common gendered – continental – rhetoric make this point clearly, and many more could be given. The first, 'Australasia' (1823) by W. C. Wentworth, describes the colonial pastoralist working on the land:

> Be their's the task to lay with lusty blow
> The ancient giants of the forest low,
> With frequent fires the cumber'd plain to clear,
> To tame the steed, and yoke the stubborn steer,
> With cautious plough to rip the virgin earth,
> And watch her first born harvest from its birth, (lines 343–348)

Wentworth's georgic vision performs the claim on land according to the law of *ferae bestiae*, which is figured as a violent conflict between man and nature in a metaphor of rape. Eighty years later, in Joseph Furphy's Australian classic *Such Is Life* (1903), narrator Tom Collins rhapsodizes on Australia: 'Our virgin Continent, How long she has tarried her bridal day!' (Furphy 1991, 65). In Tom's paean, which presumes *terra nullius*, the gendered relation is between Australia as the feminine land waiting for masculine history to arrive and take possession. Though very different in sensibility, each case presents a gendered tension between space and the European colonizer, by which colonial occupation is naturalized and authorized.

In addition to this virginal construction of space, and as Wentworth's lines clearly show, the Australian land has also been constructed according to tropes of the maternal earth. In this mode, however, as Kay Schaffer elaborates in *Women and the Bush*, the earth is often a bad mother for Australian colonials, one that does not readily nurture her new white children (1988, 65, 84, 106). So, too, this white Australian mother must compete with the original or British mother for primacy. In any case, one or both mothers are repeatedly and ritually repudiated in narratives which trace the development from fledging colony to nation and the 'new chum' on his journey to Australian manhood. Moreover, in the myths of the fall that are a conventional device of colonial constitution, the narrative of colonial individuation and maturation is often written on and through the bodies of the daughters of the earth, namely Aboriginal women, who enable the transition from boy (of the unloving mother) to manhood. It is an overtly oedipal process in which the male subject negotiates various forms of otherness in the ultimate allegiance to the father and the homosocial order.

Not so on the island. This elision of gendered difference on the island is both specific and structural, that is, it is at once an active repression of the feminine and a symptom of the elision of all systems of difference. The island as colony promises to provide a perfect alignment of ego and geography. As encapsulated in Cowper's poem of the island monarch in the Western imaginary, the island is a territory where a man can be king. This not the same process of achieving mastery over the feminine land and/as the other but of experiencing the mastery of self in a condition of reflexivity, of self to self in an imagined alignment. There are numerous products of this parthenogenesis and intransitivity. Blumenberg's philosophical exemplars from Aristippus to Lorenzen testify to the paradigm of the 'shipwrecked man who, by virtue of his self-possession alone, comes out of the catastrophe unharmed' (1997, 17). Of Blumenberg's list, it is Nietzsche who is coincident with the Australian colonial period. In *Thus Spake Zarathustra* (1885) he writes:

> Once, when Zarathustra as a result of shipwreck was spat out on the land and rode on a wave, he said in wonder: What is my fate now? I do not know where I should go. I am losing myself. He threw himself into turmoil. Then, overcome by disgust he sought some consolation – himself. (Nietzsche quoted in Blumenberg 1997, 19)

Nietzsche's futuristic hero is self-reliant in the manner of island maroons, and it is the unknown and unsought island that enables this self-transitivity. Despite radical differences in the conception of the human subject, Nietzsche's nihilism resonates with Hopkins's conception of the Deutschland disaster in that, for both, life is the experience of shipwreck and drowning an expected endpoint.

But Nietzsche's hero does reach land and is accorded the distance of perspective. Unlike the earlier instances of the shipwreck spectator, however, this perspective is not directed out to sea but onto the observing self; it is in this land that Nietzsche's Übermensch takes form, exercising his will to self-mastery. In its negative cast, it is this space that welcomes and fosters the despot. It gives him ground, a spatialization of the fascist illusion of self-possession and autonomy: rigid borders, homogeneity and sovereignty. Unlike the narrative of the continental colonial who, in the Australian instance, commonly performs a process of realignment from the (biological, elemental, national, imperial) mother to the homosociality of Australian mateship, the island colonist is not born but arrives fully formed, already made, like the parthenogenic egg of the island itself. As D. H. Lawrence writes in his fable 'The Man Who Loved Islands', 'an island is a nest which holds one egg, and one only. This egg is the islander himself' (2006). Various fields of inquiry, most especially psychoanalysis, postcolonialism and gender theory, have revealed the numerous ways the colonizer/settler subject constructs an identity via the binary of self and other. This 'other' may occupy any and all of the categories against which the colonizer defines himself: feminine gender, 'racialized other', native occupant rather than national citizen, foreigner. In the case of the island castaway, however, these categories of otherness are (impossibly) erased and replaced with the illusion of self-definition.

The operations of this particular subjectivity and its form of dominion are played out to macabre effect in H. G. Well's *The Island of Dr Moreau* (1896) in which the shipwrecked narrator, Edward Prendick, comes to understand the promethean project of the island's owner, Dr Moreau, who practices the vivisection of animals to create new human-like beings. Unlike Dr Frankenstein, Dr Moreau does not use composite corpses but joins two live animals. The novel's explicit and impossible experimentation with hybridism, and the gender exclusivity of the island, acts out the ontological impossibility of transitive identity on the island, for duality cannot survive in that place. Both meaningfully and ironically, Moreau's experiments signal that, on an island colony/laboratory, duality is both symptom and cause of perverse generation. Dr Moreau's tragic creatures are doomed because they cannot become single beings, the trace of their dual origin cannot be erased.

As Julia Kristeva argues (1982) in relation to the fascism of Louis-Ferdinand Céline, the fascist subject insists on the perfect concordance of identity, the pure singularity of self, the father and the state as fatherland.[10] The (illusory) achievement of this fantasy requires the expulsion of everything and everyone who threatens homogeneity: women, particularly the maternal who belies masculine parthenogenesis, and 'foreigners'. It also denies the doubleness of human consciousness, the awareness of the gap between ourselves as subjects and as social objects. Indeed, it is the denial of the duality of consciousness that enables the fascist subject to relinquish autonomy to the state, for he does not countenance distinction between it and himself.

This tension of this doubleness is played out in the first novel of one of Australia's great adventure writers, Ion Idriess's *Madman's Island* (1927), which was promoted by publishers Angus and Robertson as 'more than a modern Robinson Crusoe' ('An Australian Story' 1938, 1).[11] Originally written as nonfiction, the account was compiled from the diaries Idriess kept to preserve his sanity when marooned on Howick Island in the Great Barrier Reef for six months with a friend whose mental health collapsed soon after their arrival. Idriess used a log book he found on the wreck of the *Sea Foam* (1922) as his diary, writing on blank pages and in and around used pages. A page of this palimpsest of wrecks and maroons is reproduced in the 1938 nonfiction edition (see Figure 4.2). Angus and Robertson persuaded Idriess to rewrite the memoir as a novel and to include a romance subplot, which was expunged

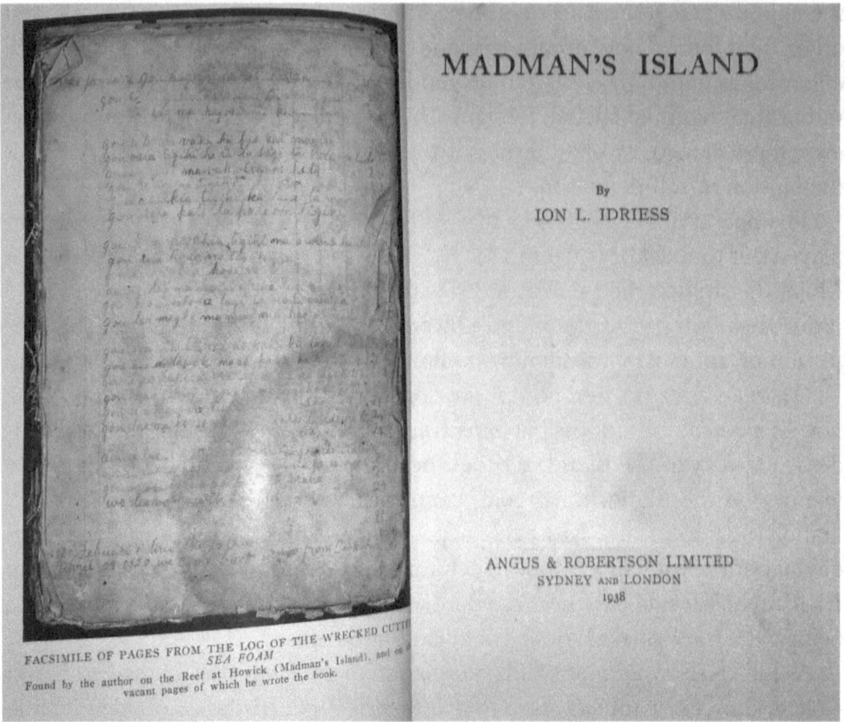
FACSIMILE OF PAGES FROM THE LOG OF THE WRECKED CUTT
SEA FOAM
Found by the author on the Reef at Howick (Madman's Island), and on
vacant pages of which he wrote the book.

MADMAN'S ISLAND

By
ION L. IDRIESS

ANGUS & ROBERTSON LIMITED
SYDNEY AND LONDON
1938

**Figure 4.2** Inside front cover of the 1938 edition of *Madman's Island* by Ion Idriess showing his writing of the text on a ship's log book he found while in hiding on Howick Island. Courtesy the publishers ETT Imprint, Sydney.

in the 1938 version. The 1927 novel follows the fortunes of Jack Burnet who embarks on a tin prospecting venture with a friend to an uninhabited island in the Barrier Reef. Not long after the pair arrives, the friend develops or exhibits a homicidal mania, and Jack has to flee and live in the mangrove swamp until he is eventually rescued. He then embarks on a brief life of crime, only to see the error of his ways and take up with an exemplary young woman.

While it would be heavy-handed to frame *Madman's Island* through Kristevan theory, Idriess's novel does play out, ironically or otherwise, the impossibility of an equal pair of men on the island. There is room for one only, and in this story, based as it is on Idriess's direct experience, the one who rules is the despot. As the island experience is, in part, responsible for his onset of madness, the novel serves as a salutary lesson against the delusion of aligning the self with geography. In any case, the island will always refuse this attempt at identification. As Deleuze argues, the impossibility of becoming one with the island is experienced as a rejection from the island itself. The failure to 'give the island a dynamic image of itself" – a unity of geography and imagination – is necessary, Deleuze argues, to the preservation of the island's perfection. By remaining separate from the human, the island is preserved from self-consciousness and dependency (Deleuze 2004, 10–11).

This is the precise dilemma that confronts Mac Hope in Thea Astley's 'The Genteel Poverty Bus Company', one of the two novellas that comprise her *Vanishing Points* (1992).[12] Mac retreats from the mainland Gulf country to Little Brother Island, with which he identifies and 'embrace[s] whole'. In a further nesting impulse, he then constructs a maze to protect the core of the island, which is, in effect, another mirror of himself within the larger mirror of the island. When he is eventually evicted from the island, the island is impervious to him:

> It gave nothing back. Nothing. It remained floating above the sea, tiny, perfect and unknowable, indifferent to the tearing he felt in the heart of him. 'I love you,' he said to the island. Its perfection remained unmoved. (Astley 1992, 121)

The dangers of insular self-sovereignty are evident in the many actual stories of lone dwellers on Australian islands. In 2010 the Queensland state government reclaimed for national parkland most of Middle Percy Island, described as 'a Robinson Crusoe island rising from the indigo depths of the Coral Sea' located 70 nautical miles off the central Queensland coast (Robson 2012). The island had been mired in a dispute about ownership involving the reclusive Andy Martin, an eccentric, Eton-educated Englishman who represented England in the 1948 Olympics and who bought the island lease in 1964. The lease had been intended for a group of utopianists, but the group quarrelled. Martin, dubbed 'Lord Percy', lived on the island until 1996, a period when the island was known as a safe haven for sailors; Martin had even constructed a large open A-frame shelter for passing sailors. In 1996, however, after years of increasing obsession, Martin returned to England in a state of religious mania in a bid to save his motherland from damnation. He had become a follower of British Israelism, which espoused the direct antecedence of white races, especially the British, from the Ten Lost Tribes of Israel and subscribed to the millenarian prophecies of their return.

Martin revised his self-understanding from prophet to infidel when his own prediction of Princess Diana's resurrection was not fulfilled. Martin's niece told Frank Robson that her uncle had visited Diana's burial place, an island in an ornamental lake at her family home, on the day of the British Israelite Feast of the Trumpets and there made the connection between the burial island, Middle Percy Island and the islands of prophecy (Robson 2012). In his desire to align these narratives – self, race, state and geography – he had planned for the risen Princess and her children to live with him on Middle Percy Island which he also called 'little England' (Robson 2012). In this royal connection, he performs a sad travesty of the monarch of all he surveyed.

It was while he was in this parlous and distressed condition that he was accosted by a Queensland man, Mick Cotter, who wanted the island for himself and he pressured Martin to sell him the lease, valued at $320,000, for $10.00. In response to criticisms about the subsequent decline of the island, Cotter replied: 'everybody thinks they own some part of this island. In fact they do not. I do. I own all of it' (Robson 2012). Like Mac Hope, he had embraced it whole. After seven years Cotter was forced to leave the island.

The battle for ownership of Middle Percy Island, while intense, merely exaggerates the dilemma posed by the fantasy of island possession as it is constructed by the illusion of a seamless concordance of self, state and place. At the heart of this perception is the contradiction that monadic isolation produces a subject who can be absorbed whole within the ideology of the state. Ironically, without the friction of otherness, of duality or multiplicity within the self and between the self and others, the subject is annihilated and becomes a shell of ideology. He cannot live with himself or others, only rule over them. In Lawrence's fable, the eponymous 'man who loves islands' imports minions to the first island he owns in order to be their 'Master'. As the tale progresses, however, even this semblance of human contact is rejected for complete isolation. Ultimately the only challenge to his will to isolation is posed by nature, which he cannot command.

As discussed in Chapter 1, there is no direct female equivalent to the male Robinsonade mainly because there is no perceived equivalence between the female subject and the island. There are Australian castaway stories that include female characters, but they are all written by men, underscoring the gendered structure of this imaginary. The 'female Robinsonade' operates quite differently in that the women are generally not alone, and their stories are commonly framed by romance conventions, which, by definition, involve more than one person. There are numerous such cases in the Australian archive. An issue of the *Australian Journal* in 1883 includes a short story by W. C. Fulton titled 'How It Ended', in which a young man rescues two young women who have been marooned on an island. He falls in love with one, who rejects him, but the pair meet again in the course of their normal lives and unite (Fulton 1883). A more controversial narrative was offered by Norman Lindsay in 1932 in his comic novel *The Cautious Amorist*, which was banned by the Australian Customs Department, though freely sold in Britain and the United States ('Novel Banned' 1934, 9). The novel tells the story of four survivors from a cruise ship who are marooned on a desert island: three men and one woman, making it more of an ensemble piece than a conventional castaway narrative. Two of the men make a play for the woman, but she falls for the third (of course), but he refuses her. The four are eventually rescued, but the romantic couple is shipwrecked again on the same island, this time on their own. The novel was adapted for film by Renown Film Productions (UK) in 1954 with a star-studded cast including Joan Collins, Kenneth More, George Cole and with Peter Sellers doing the voice of the island parrot. The film was shot in Britain and Majorca (see Figure 4.3).

There are, however, texts centred on, or projected onto, female characters that deploy aspects of the male island castaway *topos*, generally to irresoluble effect. One such story is 'The Castaway of the Barrier' by David G. Falk, published in the December 1889 edition of *Centennial Magazine* and developed into a novel published in 1896. The story is set in the Barrier Reef islands and focuses on the heroine Jess's encounter with a French castaway, who is revealed to be an escaped convict. Rivalling this first – and impossible – romantic attachment is Jess's relationship with the islands themselves, which ultimately retain their hold. She allows her castaway lover to escape but will not allow him to stay and she will not leave. Like Mac Hope in Astley's novella, Jess loves the islands. Jess's particular self-containment – a figure of her ultimate aloneness or self-transitivity – is shown in a scene of ascent and panoramic survey early in the story. After a long and ecstatic description of the sea and islands, we read a version of the monarchical possession:

> Jess looked long and silently at this marvelous scene, shifting her gaze from point to point of the vast rocky panorama, taking in its grandeur with her whole soul. It was a scene long familiar to her and one she never tired of. She knew it so well, she loved it so dearly. It seemed somehow to belong to her alone: there was none other who shared her delight of possession. (Falk 1889, 330)

Jess's gaze is a textbook exemplar of colonial, monarchical possession. The reader has earlier been told of her loneliness and her desire for company and experience, but we nevertheless recognize this scene of panoramic mastery as a form of perfect reflexivity between the human subject and the island landscape. Despite the strong draw of the romantic plot, there is no room for a third party here. The alignment between Jess and the island is reinforced by the unnaturalness of her human family: her mother is dead and her father is rough and unloving. She is instead 'a child of the bush and the sea; they had formed her kingdom' (Falk 1889, 329). She has been made by the island itself, is one with it. From the opening description of Jess she blends into the landscape in such a way that all her distinguishing details and flaws are 'lost in the bright harmony of the picture she made' with her island home (Falk 1889, 328).

**Figure 4.3** Joan Collins in *Our Girl Friday* (Twentieth Century Fox, 1953), an adaptation of *The Cautious Amorist* by Norman Lindsay. Courtesy Photofestnyc.

Tom Shapcott's novel of a female castaway, *Theatre of Darkness* (1998), also plays with the gendered conventions of the genre. Based on historical events, the novel narrates the plight of the American opera diva, Lillian Nordica, whose boat crashed onto coral reef in the Torres Strait on her return voyage from Australia to the United States in 1913. Nordica suffered hyperthermia in the incident and did not ever fully recover. She spent some months on Thursday Island in the aim of recovering her health and did eventually travel on to Batavia (Jakarta) but died there. Shapcott's novel is an intense study of interiority, befitting an insular narrative, and stages the interplay of external and masterful performances of the operatic voice, internal voices and silence. The theatres of life and of performance retreat to the 'theatre of the mind' as Nordica learns the island wisdom of 'passivity' (Shapcott 1998, 23), of allowing the self to be acted on rather than 'acting out' – the latter process understood in Freud's sense of a subject's defensive, often anti-social behaviour by which she or he unconsciously dramatizes the past in a symbolic way in order not to remember it. In *Theatre of Darkness* Thursday Island is the site of an enforced sojourn by which the central character, a performer defined by the public sphere, redresses the disequilibrium by which her exterior self has distracted her from the self-knowledge of her interiority. The island is both site and figure of this interiority and where her former tyrannies are crystallized.

Historically, women have been of greater interest when their marooned status means they are the European focus in first contact narratives, as with the legendary 'white woman of Gippsland', and in the island context Eliza Frazer and Barbara Crawford Thompson. Earlier than these women, the restrained deposition of American Elizabeth Morey made the front page of the *Sydney Gazette* in 1804 (Hughes 1999, 45). Morey spent two years on Tongatapu, from 1802 to 1804; the ship she was travelling in was attacked after reaching the island. She was the only European survivor. Local knowledge and oral history indicate that Elizabeth had three children to Chief Teukava of Kolovai (Hughes 1999, 50). Although she was 'rescued' in 1804, it would also appear that she freely and deliberately elected to leave Port Jackson and return to Tonga in 1805 (Hughes 1999, 54).

Morey's reserved account of her experiences and her disappearance from Sydney contributed to her almost fading from view. There is one fictional account, 'The Adventure of Elizabeth Morey, of New York', which presents the story as Elizabeth's kidnap and captivity by the Tongans (Becke and Jeffrey 1901). Later incidences of shipwrecked women, Eliza Frazer and Barbara Crawford Thomson, repeat and amplify this construction. In the narrativization of these events, the woman is most often cast as representative of European civilization itself, her fate being the subject of prurient fascination and used as a justification for the colonizing mission as well as violence against Indigenous peoples in the aim of 'recovery' of a vulnerable whiteness. Fraser was a survivor of the ship *Stirling Castle*, which was wrecked in a storm, 800 kilometers off the coast of what is now Queensland in 1836. After four weeks in a leaky lifeboat with few provisions, they landed on (what was subsequently named) Fraser Island. Her stay on the island lasted 52 days during which time her husband was killed. She was rescued by either one or two escaped convicts. As Kay Schaffer summarizes, she then married another sea captain, returned to England, and lived off her notoriety until she pushed her luck too far once too often and was accused of being a fraud. The last record of a woman purporting to be Eliza Frazer of the Stirling Castle is from a sideshow attraction in Hyde Park in the late 1830s (Schaffer 1998, 8), though her recorded date of death is, with no certainty, given as 1848. In any case, the whole 'adventure' did not last long, and in many ways it is not as remarkable as other similar narratives such as that Barbara Crawford Thomson. However, the particular configuration of elements – shipwreck, island castaway, a white woman amongst Aboriginal people, but also her return to England and her manipulation of identity and veracity – became the stuff of colonial legend as well as the site onto which a range of texts have sought to address and redress colonial history and historiography.

The discursive history of Eliza Frazer, including its many fictional treatments, has been comprehensively documented by Kay Schaffer as an indicative 'first contact' narrative. Such narratives provided the means of appropriating Indigenous people into western structures of meaning and interpretation. Schaffer also identifies the ways this racial agenda intersected with the shoring up of Victorian conceptions of gender and class. The evident distance between Mrs Frazer's actual background and circumstances and her self-representation as a lady affronted serves to expose the multiple operations at work. This discrepancy is not unusual in itself and was a common enough practice used by men: William Dampier successfully transformed himself from an unscrupulous buccaneer to a gentleman adventurer in exactly this way, and generations of Australian school children (including this author) learned of him some centuries later in the precise terms of his own fabrication. However, there is a greater expectation for women's lives to accord with their words, and female celebrities then as now were, in themselves, metonymic of discursive circulation and fame (McMahon 2005, 174). It is this expectation and its inevitable registration of disparity that accords to these female narratives a particular mobility. It also promotes questions that may result in emphatic acclamations that cover over doubt but may also call the reader to investigate the story.

A short story by Darwin-based writer Marie Munkara titled 'The Castaways' (2009) achieves, in relative brevity, a thoroughgoing riposte to the conventions of shipwreck and castaway narratives framed within imperial and colonial structures, anxieties and ambitions. The story is from her first collection of short fiction, *Every Secret Thing*, set in the Tiwi Islands, 80 kilometers north of Darwin where the Arafura Sea joins the Timor Sea, returning us to the overcrowded scenes of castaways in the convict escape story that prefaces the chapter. 'The Castaways' opens with Brother Angus from the 'mission mob' going on a fishing trip with Caleb from the 'bush mob'. However, word has spread about the trip and numerous others join the party, and eventually the truck is impossibly overcrowded with people inside and out and on top, like a scene from the Marx Brothers. When they arrive Brother Angus 'gazes at the beautiful white beach where no other murantani [non-Indigenous person/outsider] had set their clean white shoeless feet before' (Munkara 2009, 129). However, the fantasy of making the first imprint of a white man is quickly dispelled by the sight of a damaged yacht, indicating a rough trip over the reef and possibly injured castaways:

> 'Might be lost or something,' volunteered Lazarus.
>
> They'd certainly never seen anything like it. Nor had Brother Angus seen anything like the two naked murantani locked in the throes of noisy passion, totally oblivious to their audience. The woman was the first to notice the spectators and, shoving the poor bloke off without any warning, rushed to embrace and frantically kiss the mortified Brother Angus. (Munkara 2009, 130)

The gaze is multiply displaced in this scene. First, Brother Angus's gaze upon his fantasy of an uninhabited island paradise is disrupted. Not only is he accompanied by numerous inhabitants of the island but other murantani have preceded him to this very location. This initial de-rangement of expectation and prerogative is followed by an Ur-reversal of the castaway's imperial gaze; the islanders gaze upon the 'castaways' who are exposed in their act of noisy passion, ironically reframing that most famous scene of island passion in *From Here to Eternity* (Zinnemann 1953). This is the first step that enables connection between the castaways and the islanders. The second is when the castaways share their 'strange-smelling, weedy-looking tobacco' (Munkara 2009, 131) with some of the bush mob, even harvesting seeds for one of the men who grows a crop of marijuana on the island. This relationship of shared pleasure also eclipses the eye of the law, thereby undoing another prerogative of the colonial gaze.

The narrative continues to build more levels of connection until a baby is born to Odile, the female castaway. As the baby arrives prematurely there is no chance for Odile to reach the mainland hospital, with the result that 'she had to put up with what the bush mob had to put up with'. The baby is born with a 'tiny woolly head and little black eyes' and 'deep honey-coloured skin' – features very unlike those of Odile or Jean-Claude, her white partner and the presumed father until this point (Munkara 2009, 137). Finally, when the baby dies, Odile 'experienced the extreme sadness that the bush mob had already been through with the loss of their children' and they comfort her (Munkara 2009, 138).

The announcement of the pregnancy in the narrative implicitly refers the reader back to back to the early scene of the murantani having sex on the beach. Initially, the imminent birth of the baby appears to be a kind of narrative corollary in a chain that links the beginning and the end of the story. However, just as that original sex act was interrupted, the story's lines of cause and effect are broken. The teleological trajectory of the gaze is proven wrong. Moreover, the actual sex act that produced the child is not recorded, alerting the reader too late that there are other stories in the shadow of the one before us, ones that evade the gaze completely.

With an overdetermined clarity, the story extinguishes the gaze of the murantani through a series of spectatorial jokes that deflect attention like a magician's trick: the overcrowded van, the beach sex scene, the shared smoking sessions. As Freud observes, jokes enable us to bypass the censor regarding strong affects and drives. In this instance these include unwritten sexual experience but also, and uncomically, colonial history and the removal of children who could 'pass' from their Aboriginal families. The initial 'joke' of the reversed gaze reaches its endpoint in shared grief. The colonial gaze that connects vision, desire, possession and meaning – the prerogative of the 'monarch of all I survey' – is systematically undone in Munkara's story.

'The Castaways' deals with religious colonization on the islands with good humour and a steely eye. The mission on the island is mainly depicted as a social structure, and its theology is not the focus. The kindly portrayal of Brother Angus understands his personal predilection for solitude, but the world of 'Every Little Thing' pays short shrift to the sacralized conception of celibate clerical life, as the opening sex scene clearly shows. But 'The Castaways' certainly raises questions about the fidelity of continuance in its reminders of the forced removal of Aboriginal children, as indeed Munkara herself experienced as a child. This question reframes the island's elision of the maternal in conventional castaway stories and the conventional metaphorics of unnatural birth into the unnatural process on this Tiwi island where birth brings grief and death. Munkara's story takes the 'island' of the Western imaginary into an island of actual inhabitation to show the indivisibility of these spaces in history and representation.

# Chapter 5

# THE BEST AND WORST OF TIMES: UTOPIAS, DYSTOPIAS, ARCHIPELAGOS

Five hundred years ago Thomas More wrote his *Utopia*, a text about an ideal society (see Figure 5.1). One of the first things King Utopos undertakes in the construction of Utopia is the building of a trench that insulates Utopia from the surrounding world to make it an island. Reasons for this insular containment are provided within the narrative, and more still become apparent from the analysis of its operations, which we can see repeated across utopian fiction and its numerous posterities within speculative imaginaries. For as Fredric Jameson observes, *Utopia* is one of those rare texts that 'inaugurates a whole new genre' (1977, 4).

One of the truisms of utopian fiction is its inevitable invocation of its dystopian opposite. Readers or viewers of fictions of ideal islands know that the patina of perfection only disguises the lurking menace that lies waiting for the hapless visitors, castaways and planetary explorers dazzled by its allure.[1] The artificiality of this carapace is especially apparent in outmoded science fiction films and television series, where the time lag accentuates the cultural specificity of the nominated priorities of greatest human need and value presented as essential in an ideal world. However, if truth be told, elements of utopian artificiality were always apparent in these texts. Even at the time of their release, film and televisual depictions of these perfect worlds seemed unconvincing, but this half-recognition was easily displaced onto the medium of representation. Somehow, it was the televisual deficiency that compromised the reality of perfection. The screen itself was the patina that complicated assessment regarding what was always in plain view – the necessarily imperfect condition of all utopias.

Louis Marin's theorization of utopian texts, followed by Jameson's detailed explications of Marin and his own work on the genre over decades, accounts for this relationship between utopian and dystopian elements and the hypervisibility of their internal and mutual contradictions. These formulations and reading practices have far-reaching implications for reading island fiction

**Figure 5.1** Cover of the first edition of Thomas More's *Utopia* (1516). Courtesy Ashmolean Museum.

including but also beyond those texts explicitly engaged with projections of ideality. Central to all the textual operations and reading practices put forward by both Utopian theorists is Marin's argument that utopian discourse is inherently figural rather than conceptual: He writes:

> Utopia is a discourse, but not a discourse of the concept. It is a discourse of the figure: a particular figurative mode of discourse. It is fiction, fable-construction,

> 'anthropomorphised' narratives, concrete descriptions, exotic, novel, and pictorial representation, these are all of its nature. It is one of the regions of discourse centred on the imaginary and no matter how forceful or precise, how correct or coherent, are its theses, utopia will never become a concept. It will always stay wrapped in fiction and fable-making. (Marin 1984, 8)

Focusing on More's *Utopia*, Marin and, in turn, Jameson deploy Algirdas Greimas' semiotic square to identify three intrinsic structural contradictions within the utopian genre that are of direct, broader relevance to utopic islands and the representation of islands more generally.[2] The first concerns the opposition set up between utopian and dystopian qualities, which prove to be, ironically, interconnected. When we identify a possible flaw in a utopian world – for instance, the absence of labour might first seem ideal but on closer inspection may also be a means of denying the inhabitants motivation and satisfaction – we are led to consider the opposite scenario as a possible antidote. In the given instance, this would be the presence of labour, which, however fruitful, diminishes freedom. Both sides of the binary have some merit though not necessarily in equal measure. Further, as this example reveals, the relationship between utopia and dystopia is not a simple binary but a doubled system of negatives in that each oppositional term is inherently contradictory in and of itself as well as contradicting its putative opposite. In the example of labour, a utopia of no work contains the internal negative of pointless leisure and the opposite ideal of productive labour contains the internal negative of slavery and inequality. Hence we do not have two contested concepts but four, which, in Marin's formulation, produce an effect of neutralization or cancellation.

This neutralization process is clarified by a comparison with the operation of what Levi-Strauss identified as the founding mediation of myth between (cultural) infrastructure and (cosmological) superstructure (Jameson 1977, 4). Taking the myth of Eos, I illustrate this point. Eos (Aurora or the Dawn) successfully bids for the immortality of her human lover Tithonus but, as she forgets to ask for eternal youth, she unwittingly condemns him to an endless senescence. The myth thus opposes life and death, eternal becoming (the dawn) against the eternal twilight of dying in the incommensurability of the relationship between human and divine operations. The tale compels the reader or listener to deliberate the distinction between death *in* life and as an end *to* life, between the gift and curse of Dawn's endless renewal and of death's singular finality. The reader creates a mental assemblage of the various qualities to produce a resolution, including the benefits of timely death even in the face of ongoing dreams of eternal life, and the dangers of trying to overreach the constraints of the different orders of life and death.

Utopian fictions, however, do not produce this resolution or complexity because the structure of contradictory opposites works to cancel out all propositions as viable alternatives, let alone (re)solutions (Jameson 1977, 4–5). Further, the cancellation of each alternative is endless as the reader or viewer entertains each possibility only to dismiss it and move on to another, which also proves unsatisfactory. For Marin, this reading process *is* the structure of utopian fiction. He writes:

> Utopic discourse occupies the empty – historically empty – place of the historical resolution of a contradiction. It is the degree zero of the dialectical synthesis of contraries. It edges its ways in between the contraries and thus in the discursive expression of the *neutral* (defined as neither one nor the other of the contraries). (Marin 1984, xiii)

Utopia, bounded as an island, and which appears to be an object we can obtain, is, of course, designated by nomenclature as 'No-place', a cancelled space. The reader is not meant to be persuaded by the clunky perfection offered by the island utopia, as any viewer of *Star Trek* or *Blake's 7* senses, even if they are distracted and seduced into misrecognition. The utopian text is characterized by elaborate descriptions of the ideology and practices of a bounded state (island or planet), and these insistent boundaries direct the reader to look to the *mise en scène* for meaning, imitating Utopia's own exclusion of the outside world. However, the meaning of the utopian text actually resides in 'no place', for it is a process rather than an object of knowledge; it is the reader's relentless practice of deliberation and cancellation of each possibility of ideality or deficiency the text presents.

The identification of Utopia's 'no place' as a process rather than a bounded space provides a way of undoing the object status of islands in and beyond the context of utopian genres. The cancellation of Utopia's constructed ideality may enable the identification of what is imagined to be the island's intrinsic ideality, which, of course, is why it is the perfect textual space for utopian speculation in the first place. The figuration of island ideality as a homeland for imaginative creativity enables reflective contemplation and invention as we see from the *Odyssey* to *The Tempest* to Gregory Day's 2015 novel, *Archipelago of Souls*. However, this understanding may be coincident with the raft of related desires, such as colonial possession, that have been the focus of this book. In this more problematic cast, the perception of islands as trinkets for acquisition or as natural prisons and the inevitable reflexivity of that binary can only produce variations of stasis and stagnation. The relationship between the island and the Utopian text remobilizes the island in time and space by locating processual and futural possibilities as qualities always-already within the very heart of dominant and limiting island imaginaries. In modernity this utopian and futural potential has been obscured by colonial desire. Within the Western imaginary where, as Yi-Fu Tuan notes, this conception of islands has the strongest hold (1998, 118), the viewer is like an ancient sailor drawn in by the sirens, for they have been 'taken in' by the island's allure as a site of fantasy and, in seeming contradiction, by its metafigural capacity to embody materiality itself: the perfect spatial commodity. Re-viewing the island as a utopian No-place displaces and re-places both the gazing subject and the island object into a shifting dynamic, which may include the inversion of subject-object positions within the spectrum of permutations.

As the spatial commodity fetish, the island also figures what Michael Taussig terms 'State fetishism', providing another inflection of the island state or imaginary commonwealth. For Taussig, the state fetishist, including the social anthropologist of Australian tribal fetishism, Emile Durkheim (1858–1917) the proper national citizen and perhaps Hythloday in More's *Utopia*, gazes upon the state whose aura holds them in thrall. This aura, and the perennial distances it creates, obscures all labour, whether this is the labour of the working class in state capitalism, according to Marx, and which we find as a burgeoning dilemma in More's text, or the labour of narratives by which the ideology of the state is rendered coherent and appears whole and bounded (Taussig 1993, 227–28; Livett 2006, 40). The citizens of the modern nation state thus hold the (hidden) Figure of the State in awe in the same way as tribal cultures hold the secreted fetish object of the gods. Viewed in this way, the island of Utopia persuades us of the objective material reality of the State, as Philip Steinberg has argued regarding the perception of islands (2005), at the same time as it shows us it is no-place.

In ostensible opposition to this elusive no-place, the second quality of utopian fiction identified by Marin and Jameson, relevant to the representation of islands, pertains to the role of the historical 'Real' in constructing the text's meaning. Jameson claims that the topical allusions and footnotes in utopian fiction are not extraneous addenda but are 'structurally indispensable in the constitution of the utopian text' and mark its distinction from its 'generic neighbours of fantasy or idyll' (1977, 7). Some twenty-first century readers may be less than enthralled by footnotes that explain the link between a fictional character in More's text and a historical personage. These links are, after all, 500 years old and far removed from the twenty-first century context. In this deflection, however, the reader is again enticed into turning away from what is in plain view, for the footnotes are as necessary now as they were in 1516 in their function of introducing the facticity of the real, the historical context of the text's present time, into the neutralization process.

The dialogue between text and context, set up by the topical allusions, denies the borders of the island text, which initially appear as absolute as the trench built by King Utopos, to enter into history. In relation to the wider issue of the representation of islands, Marin's and Jameson's arguments direct the reader's attention to the seemingly extraneous details of context provided by the fictional text and the ways they construct the relationship between fact and fiction, figure and ground, in the utopian reading process of neutralization. These external references disrupt the borders of the text's pronounced self-coherence. Further, the reader necessarily considers debates in relation to their own experience and historical moment, thereby implicating the reader her/himself and the time of reading in the process of deliberation and neutralization.

The third defining property of utopian fiction of relevance to the current discussion is its uneven relationship between narrative and description. Whereas the utopian place is reached through travel, a conventional structure of narrative progression, as discussed in the previous chapter, the utopian world itself is generally represented by extensive description. It is static because action would compromise its order. Indeed, the arrival of the visitor may itself be the action that sets in train its destabilization. It is static and descriptive also because it must hide the labour of its constitutive narratives to maintain its aura. Hence, description attempts to absorb narrative in the utopian text but, as both Marin and Jameson claim, it does not do so completely, and the residue or imbalance leads us to a range of internal inconsistencies in the text's account of its social structures, political organization and economic systems. In More's *Utopia* these include, inter alia, the presence of an island centre and a prince in what is supposed to be a federation of equal states, and the status of the market-place, which is discussed in one section of the text but absent in another. These contradictions are not clumsy errors on More's part but point to meaningful *aporia*. For Marin and Jameson the absence of the market-place indicates an epistemic blind spot, namely the 'notion of capitalism itself' (Jameson 1977, 18) which is emergent but has not yet taken form in 1516. Marin thus identifies the anticipatory property of utopian fiction, which is only evident in hindsight (Marin 1984, 269; Jameson 1977, 18). This viewing platform is also enabling for reading island fictions more generally as we look back to narratives of the past to identify the germ of ideas, ideologies and practices that continue to play out in our own time, again disrupting the perception of the island's circumscribed borders and its ahistoricity.

Historical and fictional islands lie in the long shadow of desire as it commonly attaches to tropical and desert islands. Ironically, however, this static fantasy becomes mobilized when it is read through the dialectics of utopian reading practice, as these are identified by Marin and Jameson. The ensuing discussion will negotiate this contradiction by accepting the textual invitation to view the island in its bounded materiality as either ideal or site of horror and then undo this construction through a utopian ethics of reading. This process begins with a consideration of island fetishism through a range of theorists.[3] Island objects and fictions will be viewed as commodity fetishes as understood by the related theses of Marx, Benjamin and Taussig, all of which begin from the assumption of the figurative, rather than conceptual, nature of fetishism, which Marin argues is the operation of Utopia. These will then be examined in relation to theories and practices of defetishization, including the germ of the future that Jameson identifies in utopian texts when they are viewed in retrospection. Ultimately, I want to argue that the complication of the island imaginary through these modes of reading identifies mobility and futurity within real and imaginary islands in the very heart of what is imaged as their bounded stasis.

## Bounded Island Fetishism

In both history and representation islands show us the economy between aurified and nonaurified spaces in that they are simultaneously the most fetishized and the most discarded of sites. Once favoured in the Age of Discovery as perfect sites for colonies, small islands have been left behind in the continental power of late modernity (Gillis 2004, 124; McMahon 2012). Just as they performed the role of stepping stones across the Atlantic in the Age of Sail, they have been cast as the stepping stones into the future of a modernity to which they themselves have little access. They are part of capitalism's collateral damage: facing inundation from rising oceans, economically disadvantaged and decreasing in population. In the discourse of commodity fetishism, the exchange value of islands has been reduced to zero and they have become another of the disposable objects of capitalism. Simultaneously, they fulfil the role that Althusser, following Marx, identified as capitalism's illusion of escape built within the value of wages – in this case, the island getaway (Althusser 2014, 50). So, too, as we discussed in the previous chapter, the island is a precious object: a hypostatisation of the desire for singular, bounded objects of possession. Islands are, accordingly, fetish objects according to the related formulations of Marx (commodity fetishism), Benjamin (the aura of the object in industrial modernity) and Taussig's State fetishism. The relationship between this compound figure of desire and its evacuated antithesis constructs the primary binary opposition of the island's utopian operation as it shifts from paradisal jewel to bounded prison-house.

Following Marx, Benjamin's identification of the aura attached to fetishized objects stresses the necessity of distance to aurification (Hansen 2008, 339).

Distance defines the very condition of desire, which is inherently anticipatory, and it also obscures the labour of creative work, such as the individual brushstrokes in a painting. Aura and distance are properties of islands perceived through the acquisitional gaze. In this imaginary they are seen from afar, and must remain *always* afar, even when occupied, in order to sustain their aura. This desiring gaze habitually fetishizes islands as 'jewels' (McMahon 2001b, 115–16), as in the title and narrative drive of Robert Louis Stevenson's *Treasure Island* (1881–83) and in the ambiguous auras that surround the islands in Eliot Bliss's *Luminous Isle* (1934) and Phyllis Shand Allfrey's *The Orchid House* (1953), examined in Chapter 3. Islands continue to be viewed as commodity fetishes within globalized modernity, as we see in reported lists of celebrity island ownership (Ranker n.d.; Morrison n.d). One of these, titled '23 Celebrities Who Have Their Own Private Islands', includes businessman Richard Branson, who bought Necker Island in the British Virgin Islands in 1978. Branson describes it elsewhere as the 'brightest jewel I've ever found' (*Telegraph* 2002, 20).

In colonial accounts, Tasmania, which is perennially distant for boreal gaze, is often cast as a jewel relative to other imperial trinkets such as Ireland and Ceylon. In *his Travels under the Southern Cross*, American writer Maturin Ballou makes such a comparison: 'As Ceylon is called the pearl of India so Tasmania may justly be called the jewel of Australia' (Ballou 1892, 252), a view shared by Scottish novelist Hume Nisbet but with an edge:

> Tasmania is about one-sixth part smaller than Ireland, and a little larger than Ceylon. I don't know why Ireland and Ceylon should be clubbed together by way of comparing size, unless it be that both islands are considered to be gems in some way, Ireland as the Emerald of Britain and Ceylon as the Pearl of India. Tasmania may be termed the Ruby of Australia in commemoration of the blood that has been shed there in past times, now it is as sleepy as a cat gorged with mice. (1896 270–71)

Nisbet's repulsive metaphorics effectively defetishize the island jewel by questioning and unpacking the figure of the island jewel itself, which he replaces with the gorged cat – an image befitting a writer of thrillers.[4]

Hal Porter continues the critique of the Tasmanian jewel metaphor in his historical novel about the transported forger and poisoner Thomas Wainwright, *The Tilted Cross*, which opens with a description of Van Diemen's Land as 'an ugly trinket suspended at the world's discredited rump' (1961, 9). No alluring shine here. As the opening statement of the text, the text's deflation of the jewel metaphor establishes the narrative's perspective as one immersed in the actual conditions of the island, as being close up, *in* the island rather than distant. Porter, like Nisbet, destroys the aura of the island jewel by telescoping in on the details of Tasmania's history including the unfree labour by which it was established.

Tasmania retains traces of its depiction as a faraway island jewel in its enduring self-representation as a miniaturized object, which can be read as encapsulating the historical and current dilemma of desire, distance, commodification and possession. While the continental mainland tends toward giganticization (the Big Banana at Coffs Harbour, the Big Merino at Goulburn, the Big Pineapple on the Sunshine Coast, the Big Lobster in Kingston, South Australia), Tasmania represents itself through myriad forms of miniaturization. One of the most legible of these traces is the proliferation of miniature 'model' villages for tourists.[5] In one sense, a miniaturized world is always an island. Indeed, as Susan Stewart attests, it cannot be otherwise because '[t]he miniature world remains perfect and uncontaminated by the grotesque [only] so long as absolute boundaries are maintained' (1993, 68) – as King Utopos understands. Like islands, miniatures operate as the representation of distance that is the space of desire and longing. Gaston Bachelard writes:

> Distance, too, creates miniatures at all points on the horizon, and the dreamer, faced with these spectacles of distinct nature, picks out these miniatures as so many texts of solitude in which he dreams of living. (1994, 172)

Miniatures, including the perception of small islands as miniatures in accordance with their horizontal scale, are sites of such speculation and dreams of shelter where, as discussed in Chapter 2 when Charles O'Hara Booth, commandant of convicts at the Port Arthur penal colony (1833–39), looks out from the coast of Port Arthur to a small island in the distance and longs to settle there with a 'good tempered little partner' (1981, 221).

Miniatures draw the viewer in closer and closer. However, distance does not diminish with proximity because of the confusion of scale between viewer and miniature object. This allure is integral to the discourse of miniature villages, which coaxes the viewer to observe the scene with more attention and in greater detail: 'Can you see the man being bitten by a snake?' asks Old Hobart model village in Richmond Tasmania. 'Can you see the famous person who lives in the cottage?' asks The Tudor Court Village in Tasmania's Huon Valley (McMahon 2001, 81–83). The miniature's perfection resides in its absolute materiality as a bounded object yet its capacity to retain the distance of desire. For peer as we might we cannot enter into the miniature world because we are, like Gulliver in Lilliput, too large.[6]

These 'model' worlds simultaneously avow and deny labour in multiple ways – the simultaneous and paradoxical movement that characterizes fetishism (Freud 1905). The term 'model village', though referring to the

**Figure 5.2** Miniature World in the hothouse of the Royal Tasmanian Botanical Garden, Hobart, during World War II. Courtesy Archives Office of Tasmania.

twentieth-century practice of building miniature replicas,[7] is also the homonym for villages built by industrialists and landowners to house workers from the late eighteenth century, often nearby the workers' site of labour (Darley 1975; Burchardt 2002, 58*ff.*). Tasmania's island boundedness, which sees it lauded as an idyll and used as a prison, is a readymade model on these terms, as we see also in its adoption of Bentham's 'model prison' at the Port Arthur penal settlement in 1853. The shared status as modern-day tourist sites of historical interest links model villages and Port Arthur's model prison and reveals the dual operations of industrial capitalism and biopower which mark the origins of modern Tasmania.

The model village's affirmation of labour is evident also in the choice of depicted scenes. The villages are resolutely bounded in a space and time prior to industrialized labour and are, hence, ostensibly removed from the economies of the present, though they usually charge admission fees. The village layout is organized around the artisanal roles of its inhabitants: baker, blacksmith, butcher, etc. The Mole Hill Fantasy at Launceston comprises *tableau vivant* of humanized moles going about their daily work. Indeed the very title suggests industriousness by dint of the collective term 'a labour of moles'.[8]

Where the moles may pertain to a perceived seasonal cycle of labour, even if the seasons accord with Britain rather than Tasmania, Old Hobart Town is built around the historical foundation of Hobart including the unfree convict labour used in the project. However, the explicit narratives of active work and history are leached of action in the miniature scene just as the dystopian elements of the penal colony are rendered charming in their proportions as children's toys. Although historical commemoration is the explicit intention of the Old Hobart site, brutality is minimized and fetishized by its miniaturization. Conversely, the incursion of violent historical content could be understood as an admission of the grotesque and the monumental into the model village, compromising the very terms of its construction and undermining its perfect materiality. The binary of (monumental and brutal) history and (miniaturized and charming) representation become interconnected, though this is more in the order of paradox than neutralization in this instance. It is, nevertheless, a function of the island boundedness that is the shadowy containment of all such late modern tourism in Tasmania.

The model villages also include a form of metacommentary or addenda about labour that is essential to the operations of utopian neutralization by its referral to the world of the maker/author. The Mole Hill Fantasy at Launceston begins: 'Fifteen months and hundreds of hours were spent in constructing the Mole Hill searching the bush for twisted roots and branches to make the caves look realistic, and to make the furniture' (Staines, n.d). Old Hobart Town model village writes: 'This unique Historical Model Village is a result of 3 years full time work by John and Andrew Quick' (Old Hobart Town). The model Village of Lower Crackpot at Tasmazia, located at Promised Land in Tasmania's north west, includes a dedication regarding work:

> The village is dedicated to all those in middle life who, in this new economic age, are adjusted out of their jobs, professions, businesses, farms, careers and thrown onto the economic scrap heap. (Tasmazia n.d.)

Seeming to explicitly describe capitalist conditions of economic production and their dumping outside the productive social space of value of that which no longer has either use or exchange value, this dedication emanates from a point of inexplicability – the reasons why mining operations or large companies suddenly pull out of Tasmania and make hundreds of workers redundant overnight. There is a foggy obscurity as to the real connections between the island State's internal economy and those of the broader Australian society.

The labour that is hidden through skill while also highlighted is vital to the miniature's claim to an authentic, artisanal labour of craft before mass production and before 'the new economic age' and the alienation of labour. Allegiance to the authenticity of artisanal labour and the correlation between the manufactured world and the real world is emphasized by the labour of scale, so that, for instance, Old Hobart Town was 'designed and built from actual historical plans' (Old Hobart n.d.). These metatexts constitute another form of invitation to view the exhibit more closely and direct the viewer to the world beyond the boundaries of the miniature world, in much the same way that Jameson argues is achieved by the historical footnotes in More's *Utopia.* They call the viewer to a mode of observation needed to undo the fetishized commodity and replace it with the *speculum superius* of the visionary and the primal longing for home, which we can never realize in our oversized belatedness.

## Working in the Island

When an island is bounded, letting no one in or out, and when it has the shine of the fetish, you cannot properly reach it. Proximity and domestication, however, destroy the aura of the island – as Robinson Crusoe discovers. Though, as Marx comments, Crusoe's labour is that of the modern 'independent man' who can control the terms of his labour (1867, Section 4). The appeal of the unreachable island, forever in the distance, has been noted in tourism studies where Tom Baum notes that island tourists often want to travel from the island they are on to another smaller island in the distance (1997, 210).

The experience of living on the fetish object, of being *in* the island, is that of immersed labour. As Derek Walcott writes:

> The Caribbean is not an idyll, not to its natives. They draw their working strength from it organically, like trees, like the sea almond or the spice laurel of the heights. Its peasantry and its fishermen are not there to be loved or even photographed; they are trees who sweat, and whose bark is filmed with salt. (1992a)

Indeed, to exist on an island that maintained its impermeability as a fetish would be to perish – unless one could afford the displaced labour of island resorts, as Jamaica Kincaid protests in *A Small Place* (1988) and which Robert Gray parodies in 'Malthusian Island' (1993, 31). Narrative and labour mobilize the island into time, as Crusoe's diary makes clear. Crusoe begins with the fantasy of the island of self, but the narrative must necessarily be the labour of the production of self and text, thereby effecting the defetishization of ego and island, at the same time as he refetishizes the island as its monarch and by Defoe's novel itself.

Ralph de Boissiere's novel *Crown Jewel* (1952), published by the leftist Australasian Book Society, is a narrative of the working class struggle in de Boissiere's home island of Trinidad. *Crown Jewel* defetishizes the trinket status of islands from the outset by the irony of the title and by the sharp delineation between the prologue and the main narrative. The prologue begins in 1498, the year Columbus claimed the island, and summarizes in under three pages the history of Western colonial acquisition of the island 'jewel' built on dispossession, slavery and indentured labour. The prologue concludes with a long, poetic paragraph describing the natural beauty of the island, and ends with the night sky: 'Then the stars, unveiled, would shine like those jewels in the El Dorado of dead men's dreaming' (de Boissiere 1981, 3). The next chapter, set in 1935, the present of the main narrative, begins overleaf and opens mid-action:

> They gripped the spokes of the two-wheeled timber cart and threw their bodies forward.
>
> Heave! … And again! … *And* again!'
>
> The flooring boards projected five feet front and rear. Grasping the boards with his massive hands, the helmsman struggled with an angry desperate look to balance the cart while steering it through the traffic according to the wheelman's shouted orders. (de Boissiere 1981, 4)

The sequence from the prologue to the main narrative juxtaposes the gazing apprehension of the island as fetish object with the experience of being *in* the island immersed in labour. This movement is from the description of 'timeless' island qualities to everyday activity and from the erased history of an unfree labour force to the centrality of daily work among free men. Ironically, key to these reversals is the author's distance. De Boissiere writes of his own writing practice that he preferred the perspective informed by temporal delay and hindsight rather than one immersed in the 'heat of the fray'. He believed that '[t]he writer has to analyse and think about the life around him to achieve some clarity about the social mess in which we live' (de Boissiere 1982, 6, 9). Specifically, he claims that the experience of viewing Trinidad from Australia shaped *Crown Jewel*. He writes that Australia's 'developing industry and highly developed trade union movement […] with strong militant traditions […] gave me a heightened appreciation of what West Indian workers were capable of achieving (de Boissiere 1982, 10). Paradoxically, distance enables him to immerse himself in the island and its racialized politics of labour. The gains and losses of this perspective were noted in the obituary for de Boissiere by

Nicholas Laughlin in *The Caribbean Review of Books* who noted that his novels 'portray Trinidad society in the 1930s and 40s with a vast historical scope and ambition very few West Indian writers have attempted' (2008). Further, Laughlin speculates:

> Had de Boissiere's major novels not been published by a small Australian press in the 1950s, had they not languished in relative obscurity until the 1980s, he might have been a major influence on two generations of West Indian writers and substantially changed the direction of West Indian literature. (2008)

Laughlin's lament can be understood in relation to the matter of the novel itself also. His gesture to de Boissiere's absence directs us to ramifications of dislocating the commodity object from the terms of its own labour, especially marked in the postcolonial context. De Boissiere's *Crown Jewel*, in its geographical and cultural alienation from the West Indian labour force that it speaks of, is rendered harmless in its capacity to galvanize the next generations of West Indians who, in reading it, would have had a tactile engagement with its descriptions of labour that were their own. This de-aurified presentation of the labour of the economic base is what Marx and Benjamin identify as one of the necessary conditions to revolution of the economic structure.

In the context of the Australian tradition, as David Carter has discussed, *Crown Jewel* is aligned to the most successful novels of Australian communism, Katherine-Susannah Prichard's *Working Bullocks* (1926) and Frank Hardy's *Power Without Glory* (1950) in that it is structured as a 'precommunist' story and includes documentary elements. Yet is also markedly different from its predecessors in its 'absolute lived understanding of the fine calibrations of race and colour as these cut across the boundaries of class' (Carter 2002, 102). While his influence on West Indian literature may have been delayed, de Boissiere's novels introduced new perspectives and politics into Australian literature, well beyond its imagined borders.

The novel ends with a complex conversation between two women, Aurelia and Miss Richards, regarding work and whether to leave Trinidad for New York at the time of the approaching War. It concludes:

> Neither of them had any suspicion of the enormous events that were unfolding in Europe and would soon overturn and refashion the life to which they and all Trinidad had so long been accustomed. (de Boissiere 1981, 361)

This retrospective prospection leaves the future open to world history, which the twenty-first century reader knows, but it does not shut down the futurity of class revolution. The significance of this endpoint is underscored by de

Boissiere's account of the War as a turning point in the history of Trinidad, which finally broke the hold of the colonial 'system' and effected a 'Revolution'. It was 'an enormous confrontation between old and new values that signalled the end of an era' (de Boissiere 1982, 4).

Compound layers of retrospection and memory also perform the work of island defetishization in Antigone Kefala's 1984 novella *The Island* (the unnamed north island of New Zealand), written decades after Kefala settled in Sydney. Here, too, the text disallows the gaze of distant longing but draws us into the island from the opening scene, which is also an account of daily work. The novel's young protagonist, Melina Pappa, a university student who has taken on her first holiday job, negotiates cross-cultural relationships and expectations and the striations of memories and losses shared by her family and other postwar immigrants from Europe. The novella thus splices this fragment of a *Künstleroman* – a form of progressive movement – with the retrospection of melancholy and mourning of earlier, irrecoverable lives, family and friends. In this way, the island of the title, which suggests the containment of event and experience, is rendered open-ended. The island becomes a site of transition, an interstitial zone where memories of Europe are more vivid than the present (Kefala 1984, 28) and where an imagined future is more compelling than present scenarios of potential becoming, such as that offered by the romance narrative. As with *Crown Jewel*, this temporal manipulation locates the island as a midpoint in space and time, positioned within the movement of lives, chronology and history. Also like *Crown Jewel*, this mobility is the result of forced and voluntary diaspora. Both novels refuse the boundaries of the island, which fend off incursion, by layers of racialized difference and ongoing migration.

The Wellington City setting of *The Island* and the narrative of a young woman's working life and cross-cultural negotiation recalls Patricia Grace's *Mutuwhenua* (The Moon Sleeps) (1978), which is directly concerned with island fetishism of a very different kind. At the centre of Grace's novel is a sacred object, a *pounamu patu* in Māori and a totem or fetish object in the discourse of Western anthropology. In *Mutuwhenua*, this object's circulation in the community of the heroine, Refika, inverts the operations of the island jewel as it is constructed in Western desire. In *Mutuwhenua*, Refika's family returns the discovered stone to 'far back in the hills', down in a deep gully (Grace 2004, 8), as it must be hidden. Refika reflects that she, herself, is like the stone and she is part of her community because of the shared sense of the 'rightness of what had been done to the stone' (Grace 2004, 9). The novel explicitly pits the sacred fetish against commodity fetishism and State fetishism in a scene where the family staunchly resists attempts to capitalize on the discovery of the precious stone.

*Mutuwhenua* is a narrative about home place and belonging. Although it recounts Refika's romance and marriage to a *Pakeha* (fair skinned or non-Mãori New Zealander) man, the drive of character and plot does not express any desire to move outside the island or away from family. It is, rather, a story where the *pounamu patu*, a literal jewel hidden in the island, orientates and coordinates the people it connects. The *pounamu patu* undoes the trajectory of the Western gaze on the island. It is, in one key sense, a realization of the nightmarish potential of the island idyll, for it is the hidden object of desire but one that sees the interlopers, protects the island against them and reflects back to them the destruction inherent in their fundamental misrecognition of the island's existing systems of connection.

Unlike Refika, who is grounded by her island home place, this history of Palm Island, located off the far north coast of Queensland in the Great Barrier Reef, is a story of the *Unheimlich* (familiar/unfamiliar), where the majority of the population are descended from people forcibly removed from their country to this new 'island (not)-home'. Chloe Hooper captures this *Heimlich/Unheimlich* dilemma in her description of arriving on the island in *The Tall Man: Death and Life on Palm Island* (2008):

> Travelling to Palm Island had been like a sequence in a dream: the pale green so luminous and the plane flying so close I could almost see the life in it – dugongs, giant turtles, whales. All around were moored small pristine islands. Then on the horizon like a dark green wave, came a larger island. As the plane turned to land the wilderness unfolded. Mountains of forest met the palm-lined shore, which met mangrove swamps, the coral reef. Then the dream shifted. (8)

Hooper's description prepares us for the unidyllic account that is to follow, clearing away any illusions of island jewels. It also performs a reversal of the gaze. First Hooper is looking down at the clear ocean and the 'small pristine islands' but Palm Island comes upon her: 'on the horizon like a dark green wave, came a larger island', as might occur in a dream of the sublime or of monstrous horror. The island is accorded agency and exceeds the gazing span of one viewer. The small island is accorded gigantic dimensions and has the power to overturn the superior (omnipotent) viewing position of the sky.

Like Bribie Island in Tracey Moffatt's ghost trilogy *Bedevil*, Palm Island is haunted. In this instance the island is haunted by the 2004 death in custody of a man known as Mulrunji (Cameron Doomadgee while alive), which resulted in a community riot including the burning of the police station. The subsequent trial was mired in difficulty, and the police officer involved, Chris Hurley, was acquitted of the manslaughter charge. This one story has a long history. The Manbarra people are the traditional owners of Palm Island. It is thought there were about 200 people resident on the island at the time of Cook's navigation, but this number had reduced to 50 by the end of the nineteenth century (Downes 2004, 1.2). In 1914 it was gazetted as a reserve for the use of the Aboriginal people of the State and between 1918 and 1971 at least 5,000 people were transported there from Queensland, the Torres Strait and other Melanesian Islands.[9] In *The Tall Man* Hooper records that the Protector of Aborigines who recommended the island as a 'reserve' commented that 'it was the ideal place for a delightful holiday' as well as an ideal prison for 'individuals we desire to punish' (Hooper 2008, 10).

The dramatization of historical and recent events on Palm Island, *Beautiful One Day* (2012), deconstructs the original binary of idyll and prison (see Figure 5.3). In 2011, motivated by the injustice of the death in custody, three theatre companies came together: Belvoir Theatre Sydney; ILBIJERRI, Australia's leading and longest running Aboriginal and Torres Strait Islander Theatre Company, based in Melbourne; and Version 1.0, a Sydney company that stages documentary performances. The result, *Beautiful One Day*, was first staged in November 2012 and eventually staged on Palm Island itself in September 2015. The seemingly impossible project of the performance is to juxtapose historical and current violence and pain with the humour, beauty

**Figure 5.3** Paul Dwyer and Kylie Doomadgee in the 2012 production of *Beautiful One Day*. Photograph Heidrun Löhr. Courtesy Belvoir St Theatre and the actors.

and joyfulness of Palm Island, which are lodged in the hidden spaces where history, geography and resilience might meet. This combination avows and denies the carceral boundaries of the island, a move that was itself performed in the cross-genre modality of *Beautiful One Day*.

The title of the play refers to a well-known slogan of the Queensland Tourist and Travel Corporation: 'Beautiful one day, perfect the next'. The title is, of course, ironic, as the island's history conforms more to the island hellscape rather than island paradise. However *Beautiful One Day* does invite the second phrase, 'perfect the next' in a transformative reversal from one kind of island containment, the prison, into another, the island paradise, a reversal also performed in Hooper's *The Tall Man* by the reversal of conventional understandings of life and death in the sequence of the subtitle, *Death and Life on Palm Island*. *Beautiful One Day* does not perform a straight reversal, but it does transfer weight from the reality of history to the necessity to dream or speculate. In one sense the phrase 'perfect the next' denotes that perfection is futural, it occurs in the space not yet imagined, in the 'next' time after the present.

## Islands of the Future

The future is a vexed issue for many islands fashioning community and sustainability in the wake of colonialism, globalization and climate change. The future is confronting in very specific ways for islands facing inundation from rising oceans, as Marshallese poet Kathy Jetnil-Kijiner addressed in her speech at the opening ceremony of the United Nations' Climate Change Summit in September 2014. Her speech and poetic performance are structured as a generational dilemma. She describes the scene of the Marshall Islands to the assembly:

> We've seen waves crashing into our homes and our breadfruit trees wither from salt and droughts. We look at our children and wonder how they will know themselves or their culture should they lose our islands. (Jetnil-Kijiner 2014)

She continues by addressing her baby daughter in a poem, assuring her that there will be a future on the Marshall Islands. This personal assurance from one mother to her daughter is, of course, contingent on the whole world changing its practices, as the poem well knows. Here, unambiguously, the islands and their future are not contained or quarantined but a pressure point within the planet's shared fragility. Any consideration of islands and futurity undertaken in the ensuing discussion is ventured in light of the shadow of this crisis.

Jameson identifies a proliferation of utopian visions since the collapse of the Eastern bloc. Writing in 2005, he claims that the utopian form seems to have recovered its vitality as a political slogan and a politically energizing perspective (Jameson 2005, xii) and that utopianism has revitalised in the face of endgame capitalism.[10] He writes:

> The Utopians not only offer to conceive of such alternate systems: Utopian form is itself a representational meditation on radical difference, radical otherness, and on the systemic nature of the social totality, to the point where one cannot imagine any fundamental change in our social existence which has not first thrown off Utopian visions like so many sparks from a comet. (Jameson 2005, xii)

In Australian literature, also, Utopian visions of the future have proliferated and bear the continuing mark of the connection between the island and the utopian no place. These islands recognize specific connections to place but also offer the 'no-place' where the complexities of the different – incommensurable difference – may be negotiated.

Alexis Wright's magisterial, dystopian novel *Carpentaria* (2006), set in the northern Gulf country of the Waanyi people in the fictional settler town of Desperance (a metonym of Australia), carves out this creative space for speculation about the historical present and future. Events in the novel move from the edge of the continent and into the surrounding sea and islands. The novel concludes on a floating island of rubbish. The narrative of *Carpentaria* is structured around binaries as alternatives, which are accorded ethical value and assume negative or positive valency according to shifting criteria. Situated 'in the middle of a warzone' (Wright 2006, 203) the novel shows communities and interests pitted against one another. The novel makes clear which perspective is given authority, and it is the Aboriginal people who vanquish various forces of evil, though not without great cost. The reader marvels at the ingenuity, wisdom and determination of the Phantom family, leaders of the Pricklebush mob, but their nonmaterialism is problematic in its relationship to dispossession and poverty. The reader has no qualms about dismissing values and behaviour of the white community of Desperance, or of the multinational mining company that seeks to destroy the aquifers by which country and people survive. However, their wrongful sense of ownership should be transferred to the Waanyi people – except that it is a very different sense of ownership. And so on. The novel shows 'radical difference, radical otherness' (Jameson 2005, xii) as concurrent realities in the present.

Part of the largeness of the novel's sweep derives from its crossing of registers and generic conventions, including social realism, songline and allegory.[11] The novel also refers to actual historical events, as indicated by Wright's dedication to her activist 'countrymen, Murrandoo Yanner and Clarence Walden' (2006, n.p.), thereby bringing history and social reality into its grid of neutralization.[12] This structured opposition between two different worlds, both real and allegorical, and the presence of positive and negative elements in each constructs the four possibilities Marin identifies the reader must grapple with in Utopian texts. All of these are explicitly and repeatedly destroyed in the novel.

The first destruction is brought about by human agency. The mine that threatens to poison the aquifers is blown up. What was made by man is destroyed by man. So, too, as the mine had been established by the teleology of capitalism, its destruction signals finality. It has no future. The second cataclysm of the cyclone is connected to the first in that, as Simon During suggests, the only riposte to capitalism may be natural catastrophe (2010, 125). The cyclone that destroys the settlement of Desperance and sunders the people of the town and its surrounds is, thus, a sequel to the destruction of the mine. However, it is simultaneously of a different order of experience and significance. It does not signify absolute finality but is a form of destruction linked to renewal. The uncoupling of nature and culture performs the disarticulation of the constructed dystopia (of colonization and global capitalism) from an imagined intrinsic dystopia (the circumstances of the Waanyi people). The novel neutralizes all alternatives premised on colonialism, as all are flawed by definition. It does not suggest that the history can be undone but that the process of speculating on the present and future needs new ground/water to begin.

After these two forms of demolition, the novel concludes on an island – of speculation, waiting, expectation and resolve. The floating island of rubbish, on which Will Phantom lives and travels while his partner Hope searches for him, is the no place of Utopia and a figure of the book itself. Constituted by the detritus of global capitalism, Will's floating island defetishizes the island and/as the nation state, and the island's mobility and abjection prohibit its fetishization as an achievable possession or jewel. It is also the site of utopian praxis, of rebirth and worldly knowledge and labour. It is, like the space of utopian cancellation, constructed in the wake and the negation of the dystopian alternatives played out in the text. From this vantage point, the reader is directed back into the events of the novel and to imagine a space beyond it.

This island of rubbish is constituted of history's detritus. As the figure of the novel itself, as it is viewed from the conclusion, Will Phantom appears as Benjamin's Angel of History: 'Where *we* see the appearance of a chain of events, *he* sees one single catastrophe, which unceasingly piles rubble on top of rubble and hurls it before his feet' (1968, 249). Will is also a figure of Redemption. Early in the novel his mother, Angel Day, finds and restores an image of the Virgin Mary so that it looks just like her – a reclamation and reversal of Durkheim (1915, 102*ff.*) and an exchange of cultural fetishes. The novel leaves open that Will is the son in this sacralized sense, a returning Redeemer or, like King Arthur in Avalon, the culture's ultimate but absent protector. The question remains as to how to produce the Janus-faced ability to view this past and yet imagine the future. In *Carpentaria*, the future is not an image or a treatise or a litany of descriptions, but the relentless labour posed by the novel itself. The novel leaves the reader suspended, with Hope, and like her, returns us to the historical present by which these futures need to be achieved and, by dint of its figural and symbolic charge, to the domain of imaginative and conceptual contemplation. In Ernst Bloch's terms, the novel ends with the 'question of learning hope', which, in his formulation, is a condition that 'goes out of itself'. It 'requires people who throw themselves actively into what is becoming, to which they themselves belong' (Bloch 1986, 3).

## Anticipatory Illuminations in the Torres Strait

It is 426 nautical miles north from Kurumba in the Gulf Country to Thursday Island, the administrative centre of the Torres Strait Islands, whose literature also challenges the binary of sea and land and the understanding of the island as a bounded object of possession for the gazing subject. In his essay on Torres Strait islanders' management of the marine environment, Canadian anthropologist Colin H. Scott quotes one traditional owner, who spoke to him during his time on the islands, as saying: 'our feet are on the ground, but our hands are in the sea' (2004, 259). The absence of a clear boundary between land and sea means the island is not contained, does not seem graspable as an object. Researcher Nonie Sharp writes of the Meriam or eastern islands: 'Location is primary […] every person (including an unborn child) must have a *ged* or homeland. In social life these homelands are situated along the sand beaches fronting the sea and the horizons (1996, 84). This homeland is not only land but also the cays, water, fishing grounds, winds and stars. The island is not its own boundary is but located within a broader geography and cosmology.

This structure is embedded in many of the stories, past and present, which, like Grace's *Mutuwhenua*, present the operations of the fetish in the island. *Myths and Legends of Torres Strait* – compiled and translated by Margaret Lawrie (1970) at the behest of Torres Strait Islanders, and included in UNESCO's Australian Memory of the World Register – presents a complex range of stories, many of which chart land-sea trajectories of belonging and relationality. John Whop, community leader from Thursday Island, has called for these Torres Strait stories to be acknowledged as Australian stories, to be 'part of Australian heritage' (Davis, 2012). The ensuing discussion is a preliminary response to this call. It is also the search for productive models of island, archipelago and continental relations for the Australian context specifically, but with broader possible application.

One story which exemplifies the fluidity of land and sea and belonging, in which we can discern what Bloch terms 'cultural surplus' – the continuing unfulfilled potential – and enduring into our own time is 'Wamin Ngurbum' (Wami's Banana Tree), told to Lawrie by Wees Nawia at Kubin, Moa Island (also Mua), in November 1967. Wees Nawia was an elder of that community and led it in a move from Poid to Kubin on Moa Island in the interisland migrations after World War II.

In this story, a man named Wami, for many years a madub (an idle, lazy or apathetic man, characterized by a lack of success in planting) one day espies an object in the waves of the sea (Lawrie 1970, 61). It is a banana sucker. He takes it and addresses it: 'You are Wami's banana sucker.' He croons to it; indeed it is a form of love object: 'My beautiful banana sucker. I am going to dig a fine hole in the ground for you' (33). He is faithful in his attention and gazes upon it all day. As the tree emerges, Wami invents a song of ownership, which he repeatedly sings, thereby attracting the attention of the other villagers:

> *Madubul ina kuruai iudanu Bgai (gar) Wami (a) Wami.*
> (This curving stem weighed down with ripening bananas belongs to the madub. I am Wami, Wami. It is mine). (34)

The villagers request suckers from the tree but he refuses. Eventually he says:

> When the bananas are ripe, I shall cut off the bunch. After that I will give a sucker to the village people. But remember this: everyone is to call it by my name. This banana is Wamin ngurbin. (34)

The storyteller, Wees Nawia, adds to this story proper that Wami kept his word and that the madub was the first kind of banana grown on Mua Island. Similar to the retrospective prospection we encounter in *Crown Jewel*, this additional knowledge throws us back into history and stresses the prophetic charge of the text.

In 'The Work of Art in the Age of Mechanical Reproduction' (1936), Benjamin details the ways in which natural objects as well as cultural artefacts are habitually aurified (1968, 216). The banana sucker given to Wamin is such an organic fetish object and is accorded marvellous or mystic power. It is sacralized in the mode of a fetish object by the love Wami bestows upon it, by its transplantation and secretion into the earth and by its capacity to bring Wami back into his culture, transformed from madub to elder.[13] The labour is minimal: the object is given to him and grows organically, emphasizing its self-originary power beyond human construction.

Significantly, Wami will only share this plant once it has borne fruit. This distribution does not occur within the limit of the story but remains a promise, folding into the future. This future is realized in the story-teller's postscript, which assures the listener that Wami kept his promise and the banana becomes a shared and enduring plant of the island and of the community. However this temporal dialogue does not foreclose the future of the time of the story-teller. Rather, it leads us back into the surplus or hope of the story itself and its enduring capacity for generation, for the creation of the future. It is a story of future fulfilment which is ongoing.

Terri Janke's novel *Butterfly Song* (2005) reads as both a transposition and a realization of one futural possibility contained in what Ernst Bloch terms the 'generative surplus' of 'Wamin Ngurbum' and similar stories. Just as Marin and Jameson look back to More's *Utopia* to identify the anticipatory revelation of capital, we can look back form *Butterfly Song* to 'Wamin Ngurbum' to identify the dilemma of ownership, homeland, law and the operations of the fetish in the capitalist postcoloniality. The novel is set mostly in Cairns and Thursday Island, reflecting in part Janke's own family's move to the mainland after the Second World War, the same time that Wees Nawia led his community in their move from Poid Island to Moa.[14] At the heart of *Butterfly Song* is a precious object that holds within itself a narrative of love, connection and rightful ownership that is also the core of the object given to Wami and of Wami's story itself.

The narrative of *Butterfly Song* traces the experience of Tarena, living in Sydney and completing a law degree, who is called back to Cairns, and then to Thursday Island (TI) in the Torres Strait. Her mother and uncle ask Tarena to attend a family funeral on TI and to assist them with the reclamation of a family heirloom, a pearl shell with a part-formed pearl creating a small, rounded dome. The shell was carved and shaped into a butterfly by Tarena's grandfather for her grandmother but 'collected' (stolen) by a doctor who attended her grandmother in her final days. The butterfly has now reappeared for sale for a sizeable sum. Like the *pounamu patu* in Grace's *Mutuwhenua*, the pearl butterfly is a precious object that needs to be returned to its rightful place outside the economy of the commodity fetish. This pearl shell is the figure of Tarena's cultural reconnection and of the novel itself.

The novel stages a series of incidents and encounters though which Tarena reconnects to TI as her home place, whatever other homes she may create. This claim, figured by the pearl shell, is the motivation and core of this novel, as announced in the novel's opening:

> They say if you live on an island for too long, you merge with it. Your bones become the sands, your blood the ocean. Your flesh is the fertile ground. Your

> heart becomes the stories, dances, songs. The island is part of your makeup. The earth. The trees. The reef. The fish. The music. The sun, moon and stars surround you. You are only part of the integral world called life. You and those who follow you will always be a part of it. No matter where you and your children will travel, the island is always home. (Janke 2005, 1)

This overture locates us in the temporality of 'too long' and 'always', eternal or monumental time and its disavowal of linear, historical time. But the ensuing narrative inserts history into this eternal temporality, weaving both the parallels and the interplay between them, which is also to say that it becomes a novelistic narrative. This temporal overlay connects the 'surplus' at work in 'Wami Ngurbum' as it moves across modes of storytelling. From the genre of myth to that of a realist novel are shared concepts, images and desires, transposed from the earlier text into novelistic form. In this process the compounded symbolism of myth becomes dispersed across the extended narrative of *Butterfly Song*.

The novel also is a tale of ownership, about right of possession, and the components of Tarena's experience circulate between her reclamation of the sense of the island as home according to the cosmology of the novel's opening description and the rightful repossession of the butterfly. *Butterfly Song*, like 'Wami Ngurbum', charts a movement of an object from its unnatural placement – in this case it is in the wrong hands – to its right and proper place. In the novel, too, the object emerges first from the sea; it is given into human hands. The pearl is transformed by human artistry, just as Wami's banana sucker is charmed, shaped by his love and placed in the soil. The pearl butterfly becomes the talisman of creative connection between two people, as with the green stone in *Mutuwhenua*. It is only restored to its proper place when family is also restored, and this occurs through the knowledge and experience of the island home place. So, too, the object's theft and commodification is a travesty of the system of exchange by which the object has meaning. Its presentation in public view for sale also threatens to diminish its true meaning, which was personal or 'hidden' from view. Its restoration re-establishes circulations between community; it becomes again a living object.

Tarena appears to be the antithesis of the lazy, idle figure of Wami, in her ready undertaking of study and work. But, like Wami, Tarena begins this narrative outside her community and is struggling to find her place in the world. Her transformation through the novel shows that the integration of self and world is effected by her role and place in the restitution of the family talisman and her openness to its generative intensity. The operation of this 'original' spiritual fetishism is the mechanism of stability and belonging for its members, having therefore a positive character. This value was reversed by Marx and

Benjamin in their theorizations of fetishism to serve the discourse of economic theory. In contemporary globalization a remobilization of this totem function is clearly positive and productive for postcolonial subjects seeking homelands, as seen also in *Mutuwhenua* and *Carpentaria*. The re-establishment of the links enabled by the spiritual fetish as it is challenged by the commodity fetish, as each of these texts performs explicitly, also successfully contracts capitalist modernity, emblematized by its corruption of fetishistic relations.

The intense romance of Wami and the object/artefact in the earlier story, which effects his transformation and integration, has occurred prior to the narrative in *Butterfly Song*, in that it was the object of the grandparents' love, for this is a narrative of inherited meaning, a dilemma of the twenty-first century. It is also a social realist novel in which mystic connection is historicized. In *Butterfly Song* we witness the dispersal of this meaning across novelistic elements such as psychologized characters, temporality and plot and the record of everyday life. However, we can also identify radical differences from novelistic convention that are encapsulated by the pearl shell. One of the most significant is the romance narrative of Tarena and Sam, which, in some ways, reads as a contemporary replay of the romance of her grandparents, especially, as Sam is a singer and guitarist and it is the signature inscription of a guitar that identifies the rightful owners. But erotic romance and experience in *Butterfly Song* does not conform to the romance convention whereby the alignment of love and sex acts as a form of narrative resolution and closure. Nor does it conform to the convention Susan Martin has identified between land and lover in 'Ru Ro' (rural romance fiction), in which the heroine, much like Elizabeth Bennett in *Pride and Prejudice*, falls in love with her suitor at first sight – of his property (Martin 2016). In *Butterfly Song*, however, the erotic charge and sexual experience are related to the 'surplus' that confounds temporal divisions. In temporal terms, Sam and Tarena's union is a fulfilment of the past, now 'avenged and inherited, mediated and fulfilled' (Bloch 1986, 9), which is achieved also through the mutual negotiation of two systems of law that Tarena masters. Romance is not resolution of the narrative. Instead, the charge of excess is also futural just as Wami's promise to the villagers projects to the time of fruition. In *Butterfly Song* the relationship is left unresolved, each party pursuing earlier plans. So, too, this potential, while open-ended, is also intimately connected to place: Thursday Island. In this way the sex between Tarena and Sam fulfils the novel's opening: "Your bones become the sands, your blood the ocean. Your flesh is the fertile ground" (Janke 2005, 1). Intimate intensity is not presented as personally binding but is part of the charge of the place, and the process of reconnection, at the same time as it recharges this place and creates its futurity. It has, in Bloch's terms, 'utopian surplus as both heritage and anticipatory illumination' (Bloch 1988, 50). *Butterfly Song* is a novel of contemporary mobility, along the eastern seaboard of continental Australia, into the Torres Strait and beyond. This mobility is shown to be fraught, and the text indicates how cultural connectedness needs to be rehearsed to be remembered. In this rehearsal, however, *Butterfly Song* builds what Peter Sloterdijk terms a global foam (2004), one mobile, interdependent, island shelter that contains its own cultural surplus for the present and future.

In the essay 'Envisioning the Archipelago', Stratford et al. (2011a) call on scholars to become engineers of displacement in their negotiation of the interrelationality of islands, which is encapsulated in the utopianism of the archipelago. A chain of islands in the sea is not inherently ideal, of course, as Markman Ellis shows in his analysis of the 'geo-poetics of [Britain's] imperial archipelago' (2002, 49). However, the archipelago offers a mode of thinking, through a long history, of a form of relation that is dynamic, interdependent and interconnected within the material experience of space. Sloterdijk calls this global foams. His vision is aerial. The archipelago of philosophy and literature roves the terraquaceous globe through the material history of topography and topology. Both structures are utopianist, both attuned to 'anticipatory illuminations'; the archipelago seeks them in the horizons, interiorities, littorals and assemblages of islands and the excess that they can unfold into the future. Most importantly, as the discussion of this chapter has shown, this archipelagic capacity resides as potentiality in the single island as much as the island chain.

## Boundless

This final chapter on the island as 'no-place' bookends Chapter 1's focus on Donne's 'No man', so we begin and end in considerations of islands, identity and negative cancellation in the literary imagination. As discussed in Chapter 1, citing Gillian Beer, the negative term always carries its positive opposite because, as Freud identified, the unconscious mind knows no negative (Beer 1997, 13). In the unconscious we do not formulate what we do not want but what we must have. This process of negative definition is integral to the imaginary conception of islands in two key ways. First, it describes the relentless oscillation between the domains of history and representation and the holographic flickering between the material presence of islands in the world and the illusory (non)presence of the island as an imaginary figment. As this book has demonstrated in relation to the modern era, the confusion between these real islands and the island imaginary both facilitated colonial acquisition of islands and confused real places with human longing. But the island also became the site of rethinking political and historical structures as this mutual constitution progressed. This binary flickering, which outpaces our conscious minds, also includes the elements of land and water. This perception constructs islands as all middle (insular) or all boundary (fetishized objects) in their relationship to surrounding water, as contemporary theorists have noted (Hau'ofa 1993; DeLoughrey 2007; Perera 2009; Stratford et al. 2011a; Hayward 2012).

The second issue related to understanding islands though negative definition is that even the ideal island is defined against what it is not. This is in part the age-old dilemma of how to represent ideality in worldly language, but it also points to the island as a site of secondary birth or settlement, as Deleuze discusses (2004). Islands, while they also structured ancient literature such as the *Odyssey* (Homer 800 BC), have particular significance in modernity as spaces of rebirth, which may be colonial settlements from European expansion and, in related literature, Prospero's remaking of world and self in *The Tempest* (Shakespeare ca. 1611) or H. G. Wells' nightmare of man-made creation as vivisection in *The Island of Dr Moreau* (1896). The cancellation process of utopian fiction is another version of this negative definition, for as Marin argues, the cancellation is always made against a specific formulation, and so each text produces a cancellation along particular lines. In these various ways, the island both affirms and denies origin and its accompanying theologies.

Man and island in negative are, finally, expressions of literary syntax, mirror selves and worlds, which are as bounded as poems or books and as unbounded as the potential for imaginative and conceptual thought: the mirror self we need to write, the mirror space we need to write on. Islands are beautiful to think upon and think with in their various contradictions of inevitable limitation and boundlessness, as sites that present the deep time of water and land at the same time as the 'anticipatory illuminations' of the future. Of course, people also live on islands, but these people are not immune to the island's allure, as their literature makes clear, though specific distinctions are paramount. The continental power of modernity has obscured many islands and islanders so that they became, from the nineteenth century no-places and no-people on the stage of globalization. Some are facing the movement from home place to no place in the wake of rising oceans. Others have their identities negated in Australia's offshore island detention of asylum seekers. It is hard, impossible, to reconcile the idyllic island vision with these urgent and desperate matters. Understanding the rhetorical unconscious that accepts, indeed promotes these patterns, is crucial to understanding the confusion between real and imaginary geographies, which islands epitomize, and the interimplication of literature in the utterly compelling, beautiful and devastating experience of islands.

# APPENDIX

# COLONIAL TIES BETWEEN THE WEST INDIES AND AUSTRALIA

| Years of activity in Australia | Name and dates | Years and Roles/activities in West Indies | Years and Roles/activities in Australia and New Zealand |
|---|---|---|---|
| **Sub-category 1. Individuals sent directly by British Empire: government/colonial administrators/military/convicts transported** | | | |
| 1786–90 | **Robert Ross (1740?–1794)** 'officer of marines and lieutenant governor' (Macmillan 1967, vol. 2). | 1781–82 Served in the West Indies (Macmillan 1967, vol. 2). | 1786 'sailed in the *Scarborough* with the First Fleet' to serve as Lieutenant-Governor of New South Wales.<br>1790 Governor of Norfolk Island. Almost immediately proclaimed martial law. Was relieved of duty on Norfolk by mid-1791, and returned to ship-board roles until his death (Macmillan 1967, vol. 2). |
| 1786–94 | **John White (1756?–1832)** naval surgeon (Rienits 1967, 2:594). | 1781–86 Naval surgeon on ships serving in West Indies and India (Rienits 1967, 2:594). | 1786 Chief-Surgeon on First Fleet. Keen naturalist, bird-drawer. Remained in NSW until end of 1794 (Rienits 1967, 2:594–95). |
| 1786–89 | **John Shortland (1739–1803)** naval officer<br>*Six members of Shortland's family were 'associated with the colonization of Australia and New Zealand' (McMartin 1967a, 2:442). | ca. 1755–63 Served as a midshipman in the West Indies 'being present at the reduction of several islands' (McMartin 1967a, 2:442). | 1786–89 Naval agent to the transports of the First Fleet. On the ship, *Supply*, Shortland's squadron first to reach Botany Bay. 'Strongly urged the Admiralty to have the eastern coast of Australia properly charted […] to some extent responsible for the dispatch of Flinders in the *Investigator*.' 'On the voyage by way of Batavia Shortland discovered and charted many islands and reefs […] [and] sighted but did not identify the Solomon Islands' (McMartin 1967a, 2:442–43). |

| | | | |
|---|---|---|---|
| 1786–<br>1795–1800 | **Admiral John Hunter (1737–1821)**<br>Born and raised in Scotland.<br>*Was shipwrecked as a child, whilst sailing with his father off the coast of Norway.<br>*Spent a year on Norfolk Island after shipwrecking there during 1788 journey from NSW to Cape of Good Hope for supplies (Auchmuty 1966, 1:566). | 1772–74 Had extensive experience sailing around the West Indies, was master of the *Intrepid*, which sailed to East Indies.<br>1780 Served as lieutenant in the *Berwock*, a ship in the fleet that commanded the West Indies.<br>1800 After his recall to England following accusations of mismanagement of NSW, and subsequent lack of charges or trial, it 'was suggested that [Hunter] be appointed Governor of the Bermudas' (Auchmuty 1966, 1:572). | 1786 Second-captain of *Sirius*, of First Fleet, 'dormant commission' as successor to Governor Arthur Phillip in case of death or absence.<br>1795–1800 Governor of NSW (Auchmuty 1966, 1:566–72). |
| 1788–91 | **David Blackburn (1753–1795)** 'naval officer' (Hirst 2005, sup. vol.). | 1785 Served as master of the *Flora* in the West Indies (Hirst 2005, sup. vol.). | 1788 arrived in First Fleet ship *Supply*, as master. Then sailed to Norfolk Island to establish another settlement. Charted Lord Howe Island during return voyage. Gave own name to 'small offshore island'.<br>Same year, Blackburn 'returned to Norfolk Island […] in command of the transport *Golden Grove* with provisions and additional convicts'.<br>1790 sailed for Norfolk Island again, in *Supply*, with *Sirius*, which was wrecked on the way.<br>1791 sailed for England (Hirst 2005, sup. vol.). |

*Continued*

| Years of activity in Australia | Name and dates | Years and Roles/activities in West Indies | Years and Roles/activities in Australia and New Zealand |
|---|---|---|---|
| 1789–94 | **John Nicol (1755–1825)** navy and diarist (Nicol 1997, 23). | 1755 Born Scotland.<br>1776 Joined Royal Navy, serving off North America (Nicol 1997, 28).<br>1783 Discharged at end of American War of Independence (Nicol 1997, 191).<br>1784–89 Sailed around globe on whaling ship, visiting West Indies, subsequently documented in his memoirs, *The Life of John Nicol, Mariner* (Nicol 1997). | 1789 Sailed on the *Lady Juliana* convict transport (over 200 female convicts aboard) as part of Second Fleet to Port Jackson.<br>1794 Impressed into Royal Navy and fought at Cape St Vincent and 'the Nile' battles as member of the *Goliath* (Nicol 1997). |
| 1791–95 | **George Vancouver (1757–1798)** 'naval officer and hydrographer'<br>*Age 15 spent seven years under Captain Cook in Pacific (Phillips 1967, 2:550). | 1780–83 Served in the West Indies as a lieutenant.<br>1784–89 Carried out independent hydrographic surveys in Jamaica (Phillips 1967, 2:550–52). | 1790 Given permission to examine 'the extent of the coast of the south-west side of New Holland, which in the present age appears a real blot in geography'. Planned to 'determine whether it and Van Diemen's Land are joined' (Phillips 1967, 2:552).<br>1791 Gave the name to Termination Island, at western-most point of Recherche Archipelago.<br>1791 Gave name to seven islands off New Zealand, 'The Snares', and the ship he was in 'discovered' Chatham Island. On the same voyage, in the Pacific area he surveyed Tahitian and Hawaiian (Sandwich) Islands (Phillips 1967, 2:550–52). |

| | | | |
|---|---|---|---|
| 1791–1809 | **Charles Grimes (1772–1858)** surveyor-general (Dowd 1966, vol. 1). | 1812–? Paymaster of the 13th regiment serving in Canada, the West Indies and India (Dowd 1966, vol. 1). | 1791 Deputy-Surveyor of roads on Norfolk Island. Made Head Constable on Norfolk and aided Lieutenant-Governor King in administration.<br>1794 Posted to Hawkesbury River and Toongabbie to help Surveyor-General Alt, who was ill. Given land at Toongabbie.<br>1795 Magistrate and Superintendent of Public Concerns at Parramatta.<br>1801 Surveyor-General.<br>1803 Discovered Yarra River whilst examining Port Phillip for possible settlement. 'Reported unfavourably on the possibilities of settlement at both.'<br>1803 Sailed for England in the *Porpoise*, which was wrecked off Sandy Cape, north of Sydney. Transferred to the *Rolla*, arrived 1804.<br>1806 Returned to Sydney, made second comprehensive map of NSW settlements.<br>1808 Sided with Macarthur in disputes in Hobart. Joined in deposition of Macarthur. Made Acting Judge-Advocate and took part in trial of Macarthur. Resigned after criticisms of trial. Sent by Acting-Governor George Johnston back to England.<br>1811 Stuck in England. Resigned as Surveyor-General.<br>1812 Went to West Indies with 13th regiment (Dowd 1966, vol. 1). |

*Continued*

| Years of activity in Australia | Name and dates | Years and Roles/activities in West Indies | Years and Roles/activities in Australia and New Zealand |
|---|---|---|---|
| 1792–94 | | | 1792–94 Return trip to NSW to 'report on the naval defences' (Tilghman 1967, 2:621). |
| 1800–03 | **Nicolas Thomas Baudin (1754–1803)** Cartographic surveyor and naturalist (Marchant and Reynolds 1966, 1:71). | 1796 Made scientific voyage to the West Indies, where he collected specimens for museums in Paris (Marchant and Reynolds 1966, 1:71). | 1800–03 Led an expedition to complete the French cartographic survey of the coast of Australia and conduct scientific investigations there (route and return via Mauritius) (Marchant and Reynolds 1966, 1:71–73). |
| 1800–21 | **George Howe (1769–1821)** 'Printer, editor, publisher and poet' (Byrnes 1967, 2:557). | 1769 Born St Kitts, son of Thomas Howe, government printer at Basse Terre. Raised in West Indies (Byrnes 1967, 2:557). | 1799 Shopping-lifting charge. Death sentence commuted to transportation for life. Became government printer in Sydney.<br>'In 1802 he issued the first book printed in Australia, *New South Wales General Standing Orders* [...]. On 5 March 1803 he began the publication of first newspaper, the *Sydney Gazette and New South Wales Advertiser*' (Byrnes 1967, 2:557).<br>1803 Conditionally pardoned.<br>1806 'fully emancipated'.<br>1808 The *Gazette* no longer published 'due to quarrel between Governor Bligh and his enemies' (Byrnes 1967, 2:557). |

| | | | |
|---|---|---|---|
| | | | 1813 Published first 'natural history and art book printed in the colony, *Birds of New South Wales with their Natural History'* (artist John Lewin), (Byrnes 1967, 2:558).<br>1819 published *First Fruits of Australian Poetry*, 'first book of poetry published in Australia' (Byrnes 1967, 2:558). |
| 1802–04 | **Daniel Woodriff (1756–1842)** naval officer and commissioner (Tilghman 1967, 2:621). | 1782–92 Naval service in America and the West Indies.<br>1814–22 Resident Commissioner at Port Royal, Jamaica (Tilghman 1967, 2:621–22). | 1802–04 Commanded the *Calcutta* in David Collin's expedition to found a new settlement in Bass Strait. Strong advocate for creation of naval base at Port Jackson (Tilghman 1967, 2:621–22). |
| 1803—04 | **Admiral John Bowen (1780–1827)** 'naval officer and superintendent' of convicts (Flinn 1966, vol.1). | 1807–08 in ship that 'took part in the blockade of Martinique and Guadeloupe' (Flinn 1966, vol. 1) | 1803 Arrived in convict transport ship at New South Wales.<br>1803—04 Served as superintendent of Risdon Cove Settlement, Van Diemen's Land.<br>1805 Returned to England (Flinn 1966, vol.1). |
| 1803–19 | **William Collins (1760?–1819)** 'naval officer, explorer and shipowner' (Pretyman 1966, 1:240). | 1800–02 Master of navy ship the *Nereide*, serving in West Indies (Pretyman 1966, 1:240). | 1803–19 Arrived in Port Phillip as settler (with recommendation from Charles Dundas) to help establish colony. Aided in survey of Port Phillip Bay, surveyed Port Dalrymple, and helped settle Hobart as main Van Diemen's Land (VDL) township. Appointed Harbour-Master of Hobart in 1804 but resigned shortly afterwards to build the first water mill in Hobart. 'By 1805 had set up […] the first bay-whaling station on the Derwent' (Pretyman 1966, 1:240). Unsuccessful, and returned to being Naval Officer and Inspector of public works.<br>1817 Member of the Lieutenant-Governor's Court (Pretyman 1966, 1:240). |

*Continued*

| Years of activity in Australia | Name and dates | Years and Roles/activities in West Indies | Years and Roles/activities in Australia and New Zealand |
|---|---|---|---|
| 1803–38 | **Robert Knopwood (1763–1838)** 'cleric and diarist' (Monks 1967, 2:66). | 1801 Chaplain on British navy ship *Resolution*. Served in West Indies 'and elsewhere' (Monks 1967, 2:66). | 1803 Joined expedition to Port Phillip to settle. Began 'his famous diary' (Monks 1967, 2:66).<br>1803 Conducted 'first religious service in Victoria' and 'the first service in Tasmania' in Hobart in 1804.<br>1804–28 Magistrate in Hobart, whilst remaining Reverend of the parish.<br>1823 Retired.<br>1826–38 Rector of parish of Rokeby outside Hobart (Monks 1967, 2:66–67). |
| 1805–08 | **Vice-Admiral William Bligh (1754–1817)** 'naval officer and governor' (Shaw 1966b, 1:118). | 1783–87 'served Campbell in the West Indian trade' (Shaw 1966b, 1:118).<br>1787–89 Commander and purser of the *Bounty*, on expedition to procure bread-fruit for the West Indies (failed due to mutiny). After mutiny, Bligh charted 'part of the north-east coast of New Holland' (Shaw 1966b, 1:118).<br>1791–93 Master and Commander of the *Providence*, he tried again to transport breadfruit from Tahiti to the West Indies (Shaw 1966b, 1:118). | 1789 Charted part of the north-east coast of New Holland (during mutiny).<br>1791 *En route* to Tahiti again, charted the south-east coast of VDL (landing at Adventure Bay, Bruny Island, which he had visited earlier with Cook, on the *Bounty*). Also charted bits of Tahiti, Fiji and Torres Strait during this trip.<br>1805–08 Governor of New South Wales. During this time Bligh also organized the 'removal of the settlers from Norfolk Island to the Derwent [Van Diemen's Land]' (Shaw 1966b, 1:118–122). |

| | | | |
|---|---|---|---|
| 1810–21 | **Lachlan Macquarie (1762–1824)** governor. *Born on island of Ulva, in Scottish Hebrides (McLachlan 1967, 2:187). | ca. 1781–84 Posted to Jamaica with the 71st Regiment (McLachlan 1967, 2:187). | 1808 Governor of New South Wales (arrived 1810).<br>1821 Departed NSW (McLachlan 1967, 2:187–95). |
| 1810–14 | **Sir Maurice Charles Philip O'Connell (1768–1848)** commander of forces and lieutenant-governor. *Born and raised in Ireland (*ADB* 1967, vol. 2). | 1800–05 Captain in the 1st West India Regiment. Served in Surinam, Grenada and Dominica (*ADB* 1967, vol. 2). | 1810 Commissioned Lieutenant-Governor of New South Wales. Married to Mary Bligh, daughter of Governor Bligh.<br>1838–46 Commander of Forces in New South Wales (*ADB* 1967, vol. 2). |
| (1788)<br>1813–16 | **Thomas Davey (1758–1823)** lieutenant-governor (Eldershaw 1966, 1:288). | 1780 Served on the *Preston* in the West Indies (Eldershaw 1966, 1:288). | 1788 Accompanied First Fleet as a volunteer guard. Born and raised in England.<br>1813–16 Lieutenant-Governor of VDL (Eldershaw 1966, 1:288–89). |
| 1814–17 | **Hugh McDonald (1779–1819)** soldier and merchant (*ADB* 1967, vol. 2). | 1804–11 Served in the 46th Regiment in the West Indies (*ADB* 1967, vol. 2). | 1814 Quartermaster in 46th Regiment sent to Sydney.<br>1814–17 Army quartermaster. Ordered women's clothing and materials, etc., and sold them as private retailer in Sydney, until regiment sailed for India in 1817 (*ADB* 1967, vol. 2). |

*Continued*

| Years of activity in Australia | Name and dates | Years and Roles/activities in West Indies | Years and Roles/activities in Australia and New Zealand |
|---|---|---|---|
| 1814–19 | **Jeffery Hart Bent (1781–1852)** judge (Currey 1966a, vol. 1). | 1820–52 After dismissal from NSW position of Judge of the Supreme Court, returned to England and was given position as Chief Justice in Grenada.<br>1829 Suspended from this position due to opponents' petitioning in London.<br>1832 Privy Council found in his favour, and he was restored to position.<br>1832 Colonial Office transferred him to Trinidad, as Puisne Judge.<br>1833 Chief Judge of St Lucia. Tried to get nephew, Ellis, position as Attorney-General but failed. Bent's authority ignored, and asked for transfer.<br>1836 Chief Justice of British Guiana (Currey 1966a, vol. 1). | 1814 Judge of Supreme Court of Civil Judicature, NSW, a newly created court. Would not 'open' the new court (i.e., start working) until a year later, creating quarrel between himself and Governor Macquarie.<br>Due to row over harbor laws, Macquarie demanded both Bents be sacked, which they were.<br>1816 Returned to England (Currey 1966a, vol. 1). |
| 1816–24 | **William Sorell (1775–1848)** soldier and lieutenant-governor. Born in the West Indies (Reynolds 1967b, 2:459) | 1775 Born in West Indies<br>1793 Became lieutenant in British Army, fought in the West Indies (Reynolds 1967b, 2:459–62). | 1816–24 Lieutenant-Governor of VDL.<br>1824 Recalled to England due to controversial private life (Reynolds 1967b, 2:459–62). |

| | | | |
|---|---|---|---|
| 1817–23 | **James Erskine (1765?–1825)** soldier and lieutenant-governor.<br>*Born and raised in Ireland (MacMillan 1966, vol. 1). | 1791–97 Served with the 22nd Regiment in the West Indies, including San Domingo campaign in 1794 (MacMillan 1966, vol. 1). | 1817–23 Lieutenant-Governor of New South Wales (MacMillan 1966, vol. 1). |
| 1818–? | **John Anderson (?)** sailor, convict (Schaffer 2005). | According to convict John Davis, a convict by the name of Anderson, who was an overseer and convict-constable at Port Macquarie, claimed to have been 'Mate of a Whale Ship, Master of a Slaver and a west Indeaman [sic]'.<br>1818 Sentenced, in England, to seven years' transportation (Schaffer 2005). | 1819 Arrived in VDL on *Hibernia*, became convict-constable and coxswain at Port Macquarie prison.<br>1822 Two female convicts, Margaret Morgan and Sarah Griffin, made official complaints against Anderson's character, but it was the women who were 'charged with raising scandalous false reports prejudicial to the character of John Anderson Overseer' (I. Schaffer 2005). As punishment, Morgan and Griffin had to wear iron collar 'and sit in the stocks' at Macquarie Harbour, for seven days (Schaffer 2005). |
| 1818–22, 1823–24 | **Gilbert Cimitiere (?–1842)** soldier and commandant (*ADB* 1966, 1:223). | 1796(–1808?) Served in the West Indies in 48th Regiment (*ADB* 1966, 1:223). | 1818–22 Commandant of Port Dalrymple.<br>1823–24 Lieutenant-Governor of Sydney (*ADB* 1966, 1:223–224). |

*Continued*

| Years of activity in Australia | Name and dates | Years and Roles/activities in West Indies | Years and Roles/activities in Australia and New Zealand |
|---|---|---|---|
| 1819–21 | **John Thomas Bigge (1780–1843)** judge and royal commissioner (Bennett 1966 vol. 1). | 1780 Born in England, educated at Oxford.<br>1806 Called to the Bar and began to practice law, but also travelled to Madeira to study Spanish law.<br>1813–18 Chief Justice at Trinidad, where he took colonial hard line on resistance from slaves.<br>1818 Returned to England on personal business (Bennett 1966, vol. 1). | 1819 Appointed Commissioner of Inquiry into NSW colony, and arrived in NSW, where he came into conflict with Governor Macquarie.<br>1822–23 Completed three reports on the NSW colony.<br>1821 Sent to Cape Colony, Mauritius and Ceylon to perform similar inquiry.<br>1829 Returned to England where he died in 1843 (Bennett 1966, vol. 1). |
| 1820–24 | **James Hall (1784–1869)** naval surgeon (Bateson 1966, vol. 1). | 1825–29 'dispenser at the naval hospital at Bermuda, West Indies' (Bateson 1966, vol. 1). | 1820 'Surgeon-Superintendent of the convict transport *Agamemnon*'.<br>1822 Surgeon-Superintendent 'of the *Mary Ann*, which landed prisoners at Hobart Town and Sydney'.<br>1824 Spent a year in Hobart before sailing to West Indies (Bateson 1966, vol. 1). |
| 1821–25 | **Sir Thomas Makdougall Brisbane (1773–1860)** soldier and governor (Heydon 1966, 1:151). | 1795–99 Major in the British Army serving stationed in the West Indies.<br>1800–03 Commander of the 69th Regiment in Jamaica (Heydon 1966, 1:151–55). | 1821–25 Governor of New South Wales (Heydon 1966, 1:151–55). |

| | | | |
|---|---|---|---|
| 1821–56 | **George Meredith (1777–1856)** former naval officer and 'settler' (Hodgson 1967, vol. 2). | 1796 'commissioned second lieutenant in the marines and later served in the West Indies' (Hodgson 1967, vol. 2). | 1821 Arrived Hobart Town and applied for land at Oyster Bay.<br>1826 Land at Oyster Bay granted.<br>1827 Meredith and others discussed petitioning 'for an effective legislature' following the same in NSW.<br>1827 Conflict with Governor Arthur over printing press and circulation of information in colonies (Hodgson 1967, vol. 2). |
| 1821–65 | **Henry Grattan Douglass (1790–1865)** doctor of medicine and public servant.<br>*Born and raised in Dublin, Ireland (Noad 1966, 1:314). | 1811 Served 'as an assistant surgeon with the 18th Regiment' in the West Indies (Noad 1966, 1:314). | 1821 Chief of the general hospital at Parramatta and Superintendent of the Female Factory.<br>1849 Honorary physician at Sydney Hospital where 'he was one of the first teachers of clinical medicine in Australia.'<br>1854 Appointed a director of the hospital.<br>1856 Member of the first Legislative Council (Noad 1966, 1:314–16). |
| 1822–68 | **William Gunn (1800–1868)** soldier and police magistrate (Read 1966, vol. 1). | 1800 Born in Ireland.<br>1815 'Obtained a commission in the Bourbon Regiment', which was in service in the West Indies, but it was disbanded following year.<br>1822 Sought and received a letter of recommendation from the Colonial Office to take to the colonies (Read 1966, vol. 1). | 1822 Arrived Hobart on way to NSW, but decided to settle in Hobart instead, after a visit from Governor Sorell, who gave him 400 acres in the Sorell area.<br>1825 Gained distinction for informal captaining of forces defending colony against bushrangers. During one of these events his arm was wounded, leading to its amputation.<br>1826 Appointed superintendent of the prisoner's barracks, Hobart.<br>1832 Appointed manager of the Male House of Correction. |

*Continued*

| Years of activity in Australia | Name and dates | Years and Roles/activities in West Indies | Years and Roles/activities in Australia and New Zealand |
|---|---|---|---|
| | | | 1846 Clashed with Dr John Hampton, comptroller-general of convicts, over proposed changes to prison system, and was relocated to Launceston to be superintendent and visiting magistrate of convict barracks there.<br>1850 Additionally made Police Magistrate of Launceston.<br>1850 With the end of transportation Gunn's convict duties ceased, but he continued as Police Magistrate until his death in 1868 (Read 1966, vol. 1). |
| 1823–46 | **Sir George Arthur (1784–1854)** soldier and governor (Shaw 1966a, vol. 1). | 1784 Born in England.<br>1804 Joined army.<br>1812 'purchased a majority in the 7th Regiment' and became assistant-quartermaster in Jamaica.<br>1814 Appointed superintendent and commandant of British Honduras in West Indies.<br>1822 Returned to England on 'sick leave' and petitioned Colonial Office for a new post (Shaw 1966a, vol. 1). | 1823 Appointed as lieutenant-governor of VDL, succeeding Sorell.<br>1824 Arrived VDL.<br>1825 VDL designated as separate colony from NSW, giving Arthur full power over the VDL colony.<br>1825–36 Ran the colony with emphasis on using punishment of convicts as deterrent to crime in England. Ordered the creation of prisons on Maria Island and at Port Arthur. Developed extensive system of using convicts as labour, including as domestic servants for free-settlers. Also made himself extremely wealthy through land grants to himself and family/friends.<br>1836 Left VDL for new post in Canada.<br>1841 Returned to England briefly and made a Baronet.<br>1842 Appointed Governor of Bombay.<br>1846 Returned to England.<br>1854 Died in England (Shaw 1966a, vol. 1). |

| | | | |
|---|---|---|---|
| 1823–? | **Charles Wellings (ca. 1796–?)** soldier and convict (Lines and Maxwell-Stewart 2002, 49). | 1821 Court-martialled for desertion while serving in the army in Grenada. Sentenced to transportation for life (Lines and Maxwell-Stewart 2002, 49). | 1823 Arrived at VDL as convict, served as official flagellator of other convicts at Port Arthur.<br>1828 Absconded, stealing goods from the police supply hut at Oatlands and setting fire to the stock of 'cat-o-nine-tails' whips. Wellings was recaptured and sentenced to 12 months on the chain gang (Lines and Maxwell-Stewart 2002, 41–49). |
| 1824–25<br>1827–33 | **Jules Poret de Blosseville (1802–1833)** navigator, explorer and geographer (Marchant 1966, 1:122). | 1818 Served in navy in Antilles.<br>1819 Further voyage to West Indies 'whetted his appetite for exploration and scientific discovery' (Marchant 1966, 1:123). | 1822 Sailed on the 'Coquille' with L.J. Duperrey, who was ordered to report on Western New Holland as a site for possible French settlement. Blosseville made his own reports.<br>1824 Spent nearly a month in New South Wales working with Governor Brisbane in his observatory. 'Wrote a significant study of the commercial prospects of the Pacific entitled *Commerce du Grand Océan*.' Involved in plans around settlements in New Zealand.<br>1827 Explored 'in Asian waters'.<br>1833 Sailed on expedition to the Arctic which disappeared (Marchant 1966, 1:122–23). |
| 1824–32 | **John Stephen (1771–1833)** judge (Currey 1967, 2:476). | 1800s 'In early manhood John Stephen built up a lucrative practice as an attorney and barrister in Basse Terre, St Kitts, West Indies.' Returned to England 1810, but lost money and returned to Basse Terre 1815 (Currey 1967, 1:476). | 1824 Post obtained for John Stephen by his nephew James. Post created by New South Wales Act of 1823. However, Governor Brisbane had already appointed Dr Henry Grattan Douglass. Stephen given even higher position as Solicitor-General of NSW: 'first to hold that office in the colony'.<br>1824 Chairman of the Courts of Quarter Sessions.<br>1825 Appointed by Governor Brisbane as first Puisne Judge of Supreme Court of NSW.<br>1831 Resigned due to ill health (Currey 1967, 1:476–78). |

*Continued*

| Years of activity in Australia | Name and dates | Years and Roles/activities in West Indies | Years and Roles/activities in Australia and New Zealand |
|---|---|---|---|
| 1824–41 | **Sir Francis Forbes (1784–1841)** chief justice (Currey 1966b, vol. 1). | 1784 Born in Bermuda.<br>Educated in America, studied law in London.<br>1811 Appointed attorney-general of Bermuda.<br>1812 Called to the Bar in London.<br>1813 Appointed King's advocate in Vice-Admiralty Court.<br>1813 Married Amelia Sophia, daughter of a Harley-Street Doctor, 'formerly of Kingston, Jamaica', and they lived in St George, Bermuda.<br>1816 Appointed chief justice of Supreme Court of Newfoundland. Then became governor and commander-in-chief (known as 'admiral-governor') (Currey 1966b, vol. 1). | 1824 Arrived NSW to take up Colonial Office appointment as first chief judge of newly-created Supreme Court of NSW (Forbes 'construed' the Act creating Supreme Court to entail trial by jury of 12 'free' men). Was also made a member of the Legislative Council, by Colonial Office. Friends with Governor Brisbane. 'Forbes helped to shape all three of the first basic constitutional instruments in New South Wales' (Currey 1966b, vol. 1).<br>1836 Returned to England due to ill health, but continued working for Colonial Office and writing essays on transportation.<br>1837 Knighted.<br>1841 Died in Sydney, NSW (Currey 1966b, vol. 1). |
| 1825–65 | **Thomas Daunt Lord (1783–1865)** soldier and commandant (Morris 1967, vol. 2). | 1800 Joined army.<br>1801 Transferred to 2nd West India Regiment and served in the West Indies. | 1825 Arrived in Hobart, where he was made a Naval Officer, but resigned when appointed commandant of Maria Island settlement (which had just been established). |

| | | | |
|---|---|---|---|
| | | 1820 Was caught up in the 'Bradley-Arthur dispute' in Honduras, eventually selling his commission, returning to England, and then swapping sides and giving evidence for Arthur.<br>1824 Applied for land grant in VDL (Morris 1967, vol. 2). | 1825–32 Commandant of Maria Island. Accused three times of personal use of government stores, but was never prosecuted. The accusers were punished in all cases. Lord presided over building of large prison and several factories on Maria Island.<br>1832 Appointed assistant police-magistrate at Swansea.<br>1834 Suspended from position for being caught with government stores. Was acquitted, but colonial office upheld his suspension and he was removed from 'Commission of Peace' list.<br>1865 Died in VDL (Morris 1967, vol. 2). |
| 1825–27 | **William Stewart (1769–1854)** soldier and lieutenant-governor (Barker 1967, 2:482). | 1794–1802 'served in the West Indies notably at Grenada, St Vincent, St Lucia and St Eustatius', in 3rd Regiment (Barker 1967, 2:482). | 1825–27 Lieutenant-Governor of New South Wales (Barker 1967, 2:482). |
| 1825–31 | **Sir Ralph Darling (1772–1858)** military officer and governor (*ADB* 1966, 1:282). | 1793–1802 Served in the West Indies as secretary to military commanders of 45th Regiment.<br>1819–23 Commander of military government, Port Louis, Mauritius (French colonists, 70,000 African/Caribbean slaves) (*ADB* 1966, 1:282–86). | 1824 Governor of New South Wales and, as separate commission, VDL (to be administrated by the Lieutenant-Governor in his absence).<br>1830 Relieved of post (militaristic and unpopular with many) (*ADB* 1996, 1:282–86). |

*Continued*

| Years of activity in Australia | Name and dates | Years and Roles/activities in West Indies | Years and Roles/activities in Australia and New Zealand |
|---|---|---|---|
| 1825–91 | **Sir Alfred Stephen (1802–94)** chief justice and legislator (Rutledge 1976, 6:180). | 1802 Born at Basseterre, St Christopher (St Kitts). Educated in England.<br>1815 Returned to St Kitts, where he worked as a clerk to his father.<br>1817 Commissioned as a Lieutenant in the Local Fusiliers (Rutledge 1976, 6:180–87). | 1825 Solicitor-General and then Crown Solicitor in Hobart Town.<br>1832 Attorney-General of VDL.<br>? Ex Officio member of the Legislative Council.<br>1839 Sat on bench in Sydney.<br>1841 Appointed Puisne Judge.<br>1843–45 Authored a treatise *Constitution, Rules, and Practice of the Supreme Court of New South Wales.*<br>1845 Chief Justice of Supreme Court in Sydney.<br>Prominent Anglican, Temperance member, and 'social welfare' advocate.<br>1856 Appointed to new Legislative Council.<br>1870–72 Chairman of Law Reform Commission.<br>1872 Temporary Governor of colony.<br>1873 Resigned as Chief Justice.<br>1875 Appointed Lieutenant-Governor.<br>1879, 1885, 1890–91 Acting Governor.<br>1891–92 Responsible for the Divorce Extension and Amendment Act.<br>1893 Appointed Australia's second Privy Councillor (Rutledge 1976, 6:180–87). |
| 1827–35 | **James Laidley (1786–1835)** 'deputy commissary general' (G. Parsons 1967, vol. 2). | 1814–19 Deputy Commissary General of West Indies. | 1827–35 Deputy Commissary General of Sydney (G. Parsons 1967, vol. 2). |

| | | | |
|---|---|---|---|
| | | 1819 Married Eliza Jane Shepheard of Barbados at Bridgetown (G. Parsons 1967, vol. 2). | |
| 1827–54 | **John Longworth (?–1854)** soldier and convict (Lines and Maxwell-Stewart 2002, 41). | 1813 Court-martialled in England, whilst serving in 2nd Dragoons, and incarcerated on convict hulk off Isle of Wight, then sentenced to forced service in York Chausseurs.<br>1813–17 Served as member of York Chausseurs and then 60th Regiment (Bourbon) in Barbados, St Vincent and Grenada.<br>1817 Deserted (for 2nd time).<br>1818 'Surrendered' himself at Isle of Wight, to 15th Foot Regiment.<br>1818–26 Deserted (3rd time) after tour of duty in Ireland, and remained 'on the run' until arrested for stealing saddles.<br>1826 Sentenced to transportation for life to Australia (Lines and Maxwell-Stewart 2002, 41–44). | 1827 Arrived at VDL in convict transport Andromeda.<br>1827 Initially made 'Gatekeeper' of Prisoner's Barracks, but quickly ended up on Oatlands Chain Gang for insubordination to superiors and assault.<br>1828 After several further acts of disobedience, was flogged and then sent to Port Arthur, where he was also given positions of (convict) authority (overseer and convict-constable).<br>1833 'Charged with embezzling […] clothing and obtaining a set of government bedding under false pretences', but Commandant Booth intervened and charges dropped, although he was sent back to Hobart 'as punishment'.<br>1834 Granted a ticket of leave.<br>1838 Arrested and sentenced to three years' transportation for embezzling from employer. Court recommended he be sent to NSW, but was allowed to stay in VDL.<br>1854 Killed by drunken fall from cart (Lines and Maxwell-Stewart 2002, 41–44). |

*Continued*

| Years of activity in Australia | Name and dates | Years and Roles/activities in West Indies | Years and Roles/activities in Australia and New Zealand |
|---|---|---|---|
| *1828–30 [never physically in Australia] | **Sir George Murray (1772–1846)** 'soldier and politician' (colonial office) (*ADB* 1967, vol. 2). | 1795–96 Lieutenant and Captain in the 3rd Foot Guards stationed in West Indies (*ADB* 1967, vol. 2). | 1828–30 Secretary of State for the colonies, in Wellington's administration. The colony of Western Australia was founded during this period. Murray personally gifted land and positions in the Australian colonies to his friends and relations (*ADB* 1967, vol. 2). |
| 1829–39 | **Sir James Stirling (1791–1865)** governor born and raised Scotland, entered navy at age 12 (Crowley 1967, 2:484). | 1804?–18 Naval commander in West Indies, and later in East Indies (Crowley 1967, 2:484–85). | 1829–39 First Governor of Western Australia. Key player in establishing the Swan River settlement (Crowley 1967, 2:484–88). |
| 1829–53 | **Sir Edward Deas Thomson (1800–1879)** 'public servant and parliamentarian' (Osborne 1967, vol. 2). | 1828 Registrar of the Orphan Chambers in Demerara, West Indies, but this appointment was changed to one in NSW before he sailed to West Indies (Osborne 1967, vol. 2). | 1829 Clerk of the council of New South Wales.<br>1837–56 Colonial Secretary of NSW and Registrar of Records.<br>1849 Member of 'Charles Wentworth's select committee on Sydney University'.<br>1850–79 Member of Sydney University senate.<br>Member of NSW legislative council until death (Osborne 1967, vol. 2). |
| 1830–40 | **John Kinchela (1774?–1845)** attorney-general and judge.<br>*Born and educated in Ireland (*ADB* 1967, 2:51) | 1824–25 Employed by British Government in West Indies to report on the condition of slaves (*ADB* 1967, 2:51). | 1831 Attorney-General of NSW.<br>1836 Acting Puisne Judge in Supreme Court while Sir Francis Forbes on leave.<br>1837 '[W]as retired from the bench and appointed deputy-commisary in the Vice-Admiralty Court' (*ADB* 1967, 2:51–52). |

| | | | |
|---|---|---|---|
| 1830–81 | **Ronald Campbell Gunn (1808–1881)** governor (Burns and Skemp 1966, vol. 1). | 1810s (early years) Spent early childhood years at Reunion Island, off Africa.<br>ca. 1820 In his teens lived in Barbados with his father.<br>1826 Clerk in Royal Engineers, on Antigua. *Resigned from Military to travel to Australia (Burns and Skemp 1966, vol. 1). | 1830 Overseer of the prison in VDL, under his brother, William.<br>1830 Assistant Superintendent of Convicts in Launceston.<br>1833 Justice of the Peace.<br>1836 Police Magistrate at Circular Head.<br>1838 Assistant Police Magistrate in Hobart. 1839 Assistant Superintendent of Male House of Correction.<br>1855–60 Held seats in VDL parliament.<br>1860 Deputy Commissioner of Crown Lands for the north of VDL, and whole island in 1867.<br>Other public positions including Coroner of VDL in 1870 (Burns and Skemp 1966, vol. 1). |
| 1832–44<br>1857–61 | **Sir William Westbrooke (1794–1888)** judge (Allars 1966, vol. 1). | ca. 1808 Served as midshipman in British navy, on tours around world including West Indies (Allars 1966, vol. 1). | 1832 A judge on bench of Supreme Court of NSW.<br>1834 '[P]resided at the trial of the leaders of an insurrection on [Norfolk Island].'<br>1840 Authored *The State of Religion and Education in New South Wales*.<br>1844 '[L]eft Sydney to become puisne judge at Madras.'<br>1857 Returned to Sydney, made member of the Legislative Council.<br>1858 President of Legislative Council.<br>1861 Opposed Robertson Land Legislation. Resigned and returned to England, when realized it would be passed (Allars 1966, vol. 1). |
| 1833–44 | **Charles O'Hara Booth (1800–1851)** soldier, commandant (Hooper 1966, 1:125). | 1820–27 Served in West Indies with 21st Fusiliers.<br>*Booth's mother was Gibraltan (Hooper 1966, 1:125). | 1833–44 Commandant of Port Arthur Prison, VDL (Hooper 1966, 1:125). |

*Continued*

| Years of activity in Australia | Name and dates | Years and Roles/activities in West Indies | Years and Roles/activities in Australia and New Zealand |
|---|---|---|---|
| 1833–56 | **Charles Schaw (1785–1874)** soldier and police magistrate.<br>Born in Jamaica (educated Eton) (Carington Smith 1967, 2:421). | 1785 Born in Jamaica.<br>1802–12 Military service in England and the West Indies (Carington Smith 1967, 2:421). | 1833 Went to VDL with the 21st Regiment, sent to Bothwell as Coroner and Deputy-Chairman of Quarter Sessions.<br>1841–56 Police Magistrate of Richmond, VDL (as civilian) (Carington Smith 1967, 2:421). |
| 1834–39? | **Joseph Anderson (1790–1877)** soldier, commandant (Barry 1966, 1:13). | 1813 Captain and Brigade Major in the York Chasseurs in the West Indies, where fought in the recapturing of Guadeloupe in 1815.<br>1821 Captain in the 50th Regiment.<br>1826 Major in 50th Regiment (Barry 1966, 1:13–14). | 1834 Major in 50th Regiment sent to Sydney.<br>1834–39 Commandant of Norfolk Island.<br>1852–56 Nominated member of the Legislative Council of Victoria (Barry 1966, 1:13–14). |
| 1835–62 | **George Barney (1792–1862)** 'soldier and engineer', superintendent, politician (*ADB* 1966, vol. 1). | 1808 Second-Lieutenant in the Royal Engineers and served in the West Indies, including recapturing of Guadeloupe in 1815.<br>ca. 1815? Worked as a civil engineer in Jamaica for several years.<br>1825 Promoted to Captain (*ADB* 1966, vol. 1). | 1835 Arrived Sydney with Royal Engineers. Employed as a civil engineer on a number of works, incl. a circular quay at Sydney Cove. 1846 Superintendent of a new convict colony of North Australia (Port Curtis).<br>1849 Chief Commissioner of crown lands.<br>1855 Surveyor-General.<br>1851 onwards: Member of Legislative Council, Sydney (*ADB* 1966, vol. 1). |

| | | | |
|---|---|---|---|
| 1836–38 | **Rear-Admiral Sir John Hindmarsh (1785–1860)** governor (*ADB* 1966, 1:538–41) | ca. 1800 Briefly served in West Indies while aboard the *Bellerophon*.<br>1809 Went to East Indies in the *Nisus*.<br>1840–56 Governor of Heligoland.<br>1851 Received a knighthood (*ADB* 1966, 1:538–41). | 1836 Governor and Commander-in-Chief of South Australia.<br>1838 Recalled to England after multiple parties petitioned in London to have him removed (*ADB* 1966, 1:538–41). |
| 1836–56 | **George Stevenson (1799–1856)** editor (*ADB* 1967, vol. 2). | Visited West Indies during teens, returning England 1830 (*ADB* 1967, vol. 2). | 1836 Appointed 'secretary to the governor and clerk of the council' in South Australia. 'He also applied to Lord Glenelg for appointment as protector of Aborigines, because of his experience with North American Indians and his benevolent character.'<br>1836 arrived Holdfast Bay and 'read the governor's [Hindmarsh] first proclamation to assembled colonists'. Was sent to report on 'lawless state of Kangaroo Island'.<br>1837 After only three issues of *South Australian Gazette and Colonial Register* newspaper in Adelaide, edited by Stevenson, a second newspaper was founded, the *Southern Australian*, to oppose Stevenson's views.<br>After Governor Gawler arrived, Stevenson resigned official role, but continued public criticism.<br>1840–41 Twice elected to Municipal Corporation of Adelaide as alderman.<br>1842 Resigned as editor, but restarted 1845.<br>1852 The newspaper ceased production.<br>Appointed coroner in Adelaide (*ADB* 1967, vol. 2). |

*Continued*

| Years of activity in Australia | Name and dates | Years and Roles/activities in West Indies | Years and Roles/activities in Australia and New Zealand |
|---|---|---|---|
| 1838–46 | **Sir George Gipps (1791–1847)** soldier and governor (McCulloch 1966, 1:446). | 1824 Served in the West Indies (McCulloch 1966, 1:446). | 1838–46 Governor of New South Wales (McCulloch 1966, 1:446–53). |
| 1838–61 | **John Walpole Willis (1793–1877)** 'judge' (Barry 1967, vol.2). | 1831–36 'vice-president of the court of Civil and Criminal Justice of British Guiana' (Demerera, Georgetown, West Indies) (Barry 1967, vol. 2). | 1838 Judge of Supreme Court of NSW.<br>1841 Was moved to Melbourne due to 'friction' with chief justice James Dowling.<br>1841–43 Judge of Supreme Court of Port Phillip. Again, was ousted due to bad temper.<br>1845 Returned to England, name cleared and salary paid in arrears after inquiry ruling in 1846, but was given no further judicial roles (Barry 1967, vol. 2). |
| 1839–54 | **Charles Joseph La Trobe (1801–1875)** 'superintendent and lieutenant-governor' (Eastwood 1967, vol. 2). | 1837 Sent by British Government to West Indies to compile report on the situation of slavery in West Indies (Eastwood 1967, vol. 2). | 1839 Superintendent of Port Phillip area.<br>1846–47 Temporary Governor of VDL whilst replacement for Eardley-Wilmot in transit.<br>1851–54 Lieutenant-Governor of Victoria (Eastwood 1967, vol. 2). |
| 1839–67 | **Charles James Tyers (1806–1870)** surveyor and public servant (also initially in navy) (Tyers 1967, 2:542). | 1828 Ship surveyor in navy. Made a study of marine surveying and computed longitudes in the Channel, Mediterranean, West Indies | 1837 Commissioned to survey Port Essington area. Left the navy and entered colonial service. Commissioned by Governor Gipps to 'fix the 141st meridian' – the boundary of Port Phillip/South Australia.<br>1841 Surveyor in charge of Portland district. |

| | | | |
|---|---|---|---|
| | | and South Africa (Tyers 1967, 2:542–43). | 1843 Commissioner of crown lands for Gippsland.<br>1846 '[I]nvestigated suitability of Gabo Island for a lighthouse.'<br>1853 Stipendiary Magistrate.<br>1861 Warden of Gippsland Goldfields (Tyers 1967, 2:542–43). |
| 1840–42 | **William Hobson (1793–1842)** naval officer and governor (Tapp 1966, 1:545). | 1806 Spent several years as a midshipman with British Naval fleet in the West Indies.<br>1825 Commander of a flotilla in the West Indies (Tapp 1966, 1:545–46). | 1836 Requisitioned to take first officials to Port Phillip. Was hopeful of Port Phillip governorship.<br>1840 Lieutenant-Governor of New Zealand. '[A]dvocated negotiated treaties with Maori chiefs' (Tapp 1966, 1:545).<br>1840 Secured treaty of Waitangi with Maoris.<br>1841 Hobson first Governor of New Zealand as a separate colony.<br>1842 Died whilst still in role as Governor (Tapp 1966, 1:545–46). |
| 1844–61 | **Sir John Nodes Dickinson (1806–1882)** judge (McLaughlin 1972, 4:71). | 1806 Born at Grenada in West Indies, 'son of […] a British army staff surgeon'. Educated Cambridge (McLaughlin 1972, 4:71). | 1844 Made Judge of the Supreme Court of New South Wales after Sir William Burton appointed judge at Madras. 'Last judge of the New South Wales Supreme Court appointed in England.'<br>1848 Appointed to royal commission into constitution and practice of the courts of NSW.<br>1852 Wrote paper proposing 75 baronets be conferred on colonial landowners.<br>1856 Appointed to first Legislative Council, but resigned in 1858 due to public opposition to judges in politics.<br>1860–61 Acting Chief Justice of NSW.<br>1861 Returned to England (McLaughlin 1972, 4:71–72). |

*Continued*

| Years of activity in Australia | Name and dates | Years and Roles/activities in West Indies | Years and Roles/activities in Australia and New Zealand |
|---|---|---|---|
| 1846–53 | **Edward John Eyre (1815–1901)** Born and raised in England, emigrated to Australia at age 17, where became sheep-driver and explorer (Dutton 1966, 1:363–64). | 1854–60 Lieutenant-Governor of St Vincent.<br>1860–61 Acting Governor of Leeward Islands.<br>1861–64 Acting Governor of Jamaica.<br>1864 Governor-in-chief of Jamaica.<br>1865 Relieved of governorship after ordering brutal reprisals on natives after riot.<br>Retired in England (Dutton 1966, 1:363–64). | 1832–45 Sheep-driver and explorer in Australia<br>1846–53 Lieutenant-Governor of New Zealand. Quarrelled with Governor (Sir George Grey) and returned to England (Dutton 1966, 1:363–64). |
| 1846–47 | **Andrew Clarke (1793–1847)** soldier and governor.<br>Born and raised in St Kitts/Trinidad (Zalums 1966, 1:228). | 1793 Born and raised in St Kitts/Trinidad.<br>1800 Served in British Army in New South Wales, India and Europe.<br>ca. 1820 Commander of 46th Regiment, serving in Gibraltar and the West Indies.<br>1843–45 Governor of St Lucia (Zalums 1966, 1:228). | 1846–47 Governor of Western Australia. Became sick after six months in office and died (Zalums 1966, 1:228). |

| | | | |
|---|---|---|---|
| 1848–61 | **Sir Henry Edward Fox Young (1803–1870)** 'colonial administrator' (Gibbney 1976, vol. 6). | 1803 Born and educated in England, studying law, but joined father in Trinidad before admission to Bar.<br>1833 Became confidential clerk in Colonial Secretary's office in Demerera. Was also Governor's aide-de-camp and acting record for Orphan Chamber.<br>1834 Temporarily took his father's position as deputy protector of slaves.<br>1834 Became Treasurer at St Lucia, as well as acting colonial secretary and puisne judge.<br>1835 Promoted to government secretary of British Guiana (Gibbney 1976, vol. 6). | 1846 Returned to England, knighted, and made lieutenant-governor of Cape Colony, but had this shifted to South Australia.<br>1847–54 Lieutenant-governor of South Australia.<br>1854 Appointed Governor of VDL.<br>1861 Resigned and returned to London.<br>1866–68 Was original director and chairman in Australian Mercantile Land & Finance Co.<br>1870 Died in England (Gibbney 1976, vol. 6). |
| 1849–59 | **Envidale Savage Norman Campbell (1806–1859)** soldier, public servant, landowner (Refshauge 1969, vol. 3). | 1837 Captain of the 2nd Foot regiment in West Indies, where he met La Trobe (Refshauge 1969, vol. 3). | 1849 Arrived Adelaide as civilian, in position of local rep. for English copper-mining company.<br>1851 Nominated by Lieutenant-Governor Sir Henry to sit on Legislative Council of South Australia. Resigned after a year.<br>1852 Went bankrupt, taken on as private secretary to Lieutenant-Governor Charles La Trobe of Victoria.<br>1853–59 Appointed by La Trobe as 'first permanent head of the Registrar-General's Department' (Refshauge 1969, vol. 3). |

*Continued*

| Years of activity in Australia | Name and dates | Years and Roles/activities in West Indies | Years and Roles/activities in Australia and New Zealand |
|---|---|---|---|
| 1849–91 | **Moritz Richard Schomburgk (1811–1891)** 'botanist' (Middelmann 1976, vol. 6). | 1811 Born in Saxony.<br>1831–34 Military service in Berlin.<br>1840–44 Joined his brother Robert's journey to British Guiana, in capacity as botanist/historian.<br>1847 Published his three-volume travel diary/botanical observations *Travels in British Guiana 1840—44* (Middelmann 1976, vol. 6). | 1849 Emigrated with wife and other brother to South Australia, where he planted a vineyard.<br>1862 Had five acres of vineyards.<br>1865 Was made the curator of the Adelaide Botanic Gardens.<br>1876 Published *Botanical Reminiscences of British Guiana.*<br>1891 Died at his house in the Botanic Gardens (Middelmann 1976, vol. 6). |
| 1853–55 | **Sir Robert Nickle (1786–1855)** army officer (commander-in-chief of Australian military forces) (McNicoll 1974, vol. 5). | 1786 'Born at sea', son of Robert Nicholl of 17th Dragoons. Educated Edinburgh, served as ensign 1798–99 during Irish Rebellion.<br>1830 Commanded 30th Regiment in West Indies.<br>1832–33 administered St Kitts government (McNicoll 1974, vol. 5). | 1853 '[A]ppointed commander-in-chief of Australian colonial military forces, arriving at headquarters in Melbourne in 1854'.<br>1854 Took charge of dispersing tensions after storming of the Eureka stockade.<br>1855 Died in Melbourne (McNicoll 1974, vol. 5). |

| | | | |
|---|---|---|---|
| 1861–79 | **Sir Archibald Paull Burt (1810–79)** chief justice (McClemans 1969, 3:307). | 1810 Born in St Christopher, West Indies, to a planter. Educated in England, admitted to Middle Temple.<br>1830 admitted to Bar in St Christopher and Anguilla.<br>1835 Appointed Notary Public.<br>1837 Appointed 'aide to the lieutenant-governor of St Christopher with the rank of lieutenant-colonel'.<br>1845 Became member of the Legislative Council of St Christopher. Short term as Speaker of the Legislative Assembly. 1848 Attorney-General for St Christopher and Anguilla, and took silk. Also served as chancellor of the Anglican diocese of Antigua.<br>1856 provisionally appointed chief justice in St Christopher by Lieutenant-Governor Hercules Robinson. Eventually 'disqualified by the rule that no local barrister should be elevated to the bench' (McClemans 1969, 3:307–8). | 1860 Appointed civil commissioner and chairman of Quarter Sessions in Western Australia (began 1861).<br>1861 Appointed chief justice of newly-created Supreme Court of Western Australia, making him colony's 'sole judge'.<br>1866 Chairman of the Western Australian committee that prepared 'an exhibit for the Intercolonial Exhibition'. Also chairman of the Boys High School, and established the Law Library. Regarded as fair and humane judge. 'He left the colony only once in his sixteen years in office, and went then to the West Indies to endeavor to salvage a partnership in sugar estates' (McClemans 1969, vol. 3).<br>1873 His business partner, Francis Spencer Wigley, found bankrupt and Burt lost 'his entire possessions in the West Indies' (McClemans 1969, 3:307–8). |

*Continued*

| Years of activity in Australia | Name and dates | Years and Roles/activities in West Indies | Years and Roles/activities in Australia and New Zealand |
|---|---|---|---|
| 1862–64 | **Sir Robert Dalrymple Ross (1827–1887)** army officer and politician. Born at St Vincent in West Indies (Hayman 1976, 6:62). | 1827 Born at St Vincent in West Indies.<br>1864–65 Fought as officer in British Army in New Zealand war against Maoris (Hayman 1976, 6:62–63). | 1862–64 Head of the Commissariat in South Australia, and 'briefly aide-de-camp to Governor Daly'.<br>1875–76 House of Assembly representative for Wallaroo.<br>1876–77 Treasurer in Colton Ministry.<br>1881–87 Speaker of the Assembly.<br>1884–87 House of Assembly rep. for Gumeracha.<br>Ross 'actively supported schemes to lay a cable from England to Australia and to build a transcontinental railway from Adelaide to Darwin. He sought to develop foreign markets for South Australian produce' (Hayman 1976, 6:63). |
| 1862–68 | **John Stephen Hampton (1810?–1869)** navy surgeon (Boyce 1966, 1:508). | 1829–32 Assistant surgeon on ships touring West Indies. Published medical research on 'diseases of the West Indies' (Boyce 1966, 1:508). | 1846 Comptroller-General of convicts of VDL settlement.<br>1855 Took leave before he could be relieved of duty due to unpopularity.<br>1862–68 Governor of Western Australia (Boyce 1966, 1:508–9). |
| 1863–66 | **Sir Charles Henry Darling (1809–1870)** military officer and governor.<br>*Father was Major-General Henry Charles Darling, Lieutenant-Governor of Tobago, | 1833–41 Served in British Army in West Indies.<br>1833–39 Military secretary.<br>1839–41 Captain in British Army stationed in West Indies.<br>1841 Settled in Jamaica.<br>1841 Governor of Barbados and the Windward Islands. | 1863–66 Governor of Victoria (Crowley 1972, 4:19–21). |

| | | | |
|---|---|---|---|
| | mother was daughter of Charles Cameron, Governor of the Bahamas.<br>**Served as private secretary to his uncle, Governor Sir Ralph Darling (Crowley 1972, 4:19–20). | 1841 Agent-General for Immigration and Adjutant-General of militia in Jamaica.<br>1843 Member of the Legislative Council.<br>1847 Lieutenant-Governor of St Lucia.<br>1857–63 Governor of Jamaica, Honduras and the Bay Islands (Crowley 1972, 4:19–21). | |
| 1868–1912 | **Septimus Burt (1847–1919)** 'lawyer, politician and grazier' and son of chief justice Burt (de Garis and Stannage 1979, 7:494) | 1847 Born in St Kitts, West Indies. Educated in England then in Perth (de Garis and Stannage 1979, 7:494). | 1861 Brought to Western Australia as a child by parents.<br>1868 Became articled clerk.<br>1870 Admitted to WA Bar.<br>1876 Taken into partnership by Sir Edward Stone, and 'Stone & Burt quickly established itself as one of WA's leading legal firms.'<br>1874 Became member of Legislative Council.<br>1886 Temporarily attorney-general, then 'rewarded' with 'appointment as one of WA's […] reps […] at the Colonial Conference in London in 1887'.<br>1881–89 Member of the Perth City Council.<br>1880s Was a key exponent of WA Constitution and independence from Westminster.<br>1890–1900 Retained seat in Legislative Assembly.<br>1890s Was attorney-general.<br>1877– Became Pastoralist, when joined Forrest brothers in syndicate lease of 590,000 acres. Leased at least four other 'station' lands, installing family members on most of them (de Garis and Stannage 1979, 7:494–96). |

*Continued*

| Years of activity in Australia | Name and dates | Years and Roles/activities in West Indies | Years and Roles/activities in Australia and New Zealand |
|---|---|---|---|
| 1869–1912 | **Octavius Burt (1849–1940)** 'public servant' brother of Septimus, son of Archibald Paull (de Garis and Stannage 1979, 7:495). | 1849 Born at St Kitts, West Indies. Educated in England then in Perth (de Garis and Stannage 1979, 7:495). | 1861 Brought to Western Australia as a child by parents.<br>1869 '[E]ntered civil service as a clerk.'<br>1872 Clerk in Governor's Office.<br>1874–77 Private secretary to the governor and clerk to the Executive Council.<br>1877–80 Clerk of records in Survey Office.<br>1880–87 Was resident magistrate for Toodyay District.<br>1887–90 Assistant colonial secretary.<br>1890 Colonial secretary.<br>1901–12 Sheriff and comptroller of prisons, and deputy marshal of the High Court of Australia. WA's 'chief electoral officer for fifteen years', conducted Federation referendum of 1900 and the first Fed. Election in 1901 (de Garis and Stannage 1979, 7:495–96). |
| 1872–79<br>1879–80 | **Sir Hercules George Robert Robinson (1824–1897)** governor. Born and raised in Ireland (Nairn 1976, 6:48). | 1854 President of Montserrat.<br>1855 Lieutenant-Governor of St Christopher (St Kitts). Dormant commission as Governor-in-Chief of the Leeward Islands.<br>1859–65 Governor of Hong Kong (Nairn 1976, 6:48–50). | 1872–79 Governor of New South Wales.<br>1879–80 Governor of New Zealand (Nairn 1976, 6:48–50). |

| | | | |
|---|---|---|---|
| 1873–77<br>1883–88 | **Sir Anthony Musgrave (1828–1888)**<br>Born in Antigua, West Indies, and raised in WI (Gibbney 1974a, 5:324). | 1849 Appointed private secretary to the Governor of the Leeward Islands.<br>1860–61 Administrator of Nevis, St Vincent.<br>1877–83 Governor of Jamaica (*later became administrator of Newfoundland) (Gibbney 1974a, 5:324). | 1873–77 Governor of South Australia.<br>1883–88 Governor of Queensland (Gibbney 1974a, 5:324). |
| 1875–77 1880–89<br>1890–95 | **Sir William Cleaver Francis Robinson (1834–1897)** governor, educated at Royal Naval School (Crowley 1976, 6:50). | 1855 Private secretary to his elder brother Hercules, the Lieutenant-Governor of St Kitts.<br>1862 President of Monserrat.<br>1865 Administered the Government of Dominica.<br>1870–73 Governor of Prince Edward Island.<br>1874 Governor of the Leeward Islands.<br>1877 Governor of the Straits Settlements (headquarters Singapore).<br>1887 Was offered but declined governorship of Hong Kong.<br>1889 Was offered but declined governorship of Mauritius (Crowley 1976, 6:50–51). | 1875–77 and 1880–83 Governor of Western Australia.<br>1883–89 and 1890–95 Governor of South Australia.<br>1889 Acting Governor of Victoria (Crowley 1976, 6:50–51). |

*Continued*

| Years of activity in Australia | Name and dates | Years and Roles/activities in West Indies | Years and Roles/activities in Australia and New Zealand |
|---|---|---|---|
| 1877–80 | **Sir Harry St George Ord (1819–1885)** soldier and governor (Boyce 1974, 5:370). | 1837? Second Lieutenant in the Royal Engineers, stationed in West Indies.<br>1857–61 Lieutenant-Governor of Dominica.<br>1861–64 Governor of the Bermudas.<br>1867–73 Governor of the Straits Settlements (Singapore) (Boyce 1974, 5:370). | 1855 Special Commissioner to the Gold Coast (South Africa).<br>1877 Lieutenant-Governor of South Australia.<br>1878 Governor of Western Australia (Boyce 1974, 5:370). |
| 1878–84 | **Henry Ling Roth (1855–1925)** sugar grower, anthropologist, museum curator (Griffin 1988, vol. 11). | 1855 Born in England, educated London and Germany.<br>1875 Visited British Guiana in West Indies (Griffin 1988, vol. 11). | 1878 Commissioned by English businessmen to report on potential of the sugar industry in Australian colonies.<br>1878 Arrived in Queensland and settled in Mackay.<br>1880 Roth's *Report on the Sugar Cane Industry in Queensland* published.<br>1881–84 Honorary secretary of the Mackay Planters' and Farmers' Association.<br>1884 Returned to England, becoming curator of Bankfield Museum in Yorkshire.<br>1887 Roth undertaking anthropological research on Tasmanian Aborigines.<br>1890 Published *Guide to the Literature of Sugar*….<br>1893 Published paper in anthropology journal on comparative birth practices and beliefs, focusing on Australian Aborigines, and linking practices between Australia and British Guiana (Griffin 1988, vol. 11). |

| | | | |
|---|---|---|---|
| 1880–1883<br>1885–1887 | **Sir Henry Thomas Wrenfordsley (1825–1908)** judge (Louch 1976, vol.6). | 1891–1901 chief justice of the Leeward Islands (Louch 1976, vol.6). | 1880 Appointed Chief Justice of Western Australia'<br>1883 Chief Justice of Fiji.<br>1885–1887 acting-judge of Tasmania<br>1888—1891 barrister in Melbourne (Louch1976, vol.6). |
| 1887–93 | **Sir Robert George Hamilton (1836–1895)** governor and military/colonial civil servant (Refshauge 1972, vol. 4). | 1836 Born and educated in Scotland.<br>1857–78 Various positions as accountant/administrator of colonial/home offices in England.<br>1879 Member of Carnarvon's commission of colonial defences.<br>1882 Made permanent secretary to the Admiralty.<br>1883 Was 'lent to the Irish administration'.<br>1886 Removed from under-secretaryship of Ireland, partly due to his 'sympathies' for Home Rule.<br>1893 Returned from Australia to English civil service, and was appointed to royal commission on Constitution of Dominica (Refshauge 1972, vol. 4). | 1887 Appointed Governor of Tasmania, as 'compensation'. 'Helped to found the University of Tasmania and several technical schools, and opened many museums and art galleries.'<br>1895 Died at South Kensington (Refshauge 1972, vol. 4). |

*Continued*

| Years of activity in Australia | Name and dates | Years and Roles/activities in West Indies | Years and Roles/activities in Australia and New Zealand |
|---|---|---|---|
| 1901–04 | **Sir Arthur Elibank Havelock (1844–1908)** governor and officer (Cartland 1983, vol. 9). | 1873 Aide-de-camp to Governor of Mauritius.<br>1874–75 Chief Civil Commissioner of the Seychelles.<br>1876 Colonial Secretary and Receiver-General of Fiji.<br>1884–85 Governor of Trinidad.<br>1901 Offered governorships of Straits Settlements and Victoria, but refused (ill health) (Cartland 1983, vol. 9). | 1901–04 Governor of Tasmania (Cartland 1983, vol. 9). |
| 1903–08 | **Sir George Ruthven Le Hunte (1852–1925)** governor (Langmore 1986, 10:66). | 1887–94 President of Dominica.<br>1894–97 Colonial Secretary of Barbados and Mauritius (1897).<br>1899–1902 Lieutenant-Governor of British New Guinea.<br>1908–15 Governor of Trinidad and Tobago (Langmore 1986, 10:66–67). | 1903–08 Governor of South Australia (Langmore 1986, 10:66–67). |
| 1909–14 | **Admiral Sir Day Hort Bosanquet (1843–1923)** admiral and governor (Howell 1979, 7:351). | 1899–1902 Commander-in-chief of East Indies.<br>1904–07 Commander-in-chief 'on the North America and West Indies Station'.<br>*Early in his career 'was present at the taking of Canton' (Howell 1979, 7:351–52). | 1909–14 Governor of South Australia (Howell 1979, 7:351–52). |

**Sub-category 2. Individuals not directly sent: merchants/pastoralists/ship-owners/clergy/lawyers/journalists**

| | | | |
|---|---|---|---|
| 1787–92<br>1794–1800 | **John Shortland (1769–1810)** naval officer, landowner<br>*son of John Shortland (see Governors, military) (McMartin 1967b, vol. 2). | 1783–87 Served as midshipman in the West Indies (McMartin 1967b, vol. 2). | 1787 Master's Mate on *Sirius* in First Fleet. 1788–92 Serving in the colonies, including 11 months on Norfolk Island when the *Sirius* was wrecked there in 1790.<br>1794 Returned to Australia (from England) with new Governor, John Hunter.<br>1797 Gave name to river in estuary of Hunter, while chasing escaped convicts.<br>1797 Granted land.<br>1800 Returned to active service in navy (McMartin 1967b, vol. 2). |
| 1792–99 | **William Raven (1756–1814)** naval officer and merchant mariner (Parsons 1967b, vol. 2). | 1779 Served as Master of a merchant ship in West Indies.<br>*Married Lucinda Wilson, daughter of the Chief Justice of Dominica (Parsons 1967b, vol. 2). | 1792 Captain and part-owner of the *Britannica*, which sailed to NSW, and was then chartered for governmental purposes in the following several years, including trips to Norfolk Island and New Zealand.<br>1799 Master on the *Buffalo* store-ship which sailed to Port Jackson.<br>? Was granted substantial farming land in NSW, managed by James Squire (Parsons 1967b, vol. 2). |
| 1795–96 | **Joseph Gerald (1760–1796)** political reformer and convict (McDougall 2002, 1) | 1760 born in St Kitts, son of an Irish planter. 'Brought to England as a child.'<br>ca. 1780 returned to St Kitts to find inheritance 'dissipated' (McDougall 2002, 1). | 1788 onwards became 'a prominent figure in radical circles' in London, advocating parliamentary reform and sympathetic to French Revolutionaries.<br>1794 Trial for sedition, convicted and sentenced to transportation.<br>1795 After a year in Newgate gaol with Tuberculosis, was suddenly put aboard convict ship, arrived Sydney with advanced tuberculosis.<br>1796 Died (*Westminster Review* 1833, 19:353). |

*Continued*

| Years of activity in Australia | Name and dates | Years and Roles/activities in West Indies | Years and Roles/activities in Australia and New Zealand |
|---|---|---|---|
| 1816–20<br>1823–69 | **Thomas Alison Scott (1777?–1881)** 'pioneer sugar grower' (Parsons 1967c, 2:430). | 1797 'Customs searcher and waiter' in St Thomas, and also managed his father's estate in Antigua for several years.<br>1820 Investigated establishment of sugar plantation in Tahiti, then established a plantation in Raiatea, 1822 (Parsons 1967c, 2:430–31). | 1823 Engaged to grow sugar and tobacco at Port Macquarie. Sugar grown there in 1824 was the first grown in Australia.<br>1825 Suspended and investigated for mismanagement by Commission of Inquiry. Campaigned for the introduction of sugar on a commercial basis in the colony (Parsons 1967c, 2:430–31). |
| 1817–18 | **Jeremiah Francis O'Flynn (1788–1831)** 'Roman Catholic priest'.<br>Born and raised in Ireland (Parsons 1967a, 2:299). | 1813 '[O]rdained deacon and went with other Trappist monks to establish a mission in the West Indies.' British Governor expelled the mission from Martinique, but O'Flynn 'allowed to remain as pastor of Santa Cruz'.<br>1816 Was 'charged with intrusion and incompetence' by Archbishop Neale of Baltimore 'who held ecclesiastical jurisdiction over the Danish islands of the West Indies'. Went to Rome to answer charges (Parsons 1967a, 2:299–300). | 1816 Petitioned Colonial Office for permission to go to NSW. Bathurst 'refused O'Flynn's request on the grounds of his insufficient education and poor command of English' (Parsons 1967a, 2:299–300).<br>Sailed for NSW anyway. Told Macquarie on arrival that he had Bathurst's permission, but due to lack of proof Macquarie told him to leave. O'Flynn promised not to work as a priest. Macquarie agreed but then arrested O'Flynn and sent him back to London, as he had been performing lots of priest duties. Returned to Ireland and then West Indies. Banished from San Domingo, went to Philadelphia, back to San Domingo 1823, back to Phil. 1825.<br>1831 Died in Philadelphia. The publicity caused by his history in NSW influenced the British Gov. to allow first official Roman Catholic missionaries to be sent to Australia in 1820 (Parsons 1967a, 2:299–300). |

| | | | |
|---|---|---|---|
| 1817–51 | **Thomas White Melville Winder (1789–1853)** 'merchant and farmer' (Guilford 1967, 2:613). | '[T]raded for some years in the East and West Indies' (Guilford 1967, 2:613). | 1817 Arrived NSW and established the Lachlan Flour Mills at Kensington. One of the largest proprietors on the Hunter. First to hold a monopoly of coal mined in the Newcastle district (Guilford 1967, 2:613–14). |
| 1818–44 | **Jean Charles Prosper de Mestre (1789–1844)** merchant (Walsh 1966, vol. 1). | 1789 '[B]orn at sea in a British ship on the way to the West Indies […] the son of a French officer fleeing […] during the revolution.'<br>Early years in Martinique (until ca. 1804) (Walsh 1966, vol. 1). | 1818 Started successful import business in Sydney.<br>1820s Began whaling.<br>1825 Became the second person to be 'naturalized' as an Australian (had been considered American), after petitioning of Legislative Council by William Charles Wentworth.<br>1830 Applied to register ship, and his citizenship status legally challenged, but Chief Justice Sir Francis Forbes ruled that 'because he had been born on the high seas in a British ship he was a British subject'.<br>1826–42 Director of the Bank of NSW.<br>1840 Founder of Mutual Fire Insurance Co. (Walsh 1966, vol. 1). |
| 1822–38 | **Alexander Kenneth McKenzie (1769–1838)** 'banker and landowner' (ADB 1967, vol. 2). | 1792 Married Elizabeth Punnet in St Vincent, West Indies (*ADB* 1967, vol. 2). | 1822 Secretary and Cashier of Bank of NSW in Sydney.<br>1825 Treasurer of the Sydney auxiliary of the Church Missionary Society, and of the Religious Tract Society and of the Turf Club. Also collected subscriptions for the building of a Roman Catholic chapel.<br>1820s Major landowner near Bathurst.<br>1827 Became Magistrate.<br>1827 Threatened with charges for corruption after printing banknotes, and resigned from all posts.<br>1834 '[H]elped to found the Bathurst Bank' and was President of it.<br>1836 Reappointed as Magistrate.<br>1837 Retired (*ADB* 1967, vol. 2). |

*Continued*

| Years of activity in Australia | Name and dates | Years and Roles/activities in West Indies | Years and Roles/activities in Australia and New Zealand |
| --- | --- | --- | --- |
| 1822–51 | **Gilbert Robertson 1794–1851)** 'editor and agriculturalist', also gov. superintendent (Godfrey 1967, vol. 2). | 1794 Born at Trinidad, West Indies (Godfrey 1967, vol. 2). | 1825–30 Superintendent on the government farm at New Town, VDL.<br>1832 Editor and reporter for the *Colonist* newspaper.<br>1834 Published *The True Colonist and Van Diemen's Land Political Dispatch and Agricultural and Commercial Advertiser*. This became Tasmania's first daily. Later was editor of the *Victoria Colonist and Western District Advertiser.*<br>1844 Last issue of *True Colonist.*<br>1844 Superintendent of agriculture at Norfolk Island.<br>1846 Station Overseer in Victoria. Was Editor of *Victoria Colonist* when killed in 1851 (Godfrey 1967, vol. 2). |
| 1823–39 | **Richard Willis (1777–1855)** settler, landowner (Eldershaw 1967, vol. 2). | 1800 Married Anne Harper, who was born in St Kitts, West Indies (Eldershaw 1967, vol. 2). | 1823 Arrived in Hobart Town with wife and eleven children. Took possession of large amounts of land.<br>1825 Became Magistrate.<br>1832 Had 35 convicts working for him by this time.<br>1836 Appointed to Legislative Council by Governor Arthur (Eldershaw 1967, vol. 2). |
| 1824–42 | **Charles McLachlan (1795?–1855)** businessman (Macmillan and Morris 1967, vol. 2). | ca. 1815 Employed in the West Indies as a planting manager/ commercial agent by Glasgow firm Ewing & Reid (until approx. 1822) (Macmillan and Morris 1967, vol. 2). | 1822 Employed in head office of the Australian Co. in Scotland. Sent to Hobart Town to work as the principal agent in Australia. The Co. brought out hundreds of Scottish settlers.<br>1828 Promoter of the Hobart Exchange.<br>1828 Director of the Bank of Van Diemen's Land.<br>1832–42 Legislative Council member, and |

| | | | |
|---|---|---|---|
| | | | Managing Director of the Derwent Bank and the Commercial Bank of VDL. Chairman of the Hobart meeting which petitioned the British government to revoke the order of removal of Sydney convicts to VDL (Macmillan and Morris 1967, vol. 2). |
| 1828–63 | **Archibald Mosman (1799–1863)** 'merchant and pastoralist' (Stephen 1967, 2:263). | 1820s 'Archibald and his twin brother George, after spending some time growing sugar in the West Indies, arrived in Sydney' (Stephen 1967, 2:263). | 1828 Began various business ventures in Sydney, including a whaling depot (located in much of what is now the suburb Mosman), the Floating Bridge Co, the Sydney Ferry Co. and the Australian Auction Co. (Stephen 1967, 2:263). |
| 1829–65 | **Daniel Scott (1800–1865)** harbourmaster (Coles 1967, vol. 2). | 1821 captained 'a small cargo ship that plied between the Gold Coast and West Indies' (Coles 1967, vol. 2). | 1829 Arrived at Freemantle and was made Deputy Harbor-Master. His boat, the *Mary Ann*, was commissioned by Governor Stirling to transport provisions from Garden Island to mainland.<br>1836 Was largely responsible for having the first sea-going vessel built in the colony (the *Lady Stirling*). Also part-owner of a whaling vessel. Later founded Geraldton Mining & Smelting Co. (Coles 1967, vol. 2). |
| 1836–88 | **Charles Smith (1816–1897)** 'shipping merchant' (Maude 1976, 6:141). | Early 1830s Served in the West Indies with the merchant navy (Maude 1976, 6:141–42). | 1836 Worked in Flower, Saltings & Co.'s whaling fleet.<br>1850 Became manager of the whaling company.<br>1869 '[S]at on imperial royal commission into alleged kidnapping of natives of the Loyalty Islands.'<br>1890–97 Was a Director of the Bank of New South Wales (Maude 1976, 6:141–42). |

*Continued*

| Years of activity in Australia | Name and dates | Years and Roles/activities in West Indies | Years and Roles/activities in Australia and New Zealand |
|---|---|---|---|
| 1836–81 | **Henry Rotton (1814–1881)** pastoralist, publican (Lea-Scarlett 1976, vol. 6). | ca. 1835 Passenger aboard a merchant ship 'that was wrecked in the West Indies' (Lea-Scarlett 1976, vol. 6). | 1836 Arrived at Kangaroo Island, South Australia, 'as second mate in the *Emma* and soon made his way to Sydney'.<br>1839 Publican of Queen Victoria Inn at Solitary Creek.<br>1840 Became 'a mail-coach proprietor'.<br>1853 Bought estate near Bathurst using gold rush money, and became successful pastoralist.<br>1858 Elected to Leg. Assembly, supporting John Robertson.<br>1859–64 Legislative Assembly representative for Hartley.<br>1869–81 Chairman of the Bathurst Sheep Board.<br>Was a 'zealous supporter of the Baptists' (Lea-Scarlett 1976, vol. 6). |
| 1838–88 | **Christopher Rolleston (1817–1888)** 'public servant and landowner' (Cunneen 1976, vol. 6). | 1855 '[R]eputedly [...] declined the presidency of Montserrat, West Indies' (Cunneen 1976, vol. 6). | 1838 Arrived at Sydney, bought land, unsuccessfully farmed with his brother.<br>1842 Appointed as commissioner of crown lands (Darling Downs) by Governor Gipps.<br>1855 Became private secretary to governor-general Sir William Denison. Then appointed registrar-general.<br>1856 '[L]aunched compulsory registration of births, deaths and marriages.'<br>1856 onwards: Was treasurer/vice-president/ president of Philosophical (Royal) Society of New South Wales.<br>1864 Became auditor-general.<br>1883 Retired. |

| | | | |
|---|---|---|---|
| | | | 1887 Appointed to Royal Commission inquiry into civil service.<br>Was also director of Mercantile Bank of Sydney, and other commercial orgs. Was 'prominent Anglican layman' and was member of Sydney diocesan synod.<br>1872 Elected to Senate of University of Sydney (Cunneen 1976, vol. 6). |
| 1843–76 | **Robert Macintosh Isaacs (1814–1876)** 'barrister and politician' (Forbes 1972, 4:464). | 1814 Born at Tortola, Virgin Islands, West Indies. Educated England, called to Bar 1839, practiced London (Forbes 1972, 4:464). | 1843 Emigrated to Sydney, admitted to Bar of NSW.<br>1854 Visited England, shipwrecked at Cape Otway, returned to Sydney 1855.<br>1856 '[R]efused appointment as attorney-general in the first ministry in the new parliament' in favour of his law practice.<br>1857–61 Member of the Legislative Council.<br>1860 New South Wales Constitutional Association.<br>1865 Won Yass Plains seat in Leg. Assembly.<br>1866 Became Solicitor-General.<br>1869 Lost seat.<br>1871 Barrister in Hobart and Chancellor of the Anglican Archdiocese.<br>1872 Crown Prosecutor in western districts of Sydney (Forbes 1972, 4:464). |

*Continued*

| Years of activity in Australia | Name and dates | Years and Roles/activities in West Indies | Years and Roles/activities in Australia and New Zealand |
|---|---|---|---|
| 1854–83 | **James Bickford (1816–95)** 'Wesleyan clergyman' (Howe 1969, 3:162). | 1838–53 Lived and preached in West Indies (Barbados), 'was appointed to several Wesleyan stations' and 'strengthened the denominational school system' (Howe 1969, 3:162–63). | 1854 Sailed to Victoria to eventually join family in South Australia. In Victoria was superintendent of Brighton circuit. Then appointed to Ballarat.<br>1861 Went to St Kilda, where elected secretary of the Australasian Wesleyan Conference.<br>1864 Chippendale, NSW.<br>1866 Superintendent of Yarra Street, Geelong, Circuit.<br>1868 Elected president of AWC (Wesleyan Conf.), and appointed to Wesley Church, Melbourne, 1870.<br>1873 Transferred to Adelaide.<br>1875 President of General Conference and South Australian Conf.<br>1877–80 Promoted emigration to Australia. In England, using own pamphlet, *Australia: God's Gift to the English People*.<br>1880 Returned to SA (Howe 1969, 3:162–63). |
| 1855–57 | **Joseph Ravenscroft Elsey (1834–1857)** 'surgeon, explorer and naturalist' (Chisholm 1972, 4:139). | 1857 After time in Australia returned to London, was about to become Government Surgeon at the Seychelles Islands, but got sick and went instead to West Indies for natural history studies. Died soon after, in St Kitts (Chisholm 1972, 4:139). | 1855 Arrived Sydney and joined the North Australian Exploring Expedition as surgeon and naturalist.<br>1856 Trekked overland to Brisbane. Discovered the 'golden-shouldered parrot', later named so by John Gould, using Elsey's data (Chisholm 1972, 4:139). |

| | | | |
|---|---|---|---|
| 1863–1913 | **Arthur Windsor (1833–1913)** journalist (Sayers 1976, vol. 6). | 1833 '[B]orn at sea on a voyage to Barbados', where family had sugar plantations.<br>1838 onwards: Educated in England.<br>ca. 1852–55 Was a teacher at Codrington College in Barbados (Sayers 1976, vol. 6). | 1862 Appointed Editor of the Melbourne *Argus* newspaper.<br>1865 Left *Argus*, relocated to Castlemaine and became editor of *Mount Alexander Mail*.<br>1869 Returned to Melbourne.<br>1872 Became editor of the *Age*.<br>1892 Became President of the Australian Institute of Journalists.<br>1900 Retired and went back briefly to England but 'didn't like it' and so returned to Melbourne.<br>1913 Died in Melbourne (Sayers 1976, vol. 6). |
| 1873–78 | **François Louis Bugnion (1822–1880)** 'universalist missionary' (*ADB* 1969, vol. 3). | 1863–66 Travelled 'in Europe, America and the West Indies'.<br>1862–63 'served on Mauritius and Bourbon' (*ADB* 1969, vol. 3). | 1873 Arrived at Sydney.<br>1874 '[W]ith help from Dr John Le Gay Brereton he published an abridged catechism.'<br>Applied to SA gov. 'for permission to settle in the Northern Territory 40,000 Mennonites and other disciples from India, America and Mauritius'.<br>1880 Died in ship off Naples, after having organized migration of Russian Mennonites which was blocked by Russian gov. (*ADB* 1969, vol. 3). |
| 1876– | **Henry Hutton Parry (1826–1893)** Anglican bishop (Haynes 1974, 5:407–8). | 1826 Born Antigua. Son of Thomas Parry, archdeacon of Antigua and from 1843. Bishop of Barbados. | 1876 Bishop of Perth diocese.<br>1880 Prompted committee to be set up for religious education of Aboriginal people. |

*Continued*

| Years of activity in Australia | Name and dates | Years and Roles/activities in West Indies | Years and Roles/activities in Australia and New Zealand |
|---|---|---|---|
| | | 1852 Henry ordained priest.<br>1861 Made Archdeacon and same year became vicar-general of the diocese, after his father left the position due to ill health (Haynes 1974, 5:407–8). | 1884 150,000 acres set aside in Murchison area for Aboriginal Mission, but in 1892 whole plan abandoned due to lack of funds.<br>1887 Failed to get funding from England for diocese, prompting church to become self-sufficient (Haynes 1974, 5:407–8). |
| 1902– | **James Gerald Stokely Doorly (1880–1956)** master mariner, writer and musician/composer (Eastwood 1981, vol. 8). | 1880 Born Port of Spain, Trinidad, son of Rev. Doorly (who later became archdeacon of Trinidad). Educated Trinidad and later the Thames Nautical Training College. Friends with E.R.G.R. Evans, who later became Admiral Lord Mountevans.<br>1904 Spent several months on the West India Mail Service ships(?) (Eastwood 1981, vol. 8). | 1902–04 Doorly (and Evans) were junior officers on *Morning*, supply ship to *Discovery*, captained by Scott for the National Antarctic Expedition. The *Morning* freed the *Discovery* from the ice, and Doorly awarded the Polar Service medal.<br>1903 Gained 'mate's' certificate in Hobart.<br>1905 'Joined the Union Steam Ship Co. of New Zealand.'<br>1908 Married Forrestina Muriel Whitson, daughter of the company secretary, at Dunedin.<br>1911 Commander of Komata, and later 23 of the fleet's ships sailing between Australia and New Zealand.<br>1914–18 During WWI 'commanded New Zealand troop transports and Admiralty colliers'.<br>1925 Left the New Zealand co. and settled in Melbourne, joining the Port Phillip Sea Pilot's Service (Eastwood 1981, vol. 8). |

*British regiments that served in both Australian colonies and Caribbean colonies:*
46th South Devonshire (Cannon 1851, xxviii & xxxii) (Chant 2013, 144).
48th Northamptonshire (Cimitiere 1966).

40th (2nd Somerset) (Southey 1827, 3:113; Reynolds 1967a, vol. 2).

63rd (West Suffolk) (Southey 1827, 3:599; Crowley 1967, 2:487).

17th (Leicestershire) (Southey 1827, 3:129; Cranfield 1966, vol. 1).

4th (King's Own) in West Indies (Southey 1827, 3:404; Haenke 1976, vol. 6) and as 34th and 55th affiliated in Australia (Chant 2013, 107).

50th (West Kent) (Southey 1827, 3:439; Barry 1966, 1:13–14).

21st (Royal North British Fusiliers) (F. Hooper 1966, 1:125).

28th (North Gloucestershire) (National Army Museum 2014a, online).

96th (Manchester) (Tameside Metropolitan Borough 2011, online).

99th (Wiltshire) Previous regiment with designation 99th raised and then disbanded in Jamaica (Southey 1827, 3:116; ADB 1966, vol.1: 'Barney, George').

65th (2nd Yorkshire, North Riding) (Raikes 1885, 102).

77th (East Middlesex) (Woollright 1907, 53–54, 108).

73rd (McLachlan 1967, 1:187–95).

3rd (Royal East Kent) (Barker 1967, 2:482).

Royal Engineers (Southey 1827, 3:281; Barney 1966).

71st Royal (Scott and Taylor 1824, 10:418; National Library Australia 1998, Part 8:112).

57th and 77th Middlesex (Duke of Cambridge's Own) (Chant 2013, 94).

14th (Buckinghamshire/The Prince of Wales's Own) (National Army Museum 2014b, online).

# NOTES

## Introduction

1 After this book had been submitted to the publisher, Tim Winton published his Australian 'landscape memoir' titled *Island Home* (Melbourne: Penguin, 2015).

2 In *Death of a Discipline* (New York: Columbia University Press, 2003) and *An Aesthetic Education in the Era of Globalization* (Cambridge, MA: Harvard University Press, 2012) Gayatri Spivak distinguishes between the categories of globe and planet and calls for 'the planet to overwrite the globe' (2003, 72). In 'Globalization and Political Strategy' (*New Left Review* 4 (2000): 49–68) Frederic Jameson debates the role of the nation state in the era of globalization. In his earlier essay, 'Notes on Globalization as a Philosophical Issue', he posits the era of globalization as the multinational stage of capitalism (*The Cultures of Globalization*, eds Frederic Jameson and Masao Miyoshi (Durham, NC: Duke University Press, 1998), 54–80).

3 For a discussion of factual instances, see Godfrey Baldacchino 'Islands and Despots,' *Commonwealth and Comparative Politics* 50, no. 1 (2012): 103–20.

4 Paul Giles's recent study, *Antipodean America: Australasia and the Constitution of U.S.* Literature (Oxford: Oxford University Press, 2013) also expands the national literatures of the United States, Australia and New Zealand by identifying complex processes of literary circulation, influence and exchange.

## 1. What's in a Metaphor: 'No Man Is an Island'

1 A similar point is made by Noam Finkler in 'John Donne and the "Anthropomorphic Map" Tradition', *Applied Semiotics*, 3, no. 8 (1999): 207–15, and by Joseph W. Meeker in 'Subtleties of the Isle: Islands and the Imagination', *Isle: Interdisciplinary Studies in Literature and Environment*, 18, no. 1 (Winter 2011): 197–202.

2 See also Jeanne Shami, 'John Donne: Geography as Metaphor', in *Geography and Literature: A Meeting of the Disciplines*, eds William E. Mallory and Paul Simpson Housley (Syracuse: Syracuse University Press, 1987), 161–67.

3 For a critique of Eliot's discovery see Dayton Haskin, *John Donne in the Nineteenth Century* (Oxford: Oxford University Press, 2007), 9.

4 For significant engagements with Benjamin's text see Giorgio Agamben, *Homo Sacer: Sovereign Power and Bare Life*, trans. Daniel Hellor-Roazen (California: Stanford University Press, 1998), 63–69; Judith Butler, 'Critique, Coercion and Sacred Life in Benjamin's "Critique of Violence"', in *Political Theologies: Public Religions in a Post-Secular World*, eds Hent de Vries and Lawrence E. Sullivan (New York: Fordham University Press, 2006), 201–19; Simon Critchley, 'Violent Thoughts about Slavoj Žižek', on Naked Punch.com,

ed. Qalander Bux Memon (21 October 2009, accessed 28 November 2011); Jacques Derrida, 'Force of Law: The "Mystical Foundation of Authority" (1989)', in *Acts of Religion*, by Jacques Derrida, trans. Mary Quaintance, ed. Gil Anidja (London and New York: Routledge, 2002), 230–98; Beatrice Hanssen, 'On the Politics of Pure Means: Benjamin, Arendt, Foucault', in *Critique of Violence: Between Poststructuralism and Critical Theory*, by Beatrice Hanssen (New York and London: Taylor & Francis, 2000), 16–29; and Slavoj Žižek, 'Language, Violence, and Non-Violence', in *International Journal of Žižek Studies*, 2, no. 3 (2008) (accessed at ZizekStudies.org, 29 November, 2011): 1–12.

5 Donne also wrote, though did not publish, a treatise on suicide. See John Donne, *Biathanatos*, intro. and comntr. Michael Rudick and M. Pabst Battin (New York and London: Garland, 1982).

6 See also John Singe's. *My Island Home: A Torres Strait Memoir* (St Lucia: University of Queensland Press, 2003) and Catherine Titasey's play on the phrase in the title of her detective novel, *My Island Homicide* (St Lucia: University of Queensland Press, 2013).

7 See also: Judith Butler, 'Melancholy Gender/Refused Identification', in *The Judith Butler Reader*, ed. by Sara Salih with Judith Butler (Massachusetts; Oxford; Victoria: Blackwell, 2004 (1997)), pp. 243–301; and Nicolas Abraham and Maria Torok, 'Mourning or Melancholia: Introjection versus Incorporation', in *The Shell and the Kernel: Renewals of Psychoanalysis*, by Nicolas Abraham and Maria Torok, ed. and trans. and intro. Nicholas T. Rand (London and Chicago: University of Chicago Press, 1994 (1972)), pp. 125–36.

8 Marc Shell's awaited *Islandology: Geography, Rhetoric, Politics* (Stanford CA: Stanford University Press, 2014), published as this book manuscript was submitted to the publisher, contains extensive discussion of island etymologies.

9 See Geoffrey Keynes, p. 279; Robert L. Sharp, 'Donne's "Good-Morrow" and the Cordiform Maps', *Modern Language Notes*, 69, no. 7 (1954): 493–95; Donald K. Anderson Jr., 'Donne's "Hymne to God my God, in my sicknesse" and the T-in-O Maps', *South Atlantic Quarterly* 71 (1972): 465–72; Claude Gandelman, 'The Poem as Map: John Donne and the "Anthropomorphic Landscape" Tradition', *Arcadia: Zeitschrift für Vergleichende Literaturwissenschaft* 19 (1984): 244–51; Claude Gandelman, *Reading Pictures, Viewing Texts* (Bloomington: Indiana University Press, 1991); Jeanne Shami, 'John Donne: Geography as Metaphor', in *Geography and Literature: A Meeting of the Disciplines*, eds William E. Mallory and Paul Simpson Housley (Syracuse: Syracuse University Press, 1987), pp. 161–67.

10 Actually it was Charles Darwin who first made this distinction, as Beer notes (1997, 38).

## 2. The First and Last of New Worlds: The Caribbean and Australia

1 In the British context William Dampier (1651–1715) has received a deal of critical attention in this regard, partly because his account of his travels in *A New Voyage Round the World* (1697) stands in such stark contrast to the scurrilous known events of his life as a buccaneer. Dampier's textual persona was fabricated (successfully) with the clear goals of resituating himself as a proper English citizen (Neill 2000) and as a modern man of science (Hasty 2010).

2 The relevant text of Locke's *Two Treatises of Government* (1689), which uses 'America' as its case in point, reads:

> Thus in the beginning all the World was *America*, and more so than that is now; for no such thing as *Money* was any where known. Find out something that hath the *Use and Value of Money* amongst his Neighbours, you shall see the same Man will begin presently to *enlarge* his *Possessions*. (2007, 45)

3 See Grenfell-Price's discussion of the achievements of Cook's second expedition in relation to the failed Antarctic discovery: 'At this time there was still little realization that Cook had discovered a fertile shoreline of continental dimensions of the East Australian coast' (1971, 173).

4 W. J. L. Wharton, who edited the 1893 edition of Cook's *Endeavour* journal, writes: 'The main object of the voyage was the settlement of the great question of the southern Continent. Cook was directed to explore the whole region about the South Pole, starting from the Cape of Good Hope, and working eastward' (1893).

5 See Lisa Gorton's discussion of this shift in relation to John Donne in her 'John Donne's Use of Space', *Early Modern Literary Studies* 4, no. 2 (1998): 1–27. For numerous fascinating essays on this topic see *The History of Cartography Volume 3, Part 1: Cartography in the European Renaissance*, ed. David Woodward (Chicago and London: University of Chicago Press, 2007).

6 See Martin Heidegger, *On Time and Being* (New York: Harper and Row, 1972) and Paul Friedlander, 'Aletheia: A Discussion with Martin Heidegger', in *Plato: An Introduction* (New Jersey: Princeton University Press, 2015), 221–29.

7 My knowledge of Charles O'Hara Booth is indebted to Dr Jennifer Livett and her extensive research into Van Diemen's Land during the governorship of John Franklin. See her forthcoming novel *Wild Little Island* (Sydney: Allen and Unwin, 2016).

8 Throughout the remainder of his life in Van Diemen's Land Booth was involved in institutions for the welfare of children: he founded a separate prison for boys at Point Puer to protect the boys from the men; and after Port Arthur he took up the role Superintendent of the Orphan Schools of Hobart. These schools had been established by Governor Arthur in 1827 to care for the increasing numbers of illegitimate children in the colony, born and abandoned in much the same way as Booth himself had done in St Vincent.

9 Booth's journals record his many attempts to marry and settle down: one code-named 'Dearest Phoebe', with whom he had an agreement, dies (29 May 1836) and another turns him down (28 January 1838). On these occasions he describes himself as 'heart broken and miserable' and 'perfectly miserable at heart' (Booth 1981, 199, 221).

10 O'Hara Booth's experience is itself mirrored by Commandant Lieutenant John Bowen, who established the first British settlement at Risdon Cove in Van Diemen's Land in 1802 at age 24. Bowen had travelled to Port Jackson on the convict ship HMS *Glatton*, where he had 'formed an attachment' with Martha Hayes, the 13-year-old daughter of a convict, who bore him two daughters in Van Diemen's Land. The second girl was born after Bowen's departure and Bowen never saw her. In reverse sequence to Booth, Bowen went to serve in India and the Caribbean and, in 1825, in England, Bowen married Elizabeth Lindley Clowes (Clooes), a niece of the Countess of Newburgh (Flinn 1966, n.p.). The archive is full of such stories, though they are still often not explicit, which range across the spectrum from indicators of greater social fluidity away from home to exploitation.

11 Of these 147 were sent from the West Indies, another 52 were resident in Britain and one in Mauritius, though these 53 were born in the West Indies, and two were convicted in Australia (Duffield 1986, 25).

12 At the 175th Anniversary Dinner of the Supreme Court of New South Wales in 1999, Chief Justice Murray Gleeson assessed that Bent 'is generally regarded, not only as the first judge in New South Wales, but also as the worst' (1999).

13 Erstwhile naval captain in the West Indies and sometime commandant of Norfolk Island Joseph Anderson (1790–1877) took up 85,000 acres on the Goulburn River with his brother. Another naval captain who distinguished himself in Dominica, Maurice McConnell (1768–1848) arrived in Port Jackson in 1809 and six months later married Mary Bligh, daughter of former Governor Bligh. Between them they were bequeathed 5,500 acres of land, though McConnell later acted for his wife and her sisters who wanted to claim the whole town of Parramatta – and much more – as their father's heirs. Of course William Bligh himself also had many connections with the Caribbean as well as the Australian colonies.

14 One such man was Thomas Scott (1777–1881), who had managed his father's plantation in Antigua for several years and saw the potential in the Australian colonies during a visit and decided to stay. He was commissioned to establish a sugar plantation at Raiatea (Society Islands) in 1822 and then at Port Macquarie, New South Wales, in 1823, which was largely unsuccessful, though he continued to campaign for the introduction of sugar and later supplied plants and advice to its successful establishment in Queensland.As Greg Dening writes, Bligh's ill-fated voyage on the *Bounty* 'was transporting the breadfruit tree, the very symbol of a free and unencumbered life from the island of freedom, Tahiti, to the islands of bondage, the West Indies and their slave plantations (1994, 11).

15 See, for example, Anthony Trollope's racialization of West Indian people in *The West Indies and the Spanish Main* (London: Chapman and Hall, 1860), which devotes individual chapters to different shades of skins colour.

16 Winston James's discussion of 'froudacity' cites its deployment by N. Darnell Davis in a 40-page essay titled 'Mr Froude's Negrophobia; or, Don Quixote as a Cook's Tourist', published in British Guiana as a pamphlet and in the journal *Timehri* in 1888, prior to Thomas's *Froudacity* (James, 'Culture, Labor and Race in the Shadow of US Capital', in *The Caribbean: A History of the Region and Its Peoples*, eds Stephan Palmié and Francisco A. Scarano (Chicago and London: University of Chicago Press, 2011), 447). Claudia Brandenstein also notes the coinages prompted by Trollope and Froude in 'Representations of Landscape and Nature in Anthony Trollope's *The West Indies and the Spanish Main* and James Anthony Froude's *The English in the West Indies*', in *Five Emus to the King of Siam: Environment and Empire*, ed. Helen Tiffin (Amsterdam: Rodopi, 2007), 16.

## 3. Insular and Continental Interiors: The Shifting Map of Literary Universalism after the War

1 Lukács takes this phrase from Novalis: 'Philosophy is really homesickness,' says Novalis: 'it is the urge to be at home everywhere' (quoted in Lukács 1920, 3).

2 Jill Franks argues for the significance of islands for the Modernists: see her *Islands and the Modernists: The Allure of Isolation in Art, Literature and Science* (London: McFarlane, 2006).

3 Jonathan Bolton reads Auden's poem as the poet's decision to remain in England 'and attend to what he perceived as being the civic obligations of a highbrow intellectual' rather than join Christopher Isherwood on the Greek island of St Nicholas (*The Explicator* 53, no. 1 (1994): 57).

4 White plays with this distinction in numerous texts, see for example the first page of *The Twyborn Affair* (London: Penguin, 1979).

5 Brigitta Olubas makes a related point regarding the mountain panorama in her discussion of the title story from Hazzard's 1961 collection *Cliffs of Fall* (London: Macmillan, 1963) in which the heroine, also called Elizabeth, is overwhelmed with grief at the mountain summit (2012, 90–93).

6 John Frow alerts us to this practice in Hazzard's work from the very title of his essay 'Future Anterior: *The Evening of the Holiday*,' in *Shirley Hazzard: New Critical Essays*, ed. Brigitta Olubas (Sydney: Sydney University Press, 2014, 3–11), and Robert Dixon examines the operations of prolepsis in *The Transit of Venus* in 'Returning to the Scene of the Crime: On Re-reading *The Transit of Venus*,' in *Shirley Hazzard: New Critical Essays*, ed. Brigitta Olubas (Sydney: Sydney University Press, 2014, 79–93).

7 There are few such instances in the Australian archive, though Christopher Koch's first novel *The Boys in the Island* (Sydney: HarperCollins, 1958) could be read in this vein. There are numerous Australian first novels that narrate island homecomings, such as Danielle Wood's *The Alphabet of Light and Dark* (Sydney: Allen & Unwin, 2003), about Bruny Island off the Tasmanian mainland, and Terri Janke's *Butterfly Song* (Melbourne: Penguin, 2005), about Thursday Island in Torres Strait.

8 Conversely, John Maynard documents the influence of African, American and West Indian sailors on the development of Australian Aboriginal politics in the contact between men on the Sydney docks in the early twentieth century (Maynard, *Fight for Liberty and Freedom: The Origins of Australian Aboriginal Activism* (Canberra: Aboriginal Studies Press, 2007), 19–20).

9 Contemporary Australian novelist Andrew McGahan constructs a similar telescopic trajectory in his island novel, *Wonders of a Godless World* (Sydney: Allen & Unwin, 2009) in which the figure of latent evil is enclosed on the island, within a hospital, within its boiler room and under a volcano. He is embedded, nested within the island's core.

10 The role of the child in West Indian literature has been much commented upon since early postcolonial criticism. See, for example, chapter 3 of Gareth Griffith's *A Double Exile* (London: Marion Boyars, 1978). Griffiths refers to Victor Ramraj's 1971 discussion of this topic ('The All-Embracing Christlike Vision: Tone and Attitude in The Mimic Men', in *Common Wealth* ed. Anna Rutherford (Aarhus: Akademisek Boghandel, 1971), 125–34).

11 Jamaica Kincaid makes a similar point about time on Antigua in *A Small Place* (1997, 53–54).

12 This insular continent is the focus of Suvendrini Perera's critique in her *Australia and the Insular Imagination* (New York: Palgrave Macmillan, 2009).

## 4. Accidents of Empire: Shipwrecks and Castaways

1 The story of Mary Bryant, one of the few survivors of this ordeal, has been the subject of at least 15 fictional and nonfictional accounts.

2 De Gasperin cites Ernst Robert Curtius who notes that the metaphor of the ship of the mind 'was already a commonplace in late antiquity and is conscientiously preserved throughout the middle ages' (de Gasperin 2010, 82).

3 See also Godfrey Baldacchino's discussion 'Island and Despots', *Commonwealth & Comparative Politics* 50, no. 1 (2012): 103–20.

4 The original lines from Part IV of the 'The Rime of the Ancient Mariner' are:

Alone, alone, all, all alone,
Alone on a wide wide sea!
And never a saint took pity on
My soul in agony. (Samuel Taylor Coleridge, *Selected Poetry* (Oxford and New York, Oxford University Press, 1997), 56)

5 Hobbes writes:

Fear and liberty are consistent: as when a man throweth his goods into the sea for fear the ship should sink, he doth it nevertheless very willingly, and may refuse to do it if he will; it is therefore the action of one that was free. (1651, ch. 21)

6 As Golding's text also shows, the topos of the marooned group is popular with children's and young adult fiction as the island provides a contained site for testing social relations and other survival skills without parental guidance and control.

7 The most historically detailed account of the Batavia is Mike Dash's *Batavia's Graveyard: The True Story of the Mad Heretic Who Led History's Bloodiest Mutiny* (London: Weidenfeld & Nicolson, 2002).

8 Henrietta Drake-Brockman was also responsible for the eventual discovery of the *Batavia* wreck (FitzSimons 2011, xii).

9 Gregory Day's recent novel *Archipelago of Souls* (Sydney: Picador, 2015) also relates a soldier's retreat to an island, in this instance, to King Island in the Bass Strait.

10 For an extended discussion of contemporary sovereignty and fascism read through Kristeva see Kate Livett 'Thieves and Fascists: The Politics of Abjection in Radiohead's *Hail to the Thief (The Gloaming)*' in *Australian Humanities Review*, 41, 2007, http://www.australianhumanitiesreview.org/archive/Issue-February-2007/Livett.html

11 Idriess wrote of novels set on various Australian and Pacific islands. Between 1933 and 1950 Idriess published a highly successful quartet of novels set in the Torres Strait. See Robert Dixon's 'Unfamiliar Selves: Ion L. Idriess and Melanesia', in *Masks, Tapestries, Journeys: Essays in Honour of Dorothy Jones*, ed. Gerry Turcotte (Wollongong: University of Wollongong, 1996), 161–71.

12 See Paul Genoni's discussion of islands in Astley's fiction in 'Girt by Sea: Islands in the Novels of Thea Astley and Christopher Koch', *JASAL* 2000, 121–26.

## 5. The Best and Worst of Times: Utopias, Dystopias, Archipelagos

1 Aldous Huxley reversed the progression of utopias giving way to dystopian visions with the publication of his final novel *Island* in 1962 (London: Vintage) to counter the bleakness of his earlier work, *Brave New World* (New York: Vintage, 1932).

2 Jameson has discussed Greimas' semiotic rectangle in numerous publications including *The Prison House of Language* (New Jersey: Princeton University Press, 1972), 162–68; *The Political Unconscious* (New York: Cornell University Press, 1981), 47–48; and *Archaeologies of the Future* (New York: Verso, 2005), 142–43.

3 Freud's theory of the sexual fetish is also pertinent here but not the primary focus of the analysis. Specifically, the fetishist's denial and avowal of the phallic mother relates directly to island desire and the oscillation between the binary of island presence and absence. The standard trope of the island's internal jewels, which are often hidden within caves, as in Robert Louis Stevenson's *Treasure Island* (1881–83), clearly map out the psychosexual imaginary.

4 Nisbet (1849–1923) published more than 40 novels between 1888 and 1905, several set in Australia.

5 See the Mole Hill Fantasy at Launceston, Tasmazia at Promised Land, Old Hobart Town at Richmond, The Tudor Court Village and Model Train World in the Huon Valley, Alpenrail and the Swiss Model Village in Claremont. The author was sad to see that Peace Haven at Glen Huon has recently closed.

6 The Swiftian reference is apposite here as Swift located his fictional Lilliput, prior to the European discovery of Van Diemen's Land, off the coast of what is now Tasmania – an ongoing source of play for Tasmanians (McMahon 2001; Bain 2014).

7 The first model village, Bekonscot in Buckingham, England, opened in 1929 and still operates in reduced form (Bekonscot, http://www.bekonscot.co.uk/history/full/).

8 Mole Hill Fantasy was closed in 2006, but plans for the revival of the tourist site were reported in the *Launceston Examiner* in 2013 (Poskitt 2013).

9 Artist Judy Watson, whose great aunt was sent to Palm Island and whose other family lived in constant fear of Palm Island, staged an exhibition 'a complicated fall' in 2007. Artworks from this exhibition are held at the National Gallery of Australia and the Queensland Gallery of Modern Art. See also Judy Watson and Louise Martin-Chew *Blood Language* (Melbourne: Miegunyah Press, 2009).

10 One such manifestation in the academic context occurred while writing this essay in the form of a new issue of the scholarly publication, *The Fibreculture Journal*, coedited by my colleague at UNSW Andrew Murphie. The new issue, a trans-Tasman project, guest-edited by Su Ballard at Otago Polytechnic, Zita Joyce at Canterbury Christchurch and Lizzie Muller at UTS, is titled 'Networked Utopias and Speculative Futures' (Ballard, Joyce and Muller 2012).

11 For a discussion of 'novelistic songlines' in *Carpentaria* see Joe Cummins, 'The Space and Time of Imagined Sound: Australian Literature and Music, 1945 to Present' (unpublished PhD thesis, Sydney: University of New South Wales 2015), 172–99.

12 Chloe Hooper records visiting the Gulf country while researching *The Tall Man*, and being hosted by Murrandoo Yanner's youngest brother TJ (2008, 55).

13 Ken Morrison writes: 'Historically, the term fetish was first used to refer to any object that excites intense feelings of attachment of desire and which focuses or rivets attention to a single thing or object by assuming the object has powers' (*Marx, Durkheim, Weber: Formations of Modern Social Thought*, Second Edition (London: Sage, 2006), 97–98).

14 See Janke's short story about living in the Torres Strait during the World War II, 'Turtle Island' (*Southerly* 72, no. 3 (2012): 42–50).

# WORKS CITED


Abraham, Nicholas and Maria Torok. (1972) 1994. 'Mourning or Melancholia: Introjection versus Incorporation.' *The Shell and the Kernel: Renewals of Psychoanalysis*. Ed., Trans. and Intro. Nicholas T. Rand. London and Chicago: University of Chicago Press. 125–36.

Adams, Thomas. (1612) n. d. 'The White Devil, or The Hypocrite Uncased.' *The Digital Puritan*. Online: http://digitalpuritan.net/thomas-adams/, accessed 20 July 2015.

Agamben, Giorgio. 1993. *Infancy and History: The Destruction of Experience*. New York and London: Verso.

———. 1998. *Homo Sacer: Sovereign Power and Bare Life*. Trans. Daniel Hellor-Roazen. California: Stanford University Press.

'All Woman Writer'. 2001. 'Petticoat Rebellion?' *Jamaica Observer*, 6 August. Online: http://www.jamaicaobserver.com/magazines/allwoman/12276_-Petticoat-Rebellion–#ixzz1sMregbCI, accessed 6 June 2011.

Allars, K. G. 1966. 'Burton, Sir William Westbrooke (1794–1888).' *Australian Dictionary of Biography Volume 1*. Canberra: National Centre of Biography. Online: http://adb.anu.edu.au/biography/burton-sir-william-westbrooke-1857/text2159, accessed 2 September 2015.

Allfrey, Phyllis Shand. (1953) 1982. *The Orchid House*. London: Virago.

Alliez, Éric. (2007). 'Living Hot, Thinking Coldly: An Interview with Peter Sloterdijk.' *Cultural Politics* 3(3): 307–26.

'An Australian Story: *Madman's Island*.' 1938. *Geraldton Guardian and Express*. 4 October.

Althusser, Louis. 2014. *On the Reproduction of Capitalism: Ideology and Ideological State Apparatuses*. Trans. G. M. Goshgarian. London and New York.

Anderson Jr., Donald K. 1972. 'Donne's "Hymne to God My God, in My Sicknesse" and the T-in-O Maps.' *South Atlantic Quarterly* 71: 465–72.

Anon. *The Summoning of Everyman*: The Fordham University: Medieval Sourcebook: Everyman, 15th Century. Online: http://www.fordham.edu./halsall/basis/everyman.asp, accessed 28 November 2011.

Arnold, Matthew. 1961. *Poetry and Criticism of Matthew Arnold*. Boston: Houghton Mifflin.

Ashcroft, Bill, Gareth Griffiths and Helen Tiffin. (1989) 2002. *The Empire Writes Back: Theory and Practice in Post-Colonial Literatures*. London; New York: Routledge.

Astley, Thea. 1968. *A Boatload of Homefolk*. Sydney: Angus and Robertson.

———. 1992. 'The Genteel Poverty Bus Company.' *Vanishing Points*. New York: Putnam and Sons.

Auchmuty, J. J. 1966. 'Hunter, John (1737–1821).' *Australian Dictionary of Biography Volume 1*. Melbourne: Melbourne University Press. 566–72.

Auden, W. H. (1933) 1945. 'Paysage Moralisé.' *The Collected Poetry of W. H. Auden*. New York: Random House. 47–48.

Austen, Jane. (1813) 1998. *Pride and Prejudice*. Oxford Oxford University Press.

*AustLit: the Australia Literature Resource*. Online: www.austlit.edu.au/. 2002–.

*Australian Joint Copying Project Handbook: Miscellaneous (M series) 3rd Edition*. 1998. Ed. National Library Australia. Riverwood, NSW: National Library Australia. Online: https://books.google.com.au/books?id=NK436M5d3n4C&pg=PA112&lpg=PA112&dq=71st+regiment+in+australia&source=bl&ots=_lruxywVID&sig=AgmUijUFfxi7P_hKBcTnl_FdWSI&hl=en&sa=X&ved=0CFAQ6AEwCWoVChMI6NXtw7COyAIVAuemCh1MIw0n#v=onepage&q=71st%20regiment%20in%20australia&f=false, accessed 23 September 2015.

Australian National Shipwreck Database (ANSD). Department of Environment, Federal Government of Australia. Online: http://www.environment.gov.au/topics/heritage/historic-shipwrecks/australian-national-shipwreck-database, accessed 10 October 2014.

Bachelard, Gaston. (1964) 1994. *The Poetics of Space*. Trans. Maria Jolas. Boston: Beacon Press.

Bacon, Sir Francis. 1627. *New Atlantis*: Project Gutenberg Online. 20 November 2011.

Bain, Andrew. 2014. 'Three Hummock Island, Tasmania: A Small Wonder.' *Traveller*. Online: http://www.traveller.com.au/three-hummock-island-tasmania-a-small-wonder-39i3h, accessed 5 April 2015.

Baldacchino, Godfrey. 2005. 'Editorial: Islands – Objects of Representation.' *Geografiska Annaler* 87B(4): 247–52.

———. 2012. 'Island and Despots.' *Commonwealth and Comparative Politics* 50(1): 103–20.

Ballantine, James (1916) 2006. *A Law Dictionary of Words, Terms, Abbreviations, and Phrases which are Peculiar to the Law and of Those which Have a Peculiar Meaning in the Law, Containing Latin Phrases and Maxims, with Their Translations and a Table of the Names of the Reports and Their Abbreviations*. New Jersey: The Lawbook Exchange, Ltd.

Ballard, Su, Zita Joyce and Lizzie Muller. 2012. *The Fibreculture Journal: Networked Utopias and Speculative Futures* 20. Online: http://twenty.fibreculturejournal.org, accessed 3 March 2014.

Ballou, Maturin Murray. 1892. *Travels under the Southern Cross or Travels in Australia, Tasmania, New Zealand, Samoa, and Other Pacific Islands*. Boston and New York: Houghton and Mifflin.

Balutansky, Kathleen. 1989. 'We Are All Activists: An Interview with Merle Hodge.' *Callaloo* 12(4): 651–62.

Banfield, Edmund James. (1908) 1980. *The Confessions of a Beachcomber: Life on a Qld Tropical Island*. Sydney: Angus and Robertson.

Barkan, Leonard. 1975. *Nature's Work of Art: The Human Body as Image of the World*. New Haven, CT: Yale University Press.

Barker, Theo. 1967. 'Stewart, William (1769–1854).' *Australian Dictionary of Biography Volume 2*. Melbourne: Melbourne University Press. 482–83.

'Barney, George (1792–1862).' (1966). *Australian Dictionary of Biography Volume 1*, Canberra: National Centre of Biography. Online: http://adb.anu.edu.au/biography/barney-george-1744/text1931, accessed 2 September 2015.

Barry, John V. 1966. 'Anderson, Joseph (1790–1877).' *Australian Dictionary of Biography Volume 1*. Melbourne: Melbourne University Press. 13–14.

———. 1967. 'Willis, John Walpole (1793–1877).' *Australian Dictionary of Biography Volume 2*. Canberra: National Centre of Biography. Online: http://adb.anu.edu.au/biography/willis-john-walpole-2797/text3989, accessed 2 September 2015.

Bateson, Charles. 1966. 'Hall, James (1784–1869).' *Australian Dictionary of Biography Volume 1*. Canberra: National Centre of Biography. Online: http://adb.anu.edu.au/biography/hall-james-2145/text2733, accessed 2 September 2015.

Baxter, James K. 1976. *The Bone Chanter: Unpublished Poems 1945–1972*. Oxford and New York: Oxford University Press.

Becke, Louis and Walter Jeffrey. 1901. 'The Adventure of Elizabeth Morey, of New York.' *The Tapu of Banderrah*. London: C. Arthur Pearson.

Beddoe, John. (1862) 1971. *The Races of Britain*. London: Hutchinson.

Beer, Gillian. 1997. 'The Making of a Cliche: No Man Is an Island.' *European Journal of English Studies* 1(1): 33–47.

———. 2003. 'Island Bounds.' *Islands in History and Representation*. Eds Rod Edmond and Vanessa Smith. London: Routledge. 32.

Bekonscot, n.d. Bekonscot Model Village and Railway. Online: http://www.bekonscot.co.uk/history/full/, accessed 23 October 2015.

Benítez-Rojo, Antonio. (1992) 1996. *The Repeating Island: The Caribbean and the Postmodern Perspective*. Trans. James. E. Maraniss. Durham, NC: Duke University Press.

Benjamin, Walter (1928) 1998. *The Origins of German Tragic Drama*. Trans. John Osborne. London and New York: Verso.

———. (1940) 1968. 'Theses on the Philosophy of History.' *Illuminations: Essays and Reflections*. Trans. Harry Zohn. Ed. and Intro. Hannah Arendt. New York: Harcourt Brace Jovanovich. 253–64.

———. (1936) 1968. 'The Work of Art in the Age of Mechanical Reproduction.' *Illuminations: Essays and Reflections*.Trans. Harry Zohn. Ed. and Intro. Hannah Arendt. New York: Harcourt Brace Jovanovich, 217–52.

———. (1966) 1978. 'Critique of Violence.' *Reflections: Essays, Aphorism, and Autobiographical Writings*. Trans. Edmund Jephcott. New York: Schocken. 277–300.

———. (1927–40) 1999. *Arcades Project.*. Ed. Rold Tiedermann. Trans. Howard Eiland and Kevin McLaughlin. Boston: Harvard University Press.

Bennett, J. M. 1966. 'Bigge, John Thomas (1780–1843).' *Australian Dictionary of Biography Volume 1*. Canberra: National Centre of Biography. Online: http://adb.anu.edu.au/biography/bigge-john-thomas-1779/text1999, accessed 2 September 2015.

Bhabha, Homi. 1994. 'Of Mimicry and Man: The Ambivalence of Colonial Discourse.' *The Location of Culture*. London and New York: Routledge. 85–92.

Birns, Nicholas. 2014. 'Does Idealism Preclude Heroism? Shirley Hazzard's United Nations Writings.' *Shirley Hazzard*. Ed. Brigitta Olubas. Sydney: Sydney University Press.

Blackmore, Josiah. 2002. *Manifest Perdition: Shipwreck Narrative and the Disruption of Empire*. Minneapolis: University of Minnesota Press.

Blackwell, Jeannine. 1985. 'An Island of Her Own: Heroines of the German Robinsonades from 1720 to 1800.' *German Quarterly* 58(1): 5–26.

Blanchot, Maurice. 1986. *The Writing of the Disaster*. Trans. Ann Smock. Lincoln: University of Nebraska Press.

Bliss, Eliot. (1934) 1984. *Luminous Isle*. London: Virago.

Bloch, Ernst. 1986. *The Principle of Hope*. Trans. N. Plaice, S. Plaice and P. Knight. Cambridge, MA: MIT Press.

———. 1988. *The Utopian Function of Art and Literature: Selected Essays*. Trans. Jack Zipes and Frank Mecklenburg. Cambridge, MA and London: MIT Press.

Blumenberg, Hans. 1997. *Shipwreck with Spectator: Paradigm of a Metaphor for Existence*. Trans. Steven Rendall. Massachusetts: MIT Press.

Bolton, Jonathan. 1994. 'Auden's [Hearing of Harvests Rotting in Valleys]'. *The Explicator* 53(1): 57–58.

Bond, Edward. (1981) 2006. *Restoration*. London and New York: Methuen Drama.

Booth, Charles O'Hara. 1981. *The Journal of Charles O'Hara Booth*. Hobart: Tasmanian Historical Research Association.

Bourke, Richard 1835. *Proclamation*. Museum of Australian Democracy. Online: http://foundingdocs.gov.au/resources/transcripts/nsw7_doc_1835.pdf, accessed 23 December 2014.

Boyce, Peter. 1966. 'Hampton, John Stephen (1810–1869).' *Australian Dictionary of Biography*. National Centre of Biography, Australian National University. Online: http://adb.anu.edu.au/biography/hampton-john-stephen-2151/text2745, accessed 3 January 2015.

———. 1974. 'Ord, Sir Harry St George (1819–1885).' *Australian Dictionary of Biography Volume 5*. Melbourne: Melbourne University Press. 370.

Boyd, Martin. (1940) 1986. *Nuns in Jeopardy*. Melbourne; Penguin.

Brand, Dionne. 1990. Interview with Dagmar Novak. *Other Solitudes: Canadian Multicultural Fictions*. Eds Linda Hutcheon and Marion Richards. Toronto: Oxford University Press. 271–77.

———. 1996. *In Another Place, Not Here*. New York: Grove.

———. 2002a. *Thirsty*. Toronto: McClelland & Stewart.

— 2002b. *A Map to the Door of No Return: Notes to Belonging*. Canada: Vintage.

Brandenstein, Claudia. 2007. 'Representations of Landscape and Nature in Anthony Trollope's *The West Indies and the Spanish Main* and James Anthony Froude's *The English in the West Indies*.' *Five Emus to the King of Siam: Environment and Empire*. Ed. Helen Tiffin. Amsterdam: Rodopi. 15–30.

Brathwaite, Edward Kamau. 1974. *Contradictory Omens: Cultural Diversity and Integration in the Caribbean*. Mona, Jamaica: Savacou Publications.

———. 1983. 'Caribbean Culture: Two Paradigms.' *Missile and Capsule*. Jurgen Martini. Bremen: Universitat Bremen. 9–54.

Brenkman, John. 2013. '…wrestling with (my God!) my God: Modernism, Nihilism, and Belief.' *Qui Parle: Critical Humanities and Social Sciences* 21(2): 1–25.

Brennan, Bernadette. 2014. 'Heriot's Ithaka: Soul, Country and the Possibility of Home in *To The Islands*.' *Journal of the Association for the Study of Australian Literature* 14(3). Online: http://www.nla.gov.au/openpublish/index.php/jasal/article/view/3283, accessed 15 September 2015.

Brito, Bernardo Gomes de. (1735–36) 2015. *Histórica Trágico-Maritima*. Forgotten Books.

Britton, David. 2000. *Southland*. London: BBC Radio 4.

Brontë, Charlotte. (1847) 2006. *Jane Eyre*. London: Penguin.

'Bugnion, François Louis (1822–1880).' (1969). *Australian Dictionary of Biography Volume 3*. Canberra: National Centre of Biography. Online: http://adb.anu.edu.au/biography/bugnion-francois-louis-3106/text4613, accessed 2 September 2015.

Burchardt, Jeremy. 2002. *Paradise Lost: Rural Idyll and Social Change Since 1800*. London and New York: I.B. Tauris and Co.

Burnham, Michelle. 2001. 'Introduction.' *The Female American, or, The Adventures of Unca Eliza Winkfield*. Michelle Burnham. New York; Hertfordshire; Sydney: Broadview Press. 9–28.

Burns, T. E. and J. R. Skemp. 1966. 'Gunn, Ronald Campbell (1808–1881).' *Australian Dictionary of Biography Volume 1*. Canberra: National Centre of Biography. Online: http://adb.anu.edu.au/biography/gunn-ronald-campbell-2134/text2709, accessed 2 September 2015.

Burton, Robert. (1621) 1927. *The Anatomy of Melancholy*. Floyd Dell and Paul Jordan-Smith. New York: Tudor Publishing Co.

Butler, Judith. 2004. 'Melancholy Gender/Refused Identification (1997).' *The Judith Butler Reader*. Eds Sarah Salih with Judith Butler. Massachusetts; Oxford; Victoria: Blackwell. 243–301.

———. 2006. 'Critique, Coercion and Sacred Life in Benjamin's "Critique of Violence".' *Political Theologies: Public Religions in a Post-Secular World*. Eds Hent de Vries and Lawrence E. Sullivan. New York: Fordham University Press. 201–19.

Byrnes, J. V. 1967. 'Howe, George (1769–1821).' *Australian Dictionary of Biography Volume 2*. Melbourne: Melbourne University Press. 557–59.

Calvin, John. (1538) 1845. 'Of the Eternal Election, by Which God Has Predestinated Some to Salvation, and Others to Destruction.' *Institutes of the Christian Religion. Book III*. Edinburgh: Online Library of Liberty. Online: http://oll.libertyfund.org/titles/535, accessed 2 November 2014.

Caney, Diane. 1993. 'Janet Frame and *The Tempest*.' *Journal of New Zealand Literature* 11: 152–71.

Cannon, Richard. 1851. *Historical Record of the Forty-sixth, or the South Devonshire, Regiment of Foot*. London: Parker, Furnivall & Parker.

Carington Smith, Julie. 1967. 'Schaw, Charles (1785–1874).' *Australian Dictionary of Biography Volume 2*. Melbourne: Melbourne University Press. 421.

Carr, Patrick. 2005. 'Batavia and the Problem of Truth: Playscript and Exegesis.' Unpublished Masters thesis. Brisbane: Queensland University of Technology.

Carter, David. 2002. 'Communism and Carnival: Ralph de Boissiere's *Crown Jewel* and Its Australian Context.' *To the Islands: Australia and the Caribbean. Australian Cultural History* 21. Ed. Russell McDougall. St Lucia: University of Queensland Press. 97–106.

Carter, Paul. (1987) 2010. *The Road to Botany Bay: An Exploration of Landscape and History*. Minneapolis: University of Minnesota Press.

Cartland, George B. 1983. 'Havelock, Sir Arthur Elibank (1844–1908).' *Australian Dictionary of Biography Volume 9*. Canberra: National Centre of Biography. Online: http://adb.anu.edu.au/biography/havelock-sir-arthur-elibank-6600/text11365, accessed 2 September 2015.

Casanova, Pascale. 2004. *The World Republic of Letters*. Trans. M. B. DeBevoice. Cambridge, MA and London: Harvard University Press.

Caterson, Simon. 1994. 'Playing the Ancestor Game: Alex Miller Interviewed by Simon Caterson.' *The Journal of Commonwealth Literature* 29(2): 5–11.

Cervantes, Miguel de. (1605, 1615) 2011. *Don Quixote*. Trans. Tom Lathrop. London: Alma Classics.

Chant, Christopher. 2013 (1988). *The Handbook of British Regiments (Routledge Revivals)*. Abingdon and New York: Routledge. Online: https://books.google.com.au/books?id=ieeOAQAAQBAJ&pg=PA103&dq=57th+West+Middlesex+regiment&hl=en&sa=X&ved=0CCQQ6AEwAmoVChMImaKdirWOyAIVih6UCh2wkwId#v=onepage&q=57th%20West%20Middlesex%20regiment&f=false, accessed 23 September 2015.

Chisholm, A.H. 1972. 'Joseph Ravenscroft Elsey (1834–1857).' *Australian Dictionary of Biography Volume 4*. Melbourne: Melbourne University Press. 139.

Churchill, Caryl. (1979) 1995. *Cloud 9*. London: Theatre Communications Group.

'Cimitiere, Gilbert (–1842).' (1966). *Australian Dictionary of Biography Volume 1*. Melbourne: Melbourne University Press. 223–24.

Clay, Diskin. 1992. 'Columbus's Senecan Prophesy.' *The American Journal of Philology* 113(4): 617–20.

Clewell, Tammy. 2004. 'Mourning Beyond Melancholia: Freud's Psychoanalysis of Loss.' *Journal of the American Psychoanalytic Association* 52(1): 43–67.

Coetzee, J. M. 1986. *Foe*. London: Secker & Warburg.

———. 1999. 'Introduction' Oxford World's Classics edition of *Robinson Crusoe* – See Ch. 3

———. 2001. 'Robinson Crusoe.' *Stranger Shores: Literary Essays 1986–1999*. New York: Viking.

———. 2003. 'He and His Man.' Nobel Lecture. *Nobel Academy*. Online: http://www.nobelprize.org/nobel_prizes/literature/laureates/2003/coetzee-lecture.html, accessed 2 June 2014.

Coleridge, S. T. 1997. *Selected Poetry*. Ed. H. J. Jackson. Oxford and New York: Oxford University Press.

Coles, P. J. 1967. 'Scott, Daniel (1800–1865).' *Australian Dictionary of Biography Volume 1*. Canberra: National Centre of Biography. Online: http://adb.anu.edu.au/biography/scott-daniel-2638/text3661, accessed 2 September 2015.

Columbus, Christopher. (1505) 1991. *El Libro de Las Profecias*. Eds Delno West and August Kling. Gainesville: University of Florida Press.

———. 1893. *The Journal of Christopher Columbus*. Ed. Clements R. Markham. London: Hakluyt Society.

Columbus, Ferdinand. 1992. *The Life of the Admiral Christopher Columbus: by his Son Ferdinand* Revised Edition. Ed. Benjamin Keen. New Brunswick: Rutgers University Press.

Conley, Tom. 2007. 'Early Modern Literature and Cartography: An Overview.' *The History of Cartography Volume 3, Part 1: Cartography in the European Renaissance*. David Woodward. Chicago and London: University of Chicago Press. 401–11.

Connor, Michael. 2005. *The Invention of Terra Nullius: Historical and Legal Fictions on the Foundation of Australia*. Sydney: Macleay Press.

Conrad, Joseph. (1899) 2007. 'Heart of Darkness.' *The Portable Conrad*. Ed. Michael Gorra. London, New York: Penguin. 271–364.

Conrad, Peter. 1988. *Down Home: Revisiting Tasmania*. London: Chatto & Windus.

Constantakopoulou, Christy. 2007. *The Dance of the Islands: Insularity, Networks, the Athenian Empire, and the Aegean World*. Oxford and New York: Oxford University Press.

Cook, James. 1971. *The Explorations of Captain James Cook in the Pacific, as Told by Selections of His Own Journals, 1768–1779*. Ed. Archibald Grenfell Price. New York: Dover.

Cooppan, Vilashini. 2009. *Worlds Within: National Narratives and Global Connections*. Stanford, CA: Stanford University Press.

Cornwell, Gareth. 2007. '"He and His Man": Allegory and Catachresis in J.M. Coetzee's Nobel Lecture.' *English in Africa* 34(1): 97–114.

Cosgrove, Denis. 2001. *Apollo's Eye: A Cartographic Genealogy of the Earth in the Western Imagination*. Baltimore and London: The Johns Hopkins University Press.

———. 2011. 'Geography Within the Humanities, Prologue.' *Envisioning Landscapes, Making Worlds: Geography and the Humanities*. Dydia DeLyser Stephen Daniels, J. Nicholas Entrikin and Douglas Richardson. London and New York: Routledge. xxii–xxv.

Cowper, William. 1913. *The Complete Poetical Works of William Cowper*. London: Oxford University Press.

Cranfield, Louis. R. 1966. 'Clunie, James Oliphant (1795–1851).' *Australian Dictionary of Biography Volume 1*. Canberra: Australian National University. Online: http://adb.anu.edu.au/biography/clunie-james-oliphant-1907/text2259, accessed 24 September 2015.

Crew, Gary. 1990. *Strange Objects*. Port Melbourne: Heinemann.

———. 2001. 'Their Ghosts May Be Heard: A Response to Ernest Favenc's Novel *Marooned in Australia*.' *Storykeepers*. Ed. Marion Halligan. Sydney: Duffy and Snellgrove. 15–29.

Critchley, Simon. 21 October 2009. 'Violent Thoughts About Slavoj Žižek.' Original retrieved 28 November 2011 from Naked Punch.com, ed. Qalander Bux Memon.

Crowley, F. K. 1967. 'Stirling, Sir James (1791–1865).' *Australian Dictionary of Biography Volume 2*. Melbourne: Melbourne University Press. 484–88.

———. 1972. 'Darling, Sir Charles Henry (1809–1870).' *Australian Dictionary of Biography Volume 4*. Melbourne: Melbourne University Press 19–21.

———. 1976. 'Robinson, Sir William Cleaver Francis (1834–1897).' *Australian Dictionary of Biography Volume 6*. Melbourne: Melbourne University Press. 50–51.

Cummins, Joe. 2015. 'The Space and Time of Imagined Sound: Australian Literature and Music, 1945 to Present.' Unpublished PhD thesis. Sydney: University of New South Wales.

Cunneen, Chris. 1976. 'Rolleston, Christopher (1817–1888).' *Australian Dictionary of Biography Volume 6*. Canberra: National Centre of Biography. Online: http://adb.anu.edu.au/biography/rolleston-christopher-4501/text7359, accessed 2 September 2015.

Currey, C. H. 1966a. 'Bent, Jeffery Hart (1781–1852).' *Australian Dictionary of Biography Volume 1*. Canberra: National Centre of Biography. Online: http://adb.anu.edu.au/biography/bent-jeffery-hart-2228/text1985, accessed 2 September 2015.

———. 1966b. 'Forbes, Sir Francis (1784–1841).' *Australian Dictionary of Biography Volume 1*. Canberra: National Centre of Biography. Online: http://adb.anu.edu.au/biography/forbes-sir-francis-2052/text2545, accessed 2 September 2015.

———. 1967. 'Stephen, John (1771–1833).' *Australian Dictionary of Biography Volume 2*. Melbourne: Melbourne University Press. 476–78.

Dampier, William. (1697) *A New Voyage Round the World*. Adelaide: University of Adelaide Library. Online: https://ebooks.adelaide.edu.au/d/dampier/william/new-voyage-round-the-world/index.html, accessed 1 June 2015.

Dance, Daryl Cumber. 2010. '"I Going Away. I Going Home.": Austin Clarke's "Leaving This Island Place".' *Journal of Caribbean Literatures*. Online: http://www.thefreelibrary.com/%22I+Going+Away.+I+Going+Home%22%3A+Austin+Clarke's+%22Leaving+This+Island...-a0275576085, accessed 10 December 2014.

Darley, Gillian. (1975) 2007. *Villages of Vision: A Study of Strange Utopias*. Nottingham: Five Leaves.

'Darling, Sir Ralph (1772–1858).' (1966). *Australian Dictionary of Biography Volume 1*. Melbourne: Melbourne University Press. 282–86.

Darwin, Charles. 1873. *The Origin of Species by Means of Natural Selection*, 6th Edition. London: John Murray.

Dash, Mike. 2002. *Batavia's Graveyard: The True Story of the Mad Heretic Who Led History's Bloodiest Mutiny*. London: Weidenfeld & Nicolson.

Dathorne, Oscar Ronald. 1994. *Imagining the World: Mythical Belief Versus Reality in Global Encounters*. Westport, CT: Greenwood Publishing.

Daurio, Beverley. (1990) 'The Language of Resistance: In Her Poetry, Dionne Brand Is Rewriting History in a Way that Saves Our Humanity.' *Books in Canada* 19(7): 13–16.

Davis, N. Darnell. 1888. 'Mr Froude's Negrophobia; or, Don Quixote as a Cook's Tourist.' *Timehri* 2(1): 85–129.

Davis, S. 2012. Torres Strait Festival Celebrates 'Stories under Tagai.' 18 September, 10:21AM AEST, ABC Far North Queensland. Online: http://www.abc.net.au/local/stories/2012/09/18/3592396.htm, accessed 21 November 2012.

Day, Gregory. 2015. *Archipelago of Souls*. Sydney: Picador.

de Boissiere, Ralph. (1952) 1981 *Crown Jewel*. London: Picador.

———. 1982. 'On Writing a Novel.' *Journal of Commonwelath Literature* 17(1): 1–12.

de Garis, B. K. and Tom Stannage. 1979. 'Burt, Septimus (1847–1919).' *Australian Dictionary of Biography Volume 7*. Melbourne: Melbourne University Press. 494–96.

de Gasperin, Vilma. 2010. 'The Ship and the Sea in the Writing of Anna Maria Ortese: Autobiographical Experience and Literary Metaphor.' *The Italianist* 30: 81–98.

Defoe, Daniel. (1719) 2003. *Robinson Crusoe*. London: Penguin.

Deleuze, Gilles. 1997. 'Bartleby, or The Formula.' *Essays Critical and Clinical*. Trans. Daniel Smith and Michael Greco. Minneapolis: Minneapolis University Press. 68–90.

———. 2004. *Desert Islands and Other Texts 1953–1974*. Trans. Michael Taorima. Los Angeles: Semiotext(e) Foreign Agents Series. Cambridge, Mass. and London. 9–14.

Deleuze, Gilles and Felix Guattari. (1991) 1994. *What Is Philosophy?* Trans. Graham Burchell and Hugh Tomlinson. New York: Columbia University Press.

DeLoughrey, Elizabeth M. 2007. *Routes and Roots: Navigating Caribbean and Pacific Island Literatures*. Honolulu: University of Hawai'i Press.

Dening, Greg. 1994. *Mr Bligh's Bad Language: Passion, Power and Theatre on the Bounty*. Cambridge: Cambridge University Press.

Derrida, Jacques. (1967) 1978. 'Structure, Sign and Play in the Discourse of the Human Sciences.' *Writing and Difference*. Trans. Alan Bass. London and New York: Routledge. 351–370.

———. 1983. *Disseminations*. Trans. Barbara Johnson. Chicago: University of Chicago Press.

———. 2002. 'Force of Law: The "Mystical Foundation of Authority" (1989).' *Acts of Religion*. Ed. and Intro. Gil Anidja. Trans. Mary Quaintance. London and New York: Routledge. 228–98.

———. 2009. 'First Session, December 11, 2009.' *The Beast and the Sovereign Volume II*. Trans. Geoffrey Bennington. Chicago and London: University of Chicago Press. 1–30.

Dimock, Wai Chee. 2006. *Through Other Continents: American Literature Across Deep Time*. Princeton, NJ: Princeton University Press.

Dixon, Robert. 1995. *Writing the Colonial Adventure: Race, Gender and Nation in Anglo-Australian Popular Fiction, 1875–1914*. New York: Cambridge University Press.

———. 1996. 'Unfamiliar Selves: Ion L. Idriess and Melanesia.' *Masks, Tapestries, Journeys: Essays in Honour of Dorothy Jones*. Ed. Gerry Turcotte. Wollongong, NSW: University of Wollongong. 161–71.

———. 2014. 'Returning to the Scene of the Crime: On Re-reading *The Transit of Venus*'. *Shirley Hazzard: New Critical Essays*. Ed. Brigitta Olubas. Sydney: Sydney University Press. 79–93.

Dixon, Robert and Brigid Rooney. 2013. 'Introduction: Australian Literature, Globalisation and the Literary Province.' *Scenes of Reading: Is Australian Literature a World Literature?* Eds Robert Dixon and Brigid Rooney. Melbourne: Australian Scholarly Publishing. ix–xxxvi.

Donne, John. 1953. *The Poems of John Donne Volume I*. Ed. and Intro. Herbert J. C. Grierson. Oxford: Oxford University Press.

———. (1622) 1953–62. 'A Sermon Preached to the Honourable Company of the Virginian Plantation, 13th November 1622.' *Sermons*. Eds G. R. Potter and Evelyn M. Simpson, 10 vols. Berkeley: University of California Press. 4:264.

———. (1623) 1967. 'Devotions Upon Emergent Occasions: Meditation XVII.' *Selected Prose*. Eds Helen and Timothy Healy Gardner. Oxford: Oxford University Press. 100–101.

———. (1647) 1982. *Biathanatos*. Introduction and Commentary. Michael Rudick and M. Pabst Battin. New York and London: Garland.

———. 2002. *Collected Poems of John Donne.* Intro. Roy Booth. Hertfordshire, U.K.: Wordsworth Editions Ltd.

Dowd, Bernard T. 1966. 'Grimes, Charles (1772–1858).' *Australian Dictionary of Biography Volume 1.* Canberra: National Centre of Biography. Online: http://adb.anu.edu.au/biography/grimes-charles-2129/text2699, accessed 2 September 2015.

Downes, Garry, 2004. 'The Manbarra People and Great Barrier Reef Marine Park Authority and Anor [2004] AATA 268 (15 March 2004).' Administrative Appeals Tribunal of Australia. Sydney. Online: http://www.austlii.edu.au/au/cases/cth/aat/2004/268.html, acccessed 3 January 2015.

Drake-Brockman, Henrietta. 1957. *The Wicked and the Fair.* Sydney: Angus and Robertson.

Drewe, Robert. 2009a. 'Shining Narrative Sketched in Shades of Grey.' The *Age* (9 May): 3.

———. 2009b 'Creative Berth on the Bloodied Ship Batavia.' *The Age* (21 November): 5.

———. 2012. *Montebello: A Memoir.* Melbourne: Penguin.

Druett, Joan. 2007. *Island of the Lost: A Harrowing True Story of Shipwreck, Death and Survival on a Godforsaken Island at the Edge of the World.* Crows Nest, NSW: Allen & Unwin.

Duffield, Ian. 1986. 'From Slave Colonies to Penal Colonies: The West Indian Convict Transportees to Australia.' *Slavery & Abolition* 7(1): 25–45.

Duffy, Edna. 2007. '"As White as Ours": Africa, Ireland, Imperial Panic and the Effects of British Race Discourse.' *Empire and After: Englishness in Postcolonial Perspective.* Eds Graham MacPhee and Prem Poddar. New York and Oxford. Berghahn Books.

Dunton, William Herbert. 1909. *Monarch of All He Surveys.* Oil on canvas mounted on board. Jackson Hole, WY: JKM Collection, National Museum of Wildlife Art.

During, Simon. 1996. *Patrick White.* Melbourne: Oxford University Press.

———. 2010. *Exit Capitalism: Literary Culture, Theory and Post-Secular Modernity.* New York: Routledge.

Durkhein, Emile. 1915. *Elementary Forms of Religious Life.* Trans. John Ward Swain. London: George Allen and Unwin.

Dutton, Geoffrey. 1966. 'Eyre, Edward John (1815–1901)'. *Australian Dictionary of Biography Volume 1.* Melbourne: Melbourne University Press. 363–64.

Eastwood, Jill. 1967. 'La Trobe, Charles Joseph (1801–1875).' *Australian Dictionary of Biography Volume 2.* Canberra: National Centre of Biography. Online: http://adb.anu.edu.au/biography/la-trobe-charles-joseph-2334/text3039, accessed 2 September 2015.

———. 1981. 'Doorly, James Gerald Stokely (1880–1956).' *Australian Dictionary of Biography Volume 8.* Canberra: National Centre of Biography. Online: http://adb.anu.edu.au/biography/doorly-james-gerald-stokely-6002/text10251, accessed 2 September 2015.

Edge, Arabella. 2000. *The Company: The Story of a Murderer.* Sydney: Picador.

Edmond, Rod and Vanessa Smith. 2003. 'Introduction.' *Islands in History and Representation.* Eds Rod Edmond and Vanessa Smith. London: Routledge, 1–18.

Edwards, Hugh. (1966) 2002. *Islands of Angry Ghosts.* Pymble, NSW: HarperCollins.

Eldershaw, P. R. 1966. 'Davey, Thomas (1758–1823).' *Australian Dictionary of Biography Volume 1.* Melbourne: Melbourne University Press. 288–89.

———. 1967. 'Willis, Richard (1777–1855).' *Australian Dictionary of Biography Volume 2.* Canberra: National Centre of Biography. Online: http://adb.anu.edu.au/biography/willis-richard-2798/text3991, accessed 2 September 2015.

Eliot, T. S. 1932. 'The Metaphysical Poets.' *Selected Essays 1917–1932.* London: Harcourt Brace. 241–50.

Ellis, Markman. 2002. '"The Cane-land Isles": Commerce and Empire in Late Eighteenth-century Georgic and Pastoral Poetry.' *Island in History and Representation.* Eds Rod Edmond and Vanessa Smith. London and New York: Routledge. 43–62.

English, James. 2005. *The Economy of Prestige: Prizes, Awards, and the Circulation of Cultural Value.* Cambridge, MA: Harvard University Press.

Evans, Chris and Olivia Saunders. 2015. 'A World of Copper: Globalizing the Industrial Revolution, 1830–70.' *Journal of Global History.* 10(1) (March): 3–26.

Evans, Julie. 2005. *Edward Eyre, Race and Colonial Governance.* Dunedin, New Zealand: University of Otago Press.

Everett, Jim. 2014. 'Savage Nation: First Nations' Philosophy and Sovereignty.' *Southerly* 74(2): 27–42.

Falconer, William. 'The Shipwreck (1762).' National Library of Australia. Online: http://catalogue.nla.gov.au/Record/4884391, accessed 3 December 2014.

Falk, David G. 1889. 'The Castaway of the Barrier.' *Centennial Magazine* 25 December. 328–43.

Favenc, Ernest. 1896. *Marooned on Australia.* London: Blackie and Son.

Fettweiss, Christopher J. 2000. 'Sir Halford Mackinder, Geopolitics, and Policymaking in the 21st Century.' *Parameters* (Summer): 58–71.

Fielding, Sydney Glanville. 1884. 'The Castaway.' *The Castaway and Other Poems.* Sydney: Angus & Robertson. 10–37.

Finkler, Noam. 1999. 'John Donne and the "Anthropomorphic Map" Tradition.' *Applied Semiotics / Semiotique appliquee* 3(8): 207–15.

Fitzmaurice, Andrew. 1997. 'Classical Rhetoric and the Promotion of the New World.' *Journal of the History of Ideas* 58(2): 221–43.

———. 2007. 'The Genealogy of Terra Nullius.' *Australian Historical Studies.* 38 (129): 1–15.

FitzSimons, Peter. 2011. *Batavia.* Sydney: Random House.

Flannery, Tim. 2011. *Among the Islands.* Melbourne: Text Publishing.

Flinn, E. 1966. 'Bowen, John (1780–1827).' *Australian Dictionary of Biography Volume 1.* Canberra: National Centre of Biography, Australian National University. http://adb.anu.edu.au/biography/bowen-john-1811/text2065, accessed 9 October 2014.

Flint, Valerie. 1992. *The Imaginative Landscape of Christopher Columbus.* Princeton, NJ: Princeton University Press.

Forbes, Curdella. 2008. *A Permanent Freedom.* London: Peepal Tree.

Forbes, John R. 1972. 'Isaacs, Robert Macintosh (1814–1876).' *Australian Dictionary of Biography Volume 4.* Melbourne: Melbourne University Press. 464.

Foucault, Michel. (1969) 1972. *The Archaeology of Knowledge.* Trans A. M. Sheridan Smith. New York: Pantheon Books.

———. (1975) 1977. *Discipline and Punish: The Birth of the Prison.* Trans. Alan Sheridan. New York: Pantheon Books.

Frame, Janet. 2008. *Three Autobiographies: To the Is-Land, An Angel at My Table, The Envoy from Mirror City.* Sydney: Random House.

Franks, Jill. 2006. *Islands and the Modernists: The Allure of Isolation in Art, Literature and Science.* London: McFarlane.

Fraser, Robert. 2011. 'Race and Religion in the Victorian Age: Charles Kingsley, Governor Eyre and the Morant Bay Rising.' *The Victorian Web; Literature, History and Culture in the Age of Victoria.* Online: http://www.victorianweb.org/authors/kingsley/rfraser.html, accessed 1 December 2014.

Freud, Sigmund. (1905) 2000. *Three Essays on the Theory of Sexuality.* Trans. James Strachey. New York: Basic Books.

———. 'Beyond the Pleasure Principle.' (1920) 2003. *Beyond the Pleasure Principle and Other Writings.* Trans. John Reddick. Intro. Mark Edmundson. London and New York: Penguin. 43–102.

Friedlander, Paul. 2015. 'Aletheia: A Discussion with Martin Heidegger.' *Plato: An Introduction*. Princeton, NJ: Princeton University Press. 221–29.
Friedrich, Caspar David. 1818. *Wanderer Above the Sea of Fog*. Oil on canvas. Hamburg: Hamburg Kunstalle.
Froude, James Anthony. (1849) 2004. *The Nemesis of Faith*. Whitefish, MT: Kessinger Publishing.
———. (1886) 2010. *Oceana: Or, England and Her Colonies*. Cambridge: Cambridge University Press.
———. 1888. *The English in the West Indies: Or, The Bow of Ulysses*. London: Longmans, Green and Co.
Frow, John. 2014. 'Future Anterior: *The Evening of the Holiday*.' *Shirley Hazzard: New Critical Essays*. Ed. Brigitta Olubas. Sydney: Sydney University Press. 3–11.
Fulton, W. C. 1883. 'How It Ended.' *Australian Journal* 19(222): 158–60.
Furphy, Joseph. (1903) 1991. *The Annotated Such Is Life*. Melbourne: Oxford University Press.
Gandelman, Claude. 1984. 'The Poem as Map: John Donne and the "Anthropomorphic Landscape" Tradition.' *Arcadia: Zeitschrift fur Vergleichende Literaturwissenschaft* 19: 244–51.
———. 1991. *Reading Pictures, Viewing Texts*. Bloomington: Indiana University Press.
Garci Rodríguez de Montalvo (1508) 2004. *Amadís* Vol. 1. Madrid Grupo Anaya Comercial.
Garimara, Nugi / Pilkington, Doris. 2002. *Follow the Rabbit-Proof Fence*. St Lucia: University of Queensland Press.
Gaunt, Mary. 1897 (1997). *Kirkham's Find*. Sydney: SETIS, University of Sydney Library. Online: http://purl.library.usyd.edu.au/setis/id/p00027, accessed 2 June 2012.
———. 1922. *Where the Twain Meet*. London: John Murray.
———. 1932. *Reflection – In Jamaica*. London: Ernest Benn Ltd.
———. 1933. *Harmony: A Tale of the Old Slave Days in Jamaica*. London: Ernest Benn.
———. (1915) 2002. *Ends of the Earth, Stories*. Sydney: SETIS, University of Sydney Library.
Genoni, Paul. 2000. 'Girt by Sea: Islands in the Novels of Thea Astley and Christopher Koch.' *JASAL*, 121–26.
Geoscience Australia. n.d. *Islands*. Online: http://www.ga.gov.au/scientific-topics/national-location-information/landforms/islands#heading-2, accessed 1 July 2013.
Géricault, Théodore. 1819. *The Raft of the Medusa*. Oil on Canvas, 491x717cm. The Louvre, Paris.
Gibbney, H. J. 1974. 'Musgrave, Sir Anthony (1828–1888).' *Australian Dictionary of Biography Volume 5*. Melbourne: Melbourne University Press. 324.
———. 1974. 'O'Connell, Sir Maurice Charles (1812–1879).' *Australian Dictionary of Biography Volume 5*. Canberra: National Centre of Biography. Online: http://adb.anu.edu.au/biography/oconnell-sir-maurice-charles-4313/text6993, accessed 2 September 2015.
———. 1976. 'Young, Sir Henry Edward Fox (1803–1870).' *Australian Dictionary of Biography Volume 6*. Canberra: National Centre of Biography. Online: http://adb.anu.edu.au/biography/young-sir-henry-edward-fox-4902/text8207, accessed 2 September 2015
Gibbons, Luke. 2000. 'Race Against Time: Racial Discourse and Irish History.' *Cultures of Empire: A Reader*. Ed. Catherine Hall. Manchester: Manchester University Press. 207–23.
Giles, Paul. 2013. *Antipodean America Australasia and the Constitution of U.S. Literature*. Oxford: Oxford University Press.

Gillis, John. 2004. *Islands of the Mind: How the Human Imagination Created the Atlantic World.* New York and Houndmills, U.K.: Palgrave Macmillan.

———. 2007. 'Island Sojourns.' *The Geographical Review* 97(2): 274–87.

Gleeson, Murray. 1999. Address at 175th Anniversary Dinner of the Supreme Court of New South Wales. Sydney: Supreme Court. Online: http://www.supremecourt.justice.nsw.gov.au/Documents/Speeches/175_06_anniv_scnsw_1999.05.17_gleeson.pdf, accessed 3 March 2015.

Glissant, Édouard. 1997. *Poetics of Relation.* Trans. Betsy Wing. Ann Arbor: University of Michigan Press.

Godfrey, Margery. 1967. 'Robertson, Gilbert (1794–1851).' *Australian Dictionary of Biography Volume 2.* Canberra: National Centre of Biography. Online: http://adb.anu.edu.au/biography/robertson-gilbert-2595/text3563, accessed 2 September 2015.

Golding, William. (1954) 1999. *Lord of the Flies.* London: Penguin.

Goldsworthy, Peter and Richard Mills. 2002. *Batavia.* Sydney: Opera Australia.

Gordon, Andrew and Bernhard Klein. 2001. 'Introduction.' *Literature, Mapping, and the Politics of Space in Early Modern Britain.* Andrew Gordon and Bernhard Klein. Cambridge: Cambridge University Press.

Gorton, Lisa. 1998. 'John Donne's Use of Space.' *Early Modern Literary Studies* 4(2): 1–27.

Grace, Patricia. (1978) 2004. *Mutuwhenua.* Auckland, New Zealand: Penguin.

Gray, Robert. 1993. *Certain Things.* Port Melbourne, VIC: Heinemann.

Greenblatt, Stephen. 1992. *Marvelous Possessions: The Wonder of the New World.* London and New York: Oxford University Press.

Gregory, John Walter. 1906. *The Dead Heart of Australia.* London: J. Murray.

Grenfell-Price, Archibald. (Ed.) 1971. *The Explorations of Captain James Cook in the Pacific, as Told by Selections of His Own Journals, 1768–1779.* New York: Dover.

Griffin, Helga M. 1988. 'Roth, Henry Ling (1855–1925).' *Australian Dictionary of Biography Volume 11.* Canberra: National Centre of Biography. Online: http://adb.anu.edu.au/biography/roth-henry-ling-8278/text14505, accessed 2 September 2015.

Griffiths, Gareth. 1978. *A Double Exile: African and West Indian Writing Between Two Cultures.* London: Marion Boyars.

Guilford, Elizabeth. 1967. 'Winder, Thomas White Melville (1789–1853).' *Australian Dictionary of Biography Volume 2.* Melbourne: Melbourne University Press. 613–14.

Hadcraft, Cecil. (1962) 1984. 'Preface to *Quintus Servinton: A Tale Founded upon Incidents of Real Occurrence.* 3 vols. Brisbane and Melbourne: Jacaranda Press. vii–xxviii.

Haenke, Helen. 1976. 'Thorn, George (1838–1905).' *Australian Dictionary of Biography Volume 6.* Canberra: Australian National University. Online: http://adb.anu.edu.au/biography/thorn-george-4942/text7825, accessed 24 September 2015.

Haggard, Rider. (1885) 2008. *King Solomon's Mines.* Adelaide: University of Adelaide Library. Online. https://ebooks.adelaide.edu.au/h/haggard/h_rider/, accessed 12 March 2015.

Hakluyt, Richard. 1599. *Principall Navigations, Voyages, Traffiques and Discoveries of the English Nation.* Ed. Edmund Goldsmid. Adelaide: ebooks@Adelaide, University of Adelaide. Online: https://ebooks.adelaide.edu.au/h/hakluyt/, accessed 2 August 2013.

Hamner, Robert D. 1997. *Epic of the Dispossessed: Derek Walcott's* Omeros. Columbia and London: University of Missouri Press.

Hansen, Miriam Bratu. 2008. 'Benjamin's Aura.' *Critical Inquiry* 34(Winter 2008): 334–78.

Hanssen, Beatrice. 2000. 'On the Politics of Pure Means: Benjamin, Arendt, Foucault.' *Critique of Violence: Between Poststructuralism and Critical Theory.* New York and London: Taylor & Francis. 16–29.

Hardy, Frank. (1950) 2000. *Power Without Glory*. Sydney: Random House.
Harrison, Robert Pogue. 2003. *The Dominion of the Dead*. Chicago and London: University of Chicago Press.
Hartwig, Heidi. 2012. 'La Maison Moralisee in W. H. Auden's "Thanksgiving for a Habitat".' *European Journal of English Studies* 16(1): 9–19.
Haskin, Dayton. 2007. *John Donne in the Nineteenth Century*. Oxford and New York: Oxford University Press.
Hasluck, Nicholas. 1984. *The Bellarmine Jug: A Novel*. Ringwood, VIC: Penguin.
Hasty, William. 2010. 'Piracy and the Production of Knowledge in the Travels of William Dampier, c.1679–1688.' *Journal of Historical Geography* doi:10.1016/j.hg.2010.08.017: 1–15.
Hau'ofa, Epeli. 1993. 'Our Sea of Islands.' *A New Oceania: Rediscovering Our Sea of Islands*. Eds E. Waddell, V. Naidu and E. Hau'ofa. Suva, Fiji: The University of the South Pacific. 2–16.
Hayman, Noel. 1976. 'Ross, Sir Robert Dalrymple (1827–1887).' *Australian Dictionary of Biography Volume 6*. Melbourne: Melbourne University Press. 62–63.
Haynes, Mark. 1974. 'Parry, Henry Hutton (1826–1893).' *Australian Dictionary of Biography Volume 5*. Melbourne: Melbourne University Press. 407–8.
Haynes, Roslynn. 1998. *Seeking the Centre: the Australian Desert in Literature, Art and Film*. Cambridge; New York; Melbourne: Cambridge University Press.
Hayward, Philip. 2012. 'Aquapelagos and Aquapelagic Assemblages.' *Shima: The International Journal of Research into Island Cultures* 6(1): 1–10.
Hazzard, Shirley. 1974. 'Sir Cecil's Ride.' *New Yorker* 17 June.
———. (1961) 1963. *Cliffs of Fall*. London: Macmillan.
———. 1966. *The Evening of the Holiday*. London: Macmillan.
———. (1967) 1970. *People in Glass Houses*. Harmondsworth, U.K.: Penguin.
———. 1970. *The Bay of Noon*. Boston: Little, Brown & Company.
———. 1980. *The Transit of Venus*. London: Macmillan.
———. 2003. *The Great Fire*. New York: Farrar, Straus & Giroux.
Healy, J. J. 1978. 'The Lemurian Nineties.' *Australian Literary Studies* 8(3): 307–16.
Heidegger, Martin. 1972. *On Time and Being*. New York: Harper and Row.
Hemingway, Ernest. (1940) 1969. *For Whom the Bell Tolls*. London: Penguin.
Henriksen, Line. 2001. 'Fredy Neptune's Democratic Sailor and Walcott's Epic Omeros.' *Australian Literary Studies* 20(2): 87–109.
Herbert, George. 2007. 'Man (1633).' *The English Poems of George Herbert*. Helen Wilcox. Cambridge: Cambridge University Press. 332–33.
Heydon, J. D. 1966. 'Brisbane, Sir Thomas Makdougall (1773–1860).' *Australian Dictionary of Biography Volume 2*. Melbourne: Melbourne University Press. 151–55.
Heyman, Kathryn. 2003. *The Accomplice*. Sydney and London: Hodder Headline.
Hill, Samuel Prout. 1845. 'The Cataraqui.' *Colonial Times and Tasmanian* 26 December, 4.
'Hindmarsh, Sir John (1785–1860).' (1966). *Australian Dictionary of Biography Volume 1*. Melbourne: Melbourne University Press. 538–41.
Hirsh, David A. Hendrick. 1991. 'Donne's Atomies and Anatomies: Deconstructed Bodies and the Resurrection of Atomic Theory.' *Studies in English Literature, 1500–1900* 31(1): 69–94.
Hirst, Warwick. 2005. 'Blackburn, David (1753–1795).' *Australian Dictionary of Biography Supplementary Volume*. Canberra: National Centre of Biography. Online: http://adb.anu.edu.au/biography/blackburn-david-12800/text23101, accessed 2 September 2015.

Hobbes, Thomas (1651) 2013. *Leviathan*. Project Gutenberg. Online. http://www.gutenberg.org/files/3207/3207-h/3207-h.htm, accessed 22 December 2014.

Hodge, Merle. 1970 (1989). *Crick Crack Monkey*. London: Andre Deutsch.

Hodgson, David. 1967. 'Meredith, George (1777–1856).' *Australian Dictionary of Biography Volume 2*. Canberra: National Centre of Biography. Online: http://adb.anu.edu.au/biography/meredith-george-2449/text3269, accessed 2 September 2015.

Homer. 800 B.C. *The Odyssey*: Massachusetts Institute of Technology Internet Classics Archive. Online: http://classics.mit.edu/Homer/odyssey.html, accessed 15 March 2014.

Hooper, Chloe. 2008. *The Tall Man. Death and Life on Palm Island*. Camberwell, VIC: Hamish Hamilton.

Hooper, Frederic C. 1966. 'Booth, Charles O'Hara (1800–1851).'*Australian Dictionary of Biography Volume 1*. Melbourne: Melbourne University Press. 125.

Hope, A. D. 1966. *Collected Poems*. Sydney: Angus and Robertson.

———. 1943. 'Australia.' *Meanjin Papers* 2(1): 42–43.

———. 1955. *The Wandering Islands*. Sydney: Edwards & Shaw.

Hope, Emily. 25 July 2014. 'We Demand an Apology for Snub after Tasmania Is Left Off the Map Again.' *The Mercury*. Hobart, Tasmania. Online. http://www.themercury.com.au/news/tasmania/we-demand-an-apology-for-snub-after-tasmania-is-left-off-the-map-again/story-fnj4f7k1–1227000804034, accessed 3 December 2014.

Hopkins, Gerard Manley. (1885) 1978. *Gerard Manley Hopkins: Poems and Prose*. W. H. Gardner. Harmondsworth, U.K.; New York; Melbourne: Penguin.

———. 2009. *Gerard Manley Hopkins: The Major Works*. Oxford: Oxford University Press.

Horace. *Horace, The Odes: New Translations by Contemporary Poets*. Ed. J. D. McClatchy, New Jersey: Princeton University Press.

Howard, Rod. 2011. *A Forger's Tale: The Extraordinary Story of Henry Savery, Australia's First Novelist*. Melbourne: Arcade.

Howe, Renate. 1969. 'Bickford, James (1816–1895).' *Australian Dictionary of Biography Volume 3*. Melbourne: Melbourne University Press. 162–63.

Howell, P. A. 1979. 'Bosanquet, Sir Day Hort (1843–1923).' *Australian Dictionary of Biography Volume 7*. Melbourne: Melbourne University Press. 351–52.

Hubbard, Vincent K. 2002. *A History of St. Kitts: The Sweet Trade*. Northampton, MA: Interlink Group.

Hughes, Shirley. 1999. 'Elizabeth Morey: Castaway in Tonga 1802–1804.' *Journal of Pacific History* 34(1): 45–58.

Huxley, Aldous. (1932) 2007. *Brave New World*. New York: Vintage.

———. (1962) 2005. *Island*. London: Vintage.

Idriess, Ion. (1927, 1938) 1949. *Madman's Island*. Sydney: Angus and Robertson.

ILBIJERRI Theatre Company and Belvoir. 2012. *Beautiful One Day*

'Island, n.' June 2015. *OED Online*. Oxford University Press. Online: http://www.oed.com/view/Entry/99986, accessed 8 September 2015.

James, Clive. 2009. *Angels over Elsinore*. London: Picador.

James, C. L. R. 1969. 'The West Indian Intellectual.' Introduction to John Jacob Thomas *Froudacity*. London: Beacon. 23–49.

James, Winston. 2011. 'Culture, Labor and Race in the Shadow of US Capital.' *The Caribbean: A History of the Region and Its Peoples*. Ed. Stephan Palmié, Francisco A. Scarano. Chicago and London: University of Chicago Press.

Jameson, Fredric. 1972. *The Prison House of Language*. New Jersey: Princeton University Press,

———. 1977. 'Of Islands and Trenches: Neutralization and the Production of Utopian Discourse.' *Diacritics* 7(2) (Summer): 2–21.

———. 1981. *The Political Unconscious: Narrative as Socially Symbolic Act.* New York: Cornell Univesrity Press.
———. 1998. 'Notes on Globalization as a Philosophical Issue.' *The Cultures of Globalization.* Eds Frederic Jameson and Masao Miyoshi. Durham, NC: Duke University Press. 54–80.
———. 2000. 'Globalization and Political Strategy.' *New Left Review* 4: 49–68.
———. 2005. *Archaeologies of the Future: The Desire Called Utopia and Other Science Fictions.*New York: Verso.
Janke, Terri. 2005. *Butterfly Song.* Melbourne: Penguin.
———. 2012. 'Turtle Island.' *Southerly* 72(3): 42–50.
Jetnil-Kijiner, Kathy. 23 September 2014. 'We are Drawing the Line Here.' Climate Summit, United Nations. Online: http://www.un.org/climatechange/summit/?s=Kathy+Jetnil-Kijiner&lang=en&lang=en, accessed 20 December 2014.
Johnston, J. and M. Anderson, Eds 2005. *Australia Imagined. Views from the British Periodical Press 1800–1900.* Crawley: University of Western Australia Press.
Jordan, Deborah. 2010. 'Environment and Colonial Shadows: Green Island, 1932.' *Literature in North Queensland* 37 142–58.
Karskens, Grace. 2009. *The Colony: A History of Early Sydney.* Sydney: Allen & Unwin.
Kefala, Antigone. 1984. *The Island.* Sydney: Hale and Ironmonger.
Keynes, Geoffrey. 1973. *A Bibliography of Dr. John Donne.* Oxford: Clarendon Press.
Kincaid, Jamaica. 1985. *Annie John.* London: Macmillan.
———. (1988) 2000. *A Small Place.* New York: Farrar, Straus and Giroux.
'Kinchela, John (1774?–1845).' (1967). *Australian Dictionary of Biography Volume 2.* Melbourne: Melbourne University Press. 51–52.
Kingsley, Charles. 1864. *The Roman and the Teuton.* Cambridge and London: Macmillan.
———. 1867. *At Last: A Christmas in the West Indies.* Project Gutenberg. Online: http://www.gutenberg.org/ebooks/10669, accessed 15 December 2014.
Kingsley, Henry. 1865. *Eyre, the South-Australian Explorer.* London: *Macmillans Mazagine.* October and November.
Knowles, Lee. 2008. 'Batavia Islands.' *Invaders of the Heart.* Carindale, QLD: Interactive Publications. 51–55.
Koch, Christopher. (1958 revised ed. 1974) 2013. *The Boys in the Island.* Sydney: HarperCollins.
Koch, Mark. 1998. 'Ruling the World: The Cartographic Gaze in Elizabethan Accounts of the New World.' *Early Modern Literary Studies* 4(2): 11–39.
Koditschek, Theodore. 2011. *Liberalism, Imperialism, and the Historical Imagination: Nineteenth-Century Visions of a Greater Britain.* Cambridge: Cambridge University Press.
Kramer, Leonie. (1972) 1985. 'Introduction.' *Nuns in Jeopardy.* Ringwood, VIC: Penguin. v–xii.
Kristeva, Julia. 1982. *The Powers of Horror. An Essay on Abjection.* New York: Columbia University Press.
Lamming, George. (1960) 1991. *The Pleasures of Exile.* Ann Arbor: University of Michigan Press.
Landow, George P. (1982) 2014. *Images of Crisis: Literary Iconography, 1750 to the Present.* Boston: Routledge and Kegan Paul.
Langmore, Diane. 1986. 'Le Hunte, Sir George Ruthven (1852–1925).' *Australian Dictionary of Biography Volume 10.* Melbourne: Melbourne University Press. 66–67.
Laughlin, Nicholas. 2008. 'R.I.P. Ralph de Boissiere, 6 October, 1907–16 February, 2008.' *Caribbean Review of Books.* Online: http://www.meppublishers.com/content/index.

php/r-i-p-ralph-de-boissiere-6-october-1907–16-february-2008/#axzz4133ZJH2Q, accessed 4 October 2015.

Lawrence, D. H. (1928) 2006. 'The Man Who Loved Islands.' *The Woman Who Rode Away and Other Stories*. Adelaide: University of Adelaide Library. Online: https://ebooks.adelaide.edu.au/l/lawrence/dh/l41wo/chapter9.html, accessed 15 August 2015.

Lawrie, M. L. Comp. and Trans. (1970). *Myths and Legends of Torres Strait*. St Lucia: Queensland University Press.

Lea-Scarlett, E. J. 1976. 'Rotton, Henry (1814–1881).' *Australian Dictionary of Biography Volume 6*. Canberra: National Centre of Biography. Online: http://adb.anu.edu.au/biography/rotton-henry-4512/text7381, accessed 2 September 2015.

Lemon, Andrew and Marjorie Morgan. 2014. *Poor Souls They Perished: The Cataraqui, Australia's Worst Shipwreck*. Warrandyte, VIC: Burgewood Books.

Lewis, Martin W. and Kären E. Wigen. 1997. *The Myth of Continents: A Critique of Metageography*. Berkeley: University of California Press.

Leys, Simon. (2003) 2005. *The Wreck of Batavia: A True Story*. New York: Basic Books.

Lincoln, Margarette. 1997. 'Shipwreck Narratives of the Eighteenth and Early Nineteenth Century: Indicators of Culture and Identity.' *British Journal for Eighteenth-Century Studies* 20(2): 155–72.

Lindsay, Joan. 1967. *Picnic at Hanging Rock*. Melbourne: Cheshire.

Lindsay, Norman. 1932. *The Cautious Amorist*. New York: Grosset and Dunlap.

Linebaugh, Peter and Mark Rediker. (2000) 2013. *The Many-Headed Hydra: Sailors, Slaves, Commoners, and the Hidden History of the Revolutionary Atlantic*. Massachusetts: Beacon Press.

Lines, Peter and Hamish Maxwell-Stewart. 2002. 'John Longworthy's Story: The Caribbean and the Penal Station Complex'. *Australian Cultural History: To the Islands*. Ed. Russell McDougall. St Lucia: University of Queensland Press. 41–49.

Livett, Jennifer. 2016 (forthcoming). *Wild Little Island*. Sydney: Allen and Unwin.

Livett, Kate. 2006. 'Subjects, Objects, and the Fetishisms of Modernity in the Works of Gertrude Stein.' Unpublished PhD thesis. Sydney: University of New South Wales.

———. 2007. 'Thieves and Fascists: The Politics of Abjection in Radiohead's *Hail to the Thief (The Gloaming)*.' *Australian Humanities Review* 41. Online: http://www.australianhumanitiesreview.org/archive/Issue-February-2007/Livett.html, accessed 1 January 2014.

Locke, John. (1689) 2007. *Two Treatises of Government*. Minnesota: Filiquarian Publishing.

Louch, T. S. 1976. 'Wrenfordsley, Sir Henry Thomas (1825–1908)'. *Australian Dictionary of Biography Volume 6*. Canberra: National Centre of Biography. Online: http://adb.anu.edu.au/biography/wrenfordsley-sir-henry-thomas-4890/text8183, accessed 5 January 2016.

Louvre. 2014. *Raft of the Medusa*. Online: http://www.louvre.fr/en/oeuvre-notices/raft-medusa, accessed 3 April 2014.

Lukács, Georg. (1920) 1971. *Theory of the Novel*. Trans. Anna Bostock. Massachusetts: MIT.

Lyotard, Jean-Francois. (1983) 1988. *The Differend: Phrases in Dispute*. Manchester: Manchester University Press.

Mackay, William. 1798. *Narrative of the Shipwreck of the Juno*. London: J Debrett.

Mackinder, Halford J. 1919. *Democratic Ideals and Reality: A Study in the Politics of Reconstruction*. London: Constable and Company.

———. (1904) 2005 'The Geographical Pivot of History.' *The Geographical Journal* 170: 298–321.

Macmillan, David S. 1966. 'Erskine, James (1765–1825).' *Australian Dictionary of Biography Volume 1*. Canberra: National Centre of Biography. Online: http://adb.anu.edu.au/biography/erskine-james-2028/text2499, accessed 15 September 2015.

Macmillan, David S. 1967. 'Ross, Robert (1740–1794).' *Australian Dictionary of Biography Volume 2*. Canberra: National Centre of Biography. Online: http://adb.anu.edu.au/biography/ross-robert-2608/text3591, accessed 2 September 2015.

Macmillan, David S. and J. R. Morris. 1967. 'McLachlan, Charles (1795?-1855).' *Australian Dictionary of Biography Volume 2*. Canberra: National Centre of Biography. Online: http://adb.anu.edu.au/biography/mclachlan-charles-2411/text3193, accessed 2 September 2015.

MacNeice, Louis. 1947. *Holes in the Sky: Poems 1942–1947*. New York: Random House.

Mais, Roger. (1938) 1976. *George William Gordon. Time… and a Season: 8 Caribbean Plays*. Ed. Errol Hill. Trinidad: University of the West Indies Press.

Makdisi, Saree. 1998. *Romantic Imperialism*. Cambridge: Cambridge University Press.

Makkreel, Rudolf A. 1984. 'Imagination and Temporality in Kant's Theory of the Sublime.' *Journal of Aesthetics and Art Criticism* 42(3): 303–15.

Marchant, Leslie R. 1966. 'Blosseville, Jules Poret de (1802–1833).' *Australian Dictionary of Biography Volume 1*. Melbourne: Melbourne University Press. 122–23.

Marchant, Leslie R. and J. H. Reynolds. 1966. 'Baudin, Nicolas Thomas (1754–1803).' *Australian Dictionary of Biography Volume 1*. Melbourne: Melbourne University Press.71–73.

Marin, Louis. (1968) 1984. *Utopics: Spatial Play*. Trans. Robert A. Vollrath. New Jersey: Humanities Press.

———. 1993. 'Frontiers of Utopia. Past and Present.' *Critical Inquiry* 19(3): 197–220.

Markus, Julia. 2005. *J. Anthony Froude: The Last Undiscovered Great Victorian*. New York: Scribner.

Marr, David. *Utopics. Spatial Play*. Trans. Robert A. Vollrath. London: Macmillan.

Martin, Susan. 2016. 'Outback Fever: The Romance of Rural and National Literary Identity in a Networked World.' *JASAL* (forthcoming).

Mateer, John. 2015. *The Quiet Slave A History in Eight Episodes*. Trans. Nur-l-Hudda Jaffar. Perth: Spaced 2 Future Recall.

Martyr, Peter. 1912. *De Orbe Novo, Volume 1 (of 2) by Pietro Martire d'Anghiera*. Project Gutenberg. Online: http://www.gutenberg.org/files/12425/12425-h/12425-h.htm, accessed 2 December 2013.

Marx, Karl. (1867) 1887. *Capital. Volume 1*. Trans. Samuel Moore and Edward Aveling. Marx/Engels Internet Archive. Online: https://www.marxists.org/archive/marx/works/1867-c1/, accessed 2 August 2015.

'Mary's Little Lamb.' 1932. *Daily Gleaner*. 27 September. 12.

Maude, H. E. 1976. 'Smith, Charles (1816–1897).' *Australian Dictionary of Biography Volume 6*. Melbourne: Melbourne University Press. 141–42.

Maynard, John. 2007. *Fight for Liberty and Freedom: The Origins of Australian Aboriginal Activism*. Canberra: Aboriginal Studies Press.

McClemans, Sheila. 1969. 'Burt, Sir Archibald Paull (1810–1879).' *Australian Dictionary of Biography Volume 3*. Melbourne: Melbourne University Press. 307–8.

McCulloch, Samuel Clyde. 1966. 'Gipps, Sir George (1791–1847).' *Australian Dictionary of Biography Volume 1*. Melbourne: Melbourne University Press. 446–53.

'McDonald, Hugh (1779–1819).' (1967). *Australian Dictionary of Biography Volume 2*. Canberra: National Centre of Biography. Online: http://adb.anu.edu.au/biography/mcdonald-hugh-2395/text3161, accessed 15 September 2015.

McDougall, Russell. Ed. 2002. *To the Islands: Australia and the Caribbean. Australian Cultural History* 21. St Lucia: University of Queensland Press.

———. 2002. 'Introduction.' *To the Islands: Australia and the Caribbean. Australian Cultural History* 21. Ed. Russell McDougall. St Lucia: University of Queensland Press. 108–12.

McFarlane, Jill. 2006. *Islands and the Modernists: The Allure of Isolation in Art, Literature and Science.* London: McFarlane.

McGahan, Andrew. 2009. *Wonders of a Godless World.* Sydney: Allen & Unwin.

McKay, Claude. (1912) 2004. 'George William Gordon to the Oppressed Natives.' *Complete Poems.* Urbana and Chicago: University of Illinois Press. 15–16.

'McKenzie, Alexander Kenneth (1769–1838).' (1967). *Australian Dictionary of Biography Volume 2.* Canberra: National Centre of Biography. Online: http://adb.anu.edu.au/biography/mckenzie-alexander-kenneth-2407/text3185, accessed 2 September 2015.

McKernan, Susan. 1989. 'Douglas Stewart and the Bulletin.' *A Question of Commitment: Australian Literature in the Twenty Years after the War.* Sydney: Allen and Unwin. 120–40.

McLachlan, N. D. 1967. 'Macquarie, Lachlan (1762–1824).' *Australian Dictionary of Biography Volume 2.* Melbourne: Melbourne University Press. 187–95.

McLaughlin, John Kennedy. 1972. 'Dickinson, Sir John Nodes (1806–1882).' *Australian Dictionary of Biography Volume 4.* Melbourne: Melbourne University Press. 71–72.

'McLeay, Alexander (1767–1848).' (1967) *Australian Dictionary of Biography. National Centre of Biography*, Australian National University. Online: http://adb.anu.edu.au/biography/mcleay-alexander-2413/text3197, accessed 4 November 2014.

McMahon, Elizabeth. 2000. 'Transvestism and Colonial Narratives of Itinerancy and Settlement.' *Outskirts; Feminisms Along the Edge.* Perth: University of Western Australia. Online: http://www.outskirts.arts.uwa.edu.au/volumes/volume-6/mcmahon, accessed 6 June 2013.

———. 2001a. 'Tasmania Lilliputianism: Miniature Villages and Model Citizens on the Tourist Trail.' *Southerly* 61(2): 70–84.

———. 2001b. 'Tasmania: Island or Archipelago; Trinket or Chain,' *Changing Geographies: Essays on Australia.* Ed. Susan Ballyn et al. Barcelona: Universitat de Barcelona. 113–20.

———. 2003. 'The Gilded Cage: From Utopia to Monad in Australia's Island Imaginary.' *Islands in History and Representation.* Eds Rod Edmond and Vanessa Smith. London: Routledge. 190–202.

———. 2005. 'Encapsulated Space: The Paradise-Prison of Australia's Island Imaginary.' *Southerly* 65(1): 20–30.

———. 2010. 'Australia, the Island Continent: How Contradictory Geography Shapes the National Imaginary.' *Space and Culture* 13(2): 178–87.

———. 2011. 'Monstrous Symmetries: Australia's Alignment of Space and Nation.' Individual essay within Stratford, Elaine et al. 'Reading Suvendrini Perera's *Australia and the Insular Imagination: Beaches, Borders, Boats, and Bodies.*' *Political Geography.* 30(6): 329–38.

———. 2012. 'Continental Heartlands and Alex Miller's Geosophical Imaginary.' *The Novels of Alex Miller.* Ed. Robert Dixon. Sydney: Allen & Unwin. 125–37.

———. 2013. 'Reading the Planetary Archipelago of the Torres Strait.' *Island Studies Journal* 8(1): 55–66.

McMartin, Arthur. 1967a. 'Shortland, John (1739–1803).' *Australian Dictionary of Biography Volume 2.* Melbourne: Melbourne University Press. 442–43.

———. 1967b. 'Shortland, John (1769–1810).' *Australian Dictionary of Biography Volume 2.* Canberra: National Centre of Biography. Online: http://adb.anu.edu.au/biography/shortland-john-2659/text3663, accessed 2 September 2015.

McNicoll, Ronald. 1974. 'Nickle, Sir Robert (1786–1855).' *Australian Dictionary of Biography Volume 5.* Canberra: National Centre of Biography. Online: http://adb.anu.edu.au/biography/nickle-sir-robert-4301/text6967, accessed 2 September 2015.

Meeker, Joseph W. 2011. 'Subtleties of the Isle: Islands and the Imagination.' *Isle: Interdisciplinary Studies in Literature and Environment* 18(1): 197–202.

Middelmann, Raoul F. 1976. 'Schomburgk, Moritz Richard (1811–1891).' *Australian Dictionary of Biography Volume 6*. Canberra: National Centre of Biography. Online: http://adb.anu.edu.au/biography/schomburgk-moritz-richard-4543/text7445, accessed 2 September 2015.

Miller, Alex. 1993. 'Chasing My Tale.' *Kunapipi* 15(3): 1–6.

———. (2000) 2001. *Conditions of Faith*. Sydney: Allen & Unwin.

———. (1993) 2003a. *The Ancestor Game*. Sydney: Allen & Unwin.

———. (2002) 2003b. *Journey to the Stone Country*. Sydney: Allen & Unwin.

———. 2007. *Landscape of Farewell*. Sydney: Allen & Unwin.

———. 25 October 2009. 'John Masefield's Attic.' Canberra: National Library Australia: Online: http://www.nla.gov.au/events/flight/John_Masefields_Attic-Alex_Miller.pdf, accessed 2 August 2015.

Miller, E. Morris. (1957) 1999. *Australia's First Two Novels: Origins and Backgrounds* (1958). Hobart, Tasmania: Tasmanian Historical Research Association.

Milton, John. 1983. *Milton Poetical Works*. Ed. Douglas Bush. Oxford and New York: Oxford University Press.

Mizejewski, Linda. 1977. 'Darkness and Disproportion: A Study of Donne's "Storme" and "Calme".' *The Journal of English and Germanic Philology* 76(2): 217–30.

Moffatt, Tracey. 1993. *Bedevil*. Australia.

Mohaghegh, Jason. 2010. *New Literature and Philosophy of the Middle East: The Chaotic Imagination*. New York: Palgrave Macmillan.

Monks, Linda. 1967. 'Knopwood, Robert (1763–1838).' *Australian Dictionary of Biography Volume 2*. Melbourne: Melbourne University Press. 66–67.

Montgomery, Scott B. 2010. *St Ursula and the Eleven Thousand Virgins of Cologne*. Bern: Peter Lang.

More, Thomas. (1516) 1969. *Utopia*. Harmondsworth, U.K.: Penguin.

Morin, Marie-Eve. 2008. 'Cohabiting in the Globalised World: Peter Sloterdijk's Global Foams and Bruno Latour's Cosmopolitics.' *Environment and Planning D: Society and Space* 27: 58–72.

Morris, J. R. 1967. 'Lord, Thomas Daunt (1783–1865).' *Australian Dictionary of Biography Volume 2*. Canberra: National Centre of Biography. Online: http://adb.anu.edu.au/biography/lord-thomas-daunt-2372/text3117, accessed 2 September 2015.

Morris, Meaghan. 1996. *Too Soon Too Late: History in Popular Culture*. Bloomington: Indiana University Press.

Morrison, Cheyanne. n.d. 'Celebrity, Movie Stars, The World's Most Exclusive Property.' *Private Islands Online*. http://www.privateislandsonline.com/celebrities-islands.htm, accessed 20 July 2015.

Morrison, Fiona. 2014. '"This Intricate Lasting Nature": Passage, Pastoral Elegy and the Pedagogy of Loss in *The Evening of the Holiday*.' *Shirley Hazzard*. Ed. Brigitta Olubas. Sydney: Sydney University Press. 13–22.

Morrison, Ken. 2006. *Marx, Durkheim, Weber: Formations of Modern Social Thought*, Second Edition. London: Sage.

Munkara, Marie. 2009. 'The Castaways.' *Every Secret Thing*. St Lucia: University of Queensland Press. 128–39.

'Murray, Sir George (1772–1846).' (1967). *Australian Dictionary of Biography Volume 2*. Canberra: National Centre of Biography. Online: http://adb.anu.edu.au/biography/murray-sir-george-2494/text3361, accessed 2 September 2015.

Murray, Les. 1999. 'How Fred and I Wrote *Fredy Neptune.*' *Best Australian Essays 1999*. Ed. Peter Craven. Melbourne: Bookman. 364–73.

Murray, Neil and Warumpi Band. 1986. 'My Island Home.' *Go Bush*: Parole Records.

Murray-Smith, Stephen. 1969. *Bass Strait: Australia's Last Frontier*. Sydney: Australian Broadcasting Corporation.

Naipaul, V. S. 2000. *Reading and Writing: A Personal Account*. New York: New York Review of Books.

———. 2001. 'Two Worlds'. Nobel Lecture. *Nobel Academy.* Original retrieved 7 December 2014 from http://www.nobelprize.org/nobel_prizes/literature/laureates/2001/naipaul-lecture-e.html.

Nairn, Bede. 1976. 'Robinson, Sir Hercules George Robert [first Baron Rosmead] (1824–1897).' *Australian Dictionary of Biography Volume 6*. Melbourne: Melbourne University Press. 48–50.

National Army Museum. 2014a. '28th North Gloucestershire Regiment of Foot.' *National Army Museum: Research*. Online: http://www.nam.ac.uk/research/famous-units/28th-north-gloucestershire-regiment-foot, accessed 25 September 2015.

———. 2014b. 'West Yorkshire Regiment (The Prince of Wales's Own).' *National Army Museum: Research*. Online: http://www.nam.ac.uk/research/famous-units/west-yorkshire-regiment-prince-wales-own, accessed 25 September 2015.

Neill, Anna. 2000. 'Buccaneer Ethnography: Nature, Culture, and Nation in the Journals of William Dampier.' *Eighteenth-Century Studies* 33(2): 154–80.

Nellist. B. F. 1964. 'Donne's "Storm" and "Calm" and the Descriptive Tradition.' *Modern Language Review* 59(4): 511–15.

Nicol, John. 1997. *The Life and Adventures of John Nicol, Mariner*. Introduction, ed. Tim Flannery. New York: Grove Press.

Nietzsche, Friedrich. (1885) 2009. *Thus Spake Zarathustra*. New York: Thrifty Books.

Niles, Daniel and Godfrey Baldacchino. Eds. 2011. *Island Futures: Conservation and Development across the Asia-Pacific Region*. Tokyo: Springer and Research Institute for Humanity and Nature.

Nisbet, Hume. 1896. *A Colonial Tramp: Travels and Adventures in Australia and New Guinea*. London: Ward & Downey.

Noad, K. B. 1966. 'Douglass, Henry Grattan (1790–1865).' *Australian Dictionary of Biography Volume 1*. Melbourne: Melbourne University Press. 314–16.

Nobel Committee. 1973. 'Nobel Prize in Literature, 1973, Patrick White.' Online: http://www.nobelprize.org/nobel_prizes/literature/laureates/1973/press.html, accessed 10 May 2014.

———. 1992. 'Nobel Prize in Literature, 1992, Derek Walcott.' Online: http://www.nobelprize.org/nobel_prizes/literature/laureates/1992/press.html, accessed 10 Mat 2014.

Nolan, Cynthia. (1962) 1994. *Outback and Beyond: The Travels of Cynthia and Sidney Nolan*. Sydney: Angus & Robertson.

Novalis. (1920) 1923. *Schriften Vol 2.*. Ed. J. Minor. Jena: Diederichs.

'Novel Banned.' 1934. *Sydney Morning Herald* . 29 May 1934, 9.

Old Hobart Town. n.d. *Old Hobart Town* website. Online: http://www.oldhobarttown.com, accessed 5 June 2015.

Olubas, Brigitta. 2002. 'Paradoxes of Non-Existence: Questions of Time, Metaphor and the Materialities of Cultural Traditions in Wilson Harris's Discussions of Australian Literary Texts.' *To the Islands: Australia and the Caribbean. Australian Cultural History* 21. Ed. Russell McDougall. St Lucia: University of Queensland Press. 81–88.

———. 2012. *Shirley Hazzard: Literary Expatriate and Cosmopolitan Humanist*. New York: Cambria.

———. 2013. 'The Last Curve of the Globe: Deep Time and Scenes of Reading in Shirley Hazzard's *The Great Fire.*' *Scenes of Reading: Is Australian Literature a World Literature?* Eds Robert Dixon and Brigid Rooney. Melbourne: Australian Scholarly Publishing. 127–36.

Ortega y Gassett, José. (1949) 1989. 'Goethe from Within, [reprinted as] Man's Vocation.' *Philosophies of Love.* Eds David L. Norton and Mary F. Kille. New Jersey: Rowman and Littlefield. 110–17.

Osborne, M. E. 1967. 'Thomson, Sir Edward Deas (1800–1879).' *Australian Dictionary of Biography Volume 2.* Canberra: National Centre of Biography. Online: http://adb.anu.edu.au/biography/thomson-sir-edward-deas-2732/text3855, accessed 2 September 2015.

*OED Online.* Oxford University Press, March 2016. Web. 8 March 2015. .

Paravisini-Gebert, Lizabeth. 2004. 'The Caribbean Review of Books, August.' Original retrieved 14 December 2014 from http://caribbeanreviewofbooks.com/crb-archive/1-august-2004/o-stay-and-hear/.

Parkes, Henry. 1841. 'The Last'. *Australasian Chronicle,* 7(August 3 273): 1.

Parsons, George. 1967. 'Laidley, James (1786–1835).' *Australian Dictionary of Biography Volume 2.* Canberra: National Centre of Biography. Online: http://adb.anu.edu.au/biography/laidley-james-2317/text3009, accessed 2 September 2015.

Parsons, Vivienne. 1967a. 'O'Flynn, Jeremiah Francis (1788–1831).' *Australian Dictionary of Biography Volume 2.* Melbourne: Melbourne University Press. 299–300.

———. 1967b. 'Raven, William (1756–1814).' *Australian Dictionary of Biography Volume 2.* Canberra: National Centre of Biography. Online: http://adb.anu.edu.au/biography/raven-william-2574/text3521, accessed 2 September 2015.

———. 1967c. 'Scott, Thomas Alison (1777?–1881).' *Australian Dictionary of Biography Volume 2.* Melbourne: Melbourne University Press. 430–31.

Patke, Rajeev S. 2004. 'The Islands of Poetry: The Poetry of Islands.' *Partial Answers Journal of Literature and History of Ideas* 2(1): 177–94.

Paton, Diana. 2008. 'An Injurious Population: Caribbean-Australian Penal Transportation and Imperial Racial Politics.' *Cultural and Social History* 5(4): 449–64.

Perera, Suvendrini. 2009. *Australia and the Insular Imagination: Beaches, Borders, Boats, and Bodies.* New York: Palgrave Macmillan.

Phillips, Nan. 1967. 'Vancouver, George (1757–1798).' *Australian Dictionary of Biography Volume 2.* Melbourne: Melbourne University Press. 550–52.

Pilkington, Doris / Garimara, Nugi. (1996) 2002. *Follow the Rabbit-Proof Fence.* St Lucia: University of Queensland Press.

Pinet, Simone. 2003. 'On the Subject of Fiction: Islands and the Emergence of the Novel.' *Diacritics* 33(3–4): 173–87.

———. 2011. *Archipelagoes: Insular Fictions from Chivalric Romance to the Novel.* Minnesota and London: University of Minnesota Press.

Pitts, Graham. 1994. *Edge.* First performance Fremantle Maritime Museum 1 November.

Plato. (ca. 380 BC) 1968. *The Republic of Plato Second Edition.* Trans. Allan Bloom. New York: Basic Books.

Polo, Marco. (ca. 1300) 1914. *The Travels.* London: J. M. Dent.

Porter, Hal. 1961. *The Tilted Cross.* Sydney: Angus and Robertson.

Poskitt, Lucy. 2013. 'Penny Royal Revival Hopes.' *Examiner* 16 March 2013. Online: http://www.examiner.com.au/story/1368426/penny-royal-revival-hopes/, accessed 10 October 2015.

Pratt, Mary Louise. 1992. *Imperial Eyes: Travel Writing and Transculturation.* London: Routledge.

Pretyman, E. R. 1966. 'Collins, William (1760?–1819).' *Australian Dictionary of Biography Volume 1.* Melbourne: Melbourne University Press. 240.

Prichard, Katharine-Susannah. 1926. *Working Bullocks.* London: Jonathan Cape.

Pybus, Cassandra. 2002. 'His Country Marks: African Soldiers from the Caribbean Regiments Transported to the Australian Penal Colonies.' *Australian Cultural History* (21): 33–39.

———. 2011. 'Tense and Tender Ties. Reflections on Lives Recovered from the Intimate Frontier of Empire and Slavery.' *International Life Writing: Memory and Identity in Global Context.* Ed. Paul Longley Arthur. London and New York: Routledge.

Raffles, Stamford. (1817) 2010 *History of Java.* Cambridge: Cambridge University Press.

Raikes, George Alfred. 1885. *First Battalion, formerly 65th (2nd Yorkshire, North Riding) Regiment, from 1756 to 1884.* London: Richard Bentley & Son. Online: https://books.google.com.au/books?id=HbMI3vVEJw4C&dq=65th+regiment&focus=searchwithinvolume&q=west+indies, accessed 23 September 2015.

Raleigh, Walter. (ca. 1595) 2013. *Discovery of Guiana.* Project Gutenburg. Online: http://www.gutenberg.org/files/2272/2272-h/2272-h.htm, accessed 2 January 2015.

Ramraj, Victor. 1971. 'The All-Embracing Christlike Vision: Tone and Attitude in The Mimic Men.' *Common Wealth.* Anna Rutherford. Aarhus, Denmark: Akademisek Boghandel. 125–34.

Ranker. n.d. '23 Celebrities Who Have Their Own Private Islands.' Online: http://www.ranker.com/list/celebrities-who-own-private-islands/celebrity-lists, accessed 2 November 2015.

Read, K. L. 1966. 'Gunn, William (1800–1868).' *Australian Dictionary of Biography Volume 1.* Canberra: National Centre of Biography. Online: http://adb.anu.edu.au/biography/gunn-william-2135/text2711, accessed 2 September 2015.

Redhead, Steve. 2006. 'The Art of the Accident: Paul Virilio and Accelerated Modernity.' *Fast Capitalism* 2(1). Online: http://www.uta.edu./human/agger/fastcapitalism/2_1/redhead.html, accessed 6 June 2013.

Refshauge, Richard. 1969. 'Campbell, Envidale Savage Norman (1806–1859).' *Australian Dictionary of Biography Volume 3.* Canberra: National Centre of Biography. Online: http://adb.anu.edu.au/biography/campbell-envidale-savage-norman-3155/text4713, accessed 2 September 2015.

———. 1972. 'Hamilton, Sir Robert George (1836–1895).' *Australian Dictionary of Biography Volume 4.* Canberra: National Centre of Biography. Online: http://adb.anu.edu.au/biography/hamilton-sir-robert-george-3703/text5807, accessed 2 September 2015.

Reid, V. S. (1949) 1973. *New Day.* Intro. Mervyn Morris. London: Heinemann Educational Books.

Reynolds, John. 1967a. 'Montagu, John (1797–1853).' *Australian Dictionary of Biography Volume 2.* Canberra: Australian National University. Online: http://adb.anu.edu.au/biography/montagu-john-2471/text3315, accessed 24 September 2015.

———. 1967b. 'Sorell, William (1775–1848).' *Australian Dictionary of Biography Volume 2.* Melbourne: Melbourne University Press. 459–62.

Rice, Charles E. 2005. 'Walter Benjamin's Interior History.' *Walter Benjamin and History.* Ed. Andrew Benjamin. London: Continuum. 171–81.

Riding, Christine. 2013. 'Shipwreck in French and British Visual Art 1780–1842: Vernet, Northcote, Gericault and Turner.' *The Shipwreck in Art and Literature. Images and Interpretations from Antiquity to the Present Day.* London and New York: Routledge. 112–32.

Rienits, Rex. 1967. 'White, John (1756?–1832).' *Australian Dictionary of Biography Volume 2*. Melbourne: Melbourne University Press. 594–95.

Robin, Libby. 2007. *How a Continent Created a Nation*. Sydney: UNSW Press.

Robson. Frank. 2012. 'The Possibility of an Island.' *Sydney Morning Herald* 24 December. Online: http://www.smh.com.au/national/the-possibility-of-an-island-20121223–2bl9b.html, accessed 2 October 2014.

Rody, Caroline. 2001. *The Daughter's Return: African-American and Caribbean Women's Fictions of History*. Oxford: Oxford University Press.

Rosenberg, Gary D. 2001. 'An Artistic Perspective on the Continuity of Space and the Origin of Modern Geologic Thought.' *Earth Sciences History* 20(2): 127–55.

———. 2006. 'Nicholas Steno's *Chaos* and the Shaping of Evolutionary Thought in the Scientific Revolution.' *Geology* 34(9): 793–96.

———. Ed. 2009a. *The Revolution in Geology from the Renaissance to the Enlightenment: Geological Society of America Memoir 203*. Boulder, CO: The Geological Society of America, Inc.

———. 2009b. 'The Measure of Man and Landscape in the Renaissance and Scientific Revolution.' *The Revolution in Geology from the Renaissance to the Enlightenment: Geological Society of America Memoir 203*. Gary D. Rosenberg. Boulder, CO: The Geological Society of America, Inc. 13–41.

Royle, Stephen A. 2001. *A Geography of Small Islands: Small Island Insularity*. London and New York: Routledge.

Rudd, Kevin. 24 October 2011. Australia and the Caribbean Community Working Together: Joint Media Release. Foreign Affairs and Trade. Federal Government Archives: Australian Federal Government. Online: http://foreignminister.gov.au/releases/Pages/2011/kr_mr_111024.aspx?ministerid=2, accessed 1 May 2013.

Rutledge, Martha. 1976. 'Stephen, Sir Alfred (1802–1894).' *Australian Dictionary of Biography Volume 6*. Melbourne: Melbourne University Press. 180–87.

Sabine, Mark J. L. 2005. '"Once But No Longer the Prow of Europe." National Identity and Portuguese Destiny in José Saramago's *The Stone Raft*.' *José Saramago: Bloom's Modern Critical Views*. Ed. Harold Bloom. New York: Chelsea House Publications. 75–93.

Saramago, José. (1986) 1995. *The Stone Raft*. Trans. Giovanni Pontiero. San Diego; New York; London: Harcourt.

———. (1997) 1999. *The Tale of the Unknown Island*. Trans. Margaret Jull Costa. New York; San Diego; London: Harcourt Brace.

Savery, Henry. (1830) 1962. *Quintus Servinton: A Tale Founded upon Incidents of Real Occurrence*. Intro. Cecil Hadcraft. 3 vols. Brisbane and Melbourne: Jacaranda Press.

Sayer, Stuart. 1981. 'Writers and Readers: Better Late than Never.' *Age* (8 August): 26.

Sayers, C. E. 1976. 'Windsor, Arthur Lloyd (1833–1913).' *Australian Dictionary of Biography Volume 6*. Canberra: National Centre of Biography. Online: http://adb.anu.edu.au/biography/windsor-arthur-lloyd-4872/text8149, accessed 2 September 2015.

Schaffer, Irene. 2005. *The Forgotten Women Convicts at Macquarie Harbour 1821–26*. Online: http://www.tasfamily.net.au/~schafferi/index.php?file=kop28.php, accessed 15 September 2015.

Schaffer, Kay. 1988. *Women and the Bush: Forces of Desire in the Australian Cultural Tradition*. Cambridge: Cambridge University Press.

Scott, Colin. 2004. '"Our Feet Are on the Land, but Our Hands Are in the Sea": Knowing and Caring for Marine Territory at Erub, Torres Strait.' *Woven Histories, Dancing Lives: Torres Strait Islander Identity, Culture and History*. Ed. R. Davis. Canberra: Aboriginal Studies Press. 259–70.

Scott, John and John Taylor. 1824. *The London Magazine, July to December 1824, Volume 10.* London: Taylor & Hessey.

Scrymgour, Marion. 27 October 2007. 'Whose National Emergency?' Charles Perkins Memorial Oration. Original retrieved 7 December 2014 from http://www.abc.net.au/radionational/programs/awaye/charles-perkins-memorial-oration-marion-scrymgour-/3669310#transcript.

Sedgwick, Eve. 1990. *Epistemology of the Closet.* Berkeley: University of California Press.

Semmel, Bernard. 1963. *Jamaican Blood and Victorian Conscience: The Governor Eyre Controversy.* Boston: Houghton Mifflin.

Shakespeare, William. (ca. 1595) 1979. *A Midsummer Night's Dream.* Ed. Harold Brooks. London: Arden, Bloomsbury.

———. *The Tempest.* (ca. 1611) 1999. Ed. Virginia Mason Vaughan and Alden T. Vaughan. London: Arden, Bloomsbury.

———. (1616) 1995. *Antony and Cleopatra.* Ed. John Wilders. London: Arden, Bloomsbury.

———. (ca 1600) 1980. *Hamlet.* Ed. T. J. B. Spencer. London: Penguin.

Shami, Jeanne. 1987. 'John Donne: Geography as Metaphor.' *Geography and Literature: A Meeting of the Disciplines.* Eds William E. Mallory and Paul Simpson-Housley. Syracuse: Syracuse University Press. 161–67.

Shapcott, Tom. 1998. *Theatre of Darkness.* Sydney: Vintage.

Sharp, Nonie. 1996. *No Ordinary Judgment: Mabo, the Murray Islanders Land Case.* Canberra: Aboriginal Studies Press.

———. 2002. *Saltwater People: The Waves of Memory.* Sydney: Allen and Unwin.

Sharp, Robert L. 1954. 'Donne's "Good Morrow" and Cordiform Maps.' *Modern Language Notes* 69(7): 493–95.

Sharrad, Paul. 1993. 'Countering Encounter: Black Voyaging after Columbus in Australia and the Caribbean.' *Kunapipi: Journal of Postcolonial Writing* 15(3): 58–72.

Shaw, A. G. L. 1966a. 'Arthur, Sir George (1784–1854).' *Australian Dictionary of Biography Volume 1.* Canberra: National Centre of Biography. Online: http://adb.anu.edu.au/biography/arthur-sir-george-1721/text1883, accessed 2 September 2015.

———. 1966b. 'Bligh, William (1754–1817).' *Australian Dictionary of Biography Volume 1.* Melbourne: Melbourne University Press. 118–22.

Shell, Marc. 2014. *Islandology: Geography, Rhetoric, Politics.* Stanford, CA: Stanford University Press.

Shepherd, Verene A. 2007. 'Resisting Representation: Locating Enslaved and Indentured Women's Voices in the Colonial Caribbean.' *Caribbean Culture: Soundings on Kama Braithwaite.* Annie Paul. Kingston: University of West Indies Press. 265–86.

Simpson, R. A. 1972. *Diver.* St Lucia: Queensland University Press.

Singe, John. 2003. *My Island Home: A Torres Strait Memoir.* St Lucia: University of Queensland Press.

Siskind, Mariano. 2005. 'Captain Cook and the Discovery of Antarctica's Modern Specificity: Towards a Critique of Globalism.' *Comparative Literary Studies* 42(1): 1–23.

Sloterdijk, Peter. (1998) 2011. *Bubbles: Spheres Volume 1: Microspherelogy.* Trans. Wieland Hoban. Los Angeles: Semiotext(e).

———. 2004. *Sphären III – Schäume, Plurale Sphärologie.* Berlin: Suhrkamp Verlag.

———. (2005) 2013. *In the World Interior of Capital: Towards a Philosophical Theory of Globalization.* Trans. Wieland Hoban. Cambridge, U.K.; Massachusetts: Polity.

Smith, Vivian. 1983. 'Tasmania and Australian Poetry.' *Quadrant* (October): 28–36.

Souhami, Diana. (2001) 2002. *Selkirk's Island: The Original Robinson Crusoe.* London: Phoenix.

Southey, Thomas. 1827. *Chronological History of the West Indies Volume III.* London: Longman, Rees, Orme, Brown and Green.

Spivak, Gayatri. 2003. *Death of a Discipline*. New York: Columbia University Press.

———. 2012. *An Aesthetic Education in the Era of Globalization*. Cambridge, MA: Harvard University Press.

Staines, Max. n.d. *Mole Hill Fantasy* brochure. Launceston, Tasmania.

Stead, Christina. (1944) 2011. *For Love Alone*. Melbourne: Melbourne University Press.

Stedman, M. L. 2012. *The Light between Oceans*. North Sydney: Random House.

Steinberg, Philip E. 2005. 'Insularity, Sovereignity and Statehood: The Representation of Islands on Portolan Charts and the Construction of the Territorial State.' *Geografiska Annaler* 87B(4): 253–65.

Steiner, George. (1978) 1989. *Martin Heidegger: With a New Introduction*. Chicago: University of Chicago Press.

Stephen, M. D. 1967. 'Mosman, Archibald (1799–1863).' *Australian Dictionary of Biography Volume 2*. Melbourne: Melbourne University Press. 263–64.

'Stevenson, George (1799–1856).' (1967). *Australian Dictionary of Biography Volume 1*. Canberra: National Centre of Biography. Online: http://adb.anu.edu.au/biography/stevenson-george-2699/text3785, accessed 2 September 2015.

Stevenson, Robert Louis. (1881–83) 1998. *Treasure Island*. Edinburgh: Edinburgh University Press.

Stewart, Douglas. 1949. *Shipwrecked. Four Plays*. Sydney: Angus and Robertson.

Stewart, Susan. 1993. *On Longing: Narratives of the Miniature, the Gigantic, the Souvenir, the Collection*. Durham, NC and London: Duke University Press.

Stow, Randolph. (1958) 2002. *To the Islands*. St Lucia: University of Queensland Press.

———. 1971. 'The Southland of Antichrist: The Batavia Disaster of 1629.' *Common Wealth*. Ed. Anna Rutherford. Aarhus, Denmark: Akademisk Boghandel. 160–67.

Stratford (2012) '"Ah!. I could tell the wonders of an isle" … Contemplating Island Futures.' *Southerly* 72(3): 12–27.

Stratford, Elaine et al. 2011a. 'Envisioning the Archipelago.' *Island Studies Journal* 6(2): 113–30.

———. 2011b. 'Reading Suvendrini Perera's *Australia and the Insular Imagination*.' *Political Geography* 30(6): 329–38.

Stubbs, John. 2006. *Donne: The Reformed Soul*. London: Penguin.

Süskind, Patrick. (1985) 2001. *Perfume: The Story of a Murderer*. New York: Knopf.

Swift, Jonathan. (1726) 2004. *Gulliver's Travels*. Syracuse, New York: Barnes & Noble.

*Tales from 1001 Nights*. 2008. Trans. Malcolm Lyons and Ursula Lyons. London: Penguin.

Tameside Metropolitan Borough. 2011. 'Museum of the Manchester Regiment: History of the 96th Regiment of Foot, Later the 2nd Battalion.' *Tameside Museums and Galleries: Museum of the Manchester Regiment*. Online: http://www.tameside.gov.uk/museumsgalleries/mom/history/96th, accessed 25 September 2015.

Tapp, E. J. 1966. 'Hobson, William (1793–1842).' *Australian Dictionary of Biography Volume 1*. Melbourne: Melbourne University Press. 545–46.

Tasmazia. n.d. Tasmazia and the Village of Lower Crackpot website. Online: http://www.tasmazia.com.au, accessed 2 January 2015.

Taussig, Michael. 1993. 'Maleficium: State Fetishism.' *Fetishism as Cultural Discourse*. Eds Emily Apter and William Pietz. Ithaca, NY: Cornell University Press. 218–45.

Teale, Ruth. (1972) 2014. 'Froude, James Anthony (1818–1894).' *Australian Dictionary of Biography*. National Centre of Biography: Australian National University. Online: http://adb.anu.edu.au/biography/froude-james-anthony-3578, accessed 2 December 2014.

Telegraph. 2002. 'British Bliss Is an Island Escape.' *Sydney Morning Herald* (3–4 August): 20.

Thomas, John Jacob. (1889) 1969. *Froudacity: West Indian Fables by James Anthony Froude*. London: New Beacon Books.

Thomas, Nicholas. 2003. *Cook: The Extraordinary Voyages of Captain James Cook*. New York: Walker & Company.

Thompson, Carl. 2007. *The Suffering Traveller and the Romantic Imagination*. Oxford: Oxford University Press.

———. 2013. 'Shipwreck and the Forging of the Commercial Nation: The 1786 Wreck of the Halsewell.' *The Shipwreck in Art and Literature*. Ed. Carl Thompson. London and New York: Routledge.

———. Ed. 2013. *The Shipwreck in Art and Literature*. London and New York: Routledge.

Thompson, Norma. 2001. *The Ship of State: Statecraft and Politics from Ancient Greece to Democratic America*. New Haven and London:Yale University Press.

Thoreau, Henry. (1854) 2008. *Walden, Civil Disobedience and Other Writings*. New York and London: Norton.

Tierney, Brian. (Original Publication) 1994 'Natural Rights: Before and After Columbus.' *Fulton Lectures*. Chicago: University of Chicago Law School.

Tiffin, Helen and Diana Brydon. 1993. *Decolonising Fictions*. Sydney: Dangaroo.

Tilghman, Douglas Campbell. 1967. 'Woodriff, Daniel (1756–1842).' *Australian Dictionary of Biography Volume 2*. Melbourne: Melbourne University Press. 621–22.

Titasey, Catherine. 2013. *My Island Homicide*. St Lucia: University of Queensland Press.

Titlestad, Michael. 2009. '"Dead to the World, and Almost to Ourselves": William Mackay's *Narrative of the Shipwreck of the* Juno (1798).' *South African Historical Journal* 61(4): 788–801.

———. 2013 '"Changed as to a Tiger": Considering the Wreck of the Batavia.' *Antipodes* 27 (2) 149–56.

Titlestad, Michael and Mike Kissack. 2007. 'The Persistent Castaway in South African Writing.' *Postcolonial Studies* 10(2): 191–218.

Trollope, Anthony. 1860. *The West Indies and the Spanish Main*. London: Chapman and Hall.

Tuan, Yi-Fu. 1998. *Topophilia: A Study of Environmental Perception, Attitudes, and Values*. London: Columbia University Press.

Turley, Hans. 2004. 'Protestant Evangelicism, British Imperialism, and Crusonian Identity.' *A New Imperial History: Culture, Identity, and Modernity in Britain and the Empire 1600–1840*. Ed. Kathleen Wilson. Cambridge and New York: Cambridge University Press. 176–94.

Turner, Henry S. 2007. 'Literature and Mapping in Early Modern England, 1520–1688.' *The History of Cartography Volume 3: Cartography in the European Renaissance*. Ed. David Woodward. Chicago and London: University of Chicago Press. 412–26.

Tyers, Nowa. 1967. 'Tyers, Charles James (1806–1870).' Australian Dictionary of Biography Volume 2. Melbourne: Melbourne University Press. 542–43.

Veitch, Michael. 2011. *The Forgotten Islands*. Melbourne: Viking.

Vicari, Patricia. 1989. *The View from Minerva's Tower: Learning and Imagination in The Anatomy of Melancholy*. Toronto; Buffalo; London: Toronto University Press.

Virilio, Paul. 1977. *Speed and Politics: An Essay on Dromology*. New York: Semiotext(e).

———. 2007. *The Original Accident*. Cambridge: Polity.

'Vox.' 1846. 'The Cataraqui.' *Launceston Examiner* 14 March.

Walcott, Derek. 1992a. 'The Antilles: Fragments of Epic Memory.' Nobel Lecture. Nobel Academy. Online: http://www.nobelprize.org/nobel_prizes/literature/laureates/1992/walcott-lecture.html, accessed 12 August 2015.

———. (1986) 1992b. *Collected Poems 1948–1984*. London: Faber & Faber. 19–21.

———. 1990. *Omeros*. New York: Farrar Straus and Giroux.

Wallace, Alfred Russell. 1895. 'The Classification of Islands.' *Island Life: Or, The Phenomena and Causes of Insular Faunas and Floras*, 2nd Revised Edition. London and New York: Macmillan and Co.

Walsh, G. P. 1966. 'de Mestre, Jean Charles Prosper (1789–1844).' *Australian Dictionary of Biography Volume 1*. Canberra: National Centre of Biography. Online: http://adb.anu.edu.au/biography/de-mestre-jean-charles-prosper-1976/text2393, accessed 2 September 2015.

Watson, Judy. 2007. 'A Complicated Fall.'Brisbane: Milani Gallery.

Watson, Judy and Louise Martin-Chew. 2009. *Blood Language*. Melbourne: Miegunyah Press.

Watts, Pauline Moffitt. 1985. 'Prophecy and Discovery: On the Spiritual Origins of Christopher Columbus's "Enterprise of the Indies".' *The American Historical Review* 90(1): 73–102.

Weaver-Hightower, Rebecca. 2006. *Empire Islands: Castaways: Cannibals and Fantasies of Conquest.* Minneapolis: University of Minnesota Press, 2007.

Webb, Francis. (1952) 2011. 'Leichhardt in Theatre.' *Collected Poems*. Ed. Toby Davidson. Perth: University of Western Australia Press, 75–85.

———. (1961) 2011. 'Eyre All Alone.' *Collected Poems of Francis Webb*. Ed. Toby Davidson. Perth: University of Western Australia Press. 265–77.

———. (1961) 2011. 'Poet.' *Collected Poems of Francis Webb*. Ed. Toby Davidson. Perth: University of Western Australia Press. 227.

Wells, H.G. (1896) 2005. *The Island of Dr Moreau*. London and New York: Penguin.

———. (1904) 2004. 'The Country of the Blind.' *The Country of the Blind and Other Stories*. Ed. Jim Manis. An Electronic Classics Series Publication. Pennsylvania: Pennsylvania State University. 376–99.

Wentworth, W. C. (1823) 1997. *Australasia*. University of Sydney Library. Online: http://adc.library.usyd.edu.au/data-2/v00014.pdf, accessed 2 November 2015.

West, Delno C. and August Kling. 1991. 'Introduction.' *El Libro de la Profecias Columbus*. Gainesville: University of Florida Press.

*Westminster Review July-October 1833, Volume 19* (1833). London: Robert Heward. Online: https://books.google.com.au/books?id=RiM6AQAAMAAJ&printsec=frontcover&source=gbs_ge_summary_r&cad=0#v=onepage&q&f=false, accessed 26 September 2015.

Wharton, W. J. L. 1893. 'Introduction.' *Captain Cook's Journal During His First Voyage Round the World Made in H.M. Bark* Endeavour *1768–71*. London: Eliot Stock. Online: http://gutenberg.net.au/ebooks/e00043.html, accessed 23 December 2014.

White, Patrick. (1939) 2012. *Happy Valley*. Melbourne: Text Publishing.

———. (1941) 1996. *The Living and the Dead*. Sydney: Random House.

———. (1948) 2008. *The Aunt's Story*. Sydney: Random House.

———. (1957) 1960. *Voss*. London, New York: Penguin.

———. 1979. *The Twyborn Affair*. London: Penguin.

———. 1981. *Flaws in the Glass*. London and New York: Penguin.

Whitfield, Unca Eliza. (1767) 2001. *The Female American*. London: Broadview.

Winter, Sarah. 1963. 'On the Morant Bay Rebellion in Jamaica and the Governor Eyre-George William Gordon Controversy, 1865–70.' *BRANCH: Britain, Representation and Nineteenth-Century History*. Ed. Dino Franco Felluga. Extension of Romanticism and Victorianism on the Net. Online: http://www.branchcollective.org/?ps_articles=sarah-winter-on-the-morant-bay-rebellion-in-jamaica-and-the-governor-eyre-george-william-gordon-controversy-1865–70, accessed 10 December 2014.

Winton, Tim. 2015. *Island Home*. Melbourne: Penguin.
Wolfe, Patrick. 2002. 'Race and Racialisation: Some Thoughts.' *Postcolonial Studies* 5(1): 51–62.
Wood, Danielle. 2003. *The Alphabet of Light and Dark*. Sydney: Allen and Unwin.
Woodward, David. Ed. 2007. *The History of Cartography Volume 3, Part 1: Cartography in the European Renaissance*. Chicago and London: University of Chicago Press.
Woolf, Virginia. (1927) 1964. *To the Lighthouse*. London: Penguin.
Woollacott, Angela. 2003. 'Creating the White Colonial Woman: Mary Gaunt's Imperial Adventuring and Australian Cultural History.' *Cultural History in Australia*. Eds Hsu-Ming Teo, and Richard White. Sydney: UNSW Press. 186–200.
Woollright, Henry Herriott. 1907. *Records of the Seventy-seventh (East Middlesex): the Duke of Cambridge's Own Regiment of Foot*. Aldershot, Portsmouth: Gale & Polden. Google Books. Online: http://archive.org/stream/recordsseventys00woolgoog#page/n10/mode/2up, accessed 24 September 2015.
Wright, Alexis. 2006. *Carpentaria*. Sydney: Giramondo.
Yeats, W. B. (1920) 1994.'The Second Coming.' *W. B. Yeats: The Poems*. Ed. Daniel Allbright. London: Everyman. 235.
Zalums, E. 1966. 'Clarke, Andrew (1793–1847).' *Australian Dictionary of Biography Volume 1*. Melbourne: Melbourne University Press. 228.
Zamora, Margarita. 1993. *Reading Columbus*. Berkeley: University of California Press.
Zinnemann, Fred. (Dir). 1953. *From Here to Eternity*. Columbia.
Žižek, Slavoj. 2008. 'Language, Violence and Non-Violence.' *International Journal of Žižek Studies* 2(3): 1–12. ZizekStudies.org, accessed 29 November 2011.

# INDEX

www.ingramcontent.com/pod-product-compliance
Lightning Source LLC
Chambersburg PA
CBHW031938110726
47902CB00001B/220
*9781785271892*